NBER Macroeconomics Annual 2010

NBER Macroeconomics Annual 2010

Edited by
Daron Acemoglu and Michael Woodford

NBER/Macroeconomics Annual, Number 25, 2010

Published annually by The University of Chicago Press.

Standing orders
To place a standing order for this book series, please address your request to The University of Chicago Press, Chicago Distribution Center, Attn. Standing Orders/Customer Service, 11030 S. Langley Avenue, Chicago, IL 60628. Telephone toll free in the U.S. and Canada: 1-800-621-2736; or 1-773-702-7000. Fax toll free in the U.S. and Canada: 1-800-621-8476; or 1-773-702-7212.

Single-copy orders
In the U.K. and Europe: Order from your local bookseller or direct from The University of Chicago Press, c/o John Wiley Ltd. Distribution Center, 1 Oldlands Way, Bognor Regis, West Sussex PO22 9SA, UK. Telephone 01243 779777 or Fax 01243 820250. Email: cs-books@wiley.co.uk

In the U.S., Canada, and the rest of the world: Order from your local bookseller or direct from The University of Chicago Press, Chicago Distribution Center, 11030 S. Langley Avenue, Chicago, IL 60628. Telephone toll free in the U.S. and Canada: 1-800-621-2736; or 1-773-702-7000. Fax toll free in the U.S. and Canada: 1-800-621-8476; or 1-773-702-7212.

Special orders
University of Chicago Press books may be purchased at quantity discounts for business or promotional use. For information, please write to Sales Department—Special Sales, The University of Chicago Press, 1427 E. 60th Street, Chicago, IL 60637 USA or telephone 1-773-702-7723.

This book was printed and bound in the United States of America.

ISSN: 0889-3365
ISBN-13: 978-0-226-00212-5 (hc.:alk.paper)—978-0-226-00213-2 (pbk.:alk.paper)
ISBN-10: 0-226-00212-8 (hc.:alk.paper)—2-226-00213-6 (pbk.:alk.paper)

10 9 8 7 6 5 4 3 2 1

NBER/Macroeconomics Annual, Number 25, 2010

Published annually by The University of Chicago Press.

Standing orders
To place a standing order for this book series, please address your request to The University of Chicago Press, Chicago Distribution Center, Attn. Standing Orders/Customer Service, 11030 S. Langley Avenue, Chicago, IL 60628. Telephone toll free in the U.S. and Canada: 1-800-621-2736; or 1-773-702-7000. Fax toll free in the U.S. and Canada: 1-800-621-8476; or 1-773-702-7212.

Single-copy orders
In the U.K. and Europe: Order from your local bookseller or direct from The University of Chicago Press, c/o John Wiley Ltd. Distribution Center, 1 Oldlands Way, Bognor Regis, West Sussex PO22 9SA, UK. Telephone 01243 779777 or Fax 01243 820250. Email: cs-books@wiley.co.uk

In the U.S., Canada, and the rest of the world: Order from your local bookseller or direct from The University of Chicago Press, Chicago Distribution Center, 11030 S. Langley Avenue, Chicago, IL 60628. Telephone toll free in the U.S. and Canada: 1-800-621-2736; or 1-773-702-7000. Fax toll free in the U.S. and Canada: 1-800-621-8476; or 1-773-702-7212.

Special orders
University of Chicago Press books may be purchased at quantity discounts for business or promotional use. For information, please write to Sales Department—Special Sales, The University of Chicago Press, 1427 E. 60th Street, Chicago, IL 60637 USA or telephone 1-773-702-7723.

This book was printed and bound in the United States of America.

ISSN: 0889-3365
ISBN-13: 978-0-226-00212-5 (hc.:alk.paper)—978-0-226-00213-2 (pbk.:alk.paper)
ISBN-10: 0-226-00212-8 (hc.:alk.paper)—2-226-00213-6 (pbk.:alk.paper)

10 9 8 7 6 5 4 3 2 1

NBER Board of Directors

Relation of the Directors to the Work and Publications of the NBER

1. The object of the NBER is to ascertain and present to the economics profession, and to the public more generally, important economic facts and their interpretation in a scientific manner without policy recommendations. The Board of Directors is charged with the responsibility of ensuring that the work of the NBER is carried on in strict conformity with this object.

2. The President shall establish an internal review process to ensure that book manuscripts proposed for publication DO NOT contain policy recommendations. This shall apply both to the proceedings of conferences and to manuscripts by a single author or by one or more coauthors but shall not apply to authors of comments at NBER conferences who are not NBER affiliates.

3. No book manuscript reporting research shall be published by the NBER until the President has sent to each member of the Board a notice that a manuscript is recommended for publication and that in the President's opinion it is suitable for publication in accordance with the above principles of the NBER. Such notification will include a table of contents and an abstract or summary of the manuscript's content, a list of contributors if applicable, and a response form for use by Directors who desire a copy of the manuscript for review. Each manuscript shall contain a summary drawing attention to the nature and treatment of the problem studied and the main conclusions reached.

4. No volume shall be published until forty-five days have elapsed from the above notification of intention to publish it. During this period a copy shall be sent to any Director requesting it, and if any Director objects to publication on the grounds that the manuscript contains policy recommendations, the objection will be presented to the author(s) or editor(s). In case of dispute, all members of the Board shall be notified, and

the President shall appoint an ad hoc committee of the Board to decide the matter; thirty days additional shall be granted for this purpose.

5. The President shall present annually to the Board a report describing the internal manuscript review process, any objections made by Directors before publication or by anyone after publication, any disputes about such matters, and how they were handled.

6. Publications of the NBER issued for informational purposes concerning the work of the Bureau, or issued to inform the public of the activities at the Bureau, including but not limited to the NBER Digest and Reporter, shall be consistent with the object stated in paragraph 1. They shall contain a specific disclaimer noting that they have not passed through the review procedures required in this resolution. The Executive Committee of the Board is charged with the review of all such publications from time to time.

7. NBER working papers and manuscripts distributed on the Bureau's web site are not deemed to be publications for the purpose of this resolution, but they shall be consistent with the object stated in paragraph 1. Working papers shall contain a specific disclaimer noting that they have not passed through the review procedures required in this resolution. The NBER's web site shall contain a similar disclaimer. The President shall establish an internal review process to ensure that the working papers and the web site do not contain policy recommendations, and shall report annually to the Board on this process and any concerns raised in connection with it.

8. Unless otherwise determined by the Board or exempted by the terms of paragraphs 6 and 7, a copy of this resolution shall be printed in each NBER publication as described in paragraph 2 above.

Contents

Editorial

Daron Acemoglu, *Massachusetts Institute of Technology and NBER*
Michael Woodford, *Columbia University and NBER*

The twenty-fifth edition of the *NBER Macroeconomics Annual* continues with its tradition of featuring theoretical and empirical contributions that shed light on central issues in contemporary macroeconomics. As in previous years, the contributions push the frontiers of macroeconomic work in areas ranging from short-run macroeconomic fluctuations to international economic crises and long-run economic growth. Also as in previous years, the contributions address important policy-relevant questions and open new debates, which we expect to continue in the years to come. This year's volume continues one of the major themes of last year's volume and features several papers that investigate questions related to the recent financial crisis and policy responses to it. In addition, the volume also includes papers investigating the causes of rapid economic growth in Europe in the decades following World War II, the sources of product-level price rigidities, and how the U.S. economy, particularly the automobile sector, has adjusted to higher oil prices and how it responds to changes in oil prices. Each of the six papers tackles an important area in macroeconomics and advances the literature in several directions. We hope that these papers and the detailed discussions of the two experts on each paper will provide a useful starting point for the further study of these important debates.

The first paper by Rong Qian, Carmen Reinhart, and Kenneth Rogoff, "On Graduation from Default, Inflation, and Banking Crises: Elusive or Illusion?" uses a unique data set covering the history of 200 years of sovereign debt, banking, and inflation crises from around the world to investigate a question that has so far received little attention from the literature: what enables and what delays the "graduation" of a country from the typical pattern of serial crises, a common fate for many emerging markets? Qian, Reinhart, and Rogoff first document that such graduation is a slow and arduous process. Countries that suffer sovereign

978-0-226-00212-5/2011/2010-0001$10.00

debt, banking, and inflation crises in the past are typically more likely to do so again in the future. For banking crises, this type of graduation appears to never happen, while for sovereign debt and inflation crises, there are signs of a pattern of graduation after about 20 years; but even after that forms of "recidivism" are common. The paper raises several important empirical and theoretical questions. One issue concerns the causes of this type of serial crises. In particular, is it the history of crisis, so a form of path dependence? Or is it (unobserved) heterogeneity, perhaps driven by some institutional or policy characteristics of countries, causing the serial crises? The paper also raises some interesting questions about why markets agree to lend to countries that have undertaken serial default in the past and, according to this research, are likely to do so again.

In "What Fiscal Policy Is Effective at Zero Interest Rates?" Gauti Eggertsson tackles a major academic and policy question: the effectiveness of fiscal policy, particularly when further stimulus from monetary policy appears no longer to be an option, as recently in the United States and elsewhere. There has been much recent debate about whether U.S. and European fiscal stimulus packages were too small or too big and what their contributions have been to the slow recovery. Empirical estimates of the impact of the fiscal stimulus vary, and more work is required for us to have a greater understanding of what the impacts of different fiscal policies have been in the past and what they may be in the near future. But there is also a big gap in our theoretical understanding. Eggertsson's paper provides important new insights by developing a new Keynesian model in which the effect of fiscal policy is very different during crisis periods, in which the nominal interest rate has reached the zero lower bound, from what it is under more normal circumstances. Essentially, the effects of fiscal policy depend greatly on the interest rate response, and this is very different when interest rates are constrained by the zero bound than when the central bank can be expected to adjust interest rates in response to changes in the level of economic activity and/or inflation. Eggertsson shows that an otherwise standard new Keynesian model leads to several novel and perhaps surprising conclusions. Several policies commonly thought to be expansionary, such as reductions in taxes on wages or reduced capital taxes, are recessionary during a crisis. These policies encourage greater savings precisely when greater consumption is required for recovery and encourage firms to cut prices at a time when deflationary expectations are especially dangerous, because of the impossibility of lowering nominal interest rates. In contrast, fiscal policies that increase aggregate demand, for example, by increasing government spending, are more effective than under normal circumstances, because there should be less crowding out of private spending in the absence of the usual increase in interest rates. Eggertsson finds that temporary tax cuts and government spending increases should be particularly effective. Interestingly, and again somewhat paradoxically, temporary investment tax credits are less effective. Eggertsson also provides a quantitative analysis, showing that under at least some circumstances the "multiplier" effect of government purchases can be much larger than has been indicated by many previous studies. The results of this paper are both new and provocative; the discussion focused on how credible the implied numbers are and whether the channel that works through future inflationary expectations and the impact of those on savings today capture the main impact of fiscal policies.

Adam Ashcraft, Nicolae Gârleanu, and Lasse Heje Pedersen, in "Two Monetary Tools: Interest Rates and Haircuts," develop a theoretical and empirical analysis of a new dimension of monetary policy that has been important during the recent crisis: direct lending by the Fed to private borrowers on terms other than those otherwise available in the market. In particular, they discuss the Term Asset-Backed Securities Loan Facility (TALF), which sought to increase the availability of credit to the economy by financing private investors' acquisitions of asset-backed securities (ABS) on terms that involved the Fed allowing loans to be taken out backed by given ABS collateral larger than private lenders were at that time willing to allow. Despite the importance of this kind of policy during the recent crisis, very little theoretical or empirical analysis of it exists. The paper first develops a simple theoretical model that provides a simple framework for understanding how the "haircuts" required in collateralized lending can affect real activity, in addition to the more familiar effects of changes in the level of interest rates. In a production economy with multiple sectors and binding collateral constraints on intermediaries (or those investors who would otherwise be most willing to accept risk), the government can affect economic activity either by changing the interest rate or by lowering haircuts, which relaxes the collateral constraints and thus allows more risky projects to be financed. The paper then empirically investigates these ideas by looking at the effects on the required returns on commercial mortgage-backed securities of qualification for financing under the TALF, which resulted in lower haircuts for the particular securities that qualified. They find that the program reduced required returns on qualifying securities relative to those not qualifying by more than 0.7%; additional survey evidence suggests that the impact of the program could have been even larger. This paper opens the discussion of new and nonconventional monetary policies and poses the challenge of modeling the consequences of these policy tools for macroeconomic equilibria.

In "Technology Diffusion and Postwar Growth," Diego Comin and Bart Hobijn turn to a major period of economic growth for the world economy: the aftermath of World War II. This period is distinguished by the very rapid growth (recovery) of European economies but also differential growth rates both within Europe and between Europe and other areas of the world. Comin and Hobijn show that the Solow model, where convergence takes place via capital accumulation, is not a good approximation of these events. They suggest instead that technology dynamics are crucial for understanding convergence. They develop a vintage model of technology adoption and then use this model in order to guide their empirical work on the role of technology in post–World War II European growth. The patterns in the data are broadly consistent with the implications of the model. In addition, Comin and Hobijn show how U.S. policy, in particular the Marshall Plan and associated technology assistance programs, have helped the process of technology distribution to Europe and argue that this was a crucial part of the process of technology diffusion, leading to the rapid growth.

Gita Gopinath and Oleg Itskhoki in "In Search of Real Rigidities" attempt to reconcile the different approaches and results in the closed and open economy macro literatures on the prevalence and role of price rigidities. They focus on the evidence for real rigidities, meaning near invariance of suppliers' desired relative prices despite changes in the volume of sales, that may occur for a variety of reasons. Using international price data and exchange rate shocks, they document that there is considerable real rigidity in price setting. For example, the response of recent price inflation to exchange rate shocks is highly persistent. Even conditioning on changing nominal prices, individual import prices are related to exchange rate shocks prior to the last price change, creating an interesting pattern of persistence. However, aggregate reset-price inflation for imports and, as documented in the closed economy literature, aggregate reset-price inflation for consumer prices exhibit little persistence. One reason for this might be differences between wholesale and retail prices. The pattern might also be related to differences in competition patterns. Gopinath and Itskhoki show that competitors' prices affect firm pricing and that exchange rate pass-through into import prices is greater in response to trade-weighted as opposed to bilateral exchange rate changes. Motivated by these patterns, Gopinath and Itskhoki develop a simple dynamic model of price setting with sticky prices (à la Calvo) that incorporates variable markups at the wholesale level and constant markups at the retail level. Such a model has the potential of being consistent with both the closed economy and open economy evidence. They show that such a model is capable of generating real rigidities and in particular sluggish price adjustments, though quantitatively the effects seem to be small.

Finally, Valerie Ramey and Daniel Vine reexamine an important source of macroeconomic fluctuations in "Oil, Automobiles, and the U.S. Economy: How Much Have Things Really Changed?" A large literature shows that oil price hikes lead to (or precede) output contractions. Several papers have also found that the effect of oil appears to be less now than it was in the 1970s and 1980s, and this has been linked to either the declining role of oil in the economy or adjustment of technologies, making them less energy or oil dependent. Ramey and Vine, in contrast, find that there is remarkable stability in the response of aggregate real variables to oil shocks. The key to their result is that they carefully take into account the additional costs resulting from shortages and rationing, which were important in the oil price shocks of the 1970s but disappeared after price controls were lifted. To develop a better perspective on the effect of oil prices on real activity, they focus on the automobile industry, which is one of the sectors most sensitive to oil prices. Contrary to what is sometimes argued, Ramey and Vine show that the automobile industry (broadly all motor vehicles) does not have a declining share in the economy. They show that within the motor vehicle industry, oil price shocks throughout the sample period have similar effects on production. More interesting, they can also study capacity utilization and changes in production and demand across different segments (from large to small cars, e.g.). Here too, paradoxically, they find little change in the responsiveness of the automobile industry and real activity between the 1970s and today. To the extent that the 1970s were subject to larger shocks, there were larger responses, but the responsiveness does not seem to change. This raises several puzzles as to why there is this type of stability in the economy at large and in the automobile industry, despite significant changes in technology and the changing role of oil in the economy, and invites more research on this important topic.

This volume also continues last year's innovation of including a published speech of a more policy-related nature. The final chapter is a speech by former undersecretary of the Treasury (and longtime NBER researcher) John Taylor, delivered at the conference dinner. Taylor provides a lively discussion of the ways in which macroeconomic policy during the financial crisis has differed from previous practice and from prescriptions proposed by the research literature. He questions the desirability of this "Great Deviation" from standard approaches to policy and suggests that researchers need to devote more attention to the study of the political economy of macroeconomic policy in order to understand why the conclusions of the research literature do not have more influence on actual policy.

Finally, the authors and the editors would like to take this opportunity to thank Jim Poterba and the National Bureau of Economic Research for their continued support for the *NBER Macroeconomics Annual* and the associated conference. We would also like to thank the NBER conference staff, particularly Rob Shannon, for his usual excellent organization and support. Financial assistance from the National Science Foundation is gratefully acknowledged. Neil Mehrotra and Dmitriy Sergeyev provided invaluable help in preparing the summaries of the discussions. We are also grateful to Helena Fitz-Patrick for her invaluable assistance in editing and producing the volume.

Abstracts

1 On Graduation from Default, Inflation, and Banking Crises: Elusive or Illusion?

Rong Qian, Carmen M. Reinhart, and Kenneth Rogoff

This paper uses a data set of over 200 years of sovereign debt, banking, and inflation crises to explore the question of how long it takes a country to "graduate" from the typical pattern of serial crisis that most emerging markets experience. We find that for default and inflation crises, 20 years is a significant market, but the distribution of recidivism has extremely fat tails. In the case of banking crises, it is unclear whether countries ever graduate. We also examine the more recent phenomenon of International Monetary Fund programs, which sometimes result in "near misses" but sometimes end in default even after a program is instituted. The paper raises the important theoretical question of why countries experience serial default and how they might graduate.

2 What Fiscal Policy Is Effective at Zero Interest Rates?

Gauti B. Eggertsson

Tax cuts can deepen a recession if the short-term nominal interest rate is zero, according to a standard New Keynesian business cycle model. An example of a contractionary tax cut is a reduction in taxes on wages. This tax cut deepens a recession because it increases deflationary pressures. Another example is a cut in capital taxes. This tax cut deepens a recession because it encourages people to save instead of spend when more spending is needed. Fiscal policies aimed directly at stimulating aggregate demand work better. These policies include (1) a temporary increase in government spending and (2) temporary tax cuts directly aimed at stimulating aggregate demand rather than aggregate supply, such as an investment tax credit or a cut in sales taxes. The results are

978-0-226-00212-5/2011/2010-0002$10.00

special to an environment in which the interest rate is close to zero, as observed in large parts of the world today.

3 Two Monetary Tools: Interest Rates and Haircuts

Adam Ashcraft, Nicolae Gârleanu, and Lasse Heje Pedersen

We study a production economy with multiple sectors financed by issuing securities to agents who face capital constraints. Binding capital constraints propagate business cycles, and a reduction of the interest rate can *increase* the required return of high-haircut assets since it can increase the shadow cost of capital for constrained agents. The required return can be lowered by easing funding constraints through lowering haircuts. To assess empirically the power of the haircut tool, we study the introduction of the legacy Term Asset-Backed Securities Loan Facility (TALF). By considering unpredictable rejections of bonds from TALF, we estimate that haircuts had a significant effect on prices. Further, unique survey evidence suggests that lowering haircuts could reduce required returns by more than 3% and provides broader evidence on the demand sensitivity to haircuts.

4 Technology Diffusion and Postwar Growth

Diego Comin and Bart Hobijn

In the aftermath of World War II, the world's economies exhibited very different rates of economic recovery. We provide evidence that those countries that caught up the most with the United States in the postwar period are those that also saw an acceleration in the speed of adoption of new technologies. This acceleration is correlated with the incidence of U.S. economic aid and technical assistance in the same period. We interpret this as supportive of the interpretation that technology transfers from the United States to Western European countries and Japan were an important factor in driving growth in these recipient countries during the postwar decades.

5 In Search of Real Rigidities

Gita Gopinath and Oleg Itskhoki

The closed and open economy literatures work on evaluating the role of real rigidities, but in parallel. This paper brings the two literatures together. We use international price data and exchange rate shocks to evaluate the importance of real rigidities in price setting. We show that consistent with the presence of real rigidities, the response of reset-price inflation to exchange rate shocks depicts significant persistence. Individual import prices, conditional on changing, respond to exchange rate shocks prior to the last price change. At the same time aggregate reset-price inflation for imports, like that for consumer prices, depicts little persistence. Competitor prices affect firm pricing, and exchange rate pass-through into import prices is greater in response to trade-weighted as opposed to bilateral exchange rate shocks. We quantitatively evaluate sticky price models (Calvo and menu cost) with variable markups at the wholesale level and constant markups at the retail level, consistent with empirical evidence. Variable markups alone generate price sluggishness at the aggregate level, while they fall short of matching price persistence at the micro level. Finally, variable markups magnify the size of the contract multiplier, but their absolute effects are modest unless they are coupled with exogenous sources of persistence.

6 Oil, Automobiles, and the U.S. Economy: How Much Have Things Really Changed?

Valerie A. Ramey and Daniel J. Vine

This paper studies the impact of oil shocks on the U.S. economy—and on the motor vehicle industry in particular—and reexamines whether the relationship has changed over time. We find remarkable stability in the response of aggregate real variables to oil shocks once we account for the extra costs imposed on the economy in the 1970s by price controls and a complex system of entitlements that led to some rationing and shortages. To investigate further why the response of real variables to oil shocks has not declined over time, we focus on the motor vehicle industry, which is considered the most important channel through which oil shocks affect the economy. We find that, contrary to common perceptions, the share of motor vehicles in total U.S. goods production has shown little decline over time. Moreover, within the motor vehicle industry, the effects of oil shocks on the mix of vehicles sold and on capacity utilization appear to have been proportional in recent decades to the effects observed in the 1970s.

1

On Graduation from Default, Inflation, and Banking Crises: Elusive or Illusion?

Rong Qian, *University of Maryland*
Carmen M. Reinhart, *University of Maryland and NBER*
Kenneth Rogoff, *Harvard University and NBER*

I. Introduction

This paper addresses the concept of "graduation" from external default, banking, and inflation crises.[1] Employing a vast data set cataloging more than 2 centuries of financial crises for over 60 countries developed in Reinhart and Rogoff (2009), we explore the risk of recidivism across advanced economies versus middle- and low-income countries. We show that 2 decades without a relapse (falling into crisis) is an important marker. After 1800, roughly two-thirds of recurrences of external default on sovereign debt and three-quarters of recurrence of inflation crisis occur within 20 years.[2] However, crisis recidivism distributions have very fat tails, so that it takes at least 50 and perhaps 100 years to meaningfully speak of "graduation." Indeed, in the case of banking crises in particular, it is hard to argue that any country in the world has truly graduated.

Given that graduation (with its companion question, will this ever happen again?) is arguably one of the most important issues in macroeconomics and development, there has been remarkably little theoretical or empirical investigation of the subject. For example, the large theory literature on sovereign lending and default, while producing many important insights into the fundamental distinction between willingness to pay and ability to pay, largely treats a country's basic developmental and political characteristics as parametric. There is very little on explaining the political, social, economic, and financial dynamics that ultimately lead a country to be less prone to certain types of crises.

We acknowledge that the concept of graduation is a hard nut to crack. Many advanced countries had enjoyed a long hiatus from systemic

978-0-226-00212-5/2011/2010-0101$10.00

banking crises after World War II and yet had huge problems during the recent global financial crisis. After 90 years of serial default running from 1557 to 1647, Spain did not default again until 1809. Even the advanced countries had high inflation as recently as the 1970s and early 1980s, while many emerging markets had hyperinflation less than 2 decades ago. Is the advent of modern independent central banks sufficient to guarantee that fiscal dominance never again reasserts itself? Have the rich countries that have supposedly "graduated" from serial default on external debt shifted the locus of risk to de jure or de facto (via inflation or financial repression) default on domestic debt? Does the theory of sovereign default or of financial development tell us that we should expect richer and more advanced countries to be immune? Or is graduation a mirage, with the "graduates" really being at best "star pupils," and can graduates be distinguished from patients in remission?

Our goals in this paper are fairly narrowly circumscribed. Most of our analysis is based on data on the dates and duration of the crises themselves. We speculate on underlying causal factors but do not approach them empirically here.[3] Although the various types of crises often occur in clusters, our quantitative analysis mainly treats individual crises separately.

We begin the paper in Section II by defining the crises that we will catalog. In Section III of the paper, we present a summary time line of crisis, followed by a brief overview of the early history of serial default on external debt. An interesting case is France, which defaulted on its external debt no fewer than nine times from the middle of the sixteenth century through the end of the Napoleonic War but has not defaulted on external debt since. France is a canonical case of what we define as an "external default graduate." (This did not stop France from having numerous severe banking crises in the past 2 centuries.)

In the main body of the paper, we provide a broad aggregative historical overview of the data across different types of crises, distinguishing between advanced countries and emerging markets, also taking into account the advent of International Monetary Fund (IMF) programs after World War II as another marker of a debt crisis.

In Section IX of the paper, we speculate on links between graduation and development and the possibility for recidivism among richer countries. The fact that the canonical theory of sovereign default does not strongly predict smaller problems in richer countries (it does not strongly predict graduation) might be considered a flaw in theory. But it might also be taken as warning sign that graduation can be more difficult and take even more time than our data of "just" a few centuries can reveal. On banking crises, the theory needs to better explain why countries never seem to graduate.

The main empirical results from our long-dated historical time series on financial crises may be described as follows. First, the process of "graduation," that is, emergence from frequent crisis suffering status, is a long process. False starts are common and recurrent. This is especially true in the case of banking crises, for both high-income countries and middle- and low-income countries.

Second, the vulnerability to crisis in high-income countries versus middle- and low-income countries differs mostly in external default crises, to a lesser extent in inflation crises, and surprisingly little in banking crises.[4]

Third, the sequence of graduation for most countries is first to graduate from external default crisis, then from inflation crisis, and eventually from banking. The last stage of graduation is extremely difficult, even for high-income countries. Among high-income countries, even though most of them have graduated from external default crisis and inflation crisis, more than 20% recently experienced a banking crisis, and far more when weighted by size. Schularick and Taylor (2009) speculate that advanced countries continue to experience credit busts despite arguably advancing regulation and institutions, because as risks moderate, financial systems grow and restore them.

Finally, the role of IMF programs in crises in the modern period is important. The availability of IMF bridge loans certainly has increased countries' resilience to "sudden stops" but, even setting aside moral hazard problems, is by no means a cure-all. Countries entering IMF programs are still forced to undergo painful macroeconomic adjustments in an attempt to regain sound fiscal footing and regain access to private capital markets. The challenges of successfully implementing IMF programs are underscored by the fact that there are many significant cases in which countries default within 3 years of an IMF bailout. IMF programs may help facilitate orderly debt workouts but do not guarantee them. We also note that in its early history, many of today's rich countries regularly drew on IMF resources, although there has been a 3-decade hiatus.

II. Definition of Crises

External debt crisis. We distinguish between external and internal debt on the basis of the legal jurisdiction where the debt contracts are enforced. This is a convenient construct given the history and evolution of sovereign debt. Obviously it may be useful to parse the data in other ways for some exercises, and in principle our data set allows that.

Although there are exceptions and there has been some evolution in recent years, typically in our long-dated historical data set, external debt is denominated in foreign currency and held by foreign creditors. There are certainly important examples, such as Mexico's short-term Tesobono bonds in the mid-1990s, where the debt is domestic yet is denominated in foreign currency and held primarily by foreign creditors. Although we regard the U.S. abrogation of the gold clause in the early 1930s—when gold was revalued from $21 to $35 per ounce—to be a default on domestic debt, many non-U.S. residents were also holding the debt at the time. In general, following standard practice, we define an external debt crisis as any failure to meet contractual repayment obligations on foreign debts, including both rescheduling or repayments and outright default. (As both of these examples make clear, however, one ultimately needs to think carefully about whether graduation from external default may sometimes just mean a shift to episodic de facto and de jure internal default.)

In practice, most defaults on external debt end up being partial, with creditors typically (but not always) repaying 30¢–70¢ or more on the dollar, admittedly not adjusting for risk. The rationale for lumping together defaults regardless of the ultimate "haircuts" creditors are forced to absorb is that, in practice, the fixed costs of external debt default (which include difficulties in obtaining trade credits and loss of reputation) tend to be large relative to the variable costs. In principle, one could parse episodes more finely here according to, say, output or tax revenue loss depending on data availability, although we do not undertake that exercise here. See, however, Tomz (2007) and Tomz and Wright (2007).

Inflation crises. Following Reinhart and Rogoff (2004), we define inflation crises as episodes in which annual inflation exceeds 20%. This threshold is lower than the 40% we and others have used in related studies on postwar data but is a compromise reflecting that prior to World War I, average inflation rates were much lower, and 20% inflation generally represented a significant level of dysfunction. Indeed, since we are particularly interested here in inflation as a vehicle for partial default, one clearly would also want to consider lower levels of sustained unanticipated inflation such as many advanced countries experienced in the 1970s. Depending on the maturity structure of debt, sustained 10% inflation can certainly be tantamount to de facto default. A proper calibration, however, would require detailed data on the maturity structure of debt (as in Missale and Blanchard 1994) and, ideally, also on the evolution of inflation expectations. We do not attempt this here, though again, this is an important caveat to interpreting the concept of graduation from external debt crises.

Banking crises. Our definition of banking crises follows standard practice (e.g., Kaminsky and Reinhart 1999; Caprio and Klingebiel 2003). Following our own earlier work, "We mark a banking crisis by two types of events: (1) bank runs that lead to the closure, merging or takeover by the public sector of one or more financial institutions and (2) if there are no runs, the closure, merging, takeover, or large-scale government assistance of an important financial institution (or group of institutions) that marks the start of a string of similar outcomes for other financial institutions" (Reinhart and Rogoff 2009, 11). We recognize that our listing of systemic (on a national scale) banking crises may be incomplete, especially prior to 1970, especially for crises outside the large money centers that attract the attention of the world financial press.[5]

Having set out basic definitions, we are now ready to view some basic characteristics of the data. To provide context and motivation for the concept of graduation, we begin with a summary time line of financial crises since 1550, followed by a brief overview of the early history of sovereign defaults.

III. A Time Line of Financial Crises and the Early History of Sovereign Defaults

Table 1 provides a summary historical perspective that helps show how the three different varieties of financial crisis have spread over time and across country groups. Between 1550 and 1800, sovereign defaults on external debt were relatively common in Europe, but they were relatively rare elsewhere if only because (*a*) there were few other independent nations in a position to default and (*b*) given the crude state of global capital markets, relatively few countries were wealthy enough to attract international capital flows. Thus defaults were relatively insignificant in the regions that constitute today's emerging markets. Systemic banking crises, however, were relatively rare everywhere. The legal and technological underpinnings of modern private banking simply had not reached a stage of maturity and depth sufficient to cause systemic crises in most instances. (Of course, there are exceptions. Following Cipolla [1982] and MacDonald [2006], Reinhart and Rogoff [2009] discuss how England's 1340 default to Florentine bankers triggered a financial crisis in Italy.) Similarly, inflation crises were relatively

Table 1
Time Line of Crises, 1550–2010

	External Debt Crises	Banking Crises	Inflation Crises
1550–1815 (Napoleonic wars end)	Frequent in advanced economies (including the "world powers" of the time); serial in some cases	Rare	Rare
1826	Frequent in "peripheral" advanced economies and most emerging markets	Serial in advanced; rare in emerging	Rare
1850		Serial in advanced;	
1900		more frequent in emerging	
1913 (WW1 begins)		Frequent in advanced and emerging	
1945 (WWII ends)		Rare in advanced and emerging	
Post-1945			Rare
1964	Serial in some	More frequent	Frequent in
1973	emerging markets	in advanced; serial in emerging	advanced and emerging
Early 1980s			Frequent in
Early 1990s			emerging
2000			Rare
2009			
2010	??		

rare, although again there are many exceptions (see Reinhart and Rogoff 2009, chap. 12). Prior to the widespread adoption of paper currency, bouts of very high inflation were relatively difficult to engineer.

The end of the Napoleonic War in the early 1800s marks a significant transition. The largest advanced countries were increasingly able to avoid external default, albeit partly by their ability to issue an increasing share of their debt domestically. Default, however, became common in "peripheral" advanced countries such as Spain and Portugal, while newly independent emerging markets such as Greece and Latin America entered a long period of serial default. Over the same period, as advanced countries developed more sophisticated banking systems, banking crises became far more common. Emerging markets were certainly affected by advanced country banking crises but did not have so many of their own, if only because their financial systems were dominated by foreign banks.

By the turn of the twentieth century, emerging market financial institutions had developed to the point where domestic banking crises became more common. By the time of the Great Depression of the 1930s, banking crises were a worldwide phenomenon. Owing in no small part to the financial repression that followed in reaction to the Great Depression, banking crises were relatively rare during the period from the end of World War II until the early 1970s. As financial repression thawed, banking crises became more frequent in the advanced economies and serial in many emerging markets, bringing us to the recent financial crisis episode.

Finally, table 1 gives a time line of inflation crises, which of course were quite common in all countries in the 1970s and remained a problem in emerging markets until the past decade.

We thus focus our early history on sovereign external defaults. As Reinhart et al. (2003) and Reinhart and Rogoff (2009) emphasize, many of today's advanced economies had recurrent problems with default on sovereign debt during the period when they might arguably have been characterized as emerging markets. Table 2 illustrates the case

Table 2
External Defaults: Europe, 1550–1850

Country	Years of Default	Number of Defaults
Austria-Hungary	1796, 1802, 1805, 1811, 1816	5
England*	1594*	1*
France	1558, 1624, 1648, 1661, 1701, 1715, 1770, 1788, 1812	9
Germany:		
Prussia	1683, 1807, 1813	3
Hesse	1814	1
Schleswig-Holstein	1850	1
Westphalia	1812	1
Netherlands	1814	1
Portugal	1560, 1828, 1837, 1841, 1845	5
Russia	1839	1
Spain	1557, 1575, 1596, 1607, 1627, 1647, 1809, 1820, 1831, 1843	10
Sweden	1812	1

Source: Reinhart et al. (2003), Reinhart and Rogoff (2009), and sources cited therein.
Note: The table excludes Greece (which gained independence in 1829). Note that for some countries, even if there was a default on external debt, there may have been a default on domestic debt, as was the case for Denmark (1813).
*Denotes our uncertainty at this time about whether England's default involved external (as opposed to purely domestic) debt.

of Europe for the 3-century period 1550–1850, with the years listed marking the beginning of a sovereign default episode.

As one can see clearly from the table, serial default was quite common among the major European powers during the sixteenth through nineteenth centuries, with France defaulting on its external debt nine times and Spain defaulting 10 times (with three more to follow in the second half of the nineteenth century). One important observation, immediately apparent from the table, is that there is typically a substantial interval between defaults, typically decades, but sometimes centuries. (Note that we require at least 2 years between default episodes to regard them as independent events.) After defaulting in 1683, Prussia's next default episode did not follow for more than a century in 1807. Portugal, after defaulting in 1560, did not default again until 1828, when the country lapsed into a period of serial default that did not end until 1890. At this writing, Portugal has not defaulted again since. (Importantly, during a significant portion of Portugal's quiescent period, it had effectively lost its independence.)

Figure 1 gives a measure of the duration of periods of recidivism during the pre-Napoleonic era for the independent (relatively) high-income countries of our sample. The figure captures the length of time between default episodes (including cases in which there was no recidivism). As one can see from the figure, fully half of all default recurrences occurred

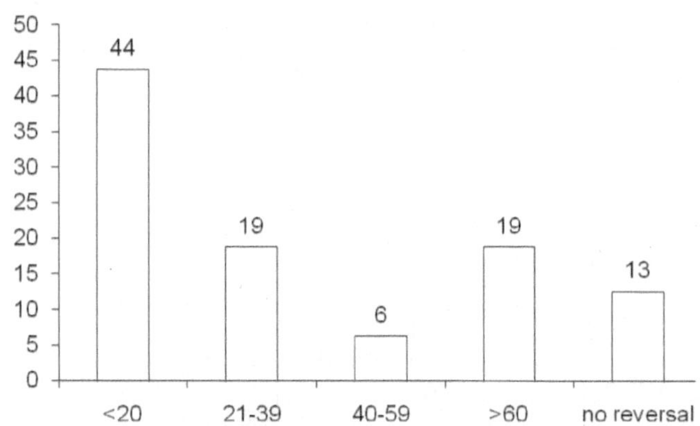

Fig. 1. External default crises: duration of tranquil time, 1300–1799, high-income countries, frequency distribution (in %). Note: Duration of tranquil time is calculated as the number of years between two consecutive external defaults' starting years. We first count the number of external default episodes, then calculate the duration of tranquil time if it was reversed, and finally calculate the frequency distribution. Sample coverage: 14 episodes of default crisis with reversal and two episodes with no reversal, six countries (United Kingdom, Spain, Germany [Prussia], Portugal, Austria, and France). Sources: Reinhart and Rogoff (2009), sources cited therein, and authors' calculations.

after a more than 20-year hiatus, with a significant percentage occurring even after a 60-year hiatus.

Advanced country external sovereign debt defaults have become much rarer events in the modern era. Germany's most recent default occurred in 1939, Austria's in 1940, and Hungary's in 1941 (Reinhart and Rogoff 2009). Especially interesting are the cases of Sweden and France. France, despite a near record level of defaults in its pre-Napoleonic era, has not defaulted on external debt since. Sweden, too, has not defaulted on external debt since its default at the end of the Napoleonic War in 1812. It would be interesting to explore whether wartime defaults are less damaging to reputation than peacetime defaults, though of course over many episodes, it is precisely the propensity to wage war that motivates many countries to build up large debts (as in the tax-smoothing model of Barro [1979]). Later, we will consider the robustness of our recidivism results to the exclusion of wartime.

Reinhart and Rogoff (2009) also show that the kind of long cycles illustrated in table 2 are quite characteristic of some of today's emerging markets, many of which have defaulted at least once during the past 2–3 decades. The number of emerging markets that have experienced external debt crises expands considerably if one includes "near-default" episodes in which countries averted technical default thanks to IMF bridge loans. In virtually all these cases, the countries still suffered massive recessions as governments were forced to tighten fiscal policy as borrowing options dried up. Importantly, we do not include these in our calculations below, although arguably from the point of view of understanding macroeconomic volatility and the dangers of excessive debt accumulation, they are equally important. We return to this issue later when we study IMF programs.

IV. The Duration and Prevalence of Crises: The Post-1800 Experience

We now proceed to focus on the more "recent" period, 1800 to the present, at the same time expanding the analysis to include banking and inflation crises, which, as shown in table 2, emerged as important in this era. The past 2 centuries also give a much broader sample of independent nations to study, as various regions of the world threw off the yoke of colonialization. In table 3, we present measures of crisis probability. Each measure takes the number of years a country experienced each kind of crisis (including all years and not just the initial one) divided by the number of years since independence (or since 1800).

Table 3
Summary Statistics of Crisis Probabilities

	External Default		Inflation		Banking	
	Average	Standard Deviation	Average	Standard Deviation	Average	Standard Deviation
World	.19	.18	.12	.12	.08	.07
High-income countries	.07	.13	.06	.05	.07	.04
Middle- and low-income countries*	.19	.17	.17	.17	.11	.09
Latin America	.34	.13	.12	.07	.04	.03

Source: Reinhart and Rogoff (2009), sources cited therein, and authors' calculations.
Note: Crisis probability is calculated as the number of years in crisis divided by the number of years since independence. Probabilities were calculated for each country since 1800 or the country's independence year. Sample coverage: 66 countries for external default crisis and 67 countries for inflation and banking crises.
*Excludes Latin America.

Table 3 shows that the biggest difference between high-income countries and the rest of the world lies in exposure to external default crisis. The average external default crisis probability of the high-income group is less than half of that of middle- and low-income countries and almost one-fifth of that of Latin American countries. The difference would be even larger if we included only twentieth- and twenty-first-century defaults. Inflation crisis probabilities are also higher in the rest of the world than in high-income countries although the gap is smaller. Interestingly, the average probabilities of banking crises in high-income countries and in the rest of the world are similar.[6] The results in table 3 are, of course, complete consistent with the time line in table 1.

Note that inflation and banking crisis probabilities are lower in part because the average duration of these crises tends to be much shorter compared to external default crises. (Note also that we are counting years in crisis, as opposed to the number of independent events.)[7]

Appendix table A1, which gives the average duration of crises, shows the striking difference between the mean and median duration of external default crises versus inflation and banking crises. The median duration of banking crises is 3 years or less across all income classes, where the world median for default crises is 8 years. For inflation crises, the median is only 1 year across all income classes. Presumably this implies that a country can find ways to trudge on in a state of sovereign default far more easily than it can continue any semblance of business as usual during a banking or inflation crisis.

Given the long duration of external default crises and their frequency, it is not surprising that large portions of the world have been in default over much of the last 200 years, as illustrated by Reinhart and Rogoff (2009, 72). Some of the major default episodes include the Napoleonic Wars in the early nineteenth century and then Latin American countries once independent, Greece, Spain, and Portugal in the first quarter of the century. The biggest default spike occurs during the era that bridged the Great Depression and World War II, when at the peak more than 40% of the world, weighted by GDP, was in default on external debt.

Figure 2 gives the share of countries in inflation crisis over the same period. Note the huge rise in inflation crises starting after World Wars I and II and again in the 1980s and early 1990s. The very recent history of low inflation throughout most of the world indeed represents a major shift from the preceding 80 years. It remains to be seen whether inflation is a scourge that has been eradicated. As Rogoff (2003) has argued, institutional changes, including especially the advent of independent central banks with a strong anti-inflation commitment, have been an important factor in this dramatic fall in inflation, but so too was the precrisis boom that alleviated political pressures on central banks to engage in unanticipated inflation. It remains to be seen whether the current period will prove merely another lull (one sees many in fig. 2) as opposed to a permanent structural shift toward universal low and stable inflation.

Fig. 2. Share of countries in inflation crisis, 1800–2008, world. Sample coverage: 66 countries that were independent in the given year. Sources: Reinhart and Rogoff (2009), sources cited therein, and authors' calculations.

Indeed, if one truly believes that fiscal dominance will never again assert itself in most countries, then, arguably, historical measures of outright default may underestimate the true probabilities (if the option of default via surprise inflation has been effectively erased). The recent explosion of public debt globally underscores this concern.

Figure 3 gives the share of the world experiencing banking crises since 1800. Note the remarkably small number of banking crises during the years of financial repression that began during World War II and continued in many countries well into the 1970s. By historical standards, this was a uniquely quiescent period. It is clear also from the figure that this era has been long but seems to be coming to an end.

The next three figures contrast the experiences of high-income countries with those of middle- and low-income countries (including Latin America). They corroborate what we have already seen in table 3 but give more detail. Figure 4 on external debt crises, for example, illustrates two points. First, as already noted, middle- and low-income countries are in technical default on external debt a significantly higher percentage of the time than high-income countries. Second, high-income countries had a dramatic drop in external defaults starting in the late 1960s with none (as of this writing!) since the advent of floating exchange rates in the 1970s. Later we shall look at evidence on distance since the last default crisis. (Note: We exclude from our middle- and low-income

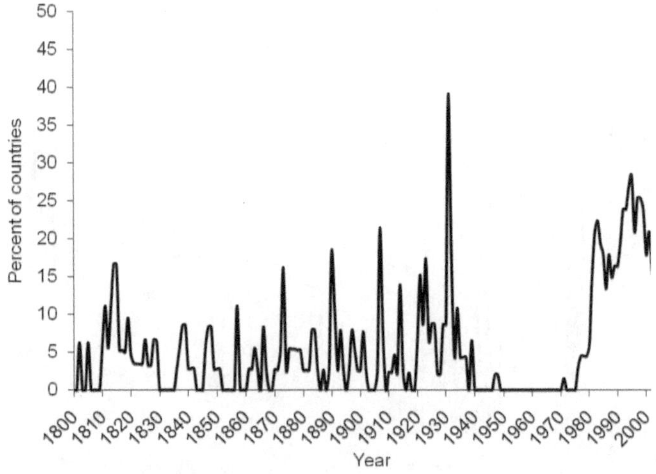

Fig. 3. Share of countries in banking crisis, 1800–2008, world. Sample coverage: 66 countries that were independent in the given year. Sources: Reinhart and Rogoff (2009), sources cited therein, and authors' calculations.

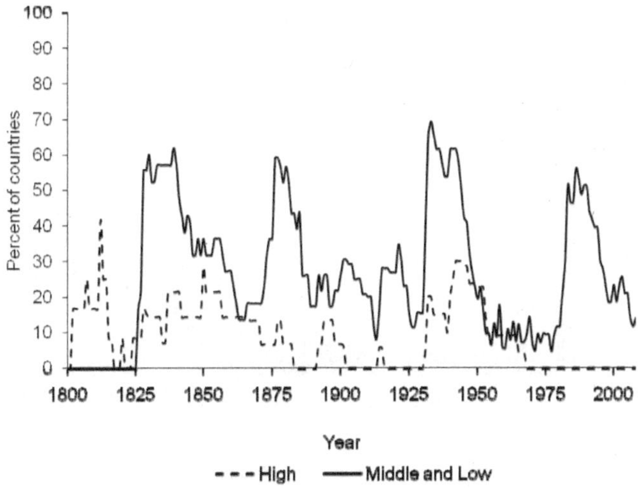

Fig. 4. Share of countries in external default crisis, 1800–2008, high-income versus middle- and low-income countries. Sample coverage: 66 countries (23 high-income and 43 middle- and low-income countries) that were independent in the given year. Sources: Reinhart and Rogoff (2009), sources cited therein, and authors' calculations.

countries very low-income countries that do not have external default by virtue of the fact that they are not able to borrow at all on private markets.)

High-income countries seem to have graduated from default crisis, or at least gone into deep remission. But most middle- and low-income countries have not yet graduated.

Figure 5 shows the frequencies of inflation crises in middle- and low-income countries versus high-income countries. High-income countries have had inflation crises more recently than external default crises, but the frequency has dropped to zero since the early 1990s. For middle- and low-income countries, a spike in the 1990s has been followed by a sharp tapering during the 2000s. Whereas figure 5 is illustrative of the frequency of very high inflation episodes, we note that it does not capture episodes of sustained high inflation below 20% that, if significantly unanticipated and depending on the maturity structure of government debt, may represent a substantial de facto default on domestic debt.

Figure 6 on banking crises tells a very different story. (Our data for developing countries begin more recently; hence the dashed line for middle- and low-income countries begins only in the 1860s. Of course, many of today's developing countries did not gain their independence until later.) One can see that in sharp contrast to external default and inflation crises, banking crises are "an equal opportunity menace" (Reinhart and Rogoff 2009, chap. 10). Although banking crises have picked up

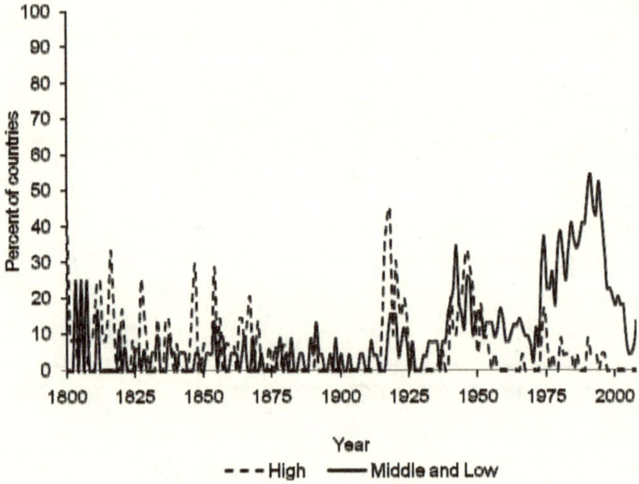

Fig. 5. Share of countries in inflation crisis, 1800–2008, high-income versus middle- and low-income countries. Sample coverage: 67 countries (23 high-income and 44 middle- and low-income countries) that were independent in the given year. Sources: Reinhart and Rogoff (2009), sources cited therein, and authors' calculations.

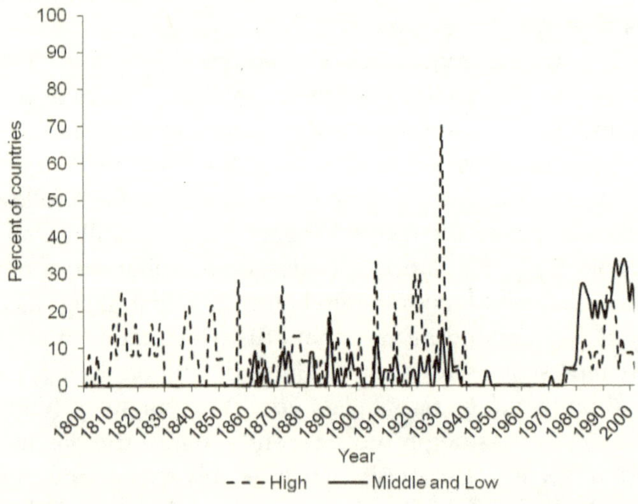

Fig. 6. Share of countries in banking crisis, 1800–2008, high-income versus middle- and low-income countries. Sample coverage: 67 countries (23 high-income and 44 middle- and low-income countries) that were independent in the given year. Sources: Reinhart and Rogoff (2009), sources cited therein, and authors' calculations.

dramatically in emerging markets since 1980, they have recently picked up in rich countries as well. Again, note the hiatus in banking crises across both groups of countries during the years of financial repression from World War II until the 1970s. Clearly, neither high-income nor middle- and low-income countries are in imminent danger of graduating from banking crises.

V. The Interval between Consecutive Crises

Having presented evidence on the incidence of crises, we next examine the duration of tranquil times or the interval between crises. In our first pass here, we do not make any attempt to deal with the possible nonstationarity of the time series and take simple averages. In particular, we do not deal with the possible structural breaks that occur at World War II, when default and banking crises frequencies sharply increased; in the early 1970s, when they rose again; and in the 1990s, when inflation crises frequencies fell dramatically. From the broader sweep of history, it is not easy to determine what constitutes a structural break, but clearly further analysis is needed. It should also be noted that in the main text, we present only unconditional measures of lulls between crises; institutions and political stability are no doubt extremely important. Yet, many of these factors, too, are highly persistent and difficult to measure, which is precisely why previous experience with crises is such a powerful predictor of future ones.[8] (We do present hazard analysis results in app. B, which in principle allow for conditioning on a broader range of variables.)

In figure 7, we look at the frequency distribution of "tranquil" periods, how long before one crisis episode stops and the next crisis starts. The figure gives the statistics separately for external default, inflation, and banking crises. The frequencies shown are conditional on having had at least one crisis of a particular type over 1800–2008. Of the 66 countries in our sample, 65 had at least one systemic banking crisis, 64 had at least one inflation crisis, and 50 had at least one sovereign default on external debt.[9] The conditional frequency distributions are similar, with a significant share of distribution falling between 10 and 20 years.

Crisis reversal and duration. The conditional frequency of recidivism (conditional on a crisis recurring) is broadly similar across different types of crises. Twenty years without a default, banking, or inflation crisis is hardly evidence of graduation. But it does appear to be a notable break, where the odds of recidivism over any medium-term period drop notably. As already mentioned and as documented in table A1 as

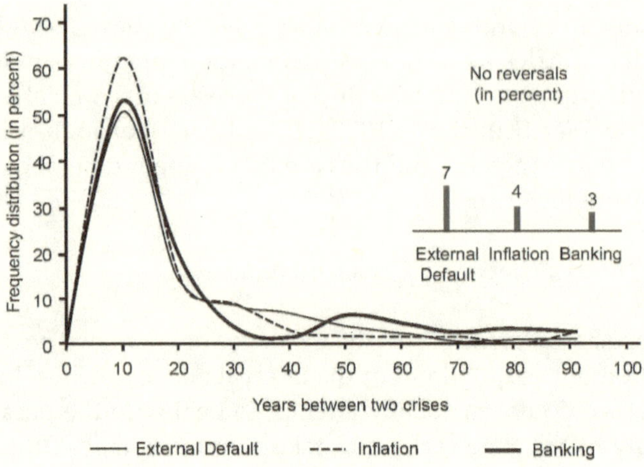

Fig. 7. Duration of tranquil times conditional on having had at least one crisis, 1800–2008, frequency distribution (in %). Note: Duration of tranquil time is calculated as the number of years between the end year of a crisis and the start of a new crisis. For example, Argentina had defaulted in 1982 and did not resolve it until 1994. In 2001 Argentina entered into default crisis again. In this case the tranquil time for Argentina was between 1994 and 2001. In other words, Argentina had default reversal in 7 years. The main figure shows the frequency distribution of years between two crises (or the number of years reversals took place). The inset smaller figure shows the frequency distribution of crises that have not reversed (for a period of more than 50 years). For each type of crisis, we count the number of crisis episodes that have reversed and those that have not for more than 50 years; then we calculate the duration of tranquil time when the crisis was reversed, and finally we calculate the frequency distribution. For example, 77% of inflation crises were reversed within 20 years; 4% of inflation crises were not reversed. Sources: Reinhart and Rogoff (2009), sources cited therein, and authors' calculations.

well as figure A1, the duration of default crises is much longer than that of inflation or banking crises.

As the inset highlights, conditional on having had at least one crisis, the percentage of no-reversal cases is significantly higher for default (7%) than for banking or inflation crises. If the 16 countries that never had an external default in the first place were counted in this tally, the graduation or no-reversal percentage gap between external default and banking and inflation crises would be far greater.

Figures 8, 9, and 10 illustrate the distribution of time between crises using a histogram and distinguishing between high-income and middle- and low-income countries. The charts give a more nuanced picture of the differences between crises than the world aggregates do. The "no-reversal" bars denote cases in which at least 50 years have passed without a crisis reversal; using a cutoff of 20 years does not lead to dramatically different

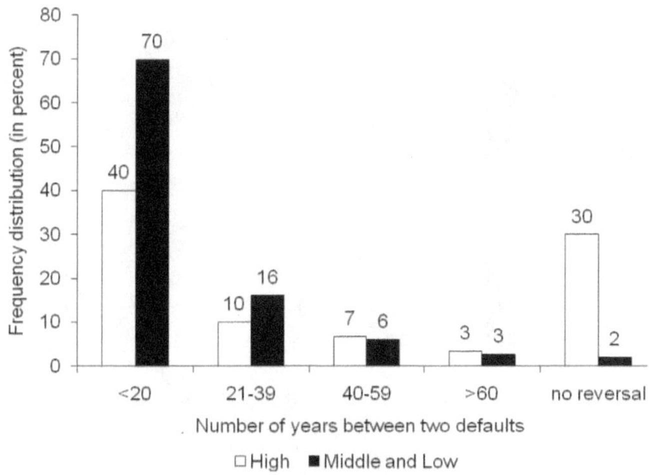

Fig. 8. External default crises: duration of tranquil time conditional on having had at least one crisis, 1800–2008, high-income versus middle- and low-income countries, frequency distribution (in %). Note: Duration of tranquil time is calculated as the number of years between two consecutive default episodes. The end of a default episode is considered as the year the country regains access to the capital market. In other words, as long as the country is excluded from the international capital market, it is not considered as having resolved its default crisis. The start of a new default episode is the year the country declares default on its external debt. For each income group, we count the number of external default episodes that have reversed and those that have not for more than 50 years, then we calculate the duration of tranquil time when default was reversed, and finally we calculate the frequency distribution. For example, for the high-income group, 40% of default crises were reversed within 20 years and 30% of default crises were not reversed. The bars do not sum to 100% because the cutoff excludes cases in which the last default occurred within 50 years but there has been no second default. Sample coverage: 167 episodes of default crisis with reversal and 12 episodes with no reversal. Sources: Reinhart and Rogoff (2009), sources cited therein, and authors' calculations.

results.[10] For external defaults, figure 8 illustrates that whereas most emerging market recurrences happen within 20 years (2 decades is an important marker), only a few countries that have once defaulted have avoided any further defaults, at least not long enough to pass the 50-year filter we use. For inflation and banking crises, the 20-year mark contains an even larger percentage of reversals, and at the same time, the cases of no reversal are scarce.

Since many crises happen during episodes of war and civil unrest, one might reasonably ask whether excluding these events dramatically affects recidivism rates or the difference between advanced and middle- and low-income economies. In appendix B, we reproduce figures 7 and 8 excluding episodes surrounding severe wars (deaths greater than 0.8% of the population). The results are little affected, as is the case

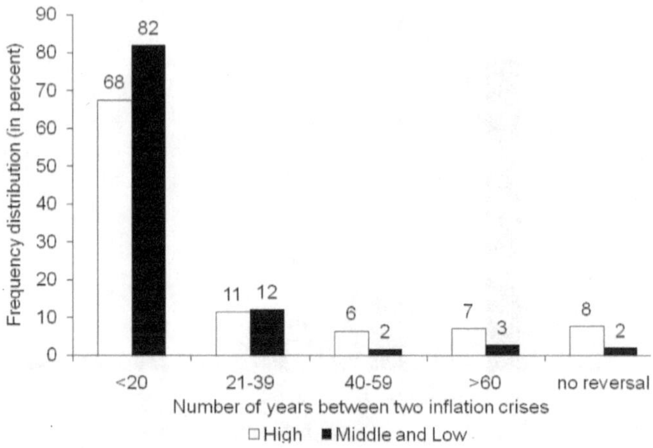

Fig. 9. Inflation crises: duration of tranquil time conditional on having had at least one crisis, 1800–2008, high-income versus middle- and low-income countries, frequency distribution (in %). Note: Duration of tranquil time is calculated as the number of years between two consecutive inflation crises. For each income group, we count the number of inflation crisis episodes that have reversed and those that have not for more than 50 years, then we calculate the duration of tranquil time when inflation crisis was reversed, and finally we calculate the frequency distribution. For example, for the high-income group, 68% of inflation crises were reversed within 20 years and 8% of inflation crises were not reversed. Sample coverage: 404 episodes of inflation crisis with reversals and 17 episodes with no reversal. Sources: Reinhart and Rogoff (2009), sources cited therein, and authors' calculations.

for the other figures. We also checked a milder war filter (deaths greater than 0.29% of the population), again without substantially changing the results. In any event, given that the risk of war is a major factor surrounding default risk and that propensity to wage war is an important risk to creditors, it is not entirely clear that this measure is more meaningful than the simpler one of the text; further study is needed.

VI. Time since the Last Crisis

To gain a deeper insight into recidivism—or its complement, graduation—we look at measures of distance since the last crisis. In figure 11, three countries, the United States, Denmark, and the United Kingdom, have been independent the entire post-1800 period and never defaulted on external debt. (Although as we have already noted, the United States and United Kingdom did effectively default on domestic debt by going off the gold standard in the early 1930s; Denmark also defaulted on domestic debt in 1813 at the end of the Napoleonic Wars.) At the other extreme, a number of African countries remain in default today. Stunningly, the

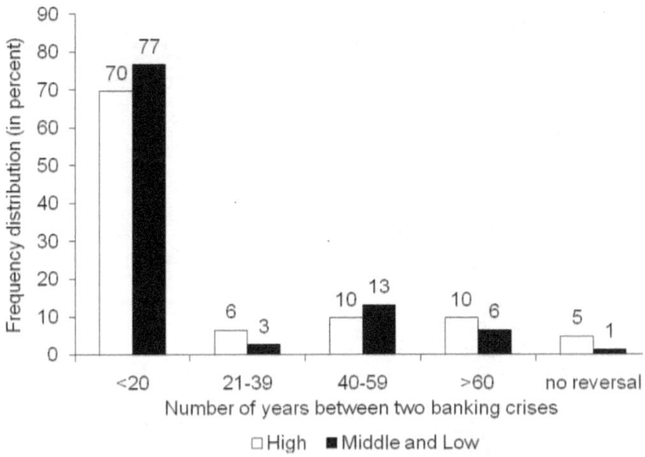

Fig. 10. Banking crises: duration of tranquil time conditional on having had at least one crisis, 1800–2008, high-income versus middle- and low-income countries, frequency distribution (in %). Note: Duration of tranquil time is calculated as the number of years between two consecutive banking crisis episodes. For each income group, we count the number of banking crisis episodes that have reversed and those that have not for more than 50 years, then we calculate the duration of tranquil time when banking crisis was reversed, and finally we calculate the frequency distribution. For example, for the high-income group, 70% of banking crises were reversed within 20 years and 5% of banking crises were not reversed. Sample coverage: 195 episodes of banking crisis with reversals and seven episodes with no reversal. Sources: Reinhart and Rogoff (2009), sources cited therein, and authors' calculations.

median time since last default is just over a century for the advanced countries (105 years) versus only 14 years for the developing countries. The world median is 23 years.

Figure 12 on inflation crises tells a similar story, with the median again being only 15 years for the middle- and low-income countries but 59 years for high-income countries. Many high-income countries, of course, had high inflation in the years after World War II, so the average time is lower than for default.

Finally, for banking crises, the difference between income groups is even smaller. Notice that even prior to the crisis, the difference between high-income countries and the rest of the world is not as large as for other types of crises. See figure 13 and table 4.

VII. Macroeconomic Volatility

What are the reasons why, at least until the recent global financial meltdown, financial crises have become less prevalent, especially in high-income

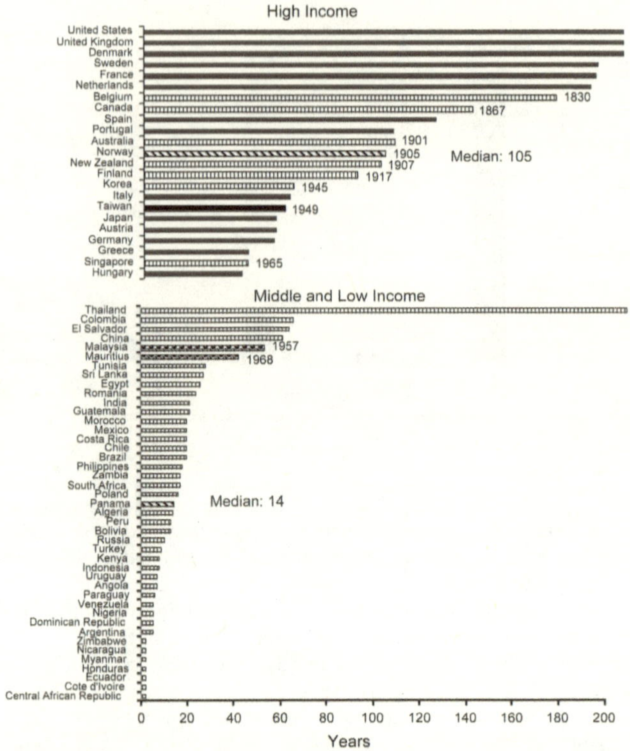

Fig. 11. Time elapsed by 2010 since the last external default crisis, 1800, or year of independence, high-income versus middle- and low-income countries. Note: Distance calculated as 2010 minus either the last year that the country was in external default crisis, 1800, or year of independence. Sample coverage: 66 countries (23 high-income and 43 middle- and low-income countries). Sources: Reinhart and Rogoff (2009), sources cited therein, and authors' calculations.

countries? Certainly, one possible reason was the general drop in macroeconomic volatility that took place particularly in the rich countries, that is, the Great Moderation, as figure 14 illustrates, particularly the drop in volatility from the 1980s in advanced countries and from the 1990s in emerging markets. The figure also illustrates, however, that our warnings about "early celebrations" for declaring countries to have graduated from financial crises may also apply to the Great Moderation. The decline in volatility from the 1970s may be due as much to a spike in the 1970s as to the Great Moderation after. The 1950s were also a period of relatively low volatility. In any event, it is clear that emerging markets face higher volatility than advanced countries.

Acemoglu et al. (2003) argue that countries that inherited more "extractive" institutions from their colonial past were more likely to

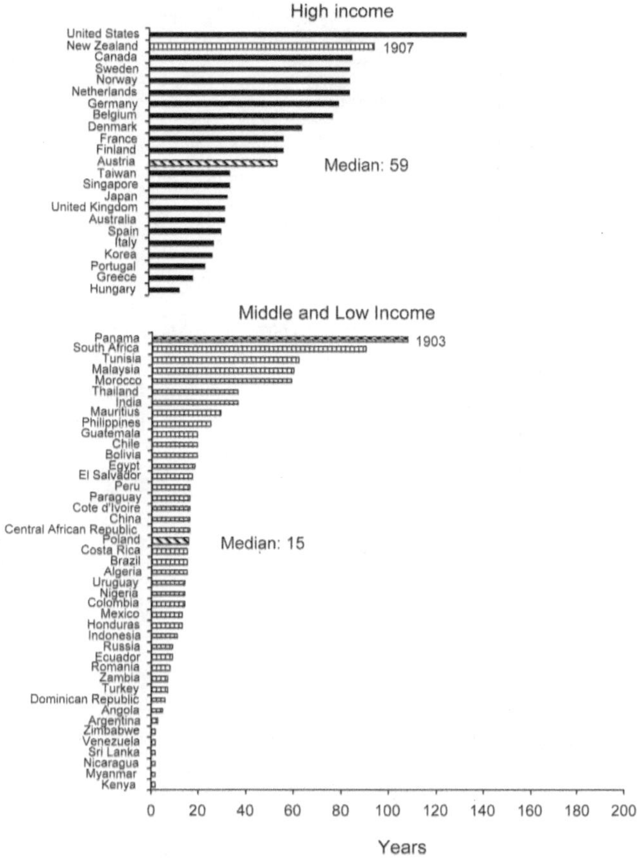

Fig. 12. Time elapsed by 2010 since last inflation crisis, 1800, or year of independence, high-income versus middle- and low-income countries. Note: Distance calculated as 2010 minus either the last year that the country was in inflation crisis, 1800, or year of independence. Sample coverage: 66 countries (23 high-income and 43 middle- and low-income countries). Sources: Reinhart and Rogoff (2009), sources cited therein, and authors' calculations.

experience high volatility, a lower growth rate, and more economic crises during the postwar period. This is an interesting hypothesis that merits further research, also on the difficulties of graduation. We note that countries with extractive resources are more likely to face very high terms of trade volatility and face higher risk of default for this reason as well (see Catao, Fostel, and Kapur 2009). Aguiar, Amador, and Gopinath (2009) argue that credibility problems may endogenously create greater persistence in productivity shocks in emerging markets, while one can also make the case that the countries with abundant natural resources

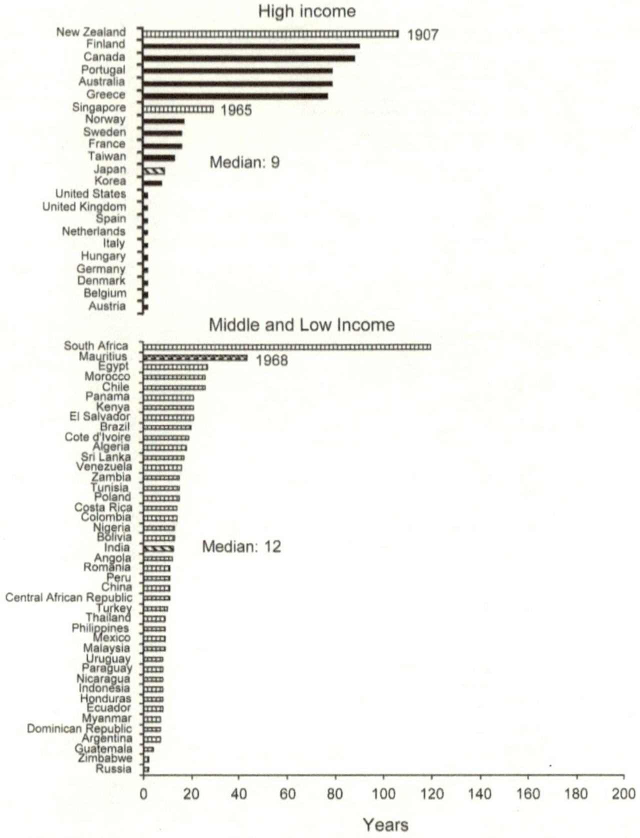

Fig. 13. Time elapsed by 2010 since the last banking crisis, 1800, or year of independence, high-income versus middle- and low-income countries. Note: Distance is calculated as 2010 minus either the last year that the country was in banking crisis, 1800, or year of independence. Sample coverage: 66 countries (23 high-income and 43 middle- and low-income countries). Sources: Reinhart and Rogoff (2009), sources cited therein, and authors' calculations.

are more likely to experience a generalized tragedy of the commons problem in governance, as emphasized in the voracity model of Tornell and Lane (1999). The institutional failure of coordinating interests of different power groups might be another reason why some countries, facing similar external shocks, are more prone to default than others, as modeled in Qian (2010). Figure 15 suggests that indeed, higher volatility in emerging market growth is not simply due to terms of trade volatility, as advanced country commodity exporters have experienced dramatically greater drops in volatility than emerging markets over the recent

Table 4
Medians of Distance (in Years) to Last Crisis in 2010

Type of Crisis	World	High-Income Countries	Middle- and Low-Income Countries
External default	23	105	14
Inflation	19	59	15
Banking	12	9	12

Source: Reinhart and Rogoff (2009), sources cited therein, and authors' calculations.
Note: Distance to last crisis is calculated as 2010 minus either the last year that the country was in crisis, 1800, or the year of independence. Medians are calculated for each income group and each type of crisis. Sample coverage: 66 countries (23 high-income and 43 middle- and low-income countries) for external default, inflation, and banking crises. Asian countries' median distance to external default crisis is 24, to inflation crisis is 21, and to banking crisis is 9. Latin American countries' median distance to external default crisis is 13, to inflation crisis is 15, and to banking crisis is 10.

period. Patterns similar to those illustrated in figures 14 and 15 emerge using swing of GDP growth rate instead of volatilities.[11]

VIII. Crisis and the Role of IMF Programs: 1952–2007

We next look at IMF programs. The presence of the IMF constitutes a major structural change. As emphasized by Bordo and Eichengreen (1999), crises have been more frequent but shorter since the advent of

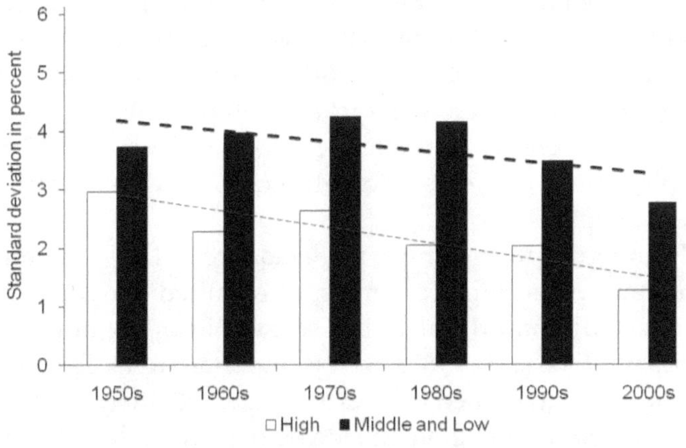

Fig. 14. Evolution of GDP growth rate volatility, 1950–2006, high-income versus middle- and low-income countries. Note: For each country the volatility is calculated as the standard deviation of its growth rate during the 10-year interval. Sample coverage: 66 countries (23 high-income and 43 middle- and low-income countries) that were independent in the given year. Sources: Maddison (2004) and Total Economy Database (http://www.conference-board.org/data/economydatabase/, 2008).

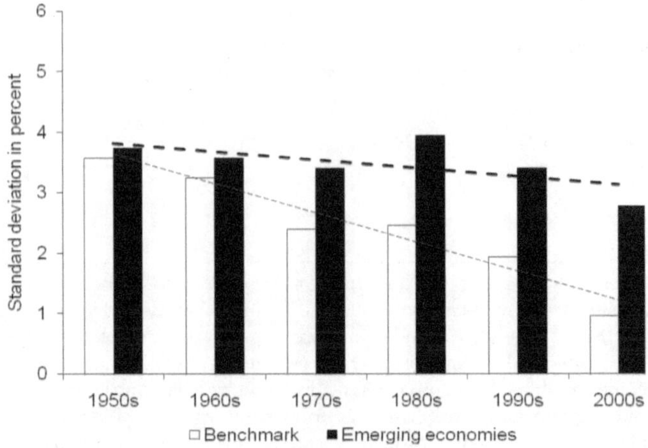

Fig. 15. Evolution of GDP growth rate volatility, 1950–2006, commodities-exporting countries: emerging versus benchmark economies. Note: For each country the volatility is calculated as the standard deviation of its growth rate during the 10-year interval. Benchmark economies: Australia and New Zealand. Emerging economies: Argentina, Bolivia, Brazil, Chile, Colombia, Cote d'Ivoire, India, Indonesia, Kenya, Malaysia, Mexico, Nigeria, Peru, Philippines, South Africa, Thailand, Uruguay, and Venezuela. Sources: Maddison (2004) and Total Economy Database (http://www.conference-board.org/data/economydatabase/, 2008).

the IMF. What is interesting is how often the introduction of the IMF program does not necessarily halt the ultimate crisis. A famous example is Argentina, which received large (as a share of GDP) bailout packages in 2000 and again in 2001 but nevertheless went ahead and defaulted in 2002. But the case of Argentina is hardly exceptional, as table 5 illustrates.

During 1952–2008, there were in total 85 default episodes and 538 IMF programs. If one restricts attention to cases in which IMF programs were implemented 1–2 years before the crisis, we have 36 cases, or 42% of all default episodes.

Finally, in figure 16, we graph the incidence of IMF programs across advanced and emerging economies. The United Kingdom famously called repeatedly on IMF help, but so too did many other advanced economies until the early 1980s. So it is important to recognize that even though countries graduated from external default, there can be a further transition period of calling on outside help in "near-default" incidents.

IX. Graduation and the Theory of Sovereign Default

Now that we have given a quantitative overview of the remarkable serial nature of sovereign default, banking, and inflation crises, what

Table 5
Examples of Cases in Which IMF Programs Are Introduced but There Is Subsequent Default

		IMF Program			
	Default Starting Year	Program Year	Approved Date	Expiration/ Cancelation Date	Amount (Millions of SDRs)
India	1958	1957	3/11/57	3/10/58	72.5
Chile	1961	1959	4/1/59	12/31/59	8.1
		1961	2/16/61	2/15/62	75
	1963	1963	1/15/63	1/14/64	40
	1966	1964	2/14/64	1/15/65	25
Costa Rica	1962	1961	10/4/61	10/3/62	15
	1981	1980	3/12/80	6/16/81	60.5
Paraguay	1968	1966	9/1/66	8/31/67	7.5
Peru	1969	1967	8/18/67	8/17/68	42.5
	1978	1977	11/18/77	9/14/78	90
	1980	1978	9/15/78	8/9/79	32.2
		1979	8/10/79	12/31/80	285
	1983	1982	6/7/82	4/26/84	650
Turkey	1982	1980	6/18/80	6/17/83	1,250
Panama	1983	1982	4/28/82	4/27/83	29.7
Uruguay	1983	1983	4/22/83	4/21/85	378
	1987	1985	9/27/85	3/26/87	122.9
	2003	2002	4/1/02	3/18/03	1,988.3
Guatemala	1989	1988	10/26/88	2/28/90	54
Venezuela	1990	1989	6/23/89	3/22/93	3,703.1
Indonesia	1998	1997	11/5/97	8/25/98	8,338.2
	2002	2000	2/4/00	1/29/02	3,638
Argentina	2001	2000	3/10/00	1/23/03	16,936.8
Dominican Republic	2005	2003	8/29/03	1/30/05	438

Note: SDRs = special drawing rights.

does theory tell us about graduation? Since by far the most striking empirical differences between advanced economies and middle- and low-income countries are for sovereign debt, we will focus mainly on this question.

At one level, the inferior performance of middle- and low-income countries is easy to explain. Emerging market countries face deeper and more permanent shocks (as Aguiar and Gopinath [2007] emphasize); at the same time, they tend to engage in procyclical macroeconomic policy, as Kaminsky, Reinhart, and Vegh (2005) document. During periods of surges in global capital flows, emerging markets rush in with a plethora of supposedly high-return projects, at the risk of being stuck with incomplete, illiquid investments if capital flows reverse or capital evaporates. Corruption and the influence of interest

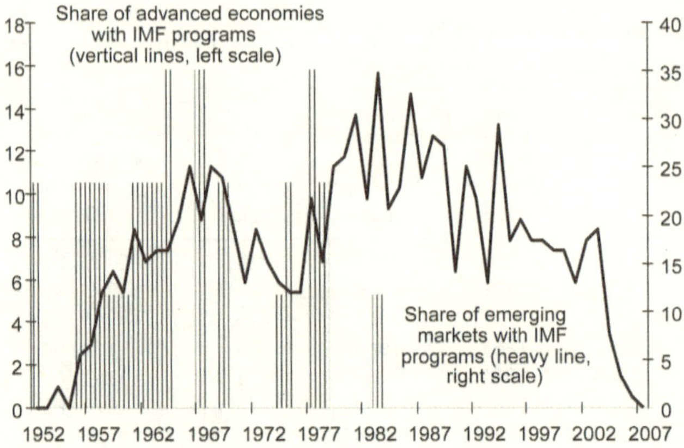

Fig. 16. The incidence of IMF programs in advanced and emerging economies, 1952–2007. Source: Reinhart (2010).

groups are other important factors in developing countries that can undermine fiscal stability and potentially lead to overborrowing as shown in Qian (2010). France's status as a centuries-long serial defaulter during its years of monarchy has often been blamed on the government's failure to establish a rational and orderly system of centralized tax collection (see MacDonald 2006). Clearly, graduation, if it can be achieved, is also linked to a country's institutions and not just its level of wealth.

At another level, explaining graduation is quite difficult because standard models of default (following Eaton and Gersovitz [1981]) do not necessarily suggest that richer countries should be able to borrow less (as a percentage of their income) or that they should necessarily be more prone to default. As detailed in Obstfeld and Rogoff (1996), the key penalty for default in the canonical model is a cutoff from international capital markets and an inability to smooth national consumption through international markets. As Obsteld and Rogoff show, the calibration of the costs to default is quite similar to that of Lucas (1987) on the gains to smoothing out business cycles. Obstfeld and Rogoff (1996, 369) find that, in fact, the empirical cost of exclusion from international markets is considerably greater for emerging markets than for rich countries. Admittedly, the canonical models illustrate model implicit contracts, so the issue of actual default is left in the background. Grossman and Van Huyck (1988) and Bulow and Rogoff (1989a) argue that if shocks are observable but not verifiable, then optimal contracts may call for a premium in good states of nature and negotiate partial default in bad states of nature, depending on the two sides' relative bargaining power. In any event, the fact that actual insolvency is seldom an issue in sovereign debt contracts and that willingness to pay is invariably the binding constraint underscores the point that countries cannot be expected to graduate simply by virtue of growing richer.

Of course, one way countries can graduate from default on external debt is by borrowing entirely (or almost entirely) through domestically administered markets. As Reinhart and Rogoff (2009) show, domestic debt has long been a quite important source of debt for most countries in the world, even though this fact has not been widely recognized. Also contrary to conventional belief, there are many cases of outright default on domestic debt (Reinhart and Rogoff document over 70). Some of these defaults involved breaking indexation clauses (to inflation, gold, etc.), but in some cases, countries prefer outright default on domestic debt to achieve the same end through inflation.

In general, the fact that rich countries tend to have far fewer problems with serial default most likely traces to collateral outside the usual type considered in the literature. (See Bulow and Rogoff [1989b] or Cole and Kehoe [1996] for discussions of possible collateral outside the direct risk-sharing gains from financial integration. For example, a breakdown in debt payments can spill over into reputation in trade relationships.) Another factor, of course, is that richer countries with better-developed domestic credit markets are in a position to rely far less on external financing, which in turn plausibly lowers the risk of external default.

At the other extreme are models of banking and financial crises that certainly do not suggest any reason why richer countries should be less crisis prone. As already noted, Schularick and Taylor (2009) argue that even where greater macroeconomic and policy stability ought to ensure a more stable environment and fewer crises, the financial system may expand to become crisis prone, offsetting the benefits of greater stability. Thus, in addition to needing a better theory of serial default on sovereign external debt and a country's ultimate graduation, it is also important to better understand the transitions countries experience as they develop, as illustrated in table 1 earlier.

X. Conclusions

In this paper, we have tried to quantify and better understand countries' risks of recidivism for different types of financial crises and the duration of time that must pass before one can consider a country to have "graduated." Twenty years without a crisis is an important marker, but the tails of the recidivism distribution are very large. Countries do seem to graduate from external default crises, although further study is required to understand how much this is due to greater institutional and macroeconomic stability and how much is due to enhanced ability to partially default in other ways (e.g., inflation and financial repression), especially as advanced countries are typically able to finance a far larger share of their debt under domestic law and in domestic currency. Of course, if one also includes borrowing under duress from the IMF as a measure of debt crisis recidivism, the evidence on graduation for advanced countries from external default crisis is less convincing. Graduation from inflation crises is a relatively recent phenomenon, and here the evidence on graduation is suggestive but less decisive. Banking crises are a completely different animal; there is no compelling evidence that any country has outgrown them. However, the very low rate of banking crises that occurred between the end of World War II and the breakup of Bretton Woods at the beginning of the 1970s is a notable phenomenon that requires further study.

Appendix A

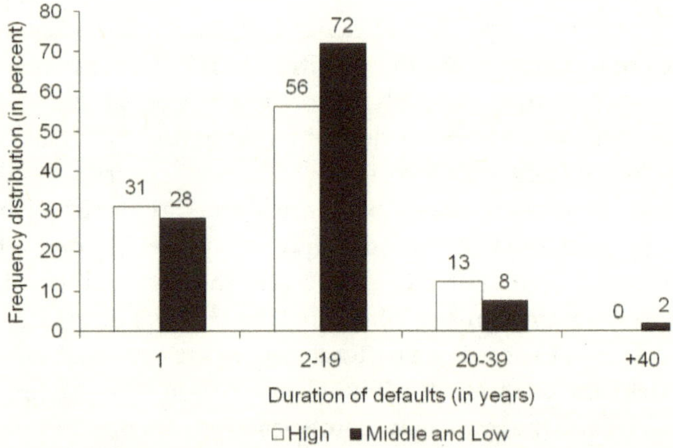

Fig. A1. Duration of external default crises, 1800–2008, high-income versus middle- and low-income countries, frequency distribution (in %). Note: Duration of defaults is calculated as the number of years between the start of a default crisis and the year that it resolved. The end of a default episode is considered as the year the country regains access to the capital market. In other words, as long as the country is excluded from the international capital market, it is not considered as having resolved its default crisis. Sample coverage: 218 episodes of default crisis (32 high-income and 186 middle- and low-income countries). Sources: Reinhart and Rogoff (2008) and authors' calculations.

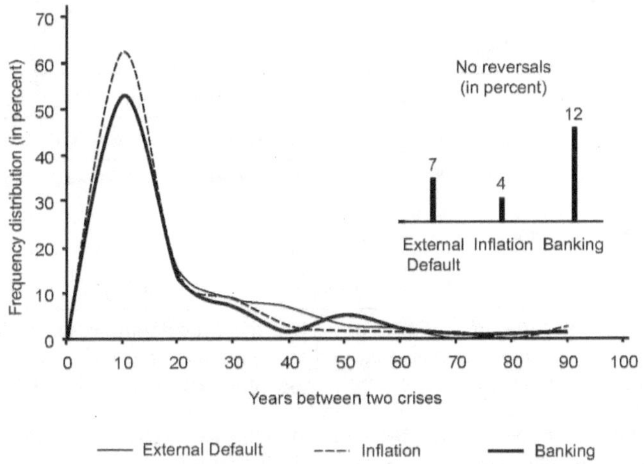

Fig. A2. Duration of tranquil times conditional on having had at least one crisis, 1800–2008, frequency distribution (in %). Excludes defaults started after and during severe wars. Note: See figure 7 in the text.

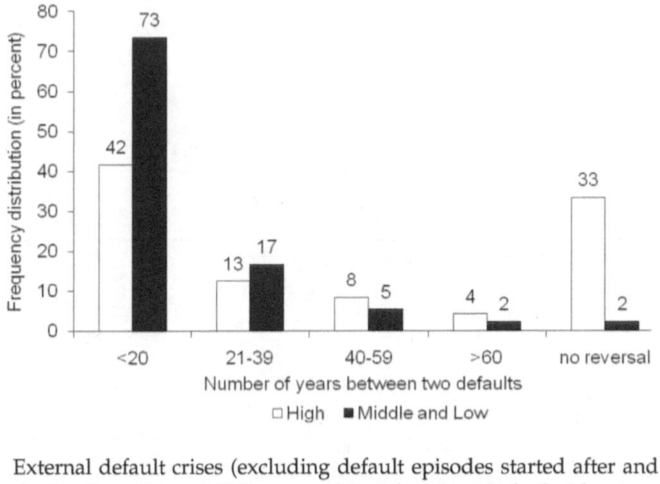

Fig. A3. External default crises (excluding default episodes started after and during severe wars): duration of tranquil times conditional on having had at least one crisis, 1800–2008, high-income versus middle- and low-income countries, frequency distribution (in %). Note: See corresponding figure 8 in the text. Sources: Reinhart and Rogoff (2009), sources cited therein, and authors' calculations.

Table A1
Average Duration of Crises

	External Default		Inflation		Banking	
	Median	Average	Median	Average	Median	Average
World	8	15.1	1	2.3	1	2.5
High-income countries	9	20.7	1	1.6	1	1.7
Middle- and low-income countries*	4	14.1	1	2.4	3	4.0
Latin America	9	14.6	1	3.2	2	2.7

Source: Reinhart and Rogoff (2008), sources cited therein, and authors' calculations.
Note: Duration of a default crisis is calculated as the number of years between the starting year and end year of the crisis. For example, Argentina had defaulted in 1982 and did not resolve it until 1993. In this case, the duration of this episode of default crisis is 12. Inflation crisis dating is straightforward per the definition in the text. As Reinhart and Rogoff (2009) note, dating the end of banking crises is very difficult, though in any event, they are typically relatively short. Sample coverage: 198 episodes of default crisis (28 high-income countries and 170 middle- and low-income countries), 462 episodes of inflation crisis (166 high-income countries and 296 middle- and low-income countries), and 201 episodes of banking crisis (108 high-income countries and 93 middle- and low-income countries).
*Excludes Latin America.

Table A2
Default Episodes That Began After and During Severe Wars

Country	War Start	War End	War Name	Death_Pop (%)	Default First Year
Angola	1975	1991	Angolan Civil War	5.57	1985
Colombia	1899	1903	Colombia vs. Liberals of 1899	2.60	1900
Germany	1939	1945	World War II	4.39	1939
Guatemala	1961	1996	Guatemalan Civil War	1.14	1986, 1989
Hungary	1941	1945	World War II	1.46	1941–67
Japan	1941	1945	World War II	2.41	1942
Mexico	1910	1914	Mexico vs. Liberals and Radicals	1.65	1914
Nicaragua	1978	1979	Nicaragua vs. Sandinistas	1.45	1979
Paraguay	1932	1935	Chaco	3.91	1932
Turkey	1914	1918	World War I	1.75	1915
Venezuela	1859	1863	Venezuela vs. Liberals	1.35	1860

Appendix B

Default Reversal: Note on Hazard Rate Analysis

Definition. The hazard rate is the probability of a country having a crisis at time $t + 1$ given that it has not had a crisis at time t. The hazard rate is calculated conditioned on the length of time since the last crisis. Thus we are looking at the subset of countries that had at least one crisis event (default in this particular calculation). For example, country A had a default crisis in 2001 and it ended in 2003. The hazard rate of crisis in 2010 for country A indicates the probability of having a crisis in 2010 conditioned on its being crisis free for 7 years.

The *nonparametric analysis* makes no assumptions about the shape of the hazard function or about how variables affect it. Instead, the hazard function is estimated on the basis of the data, using the Kaplan-Meier (1958) method. (The Kaplan-Meier method is a descriptive procedure for time to event variables, commonly used when time is considered the only salient variable.)

Figure B1 shows the hazard rate of default reversal for the entire sample (167 episodes). The vertical axis indicates the probability of having a default crisis and the horizontal axis indicates years since the end of the last default episode. For less than 60 years, the hazard rate declines with the length of the crisis-free spell. That is, the longer the country remains

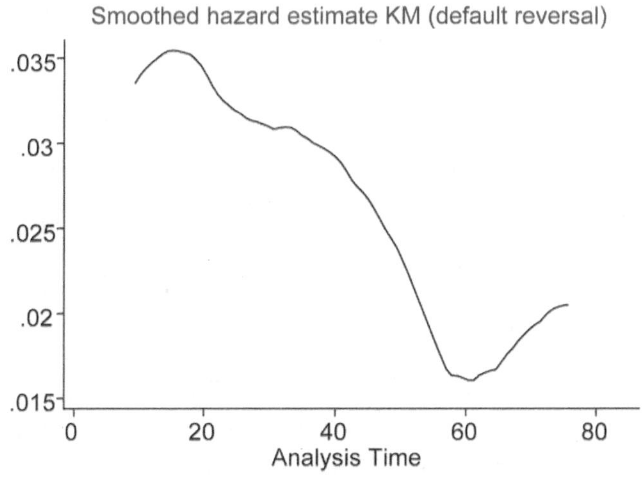

Fig. B1. Hazard rate of default reversal: full sample

crisis free, the lower the probability of its having another default crisis. But there is a break in year 60. After 60 years of being crisis free, the hazard rate increases with the length of time. This suggests that there might be a default crisis cycle every 60 years or it might be an artifact of the sparseness of the sample if countries go 60 years without a crisis.

Figure B2 separates the sample by income level. For high-income countries, the hazard function monotonically decreases with respect to the length of tranquil time, approaching zero when the country has been crisis free for more than 60 years. However, for middle- and low-income countries, the hazard function slightly declines in the first 60 years of tranquil time, but it starts to increase after year 60. This means that for countries that had been crisis free for more than 60 years, the hazard rate of having another crisis increases every year, indicating that a default cycle is highly probable for this income group. One explanation for such a pattern in the middle- and low-income group is that once a long period of time has passed since the last crisis, countries become more vulnerable to a "this time is different syndrome," with policy makers and investors not paying sufficient attention to indicators of crisis vulnerability.

Parametric analysis specifies the shape of the baseline hazard function as well as how the covariates affect the hazard function. We assume proportional hazard models. Covariates are assumed to raise or lower the hazard function in a multiplicative way. The baseline hazard function

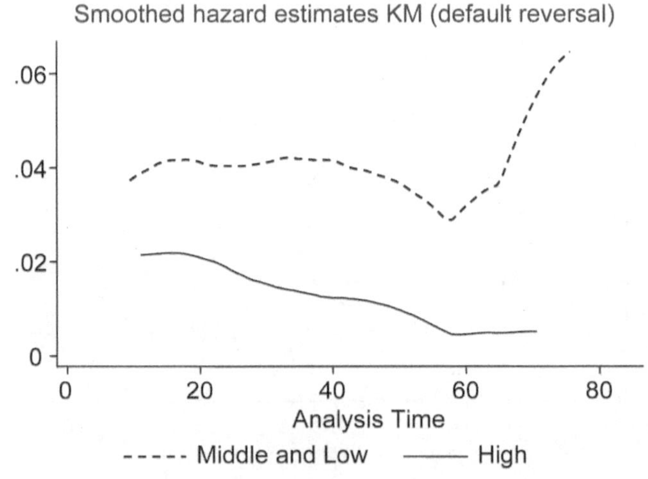

Fig. B2. Hazard rate of default reversal: high-income countries versus middle- and low-income countries.

is Weibull, which encompasses a baseline hazard function that may be flat like exponential models, monotonically increasing, or decreasing.

We use as covariates the lag world share of countries in default crisis and three dummy variables: (i) being in a severe war the year of crisis reversal, (ii) pre-1914, and (iii) income level equal to one for all high-income countries and zero for the rest of the world.

Table B1 reports the results of the parametric analysis. The coefficients have the usual interpretation: an increase of 1% in the share of countries in default crisis during the previous year increases the hazard of default reversal by roughly 2%. Both severe war and pre–World War I have coefficients close to zero and are not significant. Being a high-income country decreases the hazard of default reversal by 0.23 percentage point; however, this change is too small to be significant. The hazard ratio shows the qualitative effect of covariates to hazard rates. When it is greater than one, it increases the hazard rate; when it is less than one, it decreases the hazard rate; and when it equals one, it does not affect the hazard rate. The symbol α measures the rate of change over time of the hazard rate. In this case, $\alpha = -0.11$, indicating a decline of hazard of about 11% per year. Finally, p measures time dependence. For $p < 1$, there is negative time dependence, meaning that the longer the country stays in tranquil time (crisis free), the lower the hazard of default reversal may occur.

Table B1
Parametric Analysis: Hazard Rate of Default Reversal

	Weibull Model	
Variable	Coefficient	Hazard Ratio
Lag share of countries in default	2.04	7.68
	(.02)	
Severe war	.05	1.05
	(.87)	
Pre–World War I	.09	1.10
	(.61)	
High income	−.23	.79
	(.29)	
Constant	−2.79	
α	−.11	
p	.90	

Note: Lag share of countries in default is the percentage of countries in default crisis the year before the default reversal; severe war is a dummy variable that equals one if the country that had a default reversal was in a severe war (defined as death to population larger than 0.8%); high income is a dummy variable that equals one if the country that had a default reversal is a high-income country. In parentheses we report the p-value.

Endnotes

We are grateful to the Alfred P. Sloan Foundation and the National Science Foundation (grant 0849224) for financial support.

1. The notion of "graduation" was introduced in Reinhart, Rogoff, and Savastano (2003). An inflation crisis is defined as an annual inflation rate of 20% or higher. Given the very large correlation between exchange rate and inflation crises over this period (Reinhart and Rogoff 2004, 2010), we do not treat exchange rate crises separately in this paper.

2. Before 1800, the 20-year marker subsumes only about half of external default relapses.

3. Reinhart and Rogoff (2010) formally investigate the predictive power of past banking and sovereign default crises and future ones. Among their results is the finding that banking crises do help predict sovereign default crises, that private debt levels help predict banking crises, and that public debt helps predict sovereign default.

4. Reinhart and Rogoff (2008, 2009) emphasize that banking crises are an "equal opportunity menace."

5. We do not include domestic debt crises or exchange rate crises in this study, but some comment is warranted to put the overall exercise in perspective. Although overt de jure defaults on domestic debt have received very little attention in the literature, Reinhart and Rogoff (2008, 2009) show that they were once surprisingly common, cataloging over 70 cases of domestic default. We do not explore exchange rate crises here, in part because inflation and exchange rate crises are highly correlated (see Reinhart and Rogoff 2009, 2010). Also, it is clear that standard definitions of exchange rate crises (emphasizing very large short-term exchange rate movements) would show very few potential "graduates."

6. The similarity of banking crises across countries was first noted in Reinhart and Rogoff (2009, chap. 10). The authors also show that the macroeconomic effects of banking crises are remarkably similar as well across advanced economies and emerging markets.

7. Interestingly, as we showed in the appendix to the conference version of this paper, inflation crisis probabilities are higher among middle- and low-income countries (excluding Latin America) than in Latin America, while their default crisis probability is lower. This is partly due to the fact that low-income countries are often excluded from international capital markets; therefore, external default crises are less common.

8. Again, Reinhart et al. (2003) and Reinhart and Rogoff (2010) provide concrete empirical measures of how past crises experience measures a country's vulnerability to future crisis, an exercise we do not take up here.

9. Mauritius is the only country to have avoided a systemic banking crisis altogether; New Zealand and Panama managed to escape inflation crises.

10. The bars in figs. 8–10 add to less than 100% because they exclude episodes in which there has not yet been recidivism but the 50-year cutoff for no reversal has not yet been reached.

11. Calculated as the average swing of each group. For each country the swing is calculated as the difference between the maximum growth rate and the minimum growth rate during the 10-year interval.

References

Acemoglu, Daron, Simon Johnson, James Robinson, and Yunyong Thaicharoen. 2003. "Institutional Causes, Macroeconomic Symptoms: Volatility, Crises and Growth." *Journal of Monetary Economics* 50:49–123.

Aguiar, Mark, Manuel Amador, and Gita Gopinath. 2009. "Investment Cycles and Sovereign Debt Overhang." *Review of Economic Studies* 76 (January): 1–31.

Aguiar, Mark, and Gita Gopinath. 2007. "Emerging Market Business Cycles: The Cycle Is the Trend." *Journal of Political Economy* 115 (February): 69–102.

Barro, Robert J. 1979. "On the Determination of the Public Debt." *Journal of Political Economy* 87, no. 5, pt. 1 (October): 940–71.

Bordo, Michael, and Barry Eichengreen. 1999. "Is Our Current International Economic Environment Unusually Crisis Prone?" In *Capital Flows and the Internatonal Financial System*. Sydney: Reserve Bank of Australia.

Bulow, Jeremy, and Kenneth Rogoff. 1989a. "A Constant Recontracting Model of Sovereign Debt." *Journal of Political Economy* 97 (February): 155–78.

———. 1989b. "Sovereign Debt: Is to Forgive to Forget?" *American Economic Review* 79 (March) 43–50.

Caprio, Gerard, Jr., and Daniela Klingebiel. 2003. "Episodes of Systemic and Borderline Financial Crises." Manuscript (data set 1, January), World Bank, Washington, DC. http://go.worldbank.org/5DYGICS7B0.

Catão, Luis A. V., Ana Fostel, and Sandeep Kapur. 2009. "Persistent Gaps and Default Traps." *Journal of Development Economics* 89, no. 2:271–84.

Cipolla, Carlo. 1982. *The Monetary Policy of Fourteenth Century Florence*. Berkeley: University of California Press.

Cole, Harold L., and Patrick J. Kehoe. 1996. "Reputational Spillover across Relationships: Reviving Reputation Models of Debt." Working Paper no. 5486 (March), NBER, Cambridge, MA.

Eaton, Jonathan, and Mark Gersovitz. 1981. "Debt with Potential Repudiation: Theory and Estimation." *Review of Economic Studies* 48 (April): 289–309.

Grossman, Herschel, and John Van Huyck. 1988. "Sovereign Debt as a Contingent Claim: Excusable Default, Repudiation and Reputation." *American Economic Review* 78 (December): 1088–97.

Kaminsky, Graciela L., and Carmen M. Reinhart. 1999. "The Twin Crises: The Causes of Banking and Balance of Payments Problems." *American Economic Review* 89, no. 3:473–500.

Kaminsky, Graciela, Carmen M. Reinhart, and Carlos A Vegh. 2005. "When It Rains, It Pours: Procyclical Capital Flows and Macroeconomic Policies." *NBER Macroeconomics Annual* 19:11–82.

Kaplan, E. L., and P. Meier. 1958. "Nonparametric Estimation from Incomplete Observations." *Journal of the American Statistical Association* 53:457–81.

Lucas, Robert E., Jr. 1987. *Models of Business Cycles*. Oxford: Blackwell.

MacDonald, James. 2006. *A Free Nation Deep in Debt: The Financial Roots of Democracy.* New York: Farrar, Straus & Giroux.

Maddison, Angus. 2004. *Historical Statistics for the World Economy: 1–2003 AD*. Paris: Organization for Economic Cooperation and Development. http://www.ggdc.net/MADDISON/oriindex.htm.

Missale, Alessandro, and Olivier Blanchard. 1994. "The Debt Burden and Debt Maturity." *American Economic Review* 84 (March): 309–19.

Obstfeld, Maurice, and Kenneth Rogoff. 1996. *Foundations of International Macroeconomics*. Cambridge, MA: MIT Press.

Qian, Rong. 2010. "Why Do Some Countries Default More Often than Others? The Role of Institutions." Manuscript, University of Maryland.

Reinhart, Carmen M. 2010. "This Time Is Different Chartbook: Country Histories on Debt, Default, and Financial Crises." Working Paper no. 15815 (March), NBER, Cambridge, MA.

Reinhart, Carmen M., and Kenneth S. Rogoff. 2004. "The Modern History of Exchange Rate Arrangements: A Reinterpretation." *Quarterly Journal of Economics* 119 (February): 1–48.

———. 2008. "Banking Crises: An Equal Opportunity Menace." Working Paper no. 14587 (December), NBER, Cambridge, MA.

———. 2009. *This Time Is Different: Eight Centuries of Financial Folly.* Princeton, NJ: Princeton University Press.

———. 2010. "From Financial Crash to Sovereign Debt Crisis." Working Paper no. 15795 (March), NBER, Cambridge, MA.

Reinhart, Carmen M., Kenneth S. Rogoff, and Miguel A. Savastano. 2003. "Debt Intolerance." *Brookings Papers on Economic Activity,* no. 1:1–74.

Rogoff, Kenneth. 2003. "Globalization and Global Disinflation." In *Monetary Policy and Uncertainty: Adapting to a Changing Economy.* Kansas City: Federal Reserve Bank of Kansas City.

Schularick, Moritz, and Alan Taylor. 2009. "Credit Booms Gone Bust: Monetary Policy, Leverage Cycles and Financial Crises, 1870–2008." Working Paper no. 15512 (November), NBER, Cambridge, MA.

Tomz, Michael. 2007. *Reputation and International Cooperation: Sovereign Debt across Three Centuries*. Princeton, NJ: Princeton University Press.

Tomz, Michael, and Mark Wright. 2007. "Do Countries Default in Bad Times?" *Journal of the European Economic Association* 5 (April–May): 352–60.

Tornell, Aaron, and Philip Lane. 1999. "The Voracity Effect." *American Economic Review* 89 (March): 22–46.

Comment

Mark Aguiar, University of Rochester and NBER

I. Introduction

Qian, Reinhart, and Rogoff have assembled an impressively rich data set on external default, banking, and monetary crises. This paper is part of an ambitious project on placing crises in the proper historical perspective (e.g., Reinhart and Rogoff 2009). It is an extremely valuable research agenda since much of modern sovereign debt literature has focused on recent (post-1980) episodes, which give only a partial and potentially misleading view. One way the post-1980 perspective is misleading is that rich countries were relatively immune from many of the crises that plagued emerging markets, with the only exception being banking crises. However, as we learn from Qian et al., rich countries had more than their share of crises historically, raising the question of how a country graduates into the "stability club." This is the focus of Qian et al.

Qian et al. draw several themes from the long historical data series. I will list three that motivate my discussion:

1. Many false starts: Countries take a long time to achieve relative stability, with prolonged periods of tranquility followed by a reappearance of default or inflation. Twenty or 30 years between crises is not uncommon.

2. Rich versus poor: Rich countries appear to be less prone to external defaults and high inflations. Any complete story of graduation must link overall economic development with stability of macro policies.

3. Sequencing: Crises from sovereign default disappear first along a country's path of development, followed by high inflation. Banking crises appear to plague developed economies as well as developing economies as an "equal opportunity menace."

The issue I address in this discussion is whether these facts fit comfortably in modern macroeconomic models. I will conclude that to a

978-0-226-00212-5/2011/2010-0102$10.00

first approximation, they do. My focus will be on default. Inflation can be considered a default on the government's nominal liabilities (whether currency or nonindexed domestic currency debt) and fits within the spirit of my remarks on default. Banking crises are somewhat different, both empirically and theoretically, and I will touch on them briefly at the end.

II. A Work Horse Model of Sovereign Default

The benchmark model of sovereign default is Eaton and Gersovitz (1981). This model, with some modifications, has formed the backbone of the recent literature of quantitative models of sovereign default (e.g., Aguiar and Gopinath 2006; Arellano 2008). Recall that there are three key ingredients of the Eaton-Gersovitz model. First, the face value of debt is noncontingent; second, governments cannot commit to repaying debt, so default is always an option; and third, debt is sustained by reputational equilibria in which default triggers financial autarky.

In an endowment small open economy, for example, the government's problem can be written conditional on the stock of outstanding debt due b and current endowment y as

$$V(b, y) = \max\langle V^{ND}(b, y), V^{D}(y)\rangle,$$

where V^{ND} is the value function if the government does not default and V^{D} is the value function after default. Specifically,

$$V^{ND}(b, y) = \max_{c,b'} u(c) + \beta E_y V(b', y')$$

subject to

$$c + b \leq y + q(b'; y)b',$$

where $q(b'; y)$ is the equilibrium price of a bond issue of size b' given endowment state y; $V^{D}(y)$ is simply the autarky value function:[1]

$$V^{D}(y) = E_y \sum_{s=t}^{\infty} \beta^{s-t} u(y_s).$$

The government will default if $V^{D}(y) > V^{ND}(b; y)$. I close the model by assuming competitive risk-neutral lenders such that sovereign debt earns an expected return equal to the world risk-free rate r^*:

$$q(b'; y) = \frac{\Pr\{V^{ND}(b', y') \geq V^{D}(y')|y\}}{1 + r^*}. \quad (1)$$

An equilibrium is then a pricing function $q(b; y)$ and value functions that solve the above Bellman equations.

How does this model square with Qian et al.'s facts? On the plus side, this model predicts that more volatile economies will default more frequently, consistent with the historical data. This follows because default is the only insurance mechanism in the model. The impact on consumption of large negative shocks is mitigated by default, while the good endowment states repay at a higher rate than r^*. I will leave aside the issue of whether countries actually default in bad states (see Tomz and Wright 2007), but it is worth noting that many of the defaults documented in Qian et al.'s paper occur in response to extreme events such as war or the Great Depression. A larger problem for the model is that growth per se does not reduce the probability of default. If $u(c)$ is homogeneous, as we typically assume, the model becomes invariant to scale. That is, if we replace an endowment process y with $\tilde{y} = \lambda y$, $\lambda > 0$, the model's predictions for default do not change.

To see this, suppose that $u(c) = c^{1-\gamma}/(1-\gamma)$, $\gamma \neq 1$, and let $\tilde{b} = \lambda b$. Consider the following candidate equilibrium:

- A pricing function $q(\tilde{b}; \tilde{y}) = q(b; y)$ that is homogeneous of degree 0;
- $\tilde{V}^{ND}(\tilde{b}, \tilde{y}) = \lambda^{1-\gamma} V^{ND}(b, y)$;
- $\tilde{V}^{D}(\tilde{y}) = \lambda^{1-\gamma} V^{D}(y)$.

With such a pricing function, the value functions inherit the homogeneity of u. If the value functions are homogeneous of the same degree, then the default decision ($V^{ND} \gtrless V^{D}$) is invariant to a scaling factor. Therefore, the pricing function becomes scale invariant, making our candidate scenario an equilibrium. As $q(b; y)$ is scale invariant, the probability of default is not necessarily lower for rich economies. What matters is the volatility of income, not its level. Therefore, the Eaton-Gersovitz framework, while very useful for understanding the link between volatility and default, is not suited for understanding "graduation" from default.

III. Debt Overhang

In the Eaton-Gersovitz model, the nature of uninsurable income risk generated default probabilities, while the average level of income on its own was not a factor. However, there are potentially many reasons why high income will be associated with better insurance. I will develop one mechanism based on Aguiar, Amador, and Gopinath (2009) and Aguiar and Amador (forthcoming) that emphasizes the interplay between limited commitment in fiscal policy and political economy considerations.

We depart from the stark incomplete markets environment of Eaton-Gersovitz but continue to assume limited commitment on the part of the government. Specifically, we consider the framework of Aguiar et al. (2009), in which the government can trade a noncontingent bond and impose state-contingent taxes on capital income. This is sufficient to transfer resources across states of nature, completing the markets subject to limited commitment. The incomplete markets framework of Eaton-Gersovitz has the advantage of a clearly defined equilibrium event we can label "default." However, in practice, default is accompanied by negotiation, "haircuts," and so forth, in which payments become de facto contingent. The recent quantitative literature on sovereign debt has also deviated from Eaton-Gersovitz by introducing additional state contingency in default punishments or explicit renegotiation.[2] Equilibrium default in this framework can be viewed as anticipated or "excusable default," a concept emphasized by Grossman and Van Huyck (1988).

As in the Aguiar et al. (2009) framework, the small open economy operates a neoclassical production function as well as potentially exports an endowment commodity. Risk-neutral capitalists discount at the world risk-free interest rate r^*. The key friction in the model is that the government can expropriate installed capital and default on debt. The larger the stock of outstanding debt, the greater the incentive to expropriate. This implies that a large amount of debt is associated with low levels of equilibrium investment, as additional capital would trigger expropriation and explicit default. In equilibrium, this is implemented by the government by a high tax on capital income. If the government could commit to tax promises, the optimal distortion of capital would be zero. Even in an environment of independent and identically distributed (iid) shocks, investment will respond to current income in the presence of debt. The reason that investment is sensitive to shocks is that the government smooths income fluctuations with debt. A low-income shock raises indebtedness going forward, which lowers investment in next period's capital. Despite iid shocks, fiscal policy induces persistence in the equilibrium output. Persistent fluctuations are a hallmark of emerging market business cycles (Aguiar and Gopinath 2007).

Moreover, debt inhibits risk sharing. In particular, a heavily indebted government cannot credibly promise large payments in good states, limiting the amount it can receive in bad states. The model's implications are summarized as in table 1.

Taking stock, we see that a low-volatility/high-income economy is associated with low levels of debt. Moreover, low levels of debt are accompanied by better equilibrium insurance, making the crude insurance of default less necessary. This intuition speaks to the facts presented by Qian et al. in that graduation from default is associated with higher income and less volatility. Moreover, recent economies that have graduated from low income to middle income have typically done so by reducing external debt levels. Aguiar and Amador (forthcoming) document that, between 1970 and 2003, the developing countries that grew the most did so while paying down sovereign debt and accumulating reserves. This reduction in debt appears to be a rite of passage to middle-income status, at least in the modern era.

The analysis so far does not address the question of why some countries pay down their debt while others do not. Similarly, why do some countries take a very long time to do so, when standard growth models (like the neoclassical growth model) predict fairly fast convergence? As most external debt is sovereign debt, a reasonable place to start to answer this question is with the government. In Aguiar and Amador (forthcoming), we propose a political economy model embedded in the neoclassical growth model. The political friction we consider is that political parties prefer spending to occur while they hold power, reflecting disagreement among spending priorities as well as outright corruption. When this is combined with political turnover, the political parties become short-term impatient relative to the citizenry, as in Amador (2004). The preferences of the government matter because in equilibrium the incumbent must respect tax and debt promises made by previous

Table 1
Debt Overhang

High debt	Low investment/high capital taxation Limited risk sharing Volatility
Low debt	High investment/low capital taxation Comprehensive risk sharing Low volatility

governments. We show that while all countries may eventually converge to the frontier, the speed at which they do so is governed by the degree of political frictions. Moreover, growth is accompanied by reductions in debt levels, for the same limited commitment intuition discussed above. To attract investment, a country must pay down its debt, but the need to accommodate a sequence of impatient political parties slows this process down.

Such a framework speaks to the Qian et al. result that graduation may be a slow process, with many false starts, but in the long run, stability and high incomes can be secured. Viewed in this way, graduation to external financial stability is slow for the same reason that overall growth is slow, namely, the short-termism of political incumbents, but this short-term impatience need not prevent convergence in the long run.

IV. Rich Countries

The preceding discussion focused on graduation from low-income to middle-income status. A key feature was debt overhang, which is empirically relevant at least for recent episodes. However, many rich countries sustain extremely high debt to income ratios without the accompanying volatility, lack of investment, or default. In related work, Reinhart, Rogoff, and Savastano (2003) document that rich countries can comfortably sustain debt levels unattainable for poor countries. My view of this point is that high-income countries have other means of addressing the frictions due to limited commitment. In the environments discussed above, debt (and investment) was sustained as reputational equilibria in which deviation was punished by autarky. However, there are other mechanisms to sustain debt. I will mention two.

Sandleris (2008) argues that governments have private information regarding policy or other fundamentals that affect the prospects of the domestic economy. A default by the government, in equilibrium, is interpreted as a signal of economic weakness, inducing private agents to adjust their beliefs. This can have adverse consequences, such as igniting a domestic banking crisis. If the domestic banking system is important relative to sovereign debt, as is the case in most developed economies, the adverse consequences of default on the financial system are sufficient to sustain high levels of debt. This analysis is similar to reputation "spillover," emphasized by Cole and Kehoe (1996), in which failure to repay debt affects other relationships.

Broner, Martin, and Ventura (2010) argue that well-developed secondary markets for sovereign debt may be the key to sustain debt in equilibrium. The important element in their framework is that debt holders are anonymous, so the government cannot shield preferred bondholders from default. Default is deterred by bonds being held in equilibrium by domestic citizens (or any preferred group).

These are just two examples of how well-developed domestic financial markets support high levels of sovereign debt without the adverse consequences highlighted above. The important element in all these models is how the government solves the issue of limited commitment. For middle-income countries, this is done by holding low levels of sovereign debt; in advanced countries, a vibrant domestic financial market plays this role.

V. Inflation and Banking Crises

So far, I have focused on external debt crises. Episodes of high inflation fit naturally in the same framework. High inflation represents default on the government's nominal liabilities, whether nonindexed pensions, domestic currency debt, or currency itself. Similarly, it can be viewed as a distortionary tax, similar to capital income taxation. From this perspective, inflation arises in a limited commitment environment for the same reasons that capital is taxed or debt is not repaid.

Banking crises represent a bigger challenge, both empirically and theoretically. Empirically, they continue to affect developed economies, making it impossible to see what a country that has graduated from banking crises looks like. Theoretically, we understand that the provision of liquidity often involves leverage and maturity mismatch, making banks vulnerable to runs. In many environments, a strong central bank or an alternative lender of last resort can mitigate or eliminate banking crises. This reinforces the message that government institutions and credibility continue to be key. However, the recent crisis, as well as Japan's experience in the 1990s, suggests that there are limits to what a central bank can do.

Regulation is another important public institution that matters in the frequency and severity of banking crises. Regulation comes with costs in many instances, given the informational requirements involved in the allocation of capital and provision of liquidity. Moreover, regulators can be captured by the targets of regulation, bringing us back to the quality of public institutions and the political economy environment more generally. In short, Qian et al.'s facts on banking crises are consistent with the theme that the frequency of crises, whether banking, inflationary, or external debt related, depends sensitively on the quality of the economy's political institutions.

VI. Summing Up

The recent literature on sovereign default holds several lessons that speak to the three patterns in Qian et al.'s paper listed at the start of the discussion. Taking up the metaphor of graduation, figure 1 traces out the key stages of progression. Primary school is a low level of development accompanied by volatility, limited risk sharing, and frequent default. This is consistent qualitatively with the environment of Eaton-Gersovitz, which features limited commitment and incomplete markets. As countries pay down their debt, they can endogenously sustain higher incomes, less volatility, and improved risk sharing. This reflects the transition from low-income to middle-income status, or graduation from "primary" to "secondary" school. The key to this transition is addressing

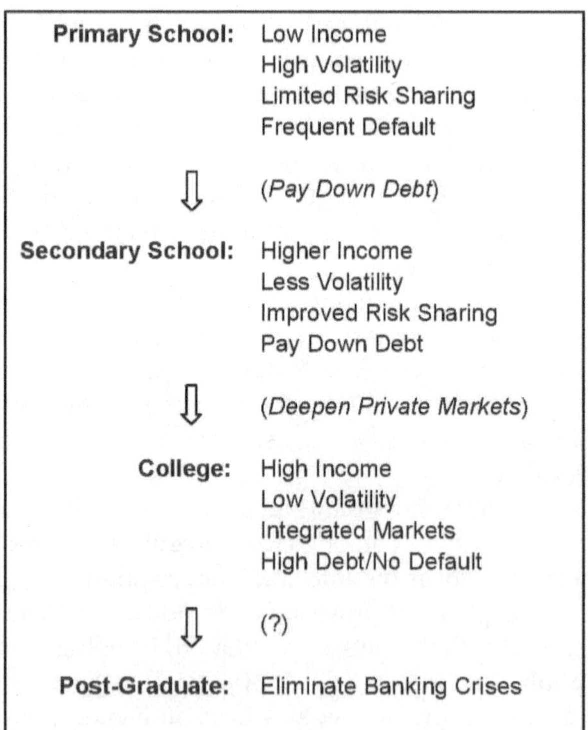

Fig. 1. Graduating from crises

commitment issues, which in practice appears to be accomplished in part by paying down external debt. The speed of this transition may be a function of the quality of the political equilibrium. The final stage observed empirically is a highly developed private financial sector and full integration ("college"). In this stage, other mechanisms become relevant in mitigating commitment issues, such as secondary markets and deep domestic financial markets. This transition requires the development of private institutions as well as continued improvement of public institutions. Given the importance of the private financial sector and the limitations of such public institutions as central banks and regulation at this stage, continued banking crises may occur. A final stage without banking crises may be attainable in theory, perhaps one in which better public institutions are combined with a decoupling of liquidity provision and leverage. Unfortunately, this stage is one that lies outside the historical record.

Endnotes

I would like to thank Manuel Amador and Gita Gopinath.

1. It is simple to alter the length of enforced autarky so punishment is no longer an absorbing state. Such an extension allows the model to match "serial defaulting," in which countries default, are excluded for a finite period, are allowed to borrow again, and then default again. See Aguiar and Gopinath (2006) for such a model and a discussion of what types of income processes are particularly prone to serial defaulting.

2. For example, Aguiar and Gopinath (2006) augment the loss of reputation with a proportional loss of income; Arellano (2008) makes the loss of output contingent on default nonlinear, increasing the state contingency; and Yue (2010) models renegotiation, which also introduces state contingency.

References

Aguiar, Mark, and Manuel Amador. Forthcoming. "Growth in the Shadow of Expropriation." *Quarterly Journal of Economics.*

Aguiar, Mark, Manuel Amador, and Gita Gopinath. 2009. "Investment Cycles and Sovereign Debt Overhang." *Review of Economic Studies* 76:1–31.

Aguiar, Mark, and Gita Gopinath. 2006. "Defaultable Debt, Interest Rates and the Current Account." *Journal of International Economics* 69:64–83.

———. 2007. "Emerging Market Business Cycles: The Cycle Is the Trend." *Journal of Political Economy* 115, no. 1:69–102.

Amador, Manuel. 2004. "A Political Economy Model of Sovereign Debt Repayment." Working paper, Stanford University.

Arellano, Cristina. 2008. "Default Risk and Income Fluctuations in Emerging Economies." *American Economic Review* 98:690–712.

Broner, Fernando, Alberto Martin, and Jaume Ventura. 2010. "Sovereign Risk and Secondary Markets." *American Economic Review* 100:1523–55.

Cole, Harold, and Patrick Kehoe. 1996. "Reputational Spillover across Relationships: Reviving Reputation Models of Debt." Working Paper no. 5486, NBER, Cambridge, MA.

Eaton, Jonathan, and Mark Gersovitz. 1981. "Debt with Potential Repudiation: Theory and Estimation." *Review of Economic Studies* 48:289–309.

Grossman, Herschel, and John Van Huyck. 1988. "Sovereign Debt as a Contingent Claim: Excusable Default, Repudiation, and Reputation." *American Economic Review* 78:1088–97.

Reinhart, Carmen, and Kenneth Rogoff. 2009. *This Time Is Different: Eight Centuries of Financial Folly.* Princeton, NJ: Princeton University Press.

Reinhart, Carmen, Kenneth Rogoff, and Miguel Savastano. 2003. "Debt Intolerance." *Brookings Papers on Economic Activity,* no. 1:1–74.

Sandleris, Guido. 2008. "Sovereign Defaults: Information, Investment and Credit." *Journal of International Economics* 76:267–75.

Tomz, Michael, and Mark Wright. 2007. "Do Countries Default in 'Bad Times'?" *Journal of the European Economic Association* 5:352–60.

Yue, Vivian. 2010. "Sovereign Default and Debt Renegotiation." *Journal of International Economics* 80:176–87.

Comment

Alan M. Taylor, *University of California, Davis, NBER, and Centre for Economic Policy Research*

I

It is a pleasure to comment on the paper by Qian, Reinhart, and Rogoff, which builds and expands on the many rich insights and the treasure trove of data developed by Reinhart and Rogoff (2009) in the course of writing their book *This Time Is Different: Eight Centuries of Financial Folly.* That book is a hard act to follow: it is no exaggeration to describe it as the most influential work in macroeconomic history of recent years, and fortuitously timed, it has deservedly won wide acclaim on its way to becoming a best seller.

Still, as the authors recognize, the project of understanding macroeconomic crises, their causes, and consequences is even now very much a work in progress. In contrast to what went before, the sudden wave of research in empirical and theoretical macroeconomics since the global financial crisis erupted in 2008 attests to a subject matter unduly neglected. Fortunately, such complacency is no longer an option, and a better understanding will have to rely on both inductive and deductive approaches to macroeconomics in which economic history will have a very important role to play (Eichengreen 2009).

The prime lesson of *This Time Is Different* and of this paper is that a retreat into introspection is not the only tool we have at hand to understand crises. Rather, with a record of such events stretching back over many centuries, we have an excellent historical laboratory in which to search for empirical regularities, stylized facts, and other clues that might lead to better-informed theoretical models and improved policy choices in the future. Indeed, this is an arena of scholarship in which economic history matters more than ever: crises of this sort are undoubtedly "rare events," and so to gain any sort of traction with an empirical

978-0-226-00212-5/2011/2010-0103$10.00

investigation one needs many years of data and many sample countries to generate any sort of statistical power.

The novel contribution of this paper is to try to address a question left tantalizingly open by the book, perhaps because that very question is so hard to tackle that answers, if not elusive, can be at best only preliminary and somewhat speculative. As of a couple of years ago, this might have been cast as the question of whether countries can in fact ever "graduate" from being crisis-prone "emerging" economies to an "advanced" economy status in which, one might have presumed, they would be immune from such problems forever. Now, of course, our innocence is lost, and we realize that not even so-called advanced economies are immune from crises and that some countries apparently cured of the crisis problem can end up suffering a relapse. Thus, perhaps the notion of graduation is a mirage? Multiple advanced countries suffered very costly banking crises in 2008; some countries are now facing escalating sovereign debt, with markets pricing in nontrivial default probabilities; and as central bankers have embraced quantitative easing strategies, some fear that the current deflationary trends may yet quickly reverse and, even in a slump, return us to 1970s-style stagflation.

In our current conjuncture, this paper, which provides a retrospective examination of the crisis record and some exploration of the capacity of countries to graduate from a "serial crisis" mode to a more stable macroeconomic environment, is welcome as a valuable and pioneering contribution to our understanding. In these comments I will endeavor to summarize and comment on the main results and, along the way, note some unanswered questions and suggest potentially useful directions for what promises to be a very broad research agenda in the years ahead.

II

The paper starts by introducing the definitions of various kinds of crises and reviewing the time line of such events, focusing mainly on the last 150–200 years. Here the authors draw on the exhaustive crisis classification work undertaken in the book *This Time Is Different*. These definitions and classifications, in turn, build on earlier antecedents due to Kaminsky and Reinhart (1999), Bordo et al. (2001), and others.

The definition of a default or sovereign crisis is at once narrow and broad. It is narrow in the sense that only cases of *external debt crisis* are considered here. It would be instructive, though much more work, to expand this to generate a complete and accurate list of all defaults. As Reinhart and Rogoff have noted in their book, there is a rich and understudied history of internal debt that shows that sovereigns have defaulted on domestic liabilities on many occasions, and the correlation with external default is not perfect. The distinction has perhaps mattered less in cases in which empirical macroeconomists have been focusing on emerging-market sovereign crises (e.g., the literature from the 1980s to the 2000s). For those cases, especially in a world of so-called original sin, the most significant debt burdens are those issued in foreign currency. However, after the global financial crisis, the specter of sovereign risk now hovers over advanced countries, where debt is issued mainly in local currency and may be held pari passu by domestic and foreign creditors alike. Thus, going forward, great interest attaches to the lessons that history offers about default in such supposedly advanced countries.

Yet at the same time, the default definition used in this paper is broad. It includes almost any deviation from the contractual terms, whether full-blown repudiation or some less consequential partial default. This problem applies to domestic and external defaults. In the space available, one cannot review a raft of cases, and indeed there has already been intense discussion—from working papers, to the letters page of the *Financial Times*, to the blogosphere—as to what really counts as a default.[1] Nonetheless, the authors' binary classification probably makes sense as a first cut at this problem, and it will be a task of future research to try to settle such disputes, explore more granular default definitions, and explore the robustness of the results under different definitions.

In terms of the failure of a nominal anchor, the preferred classification here is an *inflation crisis*, defined as inflation above 20%. Elsewhere, an alternative approach has been to rely on a currency crisis indicator, defining a crisis for the exchange rate as a steep depreciation event. In most, if not all, cases these two signals will agree. Since inflation targets have become the de facto if not de jure policy target in most advanced, and many emerging, economies, this way of defining the loss of a nominal anchor, as a breach of an inflation threshold, might be the preferred one.

Finally, to define a *banking crisis* the authors follow established convention and look for cases in which the banking sector is disrupted by widespread failures, bankruptcies or capital losses, or suspensions or else can limp through only with substantial official assistance. As with the default measure, this reduces a continuum of outcomes to a binary variable. And again some of the classifications are judgment calls.[2] However, a binary classification is the right place to start any analysis, even if it is not the final word. In the future, researchers might want to examine more carefully the intensity of different episodes of banking distress to come up with a more subtle measure of banking crises.

With these definitions in hand some of the central results in the paper are presented in the form of time lines showing the occurrences of each type of crisis in each year in their figures 4–6, where the data are broken down into high-income (advanced) and middle-/low-income (emerging/developing) countries. In these figures some key results appear, some well known, others less so. The following struck me as noteworthy historical facts that every macroeconomist should know:

- Since the 1970s no rich country has defaulted, and such a period of 30–40 years without relapse is unusual in history.
- Severe global recessions are correlated with poorer countries' defaults: the 1870s, the 1930s, and the 1980s.
- The classical gold standard era 1870–1914 stands out as the only period when inflation crises were largely averted in both rich and poor countries alike for an extended period of time.
- In the rich countries, since the end of the U.S. Civil War, extensive inflation crises have struck only three times: in each of the two world wars, but only once in peacetime, in the 1970s.
- In poorer countries, the widespread inflation crises of the 1980s have abated, but the current experience of more stable prices has not endured very long.
- There are virtually no financial crises in situations in which the financial system is small or weak (e.g., poorer countries in the nineteenth century).
- There are no financial crises in situations in which the financial system is repressed or tightly regulated (e.g., rich countries in the 1945–70 period).
- There was no sign of widespread inflation crisis in the 1930s, but banking and default crises were at their most intense in all of recorded history (something that is echoed in today's tensions between price stability objectives and the use of easy money to relieve nominal debt overhang or perform bank rescues).

The other very interesting set of results appear in their figures 7–9: these show the frequency distribution for the length of observed periods of "tranquil time" (i.e., time between crises). These frequency distributions show some similarity across the different types of crisis, with a large share of events loaded in the 10–20 year range. Thus, we are led to look at 20 years without reversal as indicative of a country having nearly graduated, although given the "short" span of data at hand and given the rare-event nature of the problem, we have very few cases of countries getting out to 30, 40, or 50 years without a crisis, whereupon we might think the odds of a reversal to be much lower. It is also evident that while richer countries have a lower propensity for inflation and default crises in the first 20 years after an event, the same cannot be said of banking crises, earning them the moniker of "equal opportunity menace." Even before the current financial crisis it was true that advanced countries have had a much harder time escaping from this particular type of crisis.

Figures 11–13 look at the issue a different way, by showing years since the last crisis as of 2010. For default it is clear that poorer countries (median 14) are completely different from rich countries (median 105). For inflation crises the gap between the distributions is not as striking but still large (median 15 vs. 59). Prior to the 2008 financial crisis, the same might have been true for banking crises, but by now the two groups are almost indistinguishable on that metric.

There is considerable scope for further research here. One suggestion would be to simply apply standard tests for equality of distributions (e.g., Kolmogorov-Smirnov) to judge whether there are shifts across the two groups of countries. And then, partitioning the data by time period, one could ask the same question for different subperiods. Clearly, the slicing cannot be taken too far, given the small sample size. Another possibility is to look at conditioning the tranquil time on other country characteristics: in essence, moving to a formal duration model. Beyond the scope of this paper, this is surely a likely target for future papers by these or other authors.

One interesting conditioning variable could be macroeconomic volatility, measured in various ways, and perhaps instrumented by terms of trade volatility and/or institutions. Section VII of the paper touches on this topic, but the question provides enough of a challenge for a paper in its own right. It is indeed striking that for both rich and poorer countries, macroeconomic volatility has fallen since the 1950s, but for both sets of countries the incidence of banking crises has gotten worse. This poses a challenge for "real-side" explanations of banking crises and offers prima facie evidence that other factors matter—for example, changes in the structure of finance over the last 50 years due to, say, "innovation" or regulation/supervision.

III

This excellent paper builds on the very timely work in *This Time Is Different*. As the economics profession digests the lessons of the global financial crisis, the stage is set for a renaissance of work in macroeconomic and financial history. To conclude these comments, I suggest two areas worthy of further consideration. Given recent events, I focus on the case of banking crises, which represents the major locus of attention in the current macrofinance debate.

First, I am sure the empirical finance and growth literature will now be revisited again. It was already the case even before the crisis that the linkages between financial liberalization and growth were subject to dispute and uncertainty (e.g., Kose et al. 2009; Rodrik and Subramanian 2009). In addition, we might also expect some further empirical exploration of the links between financial intensity and the volatility of growth (e.g., Ranciere, Tornell, and Westermann 2008) and the tradeoffs associated with capital controls (e.g., Eichengreen and Leblang 2003). Do larger or more liberalized financial systems really deliver higher growth? Do they also create more volatility? Is there a tradeoff here, and is it linear? Is there a case to be made that beyond a certain point the risks start to outweigh the gains? The raw data for advanced countries say that, despite highly repressed financial systems in the 1950s and 1960s, the immediate postwar period was one of unusually high growth and rapid capital formation. But more formal analysis of these and other episodes is certainly needed before any causal inference can be drawn. In particular, we need to devise careful methods to solve the identification problem associated with measuring the incremental costs of crises; all recessions have costs, and so we need to think in terms of the excess cost when a recession turns into a recession-plus-crisis. The construction of an appropriate counterfactual is not simple, and the same applies to any thought experiment involving counterfactual policies: for example, if policies were implemented to avert crises ex ante, would these also bring about costs in cases of a "false alarm"? I would also expect some interesting lines of research here to explore the frequency and intensity of banking crises under different exchange rate regimes and also under different capital mobility regimes, using historical variation in the solutions to the trilemma in history (Obstfeld and Taylor 2004). Clearly the debate over financial openness in general, and the specific dispute over how much blame for the current crisis lies with "global imbalances," suggest that these areas of research might be very helpful for policy makers.

Second, can we say more about the workings of the banking sector in different times and places, and can such evidence help illuminate our understanding? One of my interests here is in the role that bank credit plays in the causes and consequences of crises. In recent research based

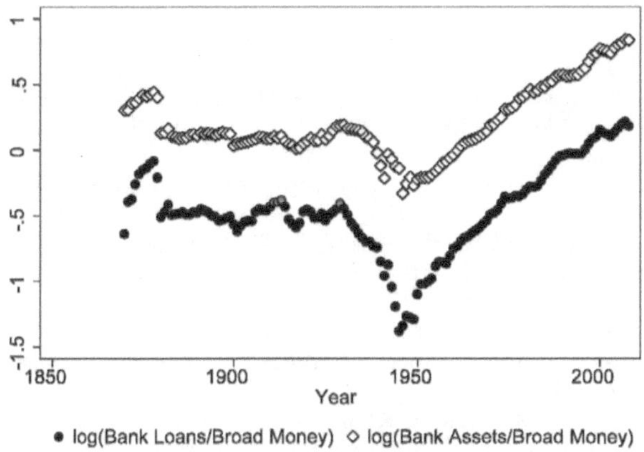

Fig. 1. Bank funding leverage in 14 countries. Note: Time trend shown by year effects, 1870–2008. Source: Schularick and Taylor (2009).

on a new long-run credit data set (Schularick and Taylor 2009), it is apparent that over the very long run the banking sectors of advanced economies have experienced profound structural changes. Figure 1 displays summary data from 14 countries for the years 1870–2008 on the ratio of loans to deposits (or assets to deposits) as a measure of the funding leverage of banks. This leverage measure was high and stable until 1929 in an era of financial instability, then fell dramatically in the 1930s and 1940s. It climbed back slowly only through the 1970s in the crisis-free postwar era of financial repression. After 1970 this ratio continued to climb past its previous peak, and we entered another era of financial instability. In addition to this correlation between leverage levels and instability, we also found that sharp increases in the growth rate of credit were significant predictors of future crises. Thus, linking the classification of banking crises used in this paper with measures of banking sector evolution could enhance our understanding further as to changes in the conditional probability of crises over the entire sample.

Endnotes

1. To take just one example: did the British have the right to call and refinance debt in the war conversion loan of 1932 and similar conversions in the nineteenth century? This is an example of a disputed domestic default. See M. R. Weale, "'Default' on UK Government Debt Was No Such Thing," *Financial Times*, letters, March 8, 2010.

2. For example, in Schularick and Taylor (2009), we elected not to classify the German giro bank failures of 1977 as a banking crisis, since we felt that the failures were not very costly, widespread, or of macroeconomic significance.

References

Bordo, Michael D., Barry Eichengreen, Daniela Klingebiel, and Maria Soledad Martinez-Peria. 2001. "Is the Crisis Problem Growing More Severe?" *Economic Policy* 32:51–82.

Eichengreen, Barry. 2009. "The Last Temptation of Risk." *National Interest* (May/June), 8–14.

Eichengreen, Barry, and David Leblang. 2003. "Capital Account Liberalization and Growth: Was Mr. Mahathir Right?" *International Journal of Finance and Economics* 8, no. 3:205–24.

Kaminsky, Graciela L., and Carmen M. Reinhart. 1999. "The Twin Crises: The Causes of Banking and Balance of Payments Problems." *American Economic Review* 89, no. 3:473–500.

Kose, M. Ayhan, Eswar Prasad, Kenneth S. Rogoff, and Shang-Jin Wei. 2009. "Financial Globalization: A Reappraisal." *IMF Staff Papers* 56, no. 1:8–62.

Obstfeld, Maurice, and Alan M. Taylor. 2004. *Global Capital Markets: Integration, Crisis, and Growth*. Cambridge: Cambridge University Press.

Rancière, Romain, Aaron Tornell, and Frank Westermann. 2008. "Systemic Crises and Growth." *Quarterly Journal of Economics* 123, no. 1:359–406.

Reinhart, Carmen M., and Kenneth S. Rogoff. 2009. *This Time Is Different: Eight Centuries of Financial Folly*. Princeton, NJ: Princeton University Press.

Rodrik, Dani, and Arvind Subramanian. 2009. "Why Did Financial Globalization Disappoint?" *IMF Staff Papers* 56, no. 1:112–38.

Schularick, Moritz, and Alan M. Taylor. 2009. "Credit Booms Gone Bust: Monetary Policy, Leverage Cycles and Financial Crises, 1870–2008." Working Paper no. 15512, NBER, Cambridge, MA.

Discussion

Carmen Reinhart began with a response to the discussants. First, she noted that even rich countries can be serial defaulters. Reinhart provided the example of Spain, which was a serial defaulter while it was a world power. The country had very volatile revenue from the trade with the New World, which was frequently interrupted by pirates. However, she noted that this example is hard to reconcile with being a world power today and being in a serial default.

Second, she made three comments about the theoretical models that would be helpful in understanding the stylized facts presented in the paper. Her first comment was that standard models (e.g., Eaton and Gersovitz 1981) assume that a country is permanently excluded from the market after it defaults. However, one can observe that, in the real world, countries return to borrowing after they defaulted and sometimes default again. Her second comment addressed particular modeling features that could be helpful. These features include politicians and private lenders' short planning horizon, public and private debt bias due to moral hazard, and cycles of behavioral optimism. Finally, Reinhart emphasized that the repeated cycles of defaults and banking crises are connected to credit cycles. Thus, models along the lines of Kiyotaki and Moore (1997) are also helpful in understanding the serial nature of defaults. Kenneth Rogoff added that Aguiar, Amador, and Gopinath (2009) advances the Eaton and Gersovitz framework by explaining endogenously why one might get the default cycles going on longer in developing countries.

Third, Reinhart mentioned that the end of the Bretton Woods system is an interesting period to look at right now. Emerging markets countries are operating much closer to full capacity than the advanced world and are importing monetary policy from advanced countries by fixing their exchange rates. Reinhart argued that it is possible that the next wave of inflation will occur in emerging markets.

Fourth, Reinhart pointed out that they did not consider the issue of sudden stops explicitly in the paper. However, since sudden stops occur

978-0-226-00212-5/2011/2010-0104$10.00

frequently with debt and banking crises, their paper captures a significant portion of sudden stop episodes.

Finally, Reinhart discussed the issue of clubs. She argued that if Greece was not treated as a developed country, its external debt would have never gotten to 160%–180% of GDP.

After acknowledging that the authors conducted a descriptive analysis, Daron Acemoglu suggested possible statistical interpretations of the graduation effect. First, the unobserved probability of default follows a duration-dependent process. Alternatively, the probability of default is affected by some other factors, and there is no duration dependence. He pointed out that it is hard to distinguish among these possibilities, and he referred to the literature started by Heckman (e.g., Heckman and Singer 1986). Acemoglu wondered if the authors can tell why the duration-dependent story seemed more plausible to them. Robert Hall reinforced Acemoglu's point by giving an example of the classic Heckman labor market issue of quits. Then he suggested that it would be useful to set up the possible explanations as hypotheses and then to show which of the explanations is correct or establish that the data are not powerful enough to distinguish between them. He mentioned that the tools are well established in labor market econometrics, making this exercise a logical next step. Reinhart agreed with this suggestion. However, she pointed out that the issue of wars should be addressed before proceeding with duration analysis given that many defaults were associated with civil or cross-border wars.

Acemoglu joined Mark Aguiar by saying that political economy factors are important for understanding debt crises. However, he argued that it is not obvious that the frequency of power turnover is key because he thought it would be easy to develop models in which the turnover effect could go either way. He argued that the relevant political frictions have to do with the constraints that are imposed on governments. The different risk premia that countries face determine their different behavior.

Frederic Mishkin posited an equilibrium story of banking crises. If good regulation built a stable, well-functioning financial system, it will create a safer environment for doing business. It will encourage people to take on greater debts and higher leverage. This may ultimately lead to a crisis. In this context, one may want to restrict the growth of credit when there is a credit boom. Thus, the idea of avoiding financial crises completely is not a good way of regulating the economy because it leads to an inefficient financial sector. Given the difficulty of eliminating financial crises completely, it is better to find ways of making them less likely and less severe. Lasse Pedersen joined Mishkin in citing the difficulty of eliminating banking crises. He added that a country must have a severely regulated financial market to avoid banking crises. Reinhart agreed with the idea. She noted that Schularick and Taylor (2009) make this point for bank credit and banking crises. In one of their recent papers, Reinhart and Rogoff come to similar conclusions in the case of external debt. She added that since one cannot do away entirely with the business cycles, one can think of financial crises as exaggerated business cycles.

Kristin Forbes highlighted two empirical facts that the authors presented in the paper. First, after a banking crisis, there is usually a sovereign debt default. Second, there are a number of countries that graduated from serial debt defaults and almost no countries that graduated from banking crises. She asked how these two facts are consistent with each other. She pointed to the existence of a group of countries that had the banking crises but then did not default on their debt, arguing that this may be due to the fact that these countries started with a low level of debt and could afford to pay for banking crises. But now with higher levels of debt these countries may no longer be able to finance another financial crisis. Reinhart replied by saying that banking crises may not lead to debt crises. However, banking crises almost always lead to an increase in government debt. She added that external versus domestic debt was a major determinant of whether countries suffered a debt default or not.

Gita Gopinath raised a question of empirical estimates of the costs of default for a country. She noted that from a theoretical point of view, default can result in reputation costs, costs of reentering the market, and other collateral damage. However, it is hard to empirically pin down the magnitude of these costs. There are countries that reenter financial markets fairly quickly with fairly low increases in the cost of borrowing. Moreover, sanctions are not very costly for them either. Reinhart replied that Reinhart and Rogoff (2009) documented that a country's growth rate is smaller around default episodes, and the growth rate is even worse if it is a domestic default. She pointed out that more analysis is needed on the duration of credibility costs that defaulters suffer. She also noted that it has became easier for a defaulter to reenter the market since World War II.

Rong Qian agreed with Aguiar's points that the political economy issues and volatility are important factors in explaining the frequency of defaults. She concluded by saying that it is possible that graduation from defaults takes a long time since institutional change is a slow process.

2

What Fiscal Policy Is Effective at Zero Interest Rates?

Gauti B. Eggertsson, *Federal Reserve Bank of New York*

I. Introduction

The economic crisis of 2008 started one of the most heated debates about U.S. fiscal policy in the past half century. With the federal funds rate close to zero—and output, inflation, and employment at the edge of a collapse—U.S.-based economists argued over alternatives to interest rate cuts to spur a recovery. Meanwhile, several other central banks slashed interest rates close to zero, including the European Central Bank, the Bank of Japan, the Bank of Canada, the Bank of England, the Riksbank of Sweden, and the Swiss National Bank, igniting similar debates in all corners of the world. Some argued for tax cuts, mainly a reduction in taxes on labor income (see, e.g., Bils and Klenow 2008; Hall and Woodward 2008; Mankiw 2008) or tax cuts on capital (see, e.g., Barro 2009; Feldstein 2009). Others emphasized an increase in government spending (see, e.g., Krugman 2009). Yet another group of economists argued that the best response would be to reduce the government, that is, reduce both taxes and spending.[1] Even if there was no professional consensus about the correct fiscal policy, the recovery bill passed by Congress in 2009 marks the largest fiscal expansion in U.S. economic history since the New Deal, with projected deficits (as a fraction of GDP) in double digits. Many governments followed the U.S. example. Much of this debate was, explicitly or implicitly, within the context of old-fashioned Keynesian models or the frictionless neoclassical growth model.

This paper takes a standard New Keynesian dynamic stochastic general equilibrium (DSGE) model, which by now is widely used in the academic literature and utilized in policy institutions, and asks a basic question: what is the effect of tax cuts and government spending under the economic circumstances that characterized the crisis of 2008? A key assumption is that the model is subject to shocks so that the short-term nominal interest rate is zero. This means that, in the absence of policy

978-0-226-00212-5/2011/2010-0201$10.00

interventions, the economy experiences excess deflation and an output contraction. The analysis thus builds on a large recent literature on policy at the zero bound on the short-term nominal interest rates, which is briefly surveyed after the introduction. The results are perhaps somewhat surprising in the light of recent public discussion. Cutting taxes on labor or capital is contractionary under the special circumstances the United States is experiencing today. Meanwhile, the effect of temporarily increasing government spending is large, much larger than under normal circumstances. Similarly, some other forms of tax cuts, such as a reduction in sales taxes and investment tax credits, as suggested, for example, by Feldstein (2002) in the context of Japan's "Great Recession," are extremely effective.[2]

The contractionary effects of labor and capital tax cuts, and the strong expansionary effect of government spending, are special to the peculiar environment created by zero interest rates. This point is illustrated by a numerical example in table 1, which shows the "multipliers" of cuts in labor taxes, cuts in capital taxes, and increases in government spending; several other multipliers are also discussed in the paper. The multipliers summarize by how much output decreases/increases if the government cuts tax rates by 1% or increases government spending by 1% (as a fraction of GDP). At positive interest rates, a labor tax cut is expansionary, as the literature has emphasized in the past. But at zero interest rates, it flips signs and tax cuts become contractionary. Similarly while capital tax cuts are almost irrelevant in the model at a positive interest rate (up to the second decimal point) they become strongly negative at zero. Meanwhile, the multiplier of government spending not only stays positive at zero interest rates but becomes almost five times larger. This illustrates that empirical work on the effect of fiscal policy based on data from the post–World War II period, such as the much cited and important work of Romer and Romer (2008), may not be directly applicable for assessing the effect of fiscal policy on output today, with important recent exceptions.[3] Interest rates are always positive in their sample, as in most other empirical research on this topic. To infer the effects of fiscal policy at zero interest

Table 1
Fiscal Policy Multipliers

	Labor Tax Cut Multiplier	Capital Tax Cut Multiplier	Government Spending Multiplier
Positive interest rate	.16	.0	.48
Zero interest rate	−1	−.1	2.3

rates, then, we can rely on experience only to a limited extent. Reasonably grounded theory may be a better benchmark with all the obvious weaknesses such inference entails, since the inference will never be any more reliable than the model assumed.

The starting point of this paper is the negative effect of labor tax cuts, that is, a cut in the tax on wages (the most reasonable interpretation of this tax is that it reflects a cut in the payroll tax paid by firms; see the discussion at the end of Sec. VII). These tax cuts cause deflationary pressures in the model by reducing marginal costs of firms, thereby increasing the real interest rate. The Federal Reserve can't accommodate this by cutting the federal funds rate, since it is already close to zero. Higher real interest rates are contractionary. I use labor tax cuts as a starting point, not only because of their prominence in the policy discussion but to highlight a general principle for policy in this class of models. *The principal goal of policy at zero interest rates should not be to increase aggregate supply by manipulating aggregate supply incentives. Instead, the goal of policy should be to increase aggregate demand—the overall level of spending in the economy.* This diagnosis is fundamental for a successful economic stimulus once interest rates hit zero in the model. At zero interest rates, output is demand determined. Accordingly, aggregate supply is mostly relevant in the model because it pins down expectations about future inflation. The result derived here is that policies aimed at increasing aggregate supply are counterproductive because they can create deflationary expectations at zero interest rates. At a loose and intuitive level, therefore, policy should not be aimed at increasing the supply of goods when the problem is that there are not enough buyers.

Once the general principle is established, it is straightforward to consider a host of other fiscal policy instruments, whose effect at first blush may seem puzzling. Consider first the idea of cutting taxes on capital, another popular policy proposal in response to the crisis of 2008. A permanent reduction in capital taxes increases investment and the capital stock under normal circumstances, which increases the production capacities of the economy. More shovels and tractors, for example, mean that people can dig more and bigger holes, which increases steady-state output. But at zero interest rate, the problem is not that the production capacity of the economy is inadequate. Instead, the problem is insufficient aggregate spending. Cutting capital taxes gives people the incentive to save instead of spend, when precisely the opposite is needed. A cut in capital taxes will reduce output because it reduces consumption spending. One might think that the increase in people's incentive to save would in turn increase aggregate savings and investment. But everyone starts saving more, which leads to lower demand, which in turns leads to lower income for households, thus reducing their ability to save. Paradoxically, a consequence of cutting capital taxes is therefore a collapse in aggregate saving in general equilibrium because everyone tries to save more.

From the same general principle—that the problem of insufficient demand leads to below-capacity production—it is easy to point out some effective tax cuts and spending programs, and the list of examples provided in the paper is surely not exhaustive. Temporarily cutting sales taxes and implementing an investment tax credit are both examples of effective fiscal policy. These tax cuts are helpful not because of their effect on aggregate supply but because they directly stimulate aggregate spending. Similarly, a temporary increase in government spending is effective because it directly increases overall spending in the economy. For government spending to be effective in increasing demand, however, it has to be directed at goods that are imperfect substitutes with private consumption (such as infrastructure or military spending). Otherwise, government spending will be offset by cuts in private spending, leaving aggregate spending unchanged.

A natural proposal for a stimulus plan, at least in the context of the model, is therefore a combination of temporary government spending increases, temporary investment tax credits, and a temporary elimination of sales taxes, all of which can be financed by a temporary increase in labor and/or capital taxes. There may, however, be important reasons outside the model that suggest that an increase in labor and capital taxes may be unwise and/or impractical. For these reasons I am not ready to suggest, based on this analysis alone, that raising capital and labor taxes is a good idea at zero interest rates. Indeed, my conjecture is that a reasonable case can be made for a temporary budget deficit to finance a stimulus plan as further discussed in the paper and note 4. The main reason increasing labor taxes may not be expansionary in the model is that this may have direct effect on demand (e.g., if a fraction of workers spend everything they earn). A similar comment apples to capital taxes.[4]

The contractionary effects of labor and capital taxes are applications of two paradoxes, one new and one old. The result on the contractionary effect of capital tax cuts is an application of the old Keynesian paradox of thrift (see, e.g., Christiano 2004).[5] The contractionary effect of labor tax cuts, however, is an application of a new paradox illustrated in Eggertsson (2010), who calls it the paradox of toil. While the paradox of thrift is that if everybody tries to save, there will be less savings in the aggregate, the paradox of toil is that if everybody tries to work more, there will be less work in the aggregate once the nominal interest rate hits zero.

The main focus of the paper is temporary tax and spending policies in response to an economic crisis. The results can be very different if instead we assume a permanent change in policy. I illustrate this by some numerical examples. While a temporary increase in government spending, for example, can be very effective at zero interest rate, an expansion in the government can instead even be contractionary if it is expected to be permanent. This explains the difference of the results reported in table 1 from some recent studies on the effect of government spending in DSGE models, as further discussed below.

II. Relation to Other Literature

The first paper to study the effect of government spending at a zero interest rate in a New Keynesian DSGE model is Eggertsson (2001). That paper characterizes the optimal policy under commitment and discretion, where the government has as policy instruments the short-term nominal interest rate and real government spending and assumes taxes are lump sum. Relative to that paper, this paper studies a much more general menu of fiscal instruments, such as the effect of various distortionary taxes, and gives more attention to the quantitative effect of fiscal policy. Moreover, the current paper does not take a direct stance on the optimality of fiscal policy but instead focuses on "policy multipliers," that is, the effect of policy at the margin, as in Christiano (2004). This allows me to obtain clean closed form solutions and illuminate the general forces at work.

This paper also builds upon a large literature on optimal monetary policy at the zero bound, such as Summers (1991), Fuhrer and Madigan (1997), Krugman (1998), Reifschneider and Williams (2000), Svensson (2001, 2003), Eggertsson and Woodford (2003, 2004), Christiano (2004), Jung, Terenishi, and Watanabe (2005), Wolman (2005), Adam and Billi (2006), and Eggertsson (2006a).[6] The analysis of the variations in labor taxes builds on Eggertsson and Woodford (2004), who study value added taxes (VAT) that show up in a similar manner. One difference is that while they focus mostly on commitment equilibrium (in which fiscal policy plays a small role because optimal monetary commitment does away with most of the problems) the assumption here is that the central bank is unable to commit to future inflation, an extreme assumption, but a useful benchmark. This assumption can also be defended because the optimal monetary policy suffers from a commitment problem, while fiscal policy does not to the same extent, as first formalized in Eggertsson (2001).[7] The contractionary effect of cutting payroll taxes is closely related to Eggertsson (2008b), who studies the expansionary effect of the National Industrial Recovery Act (NIRA) during the Great Depression. In reduced form, the NIRA is equivalent to an increase in labor taxes in this model. The analysis of real government spending also builds on Christiano (2004) and Eggertsson (2004, 2006b), who find that increasing real government spending is very effective at zero interest rates if the monetary authority cannot commit to future inflation, and Eggertsson (2008a), who argues based on those insights that the increase in real government spending during the Great Depression contributed more to the recovery than is often suggested.[8] Christiano, Eichenbaum, and Rebelo (2009), building on Christiano (2004), calculate the size of the multiplier of government spending in a much more sophisticated empirically estimated model than previous studies, taking the zero bound explicitly into account, and find relatively similar quantitative conclusions as reported here (see Denes and Eggertsson [2009] for further discussion, which describes the estimation strategy I follow in this paper and compares it to other recent work in the field). Christiano et al. also study various other issues related to the government spending multiplier, such as timing, sensitivity, and other shocks, not addressed directly here. Cogan et al. (2009) study the effect on increasing government spending in a DSGE model that is very similar to the CCR model and report small multipliers. The reason for the different finding is that they assume that the increase in spending is more permanent than the duration of zero interest rates, while this paper and Christiano et al. assume that the fiscal spending is a temporary stimulus in response to temporary deflationary shocks. This is made explicit in the analysis in Section XII that shows that an increase in government spending that is expected to be permanent can even be contractionary.

III. A Microfounded Model

This section summarizes a standard New Keynesian DSGE model.[9] (Readers familiar with this model can skip directly to the next section.) At its core, this is a standard stochastic growth model (real business cycle model) but with two added frictions: a monopolistic competition among firms and frictions in the firms' price setting through fixed nominal contracts that have a stochastic duration as in Calvo (1983). Relative to standard treatments, this model has a more detailed description of taxes and government spending. This section summarizes a simplified version of the model that will serve as the baseline illustration. The baseline model abstracts from capital, but Section XIV extends the model to include it.

There is a continuum of households of measure 1. The representative household maximizes

$$E_t \sum_{T=t}^{\infty} \beta^{T-t} \xi_T \left[u(C_T + G_T^S) + g(G_T^N) - \int_0^1 v(l_T(j))dj \right], \qquad (1)$$

where β is a discount factor, C_t is a Dixit-Stiglitz aggregate of consumption of each of a continuum of differentiated goods, $C_t \equiv \left[\int_0^1 c_t(i)^{(\theta-1)/\theta} di \right]^{\theta/(\theta-1)}$, with an elasticity of substitution equal to $\theta > 1$, P_t is the Dixit-Stiglitz price index, $P_t \equiv \left[\int_0^1 p_t(i)^{1-\theta} di \right]^{1/(1-\theta)}$, and $l_t(j)$ is the quantity supplied of labor of type j. Each industry j employs an industry-specific type of labor, with its own wage $W_t(j)$. The disturbance ξ_t is a preference shock, and $u(\cdot)$ and $g(\cdot)$ are increasing concave functions while $v(\cdot)$ is an increasing convex function. The terms G_T^S and G_T^N are government spending that differ only in how they enter utility and are also defined as Dixit-Stiglitz aggregates analogous to private consumption. The term G_t^S is perfectly substitutable for private consumption, while G_t^N is not. For simplicity, we assume that the only assets traded are one-period riskless bonds, B_t. The period budget constraint can then be written as

$$(1+\tau_t^s)P_t C_t + B_t = (1-\tau_{t-1}^A)(1+i_{t-1})B_{t-1} + (1-\tau_t^P)\int_0^1 Z_t(i)di$$

$$+ (1-\tau_t^w)\int_0^1 W_t(j) l_t(j)dj - T_t, \qquad (2)$$

where $Z_t(i)$ is profits that are distributed lump sum to the households. I do not model optimal stock holdings (i.e., the optimal portfolio allocation) of the households, which could be done without changing the results.[10] There are five types of taxes in the baseline model: a sales tax τ_t^s on consumption purchases, a payroll tax τ_t^w, a tax on financial assets τ_t^A, a tax on profits τ_t^p, and finally a lump-sum tax T_t, all represented in the budget constraint. Observe that I allow for different tax treatments of the risk-free bond returns and dividend payments, while in principle we could write the model so that these two underlying assets are taxed in the same way. I do this to clarify the role of taxes on capital. The profit tax has no effect on the household consumption/saving decision (it would only change how stocks are priced in a more complete description of the model) while taxes on the risk-free debt have a direct effect on households' saving and consumption decisions. This distinction is helpful to analyze the effect of capital taxes on households' spending and savings (τ_t^A), on the one hand, and the firms' investment, hiring, and pricing decisions, on the other (τ_t^P), because we assume that the firms maximize profits net of taxes. Households take prices and wages as given and maximize utility subject to the budget constraint by their choices of $c_t(i)$, $l_t(j)$, B_t, and $Z_t(i)$ for all j and i at all times t.

The household optimal plan needs to satisfy the following first-order conditions:

$$u_c(C_t + G_t^S) = (1+i_t)(1-\tau_t^A)\beta E_t u_c(C_{t+1} + G_{t+1}^S)\frac{\xi_{t+1}}{\xi_t}\frac{P_t}{P_{t+1}}\frac{1+\tau_t^s}{1+\tau_{t+1}^s}, \quad (3)$$

$$\frac{1-\tau_t^W}{1+\tau_t^S}\frac{W_t(j)}{P_t} = \frac{v_l(l_t(j))}{u_c(C_t + G_t^S)},$$

$$\lim_{T\to\infty} E_t \frac{B_T}{P_T(1+\tau_T^s)} u_c(C_T + G_T^S) = 0. \quad (4)$$

There is a continuum of firms in measure 1. Firm i sets its price and then hires the labor inputs necessary to meet any demand that may be realized. A unit of labor produces one unit of output. The preferences of households and the assumption that the government distributes its spending on varieties in the same way as households imply a demand for good i of the form $y_t(i) = Y_t[(p_t(i)/P_t)]^{-\theta}$, where $Y_t \equiv C_t + G_t^N + G_t^S$ is aggregate output. We assume that all profits are paid out as dividends and that the firm seeks to maximize posttax profits. Profits can be written as $Z_t(i) = p_t(i)Y_t(p_t(i)/P_t)^{-\theta} - W_t(j)Y_t(p_t(i)/P_t)^{-\theta}$, where i indexes the firm and j the industry in which the firm operates. Following Calvo (1983), let us suppose that each industry has an equal probability of reconsidering its price in each period. Let $0 < \alpha < 1$ be the fraction of industries with prices that remain unchanged in each period. In any industry that revises its prices in period t, the new price p_t^* will be the same. The maximization problem that each firm faces at the time it revises its price is then to choose a price p_t^* to maximize

$$\max_{p_t^*} E_t\left\{\sum_{T=t}^{\infty}(\alpha\beta)^{T-t}\lambda_T(1-\tau_T^P)[p_t^* Y_T(p_t^*/P_T)^{-\theta} - W_T(j)Y_T(p_t^*/P_T)^{-\theta}]\right\},$$

where λ_T is the marginal utility of nominal income for the representative household. An important assumption is that the price the firm sets is exclusive of the sales tax. This means that if the government cuts sales taxes, then consumers face a lower store price of exactly the amount of the tax cuts for firms that have not reset their prices. This maximization problem yields the following first-order condition:

$$E_t\left\{\sum_{T=t}^{\infty}(\alpha\beta)^{T-t}\frac{u_c(C_T+G_T^S)\xi_T}{P_T}\frac{(1-\tau_T^P)}{(1+\tau_T^s)}\left(\frac{p_t^*}{P_T}\right)^{-\theta-1}\right.$$
$$\left.\times Y_T\left[\frac{p_t^*}{P_T}-\frac{\theta}{\theta-1}\frac{1+\tau_t^s}{1-\tau_t^W}\frac{v_l(Y_T(p_t^*/P_T)^{-\theta})}{u_c(C_T+G_T^S)}\right]\right\}=0. \quad (5)$$

Using the assumption that a fraction of α keep their prices fixed, while $1-\alpha$ set them at p_t^*, we can express the price index as

$$P_t = [(1-\alpha)(p_t^*)^{1-\theta}+\alpha P_{t-1}^{1-\theta}]^{1/(1-\theta)}. \quad (6)$$

All output is either consumed by the government or the private sector:

$$Y_t = C_t + G_t^S + G_t^N. \quad (7)$$

Without going into details about how the central bank implements a desired path for nominal interest rates, we assume that it cannot be negative so that[11]

$$i_t \geq 0. \quad (8)$$

We assume that the central bank follows a Taylor rule, whose parameters are detailed further below, in accordance to

$$i_t = \max\left[0, \phi\left(\frac{P_t}{P_{t-1}}, Y_t, \xi_t\right)\right]. \quad (9)$$

Fiscal policy, on the other hand, is a set of functions for each of the policy variables, $\tau_t^w, \tau_t^s, \tau_t^A, \tau_t^P, T_t, G_t^N$, and G_t^S. I will be more specific about the rules that govern fiscal policy in the sections below. An equilibrium of the model can now be defined as a collection of stochastic processes for the endogenous variables $\{p_t^*, Y_t, P_t, C_t\}$ for $t \geq t_0$ given an initial condition P_{t_0-1}, an exogenous sequence $\{\xi_t\}$, a stochastic process for $\{i_t\}$ that satisfies (8)–(9) and a collection of stochastic processes for $\{\tau_t^w, \tau_t^s, \tau_t^A, \tau_t^P, T_t, G_t^N, G_t^S\}$ given the fiscal policy rules to be specified. We now describe how we approximate to model by a log-linear approximation of the equilibrium conditions around a zero-inflation steady state (summarized in proposition 1).[12]

IV. An Approximated Equilibrium

This section summarizes a log-linearized version of the model. It is convenient to summarize the model by "aggregate demand" and "aggregate supply." Aggregate demand (AD) is given by two relationships. First, there is the "IS" equation derived from the optimal consumption decision of the household (3) and the resource constraint (7)

$$\hat{Y}_t = E_t\hat{Y}_{t+1} - \sigma(i_t - E_t\pi_{t+1} - r_t^e) + (\hat{G}_t^N - E_t\hat{G}_{t+1}^N)$$
$$+\sigma\chi^s E_t(\hat{\tau}_{t+1}^s - \hat{\tau}_t^s) + \sigma\chi^A\hat{\tau}_t^A, \tag{10}$$

where i_t is the one-period risk-free nominal interest rate, π_t is inflation, and E_t is an expectation operator and the coefficients $\sigma, \chi^A, \chi^s > 0$, $\hat{Y}_t \equiv \log Y_t/\bar{Y}$, $\hat{G}_t^N \equiv (G_t^N - \bar{G}^N)/\bar{Y}$, while $\hat{\tau}_t^s \equiv \tau_t^s - \bar{\tau}^s$, $\hat{\tau}_t^A \equiv (1-\beta)^{-1}(\tau_t^A - \bar{\tau}^A)$, and r_t^e is an exogenous disturbance that is only a function of the shock ξ_t (for details, see n. 13 on the rationale for this notation).[13] Again the zero bound needs to be satisfied:

$$i_t \geq 0. \tag{11}$$

Second, there is the monetary policy rule (9) approximated by:

$$i_t = \max(0, r_t^e + \phi_\pi\pi_t + \phi_y\hat{Y}_t), \tag{12}$$

where the coefficients $\phi_\pi > 1$ and $\phi_y > 0$. When combining these relationships in coming sections, we will simply refer to the result as aggregate demand (AD) as it determines the overall level of spending in the economy given the monetary policy rule.

The aggregate supply (AS) is derived from the optimal pricing decision of the firms (5) and (6):

$$\pi_t = \kappa\hat{Y}_t + \kappa\psi(\chi^w\hat{\tau}_t^w + \chi^s\hat{\tau}_t^s - \sigma^{-1}\hat{G}_t^N) + \beta E_t\pi_{t+1}, \tag{13}$$

where the coefficients $\kappa, \psi > 0$ and $0 < \beta < 1$.

For a given policy rule for taxes and spending equations (10)–(13) close the model. An approximate equilibrium can now be defined as a collection of stochastic processes for $\{\hat{Y}_t, \pi_t\}$ that satisfy (10) and (13), given an exogenous path for $\{r_t^e\}$, a monetary policy specifying the process $\{i\}$ that satisfies (11) and (12), and fiscal policy rules that determines the path for $\{\hat{\tau}_t^w, \hat{\tau}_t^s, \hat{\tau}_t^A, \hat{G}_t^N\}$, which I will be specific about in the coming policy experiments. To summarize:

Proposition 1. The steady state of the model is a set of constants shown in the appendix. An approximate equilibrium, which is accurate up to a first order, is a collection of stochastic processes for $\{\hat{Y}_t, \pi_t, r_t^e, i_t\}$ that solve equations (10)–(13) given a path for $\{\hat{\tau}_t^w, \hat{\tau}_t^s, \hat{\tau}_t^A, \hat{G}_t^N\}$ determined by fiscal policy, where we have linearized about the steady state stated in this proposition.

Proof. See the appendix.

Observe that this list of equations for the equilibrium determination does not include the government budget constraint. I assume that Ricardian equivalence holds, so that temporary variations in either $\hat{\tau}_t^w$, $\hat{\tau}_t^s$, or $\hat{G}_t^N$ are offset either by lump-sum transfers (i.e., changes in $\hat{T}_t$) in period t or in future periods $t+j$ (the exact date is irrelevant because of Ricardian equivalence).[14] Observe also that I do not need to determine the path for $\hat{G}_t^S$ and $\hat{C}_t$ for output and inflation determination. The reason for this is that any variation in $\hat{G}_t^S$ will be offset by a corresponding reduction in $\hat{C}_t$ and hence it is irrelevant for the determination of inflation and output (more on this in Sec. VIII). Finally observe that the tax instrument $\hat{\tau}_t^P$ does not appear in any of the equations. This suggests that taxes on profits, under our assumptions, do not have a first-order effect on inflation, output, and interest rates.

V. Long-Run and Short-Run Equilibrium Allocations

This section summarizes the model's equilibrium allocation. The rest of the paper is devoted to explaining and evaluating this allocation under a variety of additional assumptions. Accordingly, the discussion of the propositions here is short and terse; the proofs and algebraic details are relegated to the appendix.

The long run in the model is defined as the time at which the shock, r_t^e, has gone to steady state. The short run is the period in which the economy is subject to temporary disturbance. More precisely, the short run is defined by $r_t^e = r_S^e$. This shock reverts back to steady state, $\bar{r}$, with probability $1-\mu$ in each period. Let us call the stochastic period in which the shocks are back to steady state T^e. Then $t \geq T^e$ is defined as the long run, while $t < T^e$ is the short run. Monetary policy follows (13), and (for now) fiscal policy is perfectly correlated with the shock, that is, we consider tax cuts/increases and government spending increases/cuts that are a direct reaction to the shock, so that, $(\hat{\tau}_t^w, \hat{\tau}_t^s, \hat{\tau}_t^A, \hat{G}_t^N) = (\hat{\tau}_S^w, \hat{\tau}_S^s, \hat{\tau}_S^A, \hat{G}_S^N)$ in the short run, $t < \tau$, and $(\hat{\tau}_t^w, \hat{\tau}_t^s, \hat{\tau}_t^A, \hat{G}_t^N) = (0,0,0,0)$ in the long run $t \geq T^e$. We are focusing, in other words, on fiscal policy that is aimed at short-run stabilization.

The assumption about a short and long run is very convenient because of the structure of the model. As we will see, it allows us to boil the model down to just a few static "short-run" equations, even if in principle we are dealing with an infinite-horizon model. This allows me to show everything in closed form and even to illustrate the key results by the aid of simple short-run diagrams.

Proposition 2. At positive interest rates, in the long run, $t \geq T^e$, there is a locally unique bounded equilibrium such that $\pi_t = \hat{Y}_t = 0$ and $i_t = \bar{r}$.

Proof. See the appendix.

We now state two conditions that are helpful to analyze the short run:

$$\text{C1} \qquad r_S^e < -\Gamma_{\tau^A}\hat{\tau}_S^A - \Gamma_{\tau^w}\hat{\tau}_S^w - \Gamma_{G^N}[\hat{G}_S^N - \sigma\chi^s\hat{\tau}_t^s],$$

$$\text{C2} \qquad L(\mu) \equiv (1-\mu)(1-\mu\beta) - \kappa\mu\sigma > 0,$$

where the coefficients $\Gamma_{\tau^A}, \Gamma_{\tau^w}, \Gamma_{G^N} > 0$ with the algebraic expressions given in the appendix. Observe that C1 imposes a condition on the fundamental shock, r_S^e, and a limit on the fiscal expansion. If there is no countercyclical short-run policy this condition simply states that $r_S^e < 0$. This condition needs to hold to ensure that the zero bound is binding.

Proposition 3. In the short run, $t < T^e$, then we consider two cases:

1. *Positive interest rates in the short run.* If C1 does not hold and the short-term interest rate is positive, there is a locally unique bounded equilibrium such that

$$\pi_t = \pi_S^p \quad \forall\ t < T^e,$$

$$\hat{Y}_t = \hat{Y}_S^p \quad \forall\ t < T^e,$$

$$i_t = i_S^p = r_S^e + \phi_\pi \pi_S + \phi_y \hat{Y}_S > 0,$$

where the analytical expression for π_S^p and $\hat{Y}_S^p$ is given in the appendix and depends on the structural parameters and $(\hat{\tau}_S^A, \hat{\tau}_S^w, \hat{\tau}_t^s, \hat{G}_S^N)$.

2. *Zero interest rates in the short run.* If C1 and C2 hold and the short-term interest rate is zero, there is a locally unique bounded equilibrium such that

$$\pi_t = \pi_S^z \quad \forall\ t < T^e,$$

$$\hat{Y}_t = \hat{Y}_S^z \quad \forall\ t < T^e,$$

$$i_t = i_S^z = 0,$$

where the analytical expression for π_S^z and $\hat{Y}_S^z$ is given in the appendix and depends on the structural parameters and $(\hat{\tau}_S^A, \hat{\tau}_S^w, \hat{\tau}_t^s, \hat{G}_S^N, r_S^e)$.

Proof. See the appendix.

I do not consider the case when C1 holds but C2 does not. In this case either the local approximation is no longer valid (the model explodes) or there is an indeterminacy of equilibria. In proposition 2 we are implicitly assuming a long-run monetary and fiscal policy regime that excludes the zero bound being binding as a long-run as steady state outcome, for example, through a monetary and fiscal commitment as in Eggertsson and Woodford (2003, 193–98). Similarly, in proposition 3, we do not consider short-run liquidity traps due to self-fulfilling expectations as in Mertens and Ravn (2010) and instead focus on traps driven by real disturbances. Proposition 3 is the heart of the paper. In fact, by manipulating it using the algebraic expression in the appendix, we can compute all the relevant fiscal multipliers. The rest of the paper is to a large extent about interpreting this proposition, both qualitatively and quantitatively.

VI. An Output Collapse in the Absence of Fiscal Interventions

Output can collapse under the special circumstances when interest rates are zero. This environment is the focus of the paper. We consider the model first when there is no fiscal intervention, that is, each of the fiscal variables is at steady state. The propositions and condition C1 suggest that when $r_t^e < 0$ then the zero bound is binding, so that $i_t = 0$. A negative r_t^e generates a recession in the model and plays a key role.

Before going further, it is natural to ask: where does this shock come from? In the simplest version of the model, a negative r_t^e is equivalent to a preference shock and so corresponds to a lower ξ_t in period t in the utility function (1) that reverts back to steady state with probability $1 - \mu$. Everyone suddenly wants to save more, so the real interest rate must decline for output to stay constant. More sophisticated interpretations are possible, however. Curdia and Eggertsson (2009), building on Curdia and Woodford (2008), show that a model with financial frictions can also be reduced to equations (10)–(13). In this more sophisticated model, the shock r_t^e corresponds to an exogenous increase in the probability of default by borrowers. What is nice about this interpretation is that r_t^e can now be mapped into the wedge between a risk-free interest rate and an interest rate paid on risky loans. Both rates are observed in the data. The wedge implied by these interest rates exploded in the U.S. economy during the crisis of 2008, providing empirical evidence for a large negative shock to r_t^e. A banking crisis—characterized by an increase in probability of default by borrowers—is my story for the model's recession.

Let us now go through the equilibrium determination informally (the formal proof is in propositions 2 and 3). Panel *a* in figure 1 illustrates assumption about the shock graphically. Under this assumption, the shock r_t^e remains negative in the short run denoted *S*, until some stochastic date T^e, when it returns to steady state. For starters, let us assume that $\hat{\tau}_t^w = \hat{\tau}_t^A = \hat{\tau}_t^s = \hat{G}_t^N = 0$. Given the shock, monetary policy takes the following form:

$$i_t = r_S^e = \bar{r} \quad \text{for } t \geq T^e, \tag{14}$$

$$i_t = 0 \quad \text{for } 0 < t < T^e. \tag{15}$$

In the periods $t \geq T^e$, the solution is $\pi_t = \hat{Y}_t = 0$. In periods $t < T^e$, the assumption about the shock implies that inflation in the next period is either zero (with probability $1 - \mu$) or the same as at time *t*, that is, $\pi_t = \pi_S$ (with probability μ).[15] Hence the solution in $t < T^e$ satisfies the *AD* and the *AS* equations:

$$AD \quad \hat{Y}_S = \mu\hat{Y}_S + \sigma\mu\pi_S + \sigma r_S^e, \tag{16}$$

$$AS \quad \pi_S = \kappa\hat{Y}_S + \beta\mu\pi_S. \tag{17}$$

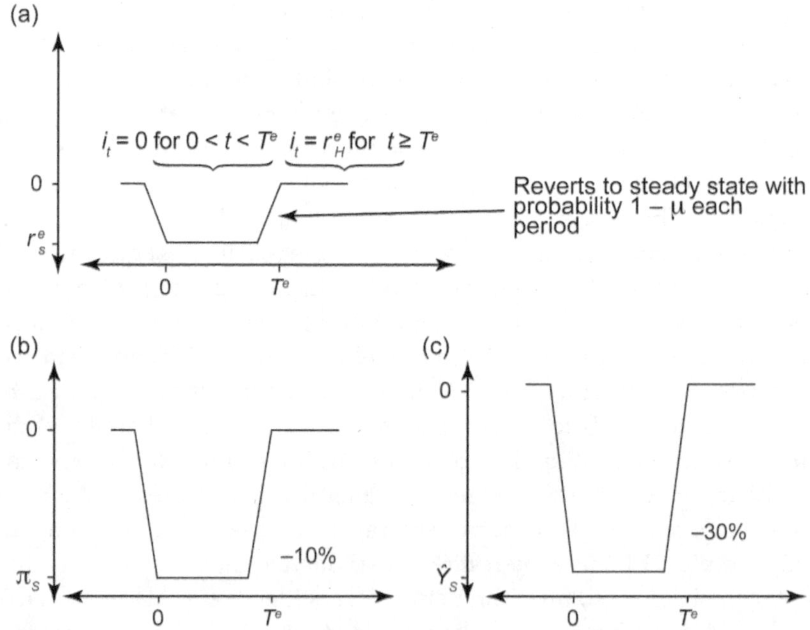

Fig. 1. The effect of negative r_t^e on output and inflation in the absence of any fiscal policy.

It is helpful to graph the two equations in $(\hat{Y}_S, \pi_S)$ space. Consider first the special case in which $\mu = 0$, that is, the shock r_S^e reverts back to steady state in period 1 with probability 1. This case is shown in figure 2. It applies only to the equilibrium determination in period 0. The equilibrium is shown where the two solid lines intersect at point A. At point A, output is completely demand-determined by the vertical AD curve and pinned down by the shock r_t^e. For a given level of output, then, inflation is determined by where the AD curve intersects the AS curve. It is worth emphasizing again: Output is completely demand-determined, that is, it is completely determined by the AD equation.

Consider now the effect of increasing $\mu > 0$. In this case, the contraction is expected to last for longer than one period. Because of the simple structure of the model, and the two-state Markov process for the shock, the equilibrium displayed in the figure corresponds to all periods $0 \leq t < T^e$. The expectation of a possible future contraction results in movements in both the AD and the AS curves, and the equilibrium is determined at the intersection of the two dashed curves, at point B. Observe that the AD equation is no longer vertical but upward sloping in inflation, that is, higher inflation expectations $\mu\pi_S$ increase output. The reason is that, for a given nominal interest rate ($i_S = 0$ in this equilibrium), any increase in expected inflation reduces the real interest rate, making current spending relatively cheaper and thus increasing demand. Conversely, expected deflation, a negative $\mu\pi_S$, causes current consumption to be relatively more expensive than future consumption, thus suppressing

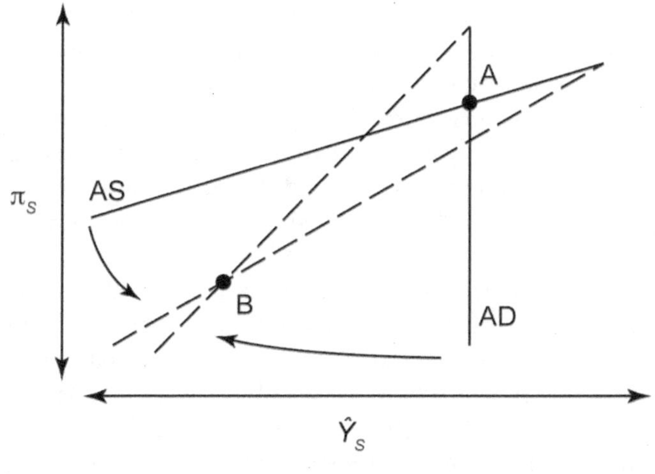

Fig. 2. The effect of multiperiod recession

spending. Observe, furthermore, the presence of the expectation of future contraction, $\mu \hat{Y}_S$, on the right-hand side of the *AD* equation. The expectation of future contraction makes the effect of both the shock and the expected deflation even stronger.

Let us now turn to the *AS* equation (17). Its slope is now steeper than before because the expectation of future deflation will lead the firms to cut prices by more for a given demand slack, as shown by the dashed line. The net effect of the shift in both curves is a more severe contraction and deflation shown by the intersection of the two dashed curves at point *B* in figure 2 (see n. 16 on why the *AD* curve has to be steeper than the *AS* curve).[16]

The more severe depression at point *B* is triggered by several contractionary forces. First, because the contraction is now expected to last more than one period, output is falling in the price level because there is expected deflation, captured by $\mu \pi_S$ on the right-hand side of the *AD* equation. This increases the real interest rate and suppresses demand. Second, the expectation of future output contraction, captured by the $\mu \hat{Y}_S$ term on the right-hand side of the *AD* equation, creates an even further decline in output. Third, the strong contraction, and the expectation of it persisting in the future, implies an even stronger deflation for given output slack, according to the *AS* equation. Note the role of the aggregate supply, or the *AS* equation. It is still really important to determine the expected inflation in the *AD* equation. This is the sense in which output is demand-determined in the model even when the shock lasts for many periods. That is what makes tax policy so tricky, as we soon will see. It is also the reason why government spending and cuts in sales taxes can have a big effect.

The two-state Markov process for the shock allows us to collapse the model into two equations with two unknown variables, as shown in figure 2 and illustrated by proposition 3. It is important to keep in mind, however, the stochastic nature of the solution. The output contraction and the deflation last only as long as the stochastic duration of the shock, that is, until the stochastic date T^e, and the equilibrium depicted in figure 2 applies only to the "recession" state, that is, the short run. This is illustrated in figure 1, which shows the solution for an arbitrary contingency in which the shock lasts for T^e periods. I have added for illustration numerical values in this figure, using the parameters from table 2. The values assumed for the structural parameters are relatively standard. (The choice of parameters and shocks in table 2 is described in more detail in Denes and Eggertsson [2009], which estimates the model using the Bayesian method.) The values are obtained by maximizing the posterior

Table 2
Parameters, Mode

	σ^{-1}	β	ω	α	θ
Parameters (mode)	1.1599	.9970	1.5692	.7747	12.7721
	ϕ_π	ϕ_y	$\bar{\tau}^s$	$\bar{\tau}^w$	$\bar{\tau}^A$
Parameters (calibrated)	1.5	.5/4	.05	.2	0
	r^e_S	μ			
Shocks (mode)	–.0104	.9030			

distribution of the model to match a 30% decline in output and a 10% deflation in the short run. Both these numbers correspond to the trough of the Great Depression in the first quarter of 1933 before President Franklin D. Roosevelt assumed power, when the nominal interest rate was close to zero. I ask the model to match the data from the Great Depression, because people have often claimed that the goal of fiscal stimulus in 2008 was to avoid a dire scenario of that kind.[17]

VII. Why Labor Tax Cuts Are Contractionary

Can fiscal policy reverse the output collapse shown in the last section? We start by considering tax cuts on labor. Before going further, it is helpful to study tax cuts under regular circumstances, that is, in the absence of the shock. Under normal circumstances, a payroll-tax cut is expansionary in the baseline model. This is presumably why this policy proposal has gained much currency in recent policy discussions. Consider a temporary tax cut $\hat{\tau}^w_t = \hat{\tau}^w_S < 0$ in period t that is reversed with probability $1 - \rho$ in each period to steady state $\hat{\tau}^w_t = 0$. Let us call the date on which the tax cut reverses to steady state T^τ. Let $\hat{G}^N_t = \hat{\tau}^s_t = \hat{\tau}^A_t = 0$. Because the model is perfectly forward-looking, this allows us again to collapse the model into only two states, the short run when $\hat{\tau}^w_S < 0$ and the long run when $\hat{\tau}^w_t = \hat{\tau}^w_L = 0$. Observe that in the steady state $t > T^\tau$ then $\hat{Y}_t = \pi_t = 0$. Substituting (13) into the *AD* equation, we can write the *AD* and *AS* equation in the short run as

$$\hat{Y}_S = -\sigma \frac{\phi_\pi - \rho}{1 - \rho + \sigma\phi_y} \pi_S, \tag{18}$$

$$(1 - \beta\rho)\pi_S = \kappa\hat{Y}_S + \kappa\psi\chi^w\hat{\tau}^w_S. \tag{19}$$

Figure 3 shows the *AS* and *AD* curves (18) and (19). This figure looks like any undergraduate textbook *AS-AD* diagram! A tax cut shifts down

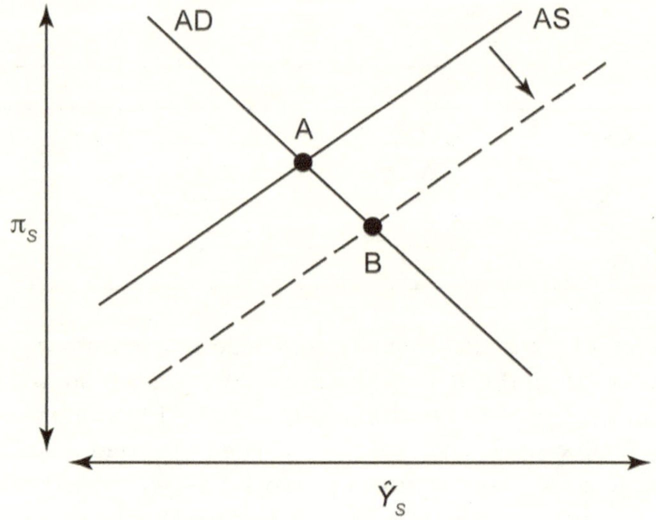

Fig. 3. The effect of cutting taxes at a positive interest rate

the *AS* curve. Why? Now people want to work more since they get more money in their pocket for each hour worked. This reduces real wages, so that firms are ready to supply more goods for less money, creating some deflationary pressure. In response, the central bank accommodates this shift by cutting interest rates in order to curb deflation, which is why the *AD* equation is downward sloping.[18] A new equilibrium is found at point *B*. We can compute the multiplier of tax cuts by using the method of undetermined coefficients. The tax cut multiplier is

$$\frac{\Delta\hat{Y}_S}{-\Delta\hat{\tau}^w_S} = \chi^w \frac{\sigma\phi_\pi\kappa\psi}{(1-\rho+\sigma\phi_y)(1-\rho\beta)+\sigma\phi_\pi\kappa} > 0. \tag{20}$$

Here, Δ denotes change relative to the benchmark of no variations in taxes. To illustrate the multiplier numerically, I use the values reported in table 2 and assume $\rho = \mu$. The multiplier is 0.16. If the government cut the tax rate $\hat{\tau}^w_S$ by 1% in a given period, then output increases by 0.16%. We can also translate this into dollars. Think of the tax cuts in terms of dollar cuts in tax collections in the absence of shocks, that is, tax collection in a "steady state." Then the meaning of the multiplier is that each dollar of tax cuts buys you a 16 cent increase in output.

We now show that this very same tax cut has the opposite effect under the special circumstances when the zero bound is binding. Again, consider a temporary tax cut but now one that is explicitly aimed at "ending the recession" created by the negative shock that caused all the trouble in the last section. Assume that the tax cut takes the following form:

$$\hat{\tau}_S^w = \phi_\tau r_S^e < 0 \quad \text{when } 0 < t < T^e, \tag{21}$$

with $\phi_\tau > 0$ and

$$\hat{\tau}_t^w = 0 \quad \text{when } t \geq T^e. \tag{22}$$

Consider now the solution in the periods when the zero bound is binding but the government follows this policy. The *AS* curve is exactly the same as under the "normal circumstance" shown in equation (19), but now we have replaced ρ with the probability of the duration of the shock, that is, $\rho = \mu$. The big difference is the *AD* curve, because of the shock r_S^e and because the zero bound is binding. Hence we replace equation (18) with equation (16) from the last section. These two curves are plotted in figure 4, and it should now be clear that the effect of the tax cut is the opposite from what we had before. Just as before, the increase in $\hat{\tau}_L^w$ shifts the *AS* curve outward as denoted by a dashed line in figure 4. As before, this is just a traditional shift in "aggregate supply" outward; the firms are now in a position to charge lower prices on their products than before. But now the slope of the *AD* curve is different from before, so that a new equilibrium is formed at the intersection of the dashed *AS* curve

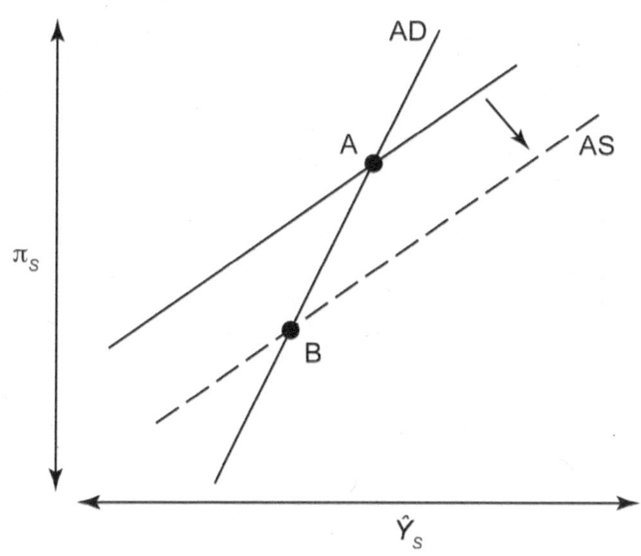

Fig. 4. The effect of cutting labor taxes at a zero interest rate

and the *AD* curve at lower output and prices, that is, at point *B* in figure 4. The general equilibrium effect of the tax cut is therefore an output contraction!

The intuition for this result (as clarified in the following paragraphs) is that the expectation of lower taxes in the recession creates deflationary expectations in all states of the world in which the shock r_t^e is negative. This makes the real interest rate higher, which reduces spending according to the *AD* equation. We can solve the *AD* and *AS* equations together to show analytically that output and inflation are reduced by these tax cuts:

$$\hat{Y}_S^{\text{taxcut}} = \frac{1}{(1-\mu)(1-\beta\mu)-\mu\sigma\kappa}[(1-\beta\mu)\sigma r_S^e + \mu\kappa\sigma\psi\chi^w\hat{\tau}_S^w] < \hat{Y}_t^{\text{notax}} \text{ if } t < T^e$$

and

$$\hat{Y}_S^{\text{taxcut}} = 0 \quad \text{if } t \geq T^e,$$

$$\pi_t^{\text{taxcut}} = \frac{\kappa}{1-\beta\mu}(\hat{Y}_t^{\text{tax}} + \psi\chi^w\hat{\tau}_S^w) < \pi_t^{\text{notax}} \text{ if } t < T^e \text{ and } \hat{\pi}_t^{\text{tax}} = 0 \text{ if } t \geq T^e.$$

Figure 5 clarifies the intuition for why labor tax cuts become contractionary at zero interest rates while being expansionary under normal circumstances. The key is aggregate demand. At positive interest rates the

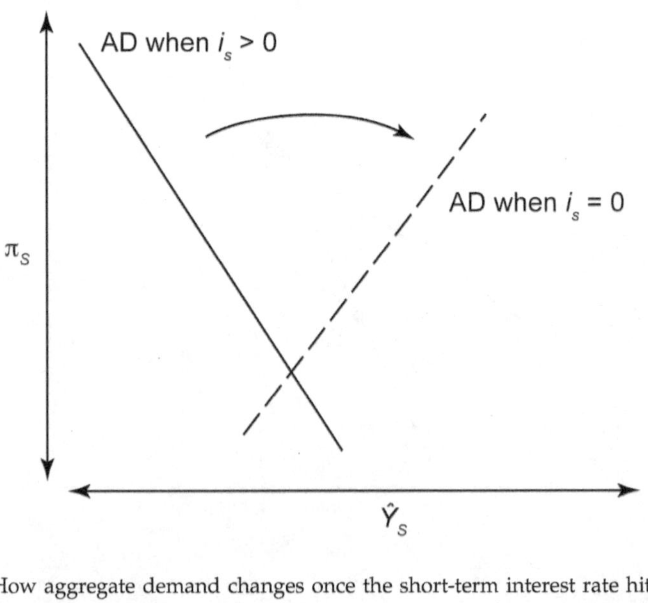

Fig. 5. How aggregate demand changes once the short-term interest rate hits zero

AD curve is downward sloping in inflation. The reason is that as inflation decreases, the central bank will cut the nominal interest rate more than 1 to 1 with inflation (i.e., $\phi_\pi > 1$, which is the Taylor principle; see eq. [12]). Similarly, if inflation increases, the central bank will increase the nominal interest rate more than 1 to 1 with inflation, thus causing an output contraction with higher inflation. As a consequence, the real interest rate will decrease with deflationary pressures and expanding output, because any reduction in inflation will be met by a more than proportional change in the nominal interest rate. This, however, is no longer the case at zero interest rates, because interest rates can no longer be cut. This means that the central bank will no longer be able to offset deflationary pressures with aggressive interest rate cuts, shifting the *AD* curve from downward sloping to upward sloping in $(\hat{Y}_S, \pi_S)$ space, as shown in figure 5. The reason is that lower inflation will now mean a higher real rate, because the reduction in inflation can no longer be offset by interest rate cuts. Similarly, an increase in inflation is now expansionary because the increase in inflation will no longer be offset by an increase in the nominal interest rate; hence, higher inflation implies lower real interest rates and thus higher demand.

We can now compute the multiplier of tax cuts at zero interest rates. It is negative and given by

$$\frac{\Delta \hat{Y}_S}{-\Delta \hat{\tau}_S^w} = -\chi^w \frac{\mu\kappa\sigma\psi}{(1-\mu)(1-\beta\mu)-\mu\sigma\kappa} < 0. \tag{23}$$

Using the numerical values in table 2, this corresponds to a multiplier of −1.02. This means that if the government reduces taxes rate $\hat{\tau}_S^w$ by 1% at zero interest rates, then aggregate output declines by 1%. To keep the multipliers (20) and (23) comparable, I assume that the expected persistence of the tax cuts is the same across the two experiments, that is, $\mu = \rho$ (see table 3).

In the model, wages are flexible. This means that it makes no difference if the labor tax is levied on the worker (labor income tax) or the firm (the

Table 3
Multipliers of Temporary Policy Changes

	Multiplier (Mode) $i_t > 0$	Multiplier (Mode) $i_t = 0$
τ_t^w (payroll tax cut)	.1612	−1.0191
G_t^S (government spending 1 increase)	0	0
G_t^N (government spending 2 increase)	.4652	2.2793
τ_t^S (sales tax cut)	.5139	2.5179
τ_t^A (capital tax cut)	−.0013	−.1012

firm's part of the payroll tax). More realistically, wages are set in a staggered fashion, as, for example, in Christiano, Eichenbaum, and Evans (2005). In this case it matters who bears the tax and how it affects the contracted (sticky) wage. Suppose variations in the tax do not change the contracted wage that is set in staggered fashion. Then the tax cut analyzed above is best approximated by the firm's payroll tax (i.e., the tax paid by the firms), since this tax variation will directly affect the marginal cost of firms almost one to one but have little effect on the wage paid to the worker. A labor income tax cut (i.e., cut in the worker's part of the payroll tax), however, will have almost no effect, since it will have a very small effect on the marginal cost of the firms and thus a small effect on expected inflation/deflation. Instead it will be absorbed almost completely by the worker, unless the workers are liquidity constrained or we introduce some other non-Ricardian features into the model.[19]

VIII. Expansionary Government Spending: Timely, Targeted, and Temporary

Let us now consider the effect of government spending. Consider first the effect of increasing $\hat{G}_t^S$. It is clear from our derivation of the model in Section IV that increasing government spending, which is a perfect substitute for private spending, has no effect on output or inflation. The reason is that the private sector will reduce its own consumption by exactly the same amount. The formal way to verify this is to observe that the path for $\{\pi_t, \hat{Y}_t\}$ is fully determined by equations (10)–(13), along with a policy rule for the tax instruments and $\hat{G}_t^N$, which makes no reference to the policy choice of $\hat{G}_t^S$. Let us now turn to government spending, which is not a perfect substitute for private consumption, $\hat{G}_t^N$.

Consider the effect of increasing government spending, $\hat{G}_t^N$, in the absence of the deflationary shock so that the short-term nominal interest rate is positive. In particular, consider an increase $\hat{G}_S^N > 0$ that is reversed with probability $1 - \rho$ in each period to steady state. Substituting the Taylor rule into the *AD* equation we can write the *AD* and *AS* equations as

$$(1 - \rho + \sigma\phi_y)\hat{Y}_S = -\sigma(\phi_\pi - \rho)\pi_S + (1 - \rho)\hat{G}_S^N, \tag{24}$$

$$(1 - \beta\rho)\pi_S = \kappa\hat{Y}_S - \kappa\psi\sigma^{-1}\hat{G}_S^N. \tag{25}$$

The experiment is shown in figure 6. It looks identical to a standard undergraduate textbook *AD-AS* diagram. An increase in $\hat{G}_S^N$ shifts out demand for all the usual reasons, that is, it is an "autonomous" increase in

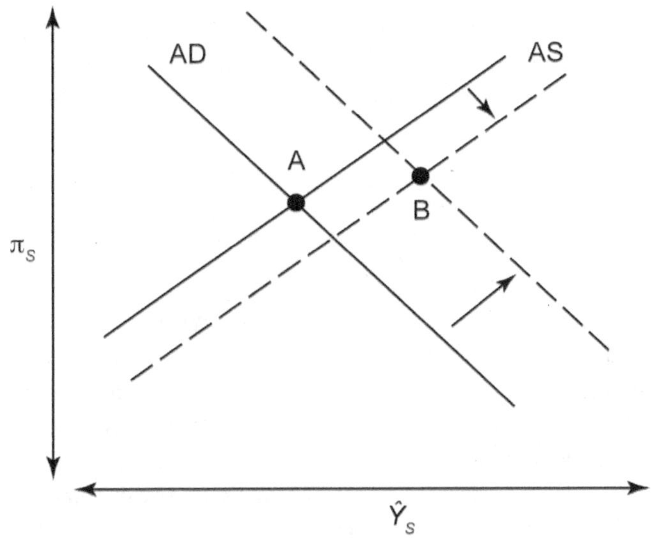

Fig. 6. Increasing government spending at positive interest rates

spending. In the standard New Keynesian model, there is an additional kick, however, akin to the effect of reducing labor taxes. Government spending also shifts out aggregate supply. Because government spending takes away resources from private consumption, people want to work more in order to make up for lost consumption, shifting out labor supply and reducing real wages. This effect is shown in the figure by the outward shift in the *AS* curve. The new equilibrium is at point *B*. Using the method of undetermined coefficients, we can compute the multiplier of government spending at positive interest rates as

$$\frac{\Delta \hat{Y}_S}{\Delta \hat{G}_S^N} = \frac{(1-\rho)(1-\rho\beta) + (\phi_\pi - \rho)\kappa\psi}{(1-\rho+\sigma\phi_y)(1-\rho\beta) + (\phi_\pi - \rho)\sigma\kappa} > 0.$$

Using the parameter values in table 1, we find that one dollar in government spending increases output by 0.46, which is more than three times the multiplier of tax cuts at positive interest rates.

Consider now the effect of government spending at zero interest rates. In contrast to tax cuts, increasing government spending is very effective at zero interest rates. Consider the following fiscal policy:

$$\hat{G}_t^N = \hat{G}_S^N > 0 \quad \text{for } 0 < t < T^e, \tag{26}$$

$$\hat{G}_t^N = 0 \quad \text{for } t \geq T^e. \tag{27}$$

Under this specification, the government increases spending in response to the deflationary shock and then reverts back to steady state once the shock is over.[20] The *AD* and *AS* equations can be written as

$$\hat{Y}_S = \mu\hat{Y}_S + \sigma\mu\pi_S + \sigma r_S^e + (1-\mu)\hat{G}_S^N, \tag{28}$$

$$\pi_S = \kappa\hat{Y}_S + \beta\mu\pi_S - \kappa\psi\sigma^{-1}\hat{G}_S^N. \tag{29}$$

Figure 7 shows the effect of increasing government spending. Increasing $\hat{G}_S^N$ shifts out the *AD* equation, stimulating both output and prices. At the same time, however, it shifts out the *AS* equation as we discussed before, so there is some deflationary effect of the policy, which arises from an increase in the labor supply of workers. This effect, however, is too small to overcome the stimulative effect of government expenditures. In fact, solving these two equations together, we can show that the effect of government spending is always positive and always greater than 1. Solving (28) and (29) together yields the following multiplier:[21]

$$\frac{\Delta\hat{Y}_S}{\Delta\hat{G}_S^N} = \frac{(1-\mu)(1-\beta\mu)-\mu\kappa\psi}{(1-\mu)(1-\beta\mu)-\sigma\mu\kappa} > 1, \tag{30}$$

that is, one dollar of government spending, according to the model, has to increase output by more than 1. In our numerical example, the multiplier is 2.3, that is, each dollar of government spending increases aggregate

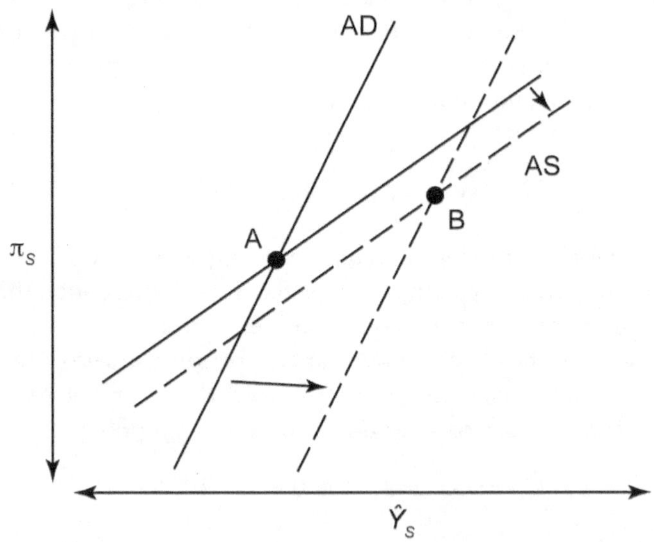

Fig. 7. The effect of increasing government spending at zero interest rates

output by 2.3 dollars. Why is the multiplier so large? The main cause of the decline in output and prices was the expectation of a future slump and deflation. If the private sector expects an increase in future government spending in all states of the world in which the zero bound is binding, contractionary expectations are changed in all periods in which the zero bound is binding, thus having a large effect on spending in a given period. Thus, expectations about future policy play a key role in explaining the power of government spending, and a key element of making it work is to commit to sustain the spending spree until the recession is over. One of the consequences of expectations driving the effectiveness of government spending is that it is not of crucial importance if there is an implementation lag of a few quarters. It is the announcement of the fiscal stimulus that matters more than the exact timing of its implementation. This is in sharp contrast to old-fashioned Keynesian models (see Christiano et al. [2009] for further discussion of this point). For discussion of sensitivity, see Denes and Eggertsson (2009).

IX. The Case for a Temporary Sales Tax Holiday

Not all temporary tax cuts are contractionary in the model. Perhaps the most straightforward expansionary one is a cut in sales taxes.[22] Observe that, according to the *AD* and *AS* equations (10)–(13), the sales tax enters these two equations in exactly the same form as the negative of government spending, except that it is multiplied by the coefficient $\sigma\chi^s$. Hence, the analysis from the last section about the expansionary effect of increases in government spending goes through unchanged by replacing $\hat{G}_t^N$ with $-\sigma\chi^s\hat{\tau}_t^s$, and we can use both the graphical analysis and the analytical derivation of the multiplier from the last section.

Why do sales tax cuts increase demand? A temporary cut in sales taxes makes consumption today relative to the future cheaper and thus stimulates spending. Observe also that it increases the labor supply because people want to work more because their marginal utility of income is higher. The relative impact of a 1% decrease in the sale tax versus a 1% increase in spending depends on $\sigma\chi^s$, and, in the baseline calibration, because $\sigma\chi^s < 1$, sales tax cuts have a bigger effect in the numerical example.

One question is of practical importance: is reducing the sales tax temporarily enough to stimulate the economy out of the recession in the numerical example? We could even finance this with a labor tax increase, so that in principle the problem of the zero bound is eliminated altogether, as in Eggertsson and Woodford (2004).[23] In the baseline calibration, however, this is not possible because it would imply a cut in the sales tax rate over 10%. Since sales taxes in the United States are typically in the range of 3%–8%, this would imply a large sales subsidy in the model. A subsidy for consumption is impractical, because it would give people the incentive to sell each other the same good ad infinitum and collect subsidies (although there may of course be ways of getting around this). However, the case for a temporary sales tax holiday appears relatively strong in the model and could go a long way toward eliminating the recession in the model. Another complication with sales taxes in the United States is that they are collected by each individual state, so it might be politically complicated to use them as a stimulative device.

It is worth pointing out that the model may not support the policy of cutting value added taxes. As emphasized by Eggertsson and Woodford (2004), VAT of the kind common in Europe enters the model differently from American sales taxes, because of how VAT typically interacts with price frictions. We assumed in the case of sales taxes that firms set their price exclusively of the tax, so that a 1% reduction in the tax will mean that the customer faces a 1% lower purchasing price for the goods he or she purchases even if the firms themselves have not revised their own pricing decisions. This assumption is roughly in line with empirical estimates of the effect of variations in sales taxes in the United States (see, e.g., Poterba 1996). This assumption is maybe less plausible for VAT, however, because posted prices usually include the tax (often by law). Let us then suppose the other extreme, as in Eggertsson and Woodford (2004), that the prices the firms post are inclusive of the tax. In this case, if there is a 1% decrease in the VAT, this will only lead to a decrease in the price consumers face if the firms whose goods they are purchasing have revisited their pricing decision (which only happens with stochastic intervals in the model). As a consequence, as shown in Eggertsson and Woodford (2004), the VAT shows up in the *AS* and *AD* equations exactly in the same way as the payroll tax, so that the analysis in Section VII goes through unchanged. The implication is that while I have argued that cutting sales taxes is expansionary, cutting VAT works in exactly the opposite way, at least if we assume that the pricing decisions of firms are made inclusive of the tax. The intuition for this difference is straightforward. Sales tax cuts stimulate spending because a cut implies an immediate drop in the prices of goods, and consumers expect them to be relatively more expensive as soon as the recession is over. In contrast, because VATs are included in the posted price, eliminating them will show up in prices only once the firm revisits its price (which happens with a stochastic probability). This could take some time. As a consequence, people may hold off their purchases to take advantage of lower prices in the future. In any event, the sensitivity of the effect of tax policy to the nature of price rigidities (i.e., if taxes are included or not in the posted price), and the absence of much empirical or theoretical literature on it, suggests a relatively big unexplored research area that may be of practical policy importance.

X. Why Capital Tax Cuts Can Be Contractionary

So far, we have only studied variations in taxes on labor and consumption expenditures. A third class of taxes is taxes on capital, that is, a tax on the financial wealth held by households. In the baseline specification, I included a tax that is proportional to aggregate savings, that is, the amount people hold of the one-period riskless bond, through τ_t^A, and then I assumed there was tax τ_t^P on dividends. Observe that even if the firm maximizes profits net of taxes, τ_t^P, it drops out of the first-order approximation of the firm Euler equation (*AS*). Capital taxes thus appear only in the *AD* equation through τ_t^A.

Consider, at positive interest rates, a tax cut in period *t* that is reversed with a probability $1 - \rho$ in each period. A cut in this tax will reduce demand, according to the *AD* equation. Why? Because saving today is now relatively more attractive than before, and this will encourage households to save instead of consume. This means that the *AD* curve shifts backward in figure 3, leading to a contraction in output and a decline in the price level. The multiplier of cutting this tax is given by

$$\frac{\Delta \hat{Y}_S}{-\Delta \hat{\tau}_S^A} = -\chi^A \frac{\sigma(1-\rho\beta)}{1-\rho+\sigma\phi_y+\sigma(\phi_\pi-\rho)\kappa} < 0$$

and is equal to −0.0013 in our numerical example, a small number. Recall that, in reporting this number, I have scaled $\hat{\tau}_S^A$ so that a 1% change in this variable corresponds to a tax cut that is equivalent to a cut in the tax on real capital income of 1% per year in steady state (see n. 13).

This effect is much stronger at zero interest rates. As shown in figure 8, a cut in the tax on capital shifts the *AD* curve backward and thus again reduces both output and inflation. The multiplier is again negative and given by

$$\frac{\Delta \hat{Y}_S}{-\Delta \hat{\tau}_S^A} = -\chi^A \frac{1-\beta\mu}{(1-\mu)(1-\beta\mu)-\mu\sigma\kappa} < 0.$$

In this case, however, the quantitative effect is much bigger and corresponds to −0.1 in our numerical example. This means that a tax cut that

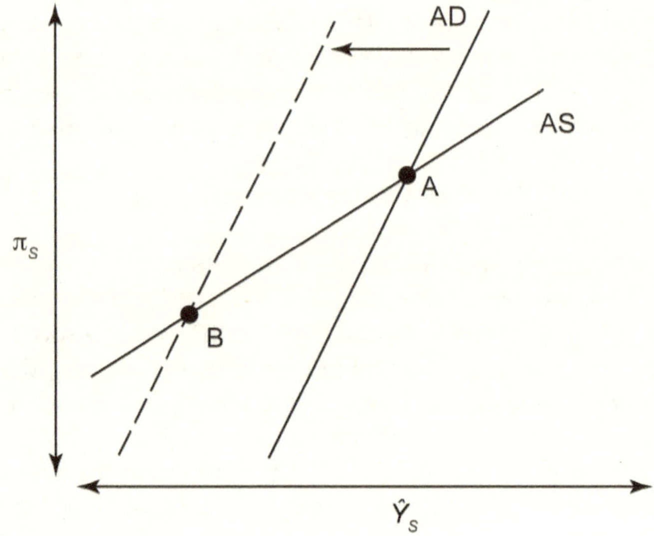

Fig. 8. The effect of cutting capital taxes

is equivalent to a 1% reduction in the tax rate on capital income (in steady state) reduces output by −0.1%.

Observe that the contractionary effect of capital tax cuts is prevalent at either positive or zero interest rates (although it is virtually absent up to two decimal points at positive interest rates). It is worth pointing out, however, that in principle the central bank can fully offset this effect at positive interest rates by cutting the nominal interest rates further, so the degree to which this is contractionary at positive interest rates depends on the reaction function of the central bank.[24] Accommodating this tax cut, however, is not feasible at zero interest rates. This tax cut is therefore always contractionary at zero short-term interest rates.

There is an important institutional difference between the capital tax in the model and capital taxes in the United States today. The tax in the model is a tax on the stock of savings. The way in which capital taxes work in practice, however, is that they are a tax on nominal capital income. Let us call a tax on nominal capital income τ_t^{AI}. In the case of a one-period riskless bond, therefore, the tax on nominal capital income τ_t^{AI} is equivalent to the tax on financial assets in the budget constraint (2) if we specify that tax as

$$\tau_t^A = \frac{i_t}{1+i_t}\tau_t^{AI}.$$

We can then use our previous equations to study the impact of changing taxes on capital income. Observe, however, that at zero interest rates this tax has to be zero by definition, because at that point the nominal income of owning a one-period risk-free bond is zero. The relevant tax rate τ_t^A on one-period bonds—which is the pricing equation that matters for policy—is therefore constrained to be zero under the current institutional framework in the United States. Hence this tax instrument cannot be used absent institutional changes. It follows that the government would need to rewrite the tax code and directly tax savings if it wants to stimulate spending by capital tax increases, a proposal that may be harder to implement than other alternatives outlined in this paper.

One argument in favor of cutting taxes on capital is that, in equilibrium, savings is equal to investment, so that higher savings will equal higher investment spending and thus can stimulate demand. Furthermore, higher capital increases the capital stock and thus the production capacities of the economy. In the baseline specification, we have abstracted from capital accumulation. Hence a cut in capital taxes reduced the willingness of consumers to consume at given prices without affecting investment spending or the production capacity of the economy.

Section XIV considers how our results change by explicitly modeling investment spending. This enriched model, however, precludes closed-form solutions, which is why I abstract from capital accumulation in the baseline model. To preview the result, I find that capital accumulation does not affect the results in a substantive way. It does, however, allow us to consider investment tax credits and also how taxes on savings affect aggregate savings, which will fall in response to tax cuts. It thus also puts a nice structure on the old Keynesian idea of the paradox of thrift.

XI. The Scope for Monetary Policy: A Commitment to Inflate and Credibility Problems

Here, I consider another policy to increase demand: a commitment to inflate the currency. Expansionary monetary policy is modeled as a commitment to a higher growth rate of the money supply in the future, that is, at $t \geq T^e$. As shown by several authors, such as Eggertsson and Woodford (2003) and Auerbach and Obstfeld (2005), it is only the expectation about future money supply (once the zero bound is no longer binding) that matters at $t < T^e$ when the interest rate is zero. Consider the following monetary policy rule:

$$i_t = \max\{0, r_t^e + \pi^* + \phi_\pi(\pi_t - \pi^*) + \phi_y(\hat{Y}_t - \hat{Y}^*)\}, \tag{31}$$

where π^* denotes the implicit inflation target of the government and $\hat{Y}^* = (1 - \beta)\kappa^{-1}\pi^*$ is the implied long-run output target. Under this policy rule, a higher π^* corresponds to a credible inflation commitment. Consider a simple money constraint as in Eggertsson (2008a), $M_t/P_t \geq \chi Y_t$, where M_t is the money supply and $\chi > 0$. A higher π^* corresponds to a commitment to a higher growth rate of the money supply in $t \geq T^e$ at the rate of π^*. The assumption about policy in (13) is a special case of this policy rule with $\pi^* = 0$.

What is the effect of an increase in the inflation target? It is helpful to write out the *AD* and *AS* equations in periods $0 < t < \tau$ when the zero bound is binding:

$$AD \quad \hat{Y}_S = \mu\hat{Y}_S + (1 - \mu)\hat{Y}^* + \sigma\mu\pi_S + \sigma(1 - \mu)\pi^* + \sigma r_S^e, \tag{32}$$

$$AS \quad \pi_S = \kappa\hat{Y}_S + \beta\mu\pi_S + \beta(1 - \mu)\pi^*. \tag{33}$$

Consider the effect of increasing $\pi^* = 0$ to a positive number $\pi^* > 0$. As shown in figure 9, this shifts the *AD* curve to the right and the *AS* curve to the left, increasing both inflation and output. The logic is straightforward: a higher inflation target in period $t \geq T^e$ reduces the real rate of interest in period $t < T^e$, thus stimulating spending in the depression state. This effect can be quite large, owing to a similar effect as described in the case of fiscal policy. The effect of π^* not only increases inflation expectations at dates $t \geq T^e$ but also increases inflation in all states of the

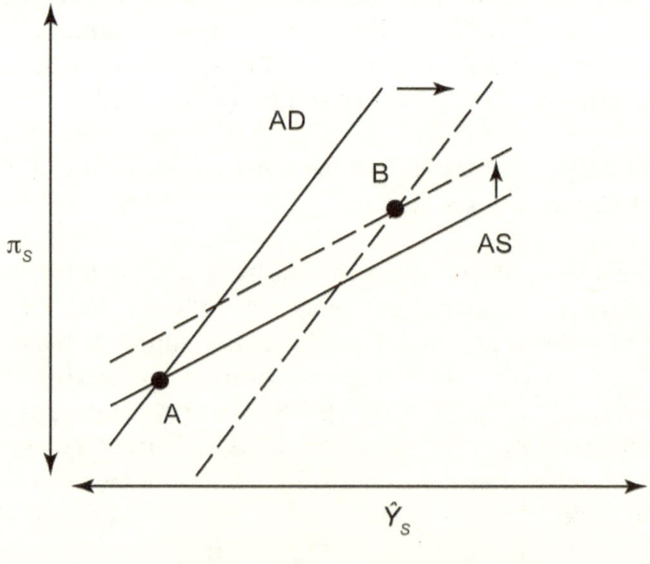

Fig. 9. Commitment to inflate at zero nominal interest rates

world in which the zero bound is binding. In general equilibrium, the effect of inflating the currency is very large for this reason.

Expansionary monetary policy can be difficult if the central bank cannot commit to future policy. The problem is that an inflation promise is not credible for a discretionary policy maker. The welfare function in the model economy is given by the utility of the representative household, which to a second order can be approximated as[25]

$$E_t \sum_{t=0}^{\infty} \beta^t \{\pi_t^2 + \lambda_Y \hat{Y}_t^2 + \lambda_G (\hat{G}_t^N)^2\}.$$

The central bank has an incentive to promise future inflation at date $t < T^e$ but then to renege on this promise at date $t \geq T^e$ since at that time the bank can achieve both zero inflation and set output at trend, which is the ideal state of affairs according to this welfare function. This credibility problem was first shown formally in Eggertsson (2006a), which calls it the "deflation bias" of discretionary monetary policy at zero interest rates. Government spending does not have this problem. In fact, the policy under full discretion will take exactly the same form as the spending analyzed in Section VIII (see, e.g., Eggertsson [2001, 2004, 2006a], who analyzes the Markov perfect equilibrium). The intuition is that fiscal policy not only requires promises about what the government will do in the future but also involves direct actions today. And those actions are fully consistent with those the government promises in the future (namely, increasing government spending throughout the recession period).

It seems quite likely that, in practice, a central bank with a high degree of credibility can make credible announcements about its future policy and thereby have considerable effect on expectations. Moreover, many authors have analyzed explicit steps, such as expanding the central bank balance sheet through purchases of various assets such as foreign exchange, mortgage-backed securities, or equities, that can help make an inflationary pledge more credible (see, e.g., Eggertsson [2006a], who shows this in the context of an optimizing government, and Jeanne and Svensson [2004], who show that an independent central bank that cares about its balance sheet can also use real asset purchases as a commitment device). Finally, if the government accumulates large amounts of nominal debt, this, too, can be helpful in making an inflation pledge credible. However, the assumption of no credible commitment by the central bank, as implied by the benchmark policy rule here, is a useful benchmark for studying the usefulness of fiscal policy in the worst case scenario in which monetary policy loses its bite.

XII. Equilibrium Allocations When Policy Changes Are Expected to Be Permanent

A key assumption in our policy exercises has been that the tax cuts, or government expansion, are temporary short-run policies. As soon as the fundamental shock, r_S^e, reverts to its long-run value, we have assumed that policy does so as well. This is natural, since much of the recent discussion has been about the appropriate "stimulus packages" in response to the economic crisis of 2008. One obvious question, however, is, how do our results change, if we assume that the policy change is permanent? Not only is this helpful to clarify through what mechanism short-run stabilization policy works in the model, it also helps illustrating the difference between the result in this paper and some recent work by Cogan et al. (2009), who argue that the multiplier of government spending is small in a model that bears close resemblance to this one. They assume that the expansion in government spending lasts for longer than the shock that causes the crisis, and permanent increase is an extreme version of this assumption that helps to clarify what is going on. As we will see, this distinction is crucial. It is so important, in fact, that we can even get a negative multiplier for government spending at a zero interest rate if it is expected to be permanent, flipping our previous result on its head. Let me stress right up front, however, that I do not think that the numerical examples reported here are a realistic description of what would happen in response to tax or spending changes, for reasons I clarify at the end of the section. They are, however, quite helpful in order to unwrap the mechanism of fiscal policy in this class of models and illustrate how important the persistence of policy can be.

The next two propositions and table 4 summarize the answer to the following question: how does a permanent change in taxes and spending affect output? The propositions show both the short- and long-run effect of the policy. In our previous analysis the long-run effect of policy was zero since we assumed that all instruments would revert back to steady

Table 4
Multipliers of Permanent Policy Changes

	Short-Run $\hat{Y}_S$ Multiplier $i_t > 0$	Short-Run $\hat{Y}_S$ Multiplier $i_t = 0$	Long-Run $\hat{Y}_L$ Multiplier	Long-Run π_L Multiplier
$\tau_t^w \downarrow$	.0195	−2.5924	.4207	−.1052
$G_t^S \uparrow$	0	0	0	0
$G_t^N \uparrow$	.0181	−2.4055	.3904	−.0976
$\tau_t^S \downarrow$	.0149	−1.9751	.3205	−.0801
$\tau_t^A \downarrow$	0	−.2495	.4207	−.0056

state in the long run. In contrast, permanent effects are now important, since the policy change is permanent. The propositions and the table also show short-run multipliers that are comparable to the statistics reported earlier in the paper.

Proposition 4. At positive interest rates, in the long run, $t \geq T^e$, there is a locally unique bounded equilibrium such that $\pi_t = \pi_L$, $\hat{Y}_t = \hat{Y}_L$, and $i_t = i_L$, where

$$\hat{Y}_t = \hat{Y}_L \quad \forall\ t \geq T^e,$$

$$\pi_t = \pi_L \quad \forall\ t \geq T^e,$$

$$i_t = i_L = \bar{r} + \phi_\pi \pi_L + \phi_y \hat{Y}_L \qquad \forall\ t \geq T^e,$$

where the analytical expressions for π_L and $\hat{Y}_L$ are given in the appendix and depend on the structural parameters and $(\hat{\tau}_L^A, \hat{\tau}_L^w, \hat{\tau}_L^s, \hat{G}_L^N)$.

Proposition 5. In the short run, $t < T^e$; then we consider two cases:

1. *Positive interest rates in the short run.* If C1 does not hold and the short-term interest rate is positive, there is a locally unique bounded equilibrium such that

$$\pi_t = \pi_S^p \qquad \forall\ t < T^e,$$

$$\hat{Y}_t = \hat{Y}_S^p \qquad \forall\ t < T^e,$$

$$i_t = i_S^p = r_S^e + \phi_\pi \pi_S + \phi_y \hat{Y}_S > 0,$$

$$i_S = r_S^e + \phi_\pi \pi_S + \phi_y \hat{Y}_S,$$

where the analytical expressions for π_S^p and $\hat{Y}_S^p$ are given in the appendix and depend on the structural parameters and $(\hat{\tau}_L^A, \hat{\tau}_L^w, \hat{\tau}_L^s, \hat{G}_L^N)$.

2. *Zero interest rates in the short run.* If C1 and C2 hold and the short-term interest rate is zero, there is a locally unique bounded equilibrium such that

$$\pi_t = \pi_S^z \qquad \forall\ t < T^e,$$

$$\hat{Y}_t = \hat{Y}_S^z \qquad \forall\ t < T^e,$$

$$i_t = i_S^z = 0,$$

$$i_S = 0,$$

where the analytical expressions for π_S^z and $\hat{Y}_S^z$ are given in the appendix and depend on the structural parameters and $(\hat{\tau}_L^A, \hat{\tau}_L^w, \hat{\tau}_L^s, \hat{G}_L^N, r_S^e)$.

Proof. See the appendix.

To focus the discussion, I mainly discuss the effect of a permanent expansion in government spending below. I then briefly comment on permanent variations in the other policy instruments. Consider first the long-run effect of an increase in government spending. According to proposition 3 it is

$$\hat{Y}_L = \frac{\kappa\psi\sigma^{-1}(\phi_\pi - 1)}{\kappa(\phi_\pi - 1) + (1-\beta)\phi_y}\hat{G}_L^N, \tag{34}$$

$$\pi_L = -\frac{\kappa\psi\sigma^{-1}\phi_y}{\kappa(\phi_\pi - 1) + (1-\beta)\phi_y}\hat{G}_L^N, \tag{35}$$

that is, a permanent increase in government spending raises permanent output (because people will work more to make up for lost private consumption), and it lowers inflation permanently (because output is now above steady state). This latter effect is highly dependent on the monetary policy commitment, for example, it disappears if either $\phi_\pi \to \infty$ or $\phi_y \to 0$ in the policy rule. The long-run multipliers in our baseline calibration are shown in table 3. A question of even greater interest, however, is, how does this change our short-run analysis?

Consider the *AD* and the *AS* equations, where short-run spending is $\hat{G}_S$, long-run spending $\hat{G}_L$, and the long-run effect of policy on output and inflation is captured by $\hat{Y}_L, \pi_L$ computed from formulas (34) and (35):

$$\begin{aligned} AD \quad \hat{Y}_S &= \mu\hat{Y}_S + (1-\mu)\hat{Y}_L - \sigma\mu\pi_S + \sigma(1-\mu)\pi_L + \sigma r_S^e \\ &\quad + \{\hat{G}_S^N - \mu G_S^N + (1-\mu)G_L^N\}, \end{aligned} \tag{36}$$

$$\pi_S = \kappa\hat{Y}_S - \kappa\psi\sigma^{-1}\hat{G}_S^N + \beta\mu\pi_L + \beta(1-\mu)\pi_S. \tag{37}$$

Again we can plot these two curves up in $(\hat{Y}_S, \pi_S)$ space, and their slope is identical to our earlier analysis, as shown in figure 10. What differs is how fiscal spending shifts these two curves. The first thing to observe is that if the increase in government spending is permanent, then $\hat{G}_S^N = \hat{G}_L^N$ and the last term in the *AD* equation disappears. Hence the spending effect we considered in Section VIII on aggregate demand is simply not there. The reason for this clarifies why government spending had an effect in our previous exercise. The main problem at the zero bound is insufficient spending, that is, the economy "needs" a negative real interest rate, which

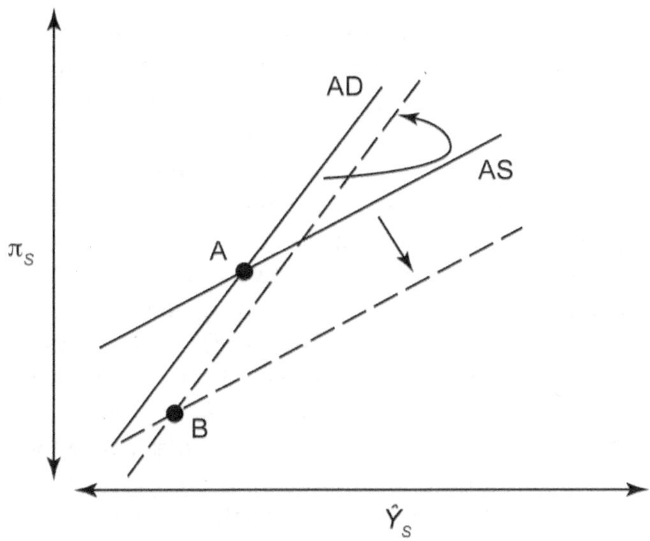

Fig. 10. Permanent increase in government spending that is contractionary

calls for higher spending today. However, this is not "insufficient spending" in the abstract. It refers to spending in the short run relative to the long run. If the government increases spending both in the long and the short run, there is no effect on spending in the short run relative to the long run and thus no effect on demand.

For aggregate demand, however, the story does not end here. In our previous example we assumed that in the long run things would go back to steady state, hence $\hat{Y}_L = \pi_L = 0$. With a permanent expansion in the government this is no longer the case, and this very fact has an influence on expectations, captured by $(1-\mu)\hat{Y}_L$ and $(1-\mu)\pi_L$, and thus aggregate demand in the short run. On the one hand, the permanent increase in government spending will increase labor supply because it takes output away from consumption to government use (thus increasing marginal utility of private consumption) and thereby increasing $\hat{Y}_L$ and shifting out demand, as shown in figure 10. On the other hand, there may be an effect on inflation in the long run, depending on how monetary policy reacts to this increase in long-run output. Our monetary commitment in equation (12) implies that monetary policy will offset the output increase to some extent, thus leading to a lower π_L, and thus moving back demand in figure 10. What is the net effect on demand? This depends on the parameters, as seen by the formulas in proposition 3. The total effect can be either positive or negative. Table 3 suggests that for the mode of our baseline calibration the net effect is $\Delta Y_L/\Delta G_L + \sigma(\Delta\pi_L/\Delta G_L) = 0.3063$, a small but nontrivial number. We can compare this to the demand effect we saw in Section VIII, where demand moved one to one with government spending increase (in that case $\Delta\hat{Y}_L/\Delta\hat{G}_L + \sigma[\Delta\pi_L/\Delta G_L] = 0$, and the effect was completely driven by change in spending in the short run vs. the long run). The demand effect of temporary government spending in response to the shock, in other words, is more than three times greater than if the change is expected to be permanent!

This is only half of the story. Let us now turn to the *AS* equation. As before, the increase in government spending shifts the *AS* curve out. Given the upward-sloping *AD* curve, however, this is contractionary in the short run, as we have already discovered. On top of this we have the effect of lower long-run inflation expectations, $\mu\pi_L$, which shifts the *AS* curve out even further. The question now becomes which force is stronger in the short run, the contractionary effect of government spending due to its negative effect on short-run inflation expectations due to the increase in aggregate supply it causes, or the positive effect of permanent spending on long-run output expectations. The answer is in table 3. In our numerical example the short-run effect of a permanent increase in government spending is contractionary according to the mode of our baseline calibration. Thus, while temporary government spending is extremely effective to battle a recession, a permanent spending increase is contractionary! Observe that the contractionary effect of a permanent increase in government spending hinges very much on the fact that it leads to a decline in long-run inflation expectations, that is, $\Delta\pi_L/\Delta\hat{G}_L < 0$. This effect was driven by the monetary policy commitment (13). We can abstract away from this channel by assuming that $\phi_\pi \to \infty$ or $\phi_y \to 0$. In this case a permanent increase in government spending is no longer contractionary but has a small positive effect. The multiplier is 0.4250. The small, or even negative, effect of a permanent increase in government spending explains why Cogan et al. (2009) report fiscal multipliers that are much smaller than I reported in Section VIII. They assume that the expansion in fiscal spending is more permanent than the duration of the zero nominal interest rates. Note that permanent sales tax cuts have exactly the same effect as government spending, but weighted by $\sigma\chi^s$.

Moving to other tax cuts, similar forces are at work for labor taxes as before, that is, in the short run a labor tax cut increases aggregate supply and creates short-run deflationary expectations. Through that mechanism a cut in labor taxes is contractionary as before. Now, however, there is an effect of these tax cuts on long-run expectations, and this can have an effect on both supply and demand. Let us focus on the demand side since this is what is new in this case. The effect comes about, as with government spending, through the term $\Delta\hat{Y}_L/\Delta\hat{\tau}_L^w + \sigma(\Delta\pi_L/\Delta\hat{\tau}_L^w) = 0.2997$ so that on net there is an increase in demand due to higher expectations of future income (because labor taxes are lower in the long run, output in the long run is also higher). As before, however, the total effect of a permanent decrease in labor taxes in the short run is negative, as can be seen in table 3. Finally we see that the multiplier of capital tax cuts is again negative but small. This is of less interest, since if one wants to take the long-run effects of capital taxes seriously, we need to take endogenous capital accumulations into account, which we do in Section XIV.

Let me conclude this section by emphasizing that I do not consider the results reported in table 4 as a reliable estimator of a "stimulus" for at least two reasons. The first, and perhaps less important, is that it seems to me to be unrealistic to assume that, for example, an increase in government spending is permanent. The fiscal stimulus in 2008 (and 1933), for example, involved a fair number of infrastructure projects that clearly seemed to be aimed at temporarily creating employment (one could argue that some entitlements spending, e.g., due to health care reforms, has a stronger persistence; that type of spending, however, would seem more accurately described as an increase in $\hat{G}_t^S$ which is substitutable with private consumption and has no effect on inflation and output). The second reason to view table 4 with some caution is that a large part of the effect is coming from the long-term monetary commitment, that is, the effect of the permanent increase in spending on long-term inflation π_L. One might argue, instead, that π_L should be some constant number that does not depend on policy (e.g., because monetary policy only responds to the deviation of output from its "natural/flexible price" level). In any event, the general point is that once we start thinking about permanent policy changes, their effect depends very much on how those policy changes affect the long-term stance of monetary policy. That assumption needs to be explicit and a key part of the analysis.

XIII. The Consequence of Deficit Spending

So far I have not modeled the dynamics of the government budget constraint. The reason I could get away with this in the context of the model is because I assumed lump-sum taxes and that any variation in government spending or one of the tax instruments would be offset by current or future lump-sum taxes. The dynamics of debt, therefore, play no role since the timing of lump-sum taxes is irrelevant due to Ricardian equivalence.

More realistically, variation in taxes and spending is not counteracted with current and/or future lump-sum taxes. Instead, it is likely that an increase in debt today will be offset by future distortionary taxes or a reduction in future government spending. How might this change the results? Will it lead us to favor or disfavor deficit spending?

The answer depends on the theory we have of how the future debt will be paid off, that is, with what combinations of tax increases and/or spending cuts or even inflation. Eggertsson (2006a), for example, points out that if the debt is nominal, then future governments have an incentive to inflate. He analyzes a Markov perfect equilibrium of the game between the government and the private sector. Since one of the main goals of policy in the short run in the model is to counteract deflationary expectations, increasing future inflation expectations through higher nominal debt can have a large positive effect on demand in the short run. Eggertsson (2008a) argues that this mechanism may in fact have played a role in the turnaround in 1933 when the United States started recovering from the Great Depression, moving from two-digit deflation into modest inflation. It is worth stressing, however, that deficit spending can also have some contractionary effects.

To the extent that future debt will be paid off by taxes that reduce output in the long run, however, this may have a negative effect on demand in the short run. Sorting out various different channels and mechanisms through which the dynamics of the government's budget constraint feed into expectations of future taxation, inflation, and output is an important direction for future research; these mechanisms may have a nontrivial effect on the estimates of fiscal multipliers in general equilibrium.

Finally, it is worth stressing that our analysis suggests that within the model it is actually possible to compute a balanced budget stimulus package that is even more stimulatory than tax cuts or spending increases that are financed by lump-sum taxes. An example of this is a temporary cut in sales taxes (which is expansionary) that is financed by a simultaneous increase in labor taxes or capital taxes (both of which are also expansionary in the model). As I have already mentioned in Section IX, this can even eliminate the problem of the zero bound altogether, provided that there is a rich and flexible enough tax structure. As noted in the introduction, however, there may be some reasons outside of the model that make such a policy counterproductive (e.g., liquidity constraints on both firms and consumers).

XIV. The Paradox of Thrift

I conclude the paper by illustrating the paradox of thrift in the extended model that allows for endogenous capital. Besides confirming the previous conclusion and illustrating the paradox of thrift, this model is also interesting because it allows us to consider investment tax credits and also gives a more important role for varying taxes on profits. Consider now an economy in which each firm uses both capital and labor as inputs in production, that is, $y_t(i) = K_t(i)^{\gamma} l_t(i)^{1-\gamma}$, and $K_t(i)$ is firm-specific capital. Following Christiano (2004) and Woodford (2003), let us assume that, in order to increase the capital stock to $K_{t+1}(i)$ from $K_t(i)$, the firm invests at time t

$$I_t(i) = \phi\left[\frac{K_{t+1}(i)}{K_t(i)}, \xi_t\right] K_t(i),$$

where the function ϕ satisfies $\phi(1, \bar{\xi}) = \zeta, \phi^I(1, \bar{\xi}) = 1, \phi^{II} \geq 0, \phi^{\xi}(1, \bar{\xi}) = 0$, and $\phi^{I\xi}(1, \bar{\xi}) \neq 0$. The variable λ corresponds to the depreciation rate of capital. At time t, the capital stock is predetermined. I allow for the shock to appear in the cost-of-adjustment function. The shock to the cost of adjustment, in addition to taxes, is the only difference relative to Christiano (2004) and Woodford (2003). Accordingly, the description of the model below is brief (readers can refer to these authors for details and also to the extended version of this paper available as Eggertsson [2010]).

Instead of one aggregate demand equation as in previous sections, there are now two Euler equations that determine aggregate demand: the investment Euler equation and the consumption Euler equation. The basic form of the two equations is the same, however; both investment spending and consumption spending depend on the current and expected path of the short-term real interest rate. The firm-pricing Euler equation is the same as in the model without capital but with an additional term involving the capital stock. An important assumption is that we assume that the shock enters the cost of adjustment of investment, which is a key difference from Christiano (2004). This assumption is consistent with the interpretation that this disturbance is due to banking troubles that raise the cost of loans, which should affect investment spending and consumption spending in the same way.

I assume the same coefficients as in the model without capital, that is, I choose parameters so that ω, σ, β, and κ correspond to one another in the two models and assume exactly the same value for shocks. I then need to choose values for τ^P, γ, λ, and ϕ^{II}. The values are summarized in table 5. The parameters λ and γ are taken from the literature, but the value for ϕ^{II} is chosen so that the output in the fourth quarter of the "contraction" is −30%. (It is assumed that investment declines in the same proportion as

Table 5
Parameter Values

	γ	ϕ^{II}	λ	$\bar{\tau}^P$
Parameters	.25	71.935	.025	.3

consumption.) Figure 11 compares the dynamics of output and inflation in the model with and without endogenous capital stock. They are almost identical, although the deflation is slightly less, reflecting that the extra terms in the *AS* equation with endogenous capital tend to increase marginal costs (and thus limit the deflation). To achieve this fit, the degree of capital adjustment is $\phi^{II} = 71.9$. Future work should include a more systematic analysis of the model, taking investment data more explicitly into account and explicitly pick the parameters to maximize the posterior of the model, as we did in previous sections. As the figure shows, capital dynamics do not add much to the analysis, at least in terms of inflation and output dynamics. This result is somewhat at odds with the findings of Christiano (2004), who finds that adding capital gives somewhat different quantitative conclusions. The main reason for this may be that I have added similar shocks to the investment Euler equation as to the consumption Euler equation (by adding the shock to the investment adjustment cost), together with the strategy I follow in calibrating the model. Table 6 shows how the multipliers change quantitatively with this extension given the calibration strategy just described. As the table reveals, they do not change much. The difference might even be smaller if we followed the same estimation strategy for the model with capital, as we used with the model with fixed capital stock.

Several things are interesting about this extension apart from confirming the robustness of the previous analysis. Endogenous investment allows us to consider one alternative instrument, that is, the investment tax

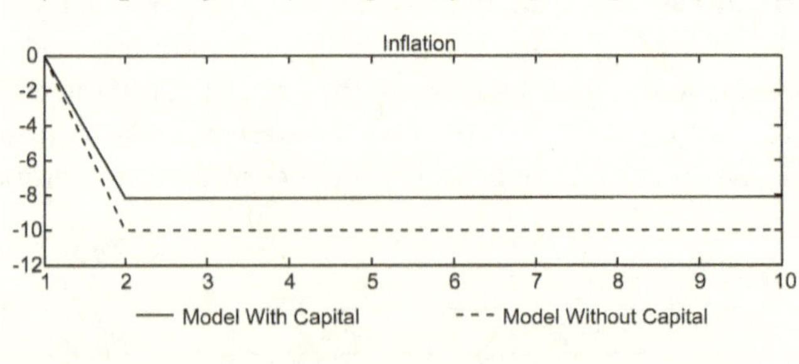

Fig. 11. Comparing the model with and without capital

Table 6
Comparing Multipliers of Temporary Policy Changes in the Model with and without Capital

	Without Capital $i_t = 0$	With Capital $i_t = 0$
τ_t^w (payroll tax cut)	−1.0191	−1.2706
G_t^S (government spending 1 increase)	0	0
G_t^N (government spending 2 increase)	2.2793	2.69
τ_t^S (sales tax cut)	2.5179	−2.73
τ_t^A (capital tax cut)	−.1012	−.0752
τ_t^P (capital tax cut)	...	−.4670
τ_t^I	...	.3116

credit. Table 6 shows the multiplier of a tax credit: a tax credit that allows firms to deduct one additional percent on top of the purchasing price of their investment from taxable profits would lead to a 0.31% increase in output. This expansionary effect occurs because an investment tax credit gives firms an incentive to invest today relative to in the future, thus stimulating spending.

Another interesting statistic is the effect of cutting the tax on savings, τ_t^A. Cutting this capital tax will give consumers an incentive to save more. Since, in equilibrium, savings must be equal to investment, one might expect that this would stimulate investment. The calibrated model, however, gives the opposite conclusion. A 1% decrease in $\hat{\tau}_t^A$ at zero interest rates will instead lower investment by 0.2384. The main reason is that even if a lower tax on capital gives the household more incentive to save, it reduces aggregate income at the same time. In equilibrium, this effect is strong enough so that even if each household saves more for a given income, aggregate saving declines. This is the classic paradox of thrift, first suggested by Keynes.

As before, a decrease in $\hat{\tau}_t^A$ results in a reduction in output, of similar order as in the model without capital, and the logic of the result is the same. The effect of cutting the tax on profits now is no longer neutral. If the tax on profits is reduced, then given the way I model this tax, the firm has an incentive to delay investment in order to pay out as much profits as possible at the lower tax rate now. Hence, to stimulate investment, the government should increase the tax on current profits, with a promise to reduce them in the future. This will give firms an incentive to spend their cash on investment today rather than on dividends payments.

XV. Conclusions

The main problem facing the model economy I have studied in this paper is insufficient demand. In this light, the emphasis should be on policies that stimulate spending. Payroll tax cuts may not be the best way to get there. The model shows that they can even be contractionary. What should be done, according to the model? Traditional change in government spending is one approach, although it needs to be targeted and temporary, or sales tax cuts and investment tax credits. Another is a commitment to inflate. Ideally, all should go together and, as we have seen, this may even eliminate the problem of the zero bound altogether for a flexible enough tax structure. Government spending, sales tax cuts, and investment credits have an advantage over inflation policy in that no credibility problems are associated with them. Inflation policy, however, has the advantage of not requiring any public spending or variations in the tax code which may be at its "first best level" in the steady state of the model studied here. Any fiddling around with the tax code should take into account that deflation might be a problem. In that case, shifting out aggregate supply can make things worse.

What should we take out of all this? There are two general lessons to be drawn from this paper in my view. The first is that insufficient demand is the main problem once the zero bound is binding, and policy should first and foremost focus on ways in which the government can increase spending. Policies that expand supply, such as some (but not all) tax cuts and also a variety of other policies, can have subtle counterproductive effects at zero interest rates by increasing deflationary pressures. This should—and can—be avoided by suitably designed policy.

The second lesson is that policy makers today should view with some skepticism empirical evidence on the effect of tax cuts or government spending based on post–World War II U.S. data. The number of these studies is high, and they are frequently cited in the current debate. The model presented here, which has by now become a workhorse model in modern macroeconomics, predicts that the effect of tax cuts and government spending is fundamentally different at zero nominal interest rates than under normal circumstances.

Appendix

Proofs

Proof of Proposition 1

For the steady state we assume that each of the fiscal instruments are equal to some constant value, that is, $\tau_t^s = \bar{\tau}^s$, $\tau_t^w = \bar{\tau}^w$, $\tau_t^P = \bar{\tau}^P$, $G_t = \bar{G}^N$, and $G_t^S = \bar{G}^S$. The value of $T_t = \bar{T}$ is then backed out as residual to solve the budget constraint (2) in the steady state. Given these values it is easy to verify that the following constants, $\Pi_t = P_t/P_{t-1} = p_t^*/P_t = \bar{\Pi} = 1$, $Y_t = \bar{Y}$, $l_t(j) = y_t(i) = Y_t = \bar{Y}$, $i_t = \bar{i} = \beta^{-1} - 1$, and $C_t = C_t = \bar{Y} - G^N - G^S$ solve equations (2)–(9) and the rest of the model where $\bar{Y}$ is the solution to

$$\frac{\theta}{\theta - 1}\frac{1 + \bar{\tau}^s}{1 - \bar{\tau}^W}\frac{v_l(\bar{Y})}{u_c(\bar{Y} - \bar{G}^N)} = 1.$$

Observe that there is no need to assume that the steady state is efficient.

The *AD* equation is a straightforward first-order approximation of the two equations (3) and (7); for details about the accuracy of this approach, which is an application of the implicit function theorem, see Woodford (2003, app. A) and for special consideration arising due to the zero bound, see Eggertsson and Woodford (2003). The derivation of the *AS* equation is slightly more involved, and the main steps are outlined briefly below (see proof of proposition 3.5 in Woodford (2003, app. B.4) for the standard case and more details for each step of the derivation).

The price index (6) can be approximated to yield

$$\log P_t = \alpha \log P_{t-1} + (1 - \alpha)\log p_t^*,$$

while an approximation of (5) yields

$$E_t\left\{\sum_{T=t}^{\infty}(\alpha\beta)^{T-t}[(1 + \omega\theta)(\log p_t^* - \log P_T) - \chi^s\hat{\tau}_T^s - \chi^w\hat{\tau}_T^s - (\omega + \sigma^{-1})\hat{Y}_T + \sigma^{-1}\hat{G}_T^N]\right\} = 0.$$

Solving this equation for $\log p_t^*$ and subtracting $\log P_t$ from both sides, and expressing the expected change in the price index over various future horizons in terms of expected inflation rate at various future dates, we obtain

$$\hat{p}_t^* = (1 - \alpha\beta)E_t\left\{\sum_{T=t}^{\infty}(\alpha\beta)^{T-t}\left[\sum_{s=t+1}^{T}\pi_s + \frac{1}{1 + \omega\theta}\chi^s\hat{\tau}_T^s + \frac{1}{1 + \omega\theta}\chi^w\hat{\tau}_T^s + \frac{\omega + \sigma^{-1}}{1 + \omega\theta}\hat{Y}_T - \frac{\sigma^{-1}}{1 + \omega\theta}\hat{G}_T^N\right]\right\}$$
$$= E_t\left\{\sum_{T=t}^{\infty}(\alpha\beta)^{T-t}\left[\alpha\beta\pi_{T+1} + \frac{1}{1 + \omega\theta}\chi^s\hat{\tau}_T^s + \frac{1}{1 + \omega\theta}\chi^w\hat{\tau}_T^s + \frac{\omega + \sigma^{-1}}{1 + \omega\theta}\hat{Y}_T - \frac{\sigma^{-1}}{1 + \omega\theta}\hat{G}_T^N\right]\right\},$$

where $\hat{p}_t^* = \log(p_t^*/P_t)$. This implies that

$$\hat{p}_t^* = \alpha\beta E_t\pi_{t+1} + \frac{(1-\alpha\beta)}{(1+\omega\theta)}\chi^s\hat{\tau}_t^s + \frac{(1-\alpha\beta)}{(1+\omega\theta)}\chi^w\hat{\tau}_l^s + \frac{(\omega+\sigma^{-1})(1-\alpha\beta)}{(1+\omega\theta)}\hat{Y}_t$$
$$- \frac{\sigma^{-1}(1-\alpha\beta)}{(1+\omega\theta)}\hat{G}_t^N + \alpha\beta E_t\hat{p}_{t+1}^*.$$

The linearization of the price index implies (subtracting $\log P_t$ from both sides) that the inflation rate is

$$\pi_t = \frac{1-\alpha}{\alpha}\hat{p}_t^*.$$

Substitute this into the equation above, and one obtains the *AS* equation in the text. QED

Propositions 2 and 3

While the steps in the proofs for propositions 2 and 3 should be familiar to most readers, they are provided here for completeness. For the reader's convenience, I first reproduce a result in linear rational-expectations models that is shown in Woodford (2003). I will use his results in my proofs of propositions 2 and 3. But first let me state the algebraic expressions for the parameters in C1,

$$\Gamma_{\tau^A} \equiv \frac{\kappa\phi_\pi + (1-\beta\mu)\phi_y}{(1-\mu+\sigma\phi_y)(1-\beta\mu)+\kappa\sigma(\phi_\pi-\mu)}\sigma\chi^A,$$

$$\Gamma_{\tau^w} \equiv \frac{(1-\mu)\kappa\psi\phi_\pi + \sigma\mu\kappa\psi\phi_y}{(1-\mu+\sigma\phi_y)(1-\beta\mu)+\kappa\sigma(\phi_\pi-\mu)}\chi^w,$$

$$\Gamma_{G^N} \equiv \frac{\kappa\sigma^{-1}(1-\mu)(\sigma-\psi)\phi_\pi + [(1-\mu)(1-\beta\mu)-\kappa\psi\mu]\phi_y}{(1-\mu+\sigma\phi_y)(1-\beta\mu)+\kappa\sigma(\phi_\pi-\mu)}.$$

Proposition A1

Consider a linear rational-expectations model of the form

$$E_t z_{t+1} = Az_t + ae_t,$$

where z_t is a two-by-two vector of nonpredetermined endogenous state variables, e_t is a vector of exogenous disturbances, A is a two-by-two matrix of coefficients, and a is two times the number of exogenous disturbances. Rational-expectations equilibrium is determinate if and only if the matrix A has both eigenvalues outside the unit circle (i.e., with modulus $|\lambda| > 1$). Denote the determinant of the matrix A as $\det(A)$ and its trace as $\mathrm{tr}(A)$.

The condition for a unique bounded solution is satisfied if and only if

Case 1 (*a*) $\det(A) > 1$ (*b*) $\det(A) - \mathrm{tr}(A) > -1$ (*c*) $\det(A) + \mathrm{tr}(A) > -1$.

Case 2 (*d*) $\det(A) - \mathrm{tr}(A) < -1$ (*e*) $\det(A) + \mathrm{tr}(A) < -1$.

Proof. See proof to proposition C.1 in Woodford (2003, 670–71).

Proof of Proposition 2

The system can be written in the form

$$E_t z_{t+1} = A z_t,$$

where

$$z_t \equiv \begin{bmatrix} \pi_t \\ \hat{Y}_t \end{bmatrix}$$

and

$$A \equiv \begin{bmatrix} \beta^{-1} & -\beta^{-1}\kappa \\ \sigma(\phi_\pi - \beta^{-1}) & 1 + \sigma(\phi_x + \kappa\beta^{-1}) \end{bmatrix}.$$

Observe that $\mathrm{tr}(A) = 1 + \beta^{-1} + \sigma\kappa\beta^{-1} + \sigma\phi_x$ and $\det(A) = \beta^{-1}[1 + \sigma(\phi_x + \kappa\phi_\pi)]$. Case 2 of proposition A1 clearly does not apply; see, for example, that condition *e* is violated. Now consider case 1. As seen above, condition *a* is satisfied because the determinant is positive. Condition *c* is also clearly satisfied since both $\det(A)$ and $\mathrm{tr}(A)$ are positive, which leaves condition *b*, which we show applies if $\phi_\pi + [(1 - \beta)/\kappa]\phi_x > 1$:

$$\begin{aligned} &\beta^{-1}[1 + \sigma(\phi_x + \kappa\phi_\pi)] - 1 - \beta^{-1} - \sigma\kappa\beta^{-1} - \sigma\phi_x \\ &\quad > -1 \Leftrightarrow \phi_\pi + [(1 - \beta)/\kappa]\phi_x > 1. \end{aligned}$$

It is now easy to confirm that the analytic solution in the proposition (which, from the discussion above, we know is unique) is the one given in the proposition, that is, $\pi_t = \hat{Y}_t = 0$ and $i_t = \bar{r}$. QED

Proof of Proposition 3

Here

$$\pi_S^p \equiv -\frac{\kappa\sigma^{-1}[(1-\mu+\sigma\phi_y)\psi-\sigma(1-\mu)]}{[(1-\mu+\sigma\phi_y)(1-\beta\mu)+\kappa\sigma(\phi_\pi-\mu)]}[\hat{G}_S^N-\sigma\chi^s\tau_S^s]$$
$$+\frac{(1-\mu+\sigma\phi_y)\kappa\psi}{[(1-\mu+\sigma\phi_y)(1-\beta\mu)+\kappa\sigma(\phi_\pi-\mu)]}\chi^w\hat{\tau}_S^w$$
$$+\frac{\kappa\sigma}{[(1-\mu+\sigma\phi_y)(1-\beta\mu)+\kappa\sigma(\phi_\pi-\mu)]}\chi^A\hat{\tau}_S^A,$$

$$\hat{Y}_S^p \equiv \frac{[(1-\mu)(1-\beta\mu)+\kappa\psi(\phi_\pi-\mu)]}{(1-\beta\mu)(1-\mu+\sigma\phi_y)+\kappa\sigma(\phi_\pi-\mu)}[\hat{G}_S^N-\sigma\chi^s\hat{\tau}_S^s]$$
$$-\frac{\sigma(\phi_\pi-\mu)\kappa\psi}{(1-\beta\mu)(1-\mu+\sigma\phi_y)+\kappa\sigma(\phi_\pi-\mu)}\chi^w\hat{\tau}_S^w$$
$$+\frac{\sigma(1-\beta\mu)}{(1-\beta\mu)(1-\mu+\sigma\phi_y)+\kappa\sigma(\phi_\pi-\mu)}\chi^A\hat{\tau}_S^A,$$

$$\pi_S^z \equiv \frac{\kappa\sigma}{(1-\mu)(1-\mu\beta)-\kappa\mu\sigma}r_S^e+\frac{\kappa(1-\mu)[(1-\psi\sigma^{-1}]}{(1-\mu)(1-\mu\beta)-\kappa\mu\sigma}[\hat{G}_S^N-\sigma\chi^s\hat{\tau}_S^s]$$
$$+\frac{\kappa\sigma}{(1-\mu)(1-\mu\beta)-\kappa\mu\sigma}\chi^A\hat{\tau}_S^A+\frac{(1-\mu)\kappa\psi}{(1-\mu)(1-\mu\beta)-\kappa\mu\sigma}\chi^w\hat{\tau}_S^w,$$

$$\hat{Y}_S^z \equiv \frac{\sigma(1-\mu\beta)}{(1-\mu)(1-\mu\beta)-\mu\sigma\kappa}r_S^e+\frac{(1-\mu)(1-\mu\beta)-\mu\kappa\psi}{(1-\mu)(1-\mu\beta)-\mu\sigma\kappa}[\hat{G}_S^N-\sigma\chi^s\hat{\tau}_S^s]$$
$$+\frac{\sigma(1-\mu\beta)}{(1-\mu)(1-\mu\beta)-\mu\sigma\kappa}\chi^A\hat{\tau}_S^A+\frac{\mu\sigma\kappa\psi}{(1-\mu)(1-\mu\beta)-\mu\sigma\kappa}\chi^w\hat{\tau}_S^w.$$

Consider the solution at time $t<\tau$. Given the result from proposition 1, we can write expectations of inflation and output as

$$E(Y_{t+1}\backslash t<\tau)=(1-\mu)E_tY_{t+1}^S+\mu\times 0=(1-\mu)E_t^SY_{t+1}^S,$$

where the notation E_t^S is used as the expectation of the variable Y_{t+1} conditional on the shock being in the S state, that is, $t+1<\tau$. Similarly, the notation Y_{t+1}^S is used to signify that this is the value of Y_{t+1} conditional on $t+1<\tau$. We can similarly write inflation as

$$E(\pi_{t+1}\backslash t<\tau)=(1-\mu)E_t\pi_{t+1}^S+\mu\times 0=(1-\mu)E_t^S\pi_{t+1}^S.$$

Hence

$$Y_t^S = \mu E_t Y_{t+1}^S - \sigma i_t^S + \sigma\mu E_t \pi_{t+1}^S + \sigma r_S^e + (1-\mu)\hat{G}_S^N - \sigma(1-\mu)\hat{\tau}_S^s + \sigma\hat{\tau}_S^A, \tag{A1}$$

$$\pi_t^S = \kappa \hat{Y}_t^S + \kappa\psi(\hat{\tau}_S^w + \hat{\tau}_S^s) - \kappa\psi\sigma^{-1}\hat{G}_S^N + \beta\mu E_t \pi_{t+1}^S, \tag{A2}$$

$$i_t^S = \max(0, r_S^e + \phi_\pi \pi_t^S).$$

Part i

Consider first part *i*, and let us conjecture that the zero bound is not binding. Then we can write

$$E_t z_{t+1}^S = A z_t^S + a e_t^S,$$

where

$$z_t^S \equiv \begin{bmatrix} \hat{Y}_t^S \\ \pi_t^S \end{bmatrix},$$

and

$$A \equiv \begin{bmatrix} \dfrac{1+\sigma(\phi_y + \kappa\beta^{-1})}{\mu} & \dfrac{\sigma(\phi_\pi - \beta^{-1})}{\mu} \\ -\dfrac{\kappa\beta^{-1}}{\mu} & \dfrac{\beta^{-1}}{\mu} \end{bmatrix},$$

$$e_t \equiv \begin{bmatrix} \hat{G}_S^N \\ \hat{\tau}_S^w \\ \hat{\tau}_S^s \\ \hat{\tau}_S^A \end{bmatrix} \quad a \equiv \begin{bmatrix} -\dfrac{\kappa\psi\beta^{-1} + 1 - \mu}{\mu} & \dfrac{\sigma\kappa\psi\beta^{-1}}{\mu} & \sigma\dfrac{\kappa\psi\beta^{-1} + 1 - \mu}{\mu} & -\dfrac{\sigma}{\mu} \\ \dfrac{\kappa\psi\sigma^{-1}\beta^{-1}}{\mu} & -\dfrac{\kappa\psi\beta^{-1}}{\mu} & -\dfrac{\kappa\psi\beta^{-1}}{\mu} & 0 \end{bmatrix}.$$

Observe that $\mathrm{tr}(A) = (1 + \beta^{-1} + \sigma\kappa\beta^{-1} + \sigma\phi_y)/\mu$ and $\det(A) = (\beta^{-1} + \sigma\kappa\beta^{-1}\phi_\pi + \sigma\beta^{-1}\phi_y)/\mu^2$. Case 2 of proposition A1 clearly does not apply; for example, condition *e* is violated. Hence, consider case 1. As seen above, condition *a* is satisfied because the determinant is positive since $\mu > 0$. Condition *c* is also clearly satisfied since both $\det(A)$ and $\mathrm{tr}(A)$ are positive. Which leaves condition *b*, which is shown to apply below:

$$\frac{\beta^{-1} + \sigma\kappa\beta^{-1}\phi_\pi + \sigma\beta^{-1}\phi_y}{\mu^2} - \frac{1 + \beta^{-1} + \sigma\kappa\beta^{-1} + \sigma\phi_y}{\mu}$$

$$> -1 \Leftrightarrow \mu^2 - (1 + \beta^{-1} + \sigma\kappa\beta^{-1} + \sigma\phi_y)\mu + \beta^{-1} + \sigma\kappa\beta^{-1}\phi_\pi + \sigma\beta^{-1}\phi_y > 0,$$

which holds for any $\mu \in [0, 1]$ as long as $\phi_\pi + [(1 - \beta)/\kappa]\phi_x > 1$. This proves that there is a unique bounded solution in the short run of the form stated in the proposition. The algebraic form of the solution in the proposition can be found using standard methods, for example, method of undetermined coefficients. Note in particular that the analytical solution for the nominal interest rate suggests that it is only satisfied as long as C1 does not apply. QED

Part ii

We now consider the case in which both C1 and C2 apply. From the solution for the nominal interest rate in part i of the proposition we see that this implies that the zero bound is binding. Then we can write

$$E_t z_{t+1}^S = A z_t^S + a e_t,$$

where

$$z_t^S \equiv \begin{bmatrix} \hat{Y}_t^S \\ \pi_t^S \end{bmatrix},$$

$$A \equiv \begin{bmatrix} \dfrac{1 + \dfrac{\sigma\kappa}{\beta}}{\mu} & -\dfrac{\sigma\beta^{-1}}{\mu} \\ -\dfrac{\kappa}{\beta\mu} & \dfrac{1}{\beta\mu} \end{bmatrix},$$

$$e_t \equiv \begin{bmatrix} r_S^e \\ \hat{G}_S^N \\ \hat{\tau}_S^w \\ \hat{\tau}_S^s \\ \hat{\tau}_S^A \end{bmatrix} a \equiv \begin{bmatrix} \sigma & -\dfrac{\kappa\psi\beta^{-1} + 1 - \mu}{\mu} & \dfrac{\sigma\kappa\psi\beta^{-1}}{\mu} & \sigma\dfrac{\kappa\psi\beta^{-1} + 1 - \mu}{\mu} & -\dfrac{\sigma}{\mu} \\ 0 & \dfrac{\kappa\psi\sigma^{-1}\beta^{-1}}{\mu} & -\dfrac{\kappa\psi\beta^{-1}}{\mu} & -\dfrac{\kappa\psi\beta^{-1}}{\mu} & 0 \end{bmatrix}.$$

Observe that $\mathrm{tr}(A) = [1 + \beta^{-1} + (\sigma\kappa/\beta)]/\mu = [1 + \beta^{-1} + (\sigma\kappa/\beta)]\mu/\mu^2$ and $\det(A) = \beta^{-1}/\mu^2$. Case 2 of proposition A1 clearly does not apply, because, for example, condition e is violated. Consider case 1. As seen above, condition a is satisfied because the determinant is positive since $1 > \mu > 0$. Condition c is also satisfied since both $\det(A)$ and tr(A) are positive. Which leaves condition b, which is shown to apply below:

$$\frac{\beta^{-1}}{(1-\mu)^2} - \frac{[1+\beta^{-1}+(\sigma\kappa/\beta)](1-\mu)}{(1-\mu)^2} > -1 \Leftrightarrow \beta\mu^2 + \mu(1-\beta+\sigma\kappa) - \sigma\kappa = \mu(1-\beta(1-\mu)) - (1-\mu)\sigma\kappa > 0,$$

$$\frac{\beta^{-1}}{\mu^2} - \frac{[1+\beta^{-1}+(\sigma\kappa/\beta)]\mu}{\mu^2} > -1 \Leftrightarrow \beta\mu^2 - \left(1+\beta^{-1}+\frac{\sigma\kappa}{\beta}\right)\beta\mu + 1 = (1-\mu)(1-\mu\beta) - \kappa\mu\sigma > 0,$$

which is condition C2. This proves that there is a unique bounded solution in the short run of the form stated in the proposition, provided C1 and C2 apply. The algebraic form of the solution in the proposition can be found using standard methods, for example, method of undetermined coefficients. QED

Proofs of Propositions 4 and 5

$$\hat{Y}_L \equiv \frac{(1-\beta)\hat{\tau}_L^A - \kappa\psi(\phi_\pi - 1)\chi^w\hat{\tau}_L^w + \kappa\psi\sigma^{-1}(\phi_\pi - 1)[\hat{G}_L^N - \sigma\chi^s\hat{\tau}_L^s]}{\kappa(\phi_\pi - 1) + (1-\beta)\phi_y},$$

$$\pi_L \equiv \frac{\kappa\chi^A\hat{\tau}_L^A + \kappa\psi\phi_y\chi^w\hat{\tau}_L^w - \kappa\psi\sigma^{-1}\phi_y[\hat{G}_L^N - \sigma\chi^s\tau_L^s]}{\kappa(\phi_\pi - 1) + (1-\beta)\phi_y},$$

$$\hat{Y}_S^p \equiv \frac{(1-\mu)(1-\mu\beta)\hat{Y}_L + (1-\mu)\pi_L + (\phi_\pi - \mu)\kappa\psi[\hat{G}_L^N - \sigma\chi^s\hat{\tau}_L^s - \sigma\chi^w\hat{\tau}_L^w] + (1-\mu\beta)\chi^A\hat{\tau}_L^A}{(1-\mu+\sigma\phi_y)(1-\mu\beta) + \sigma\kappa(\phi_\pi - \mu)},$$

$$\pi_S^p \equiv \frac{(1-\mu)\kappa\hat{Y}_L + (1-\mu)[\kappa\sigma + \beta(1-\mu+\sigma\phi_y)]\pi_L}{(1-\mu\beta)(1-\mu+\sigma\phi_y) + \sigma\kappa(\phi_\pi - \mu)}$$

$$\frac{-\kappa\psi\sigma^{-1}(1-\mu+\sigma\phi_y)[\hat{G}_L^N - \sigma\chi_L\hat{\tau}_L^s] + \sigma\kappa\chi^A\hat{\tau}_S^A + \kappa\psi(1-\mu+\sigma\phi_y)\chi^w\hat{\tau}_L^w}{(1-\mu\beta)(1-\mu+\sigma\phi_y) + \sigma\kappa(\phi_\pi - \mu)},$$

$$\hat{Y}_S^z \equiv \frac{(1-\mu\beta)(1-\mu)}{(1-\mu\beta)(1-\mu) - \sigma\mu\kappa}\hat{Y}_L + \frac{\sigma(1-\mu\beta)}{(1-\mu\beta)(1-\mu) - \sigma\mu\kappa}\pi_L + \sigma(1-\mu\beta)r_S^e] + \frac{\sigma\mu\kappa\psi}{(1-\mu\beta)(1-\mu) - \sigma\mu\kappa}\chi^w\hat{\tau}_L^w - \frac{\mu\kappa\psi}{(1-\mu\beta)(1-\mu) - \sigma\mu\kappa} \times [\hat{G}_L^N + \sigma\chi^s\hat{\tau}_L^s] + \frac{\sigma(1-\mu\beta)}{(1-\mu\beta)(1-\mu) - \sigma\mu\kappa}\chi^A\hat{\tau}_L^A,$$

$$\pi_S^z \equiv \frac{\kappa(1-\mu)}{(1-\mu\beta)(1-\mu)-\mu\sigma\kappa}\hat{Y}_L + \frac{(1-\mu)[\sigma\kappa+(1-\mu)\beta]}{(1-\mu\beta)(1-\mu)-\mu\sigma\kappa}\pi_L$$
$$+\frac{\sigma\kappa}{(1-\mu\beta)(1-\mu)-\mu\sigma\kappa}r_S^e + \frac{\sigma\kappa}{(1-\mu\beta)(1-\mu)-\mu\sigma\kappa}\chi^A\hat{\tau}_L^A$$
$$+\frac{\kappa\psi(1-\mu)}{(1-\mu\beta)(1-\mu)-\mu\sigma\kappa}\chi^w\hat{\tau}_L^w - \frac{\kappa\psi\sigma^{-1}(1-\mu)}{(1-\mu\beta)(1-\mu)-\mu\sigma\kappa}$$
$$\times[\hat{G}_L^N - \sigma\chi^s\hat{\tau}_L^s].$$

These proofs of these propositions follow exactly the same steps as proofs 2 and 3, and again one can find the algebraic solution by using the method of undetermined coefficients.

Endnotes

A previous draft of this paper was circulated in December 2008 under the title "Can Tax Cuts Deepen the Recession?" I thank Matthew Denes and Sonia Gilbukh for outstanding research assistance. I also thank Daron Acemoglu, Larry Christiano, Greg Mankiw, Lee Ohanian, Bruce Preston, and Mike Woodford for several helpful discussions on this topic and seminar participants at Columbia University, Johns Hopkins University, the Federal Reserve Bank of New York, and Princeton University. The views expressed in the paper are mine and do not necessarily reflect the position of the Federal Reserve Bank of New York or the Federal Reserve System. Any errors or omissions are my responsibility. Contact the author at Eggertsson@ny.frb.org.

1. This group consisted of 200 leading economists, including several Nobel Prize winners, who signed a letter prepared by the Cato Institute.

2. For an early proposal for temporary sales tax cuts as an effective stabilization tool, see, e.g., Modigliani and Steindel (1977).

3. See, e.g., Gordon and Krenn (2010), who report similar multipliers for 1939–41 for government spending as found here.

4. The contractionary labor tax cuts studied, although entirely standard in the literature, are very special in many respects. They correspond to variations in linear tax rates on labor income, while some tax cuts on labor income in practice resemble more lump-sum transfers to workers and may even, in some cases, imply an effective increase in marginal taxes (Cochrane 2009). Similarly, this form of taxes does not take into account the "direct" spending effect tax cuts have in some old-fashioned Keynesian models and as modeled more recently in a New Keynesian model by Gali, Lopez-Salido, and Valles (2007). A similar comment applies to taxes on capital. There could be a "direct" negative demand effect of increasing this tax through households' budget constraints. Another problem is that an increase in taxes on capital would lead to a decline in stock prices. An important channel not being modeled is that a reduction in equity prices can have a negative effect on the ability of firms to borrow, through collateral constraints as in Kiyotaki and Moore (1997) and, thus, contract investment spending. This channel is not included in the model and is one of the main mechanisms emphasized by Feldstein (2009) in favor of reducing taxes on capital.

5. The connection to the paradox of thrift was first pointed out to me by Larry Christiano in an insightful discussion of Eggertsson and Woodford (2003). See Christiano (2004). Krugman (1998) also draws a comparison to the paradox of thrift in a similar context.

6. This list is not nearly complete. See Svensson (2003) for an excellent survey of this work. All these papers treat the problem of the zero bound as a consequence of real shocks

that make the interest rate bound binding. Another branch of the literature has studied the consequence of binding zero bound in the context of self-fulfilling expectations. See, e.g., Benhabib, Schmitt-Grohe, and Uribe (2002), who considered fiscal rules that eliminate those equilibria.

7. Committing to future inflation may not be so trivial in practice. As shown by Eggertsson (2001, 2006a), the central bank has an incentive to promise future inflation and then renege on this promise; this is the deflation bias of discretionary policy. In any event, optimal monetary policy is relatively well known in the literature, and it is of most interest in order to understand the properties of fiscal policy in the "worst case" scenario if monetary authorities are unable and/or unwilling to inflate.

8. Among other papers that studied the importance of real government spending and found a substantial fiscal policy multiplier effect at zero interest rate is Williams (2006). That paper assumes that expectations are formed according to learning, which provides a large role for fiscal policy.

9. See, e.g., Clarida, Gali, and Gertler (1999), Benigno and Woodford (2003), and Christiano et al. (2005). Several details are omitted here, but see, e.g., Woodford (2003) for a textbook treatment.

10. It would simply add asset-pricing equations to the model that would pin down stock prices.

11. See, e.g., Eggertsson and Woodford (2003) for further discussion.

12. For details on the log-linearization and steady state of this class of models see, e.g., Woodford (2003), and for special considerations that arise due to the zero bound, see Eggertsson and Woodford (2003).

13. The coefficients of the model are defined as follows: $\sigma \equiv -(\bar{u}_c/\bar{u}_{cc}\bar{Y})$, $\omega \equiv \bar{v}_{ll}\bar{L}/\bar{v}_l$, $\psi \equiv 1/(\sigma^{-1}+\omega)$, $\kappa \equiv \{[(1-\alpha)(1-\alpha\beta)]/\alpha\}[(\sigma^{-1}+\omega)/(1+\omega\theta)]$, where the bar denotes that the variable is defined in the steady state. The shock is defined as $r_t^e \equiv \log \beta^{-1} + E_t(\hat{\xi}_t - \hat{\xi}_{t+1})$, where $\hat{\xi}_t \equiv \log \xi_t/\bar{\xi}$. Finally we define $\chi^A \equiv (1-\beta)/(1-\bar{\tau}^A)$, $\chi^w \equiv 1/(1-\bar{\tau}^w)$, and $\chi^s \equiv 1/(1+\bar{\tau}^s)$. In terms of our previous notation, i_t now actually refers to $\log(1+i_t)$ in the log-linear model. Observe also that this variable, unlike the others, is not defined in deviations from the steady state. I do this so that we can still express the zero bound simply as the requirement that i_t is nonnegative. For the purposes of interpretation I have scaled the fiscal policy variables in a particular way in order to have a more meaningful comparison of "multipliers" in coming sections. The term $\hat{G}_t^N$ is the percentage changes of government spending from its steady state as fraction of steady state output. We want the other tax instrument to be of a similar order to facilitate comparison of alternative fiscal actions. Because all production is consumed then, in the absence of shocks, a 1% increase in the sales tax, local to the steady state, will increase revenues by exactly the same amount as the increase in government spending, which is why we define $\hat{\tau}_t^s \equiv \tau_t^s - \bar{\tau}^s$, that is, it has the interpretation of a percentage increase in the sales tax rate (which would exactly finance an increase in $\hat{G}_t^N$ one to one). Similarly $\hat{\tau}_t^w \equiv \tau_t^w - \bar{\tau}^w$ measures the percentage increase of the tax rate on labor. Given these definitions I scale each of the tax instruments with χ^s and χ^w. Finally, I define the variable $\hat{\tau}_t^A$ so that a 1% increase in this variable corresponds to a 1% increase in the tax on capital income per year, to be comparable with the tax on labor income.

14. This assumption simplifies that analysis quite a bit, since otherwise, when considering the effects of particular tax cuts, I would need to take a stance on what combination of taxes would need to be raised to offset the effect of the tax cut on the government budget constraint and at what time horizon. Moreover, I would need to take a stance on what type of debt the government could issue. While all those issues are surely of some interest in future extensions, this approach seems like the most natural first step since it allows us to analyze the effect of each fiscal policy instrument in isolation (abstracting from their effect on the government budget). Note that by making this critical assumption, I do not need to talk in detail about several issues related to fiscal policy in the fully nonlinear model; see, e.g., Eggertsson and Woodford (2003) for a discussion.

15. This conjecture is formally proved in propositions 2 and 3.

16. The contraction is amplified without a bound as μ increases. As μ increases, the *AD* curve becomes flatter and the *AS* curve steeper, and the cutoff point moves further down in the $(\hat{Y}_S, \pi_S)$ plane in figure 2. At a critical value $1 > \bar{\mu} > 0$ when $L(\bar{\mu}) = 0$ in C2, the two curves are parallel, and no solution exists. The point $\bar{\mu}$ is called a *deflationary black hole*. In the remainder of the paper we assume that μ is small enough so that the deflationary black

hole is avoided and the solution is well defined and bounded (this is guaranteed by the inequality in assumption C2). A deflationary solution always exists as long as the shock μ is close enough to zero because $L(0) > 0$ (at $\mu = 0$, the shock reverts back to the steady state with probability 1 in the next period). Observe, furthermore, that $L(1) < 0$ and that in the region $0 < \mu < 1$ the function $L(\mu)$ is strictly decreasing, so there is some critical value $\bar{\mu} = \mu(\kappa, \sigma, \beta) < 1$ in which $L(\mu)$ is zero and the model has no solution.

17. Note that the value of τ^s, τ^w, and τ^A only matters for determining χ^A, χ^w, and χ^s, which simply scales the multipliers. Hence changing the value of these parameters will just move the multipliers I report by exactly the same amount as they change the χ's. The value of ϕ_π and ϕ_y are those suggested by Taylor (1993). Note that in his paper he expressed the rule in terms of annualized interest rates and inflation so that his interest rate referred to $4i_t$ and his inflation measure to $4\pi_t$ in my notation. Hence the coefficient on $\hat{Y}_t$ is 0.5/4 according to my notation.

18. A case in which the central bank targets a particular inflation rate, say zero, corresponds to $\phi_\pi \to \infty$. In this case, the *AD* curve is horizontal and the effect of the tax cut is very large because the central bank will accommodate it with aggressive interest rate cuts.

19. This was pointed out by Larry Christiano in his commentary on this article. Note that it is important in this thought experiment that we assume that current or future lump-sum taxes will offset the labor income tax cut so that the model is Ricardian.

20. This equilibrium form of policy is derived from microfoundations in Eggertsson (2008a) assuming a Markov perfect equilibrium.

21. Note that the denominator is always positive according to C2. See the discussion in n. 16.

22. This is essentially Feldstein's (2002) idea in the context of Japan, although he suggested that Japan should commit to raising future VAT. As documented below, there are some subtle reasons for why VATs may not be as well suited for this proposal because of how they typically interact with price frictions.

23. To see this, simply observe how labor taxes and sales taxes enter the *AD* and *AS* equations (10) and (11). This is also shown in Correia et al. (2010) in a bit more general context.

24. In the rule we assume, once $\phi_\pi \to \infty$ there is no effect. If there is a time-varying coefficient in the Taylor rule that depends on taxes, there can also be no effect.

25. See, e.g., Eggertsson and Woodford (2004). Our assumption about the shocks is such that $\hat{Y}_t^* = 0$ in their notation. See the discussion in sec. 1.2 of that paper and also Eggertsson (2008a), who discusses this assumption in some detail.

References

Adam, Klaus, and Roberto Billi. 2006. "Optimal Monetary Policy under Commitment with a Zero Bound on Nominal Interest Rates." *Journal of Money, Credit, and Banking* 38, no. 7:1877–1905.

Auerbach, Alan, and Maurice Obstfeld. 2005. "The Case for Open Market Operations." *American Economic Review* 95, no. 1:110–37.

Barro, R. 2009. "Government Spending Is No Free Lunch." *Wall Street Journal*, January 22, Opinion page.

Benhabib, Jess, Stephanie Schmitt-Grohé, and Martín Uribe. 2002. "Avoiding Liquidity Traps." *Journal of Political Economy* 110:535–63.

Benigno, Pierpaolo, and Michael Woodford. 2003. "Optimal Monetary and Fiscal Policy: A Linear Quadratic Approach." *NBER Macroeconomics Annual* 18: 271–333.

Bils, Mark, and Pete Klenow. 2008. "Further Discussion of Temporary Payroll Tax Cut during Recession(s)." Photocopy, http://klenow.com/Discussion_of_Payroll_Tax_Cut.pdf.

Calvo, Guillermo. 1983. "Staggered Prices in a Utility-Maximizing Framework." *Journal of Monetary Economics* 12:383–98.

Christiano, Lawrence. 2004. "The Zero-Bound, Low Inflation, and Output Collapse." Photocopy, Northwestern University.

Christiano, Lawrence, Martin Eichenbaum, and C. Evans. 2005. "Nominal Rigidities and the Dynamic Effects of a Shock to Monetary Policy." *Journal of Political Economy* 113:1–45.

Christiano, Lawrence, Martin Eichenbaum, and Sergio Rebelo. 2009. "When Is the Government Spending Multiplier Large?" Photocopy, Northwestern University.

Clarida, R., J. Gali, and M. Gertler. 1999. "The Science of Monetary Policy: A New Keynesian Perspective." *Journal of Economic Literature* 37:1661–1707.

Cochrane, John. 2009. "Fiscal Stimulus, Fiscal Inflation, or Fiscal Fallacies?" Photocopy, University of Chicago, http://faculty.chicagobooth.edu/john.cochrane/research/papers/fiscal2.htm.

Cogan, John, Tobias Cwik, John Taylor, and Volker Wieland. 2009. "New Keynesian versus Old Keynesian Government Spending Multipliers." Photocopy, Stanford University.

Correia, I., E. Farhi, J. Nicolini, and P. Teles. 2010. "Unconventional Fiscal Policy at the Zero Bound." Photocopy, Federal Reserve Bank of Minneapolis.

Curdia, Vasco, and Gauti Eggertsson. 2009. "What Caused the Great Depression?" Photocopy, Federal Reserve Bank of New York.

Curdia, Vasco, and Michael Woodford. 2008. "Credit Frictions and Optimal Monetary Policy." Photocopy, Columbia University.

Denes, Matthew, and Gauti Eggertsson. 2009. "A Bayesian Approach to Estimating Tax and Spending Multpliers." Staff Paper, Federal Reserve Bank of New York.

Eggertsson, Gauti. 2001. "Real Government Spending in a Liquidity Trap." Photocopy, Princeton University, http://www.ny.frb.org/research/economists/eggertsson/papers.html.

———. 2004. "Monetary and Fiscal Coordination in a Liquidity Trap." Chapter 3 of "Optimal Monetary and Fiscal Policy in the Liquidity Trap." PhD diss., Princeton University.

———. 2006a. "The Deflation Bias and Committing to Being Irresponsible." *Journal of Money, Credit, and Banking* 36, no. 2:283–322.

———. 2006b. "Fiscal Multipliers and Policy Coordination." Staff Report no. 241, Federal Reserve Bank of New York.

———. 2008a. "Great Expectations and the End of the Depression." *American Economic Review* 98, no. 4:1476–1516.

———. 2008b. "Was the New Deal Contractionary?" Photocopy, Federal Reserve Bank of New York.

———. 2010. "The Paradox of Toil." Staff Report no. 433, Federal Reserve Bank of New York.

Eggertsson, Gauti, and Michael Woodford. 2003. "The Zero Bound on Interest Rates and Optimal Monetary Policy." *Brookings Papers on Economic Activity*, no. 1:139–211.

———. 2004. "Optimal Monetary and Fiscal Policy in a Liquidity Trap." *International Seminar on Microeconomics* 1:75–131.

Feldstein, Martin. 2002. "Commentary: Is There a Role for Discretionary Fiscal Policy?" In *Rethinking Stabilization Policy*. Kansas City: Federal Reserve Bank of Kansas City.

———. 2009. "Rethinking the Role of Fiscal Policy." Working Paper no. 14684, NBER, Cambridge, MA.

Fuhrer, A. C. Jeffrey, and Brian Madigan. 1997. "Monetary Policy When Interest Rates Are Bounded at Zero." *Review of Economics and Statistics* 79 (November): 573–85.

Gali, J., D. Lopez-Salido, and J. Valles. 2007. "Understanding the Effects of Government Spending on Consumption." *Journal of the European Economic Association* 5, no. 1:227–70.

Gordon, Robert, and Robert Krenn. 2010. "The End of the Great Depression 1939–41: VAR Insight on Policy Contributions and Fiscal Multipliers." Photocopy, Northwestern University.

Hall, Robert, and Susan Woodward. 2008. "Options for Stimulating the Economy." Photocopy, http://woodwardhall.wordpress.com/2008/12/08/options-for-stimulating-the-economy/.

Jeanne, O., and L. Svensson. 2004. "Credible Commitment to Optimal Escape from a Liquidity Trap: The Role of the Balance Sheet of an Independent Central Bank." Photocopy, Princeton University.

Jung, Taehun, Yuki Terenishi, and Tsutomu Watanabe. 2005. "Zero Bound on Nominal Interest Rates and Optimal Monetary Policy." *Journal of Money, Credit, and Banking* 37:813–36.

Kiyotaki, N., and J. Moore. 1997. "Credit Cycles." *Journal of Political Economy* 105, no. 2:211–48.

Krugman, Paul. 1998. "It's Baaack! Japan's Slump and the Return of the Liquidity Trap." *Brookings Papers on Economic Activity*, no. 2:137–205.

———. 2009. "Fighting off Depression." *New York Times*, January 4, Opinion page.

Mankiw, Gregory. 2008. "The Case for a Payroll Tax Cut." December 13, http://gregmankiw.blogspot.com.

Mertens, K., and Morten Ravn. 2010. "Fiscal Policy in an Expectations Driven Liquidity Trap." Discussion Paper no. 7931, Centre for Economic Policy Research, London.

Modigliani, Franco, and Charles Steindel. 1977. "Is a Tax Rebate an Effective Tool for Stabilization Policy?" *Brookings Papers on Economic Activity*, no. 1:175–209.

Poterba, James. 1996. "Retail Price Reactions to Changes in State and Local Sales Taxes." *National Tax Journal* 49, no. 2:169–79.

Reifschneider, David, and John C. Williams. 2000. "Three Lessons for Monetary Policy in a Low Inflation Era." *Journal of Money, Credit, and Banking* 32, no. 4:936–66.

Romer, Christina D., and David H. Romer. 2008. "The Macroeconomic Effects of Tax Changes: Estimates Based on a New Measure of Fiscal Shocks." Photocopy, University of California, Berkeley.

Summers, Lawrence. 1991. "Panel Discussion: Price Stability: How Should Long-Term Monetary Policy Be Determined?" *Journal of Money, Credit, and Banking* 23, no. 3:625–31.

Svensson, Lars. 2001. "The Zero Bound in an Open Economy: A Foolproof Way of Escaping from a Liquidity Trap." *Monetary and Economic Studies* 19:277–312.

———. 2003. "Escaping from a Liquidity Trap and Deflation: The Foolproof Way and Others." *Journal of Economic Perspectives* 17, no. 4:145–66.

Taylor, John B. 1993. "Discretion versus Policy Rules in Practice." *Carnegie-Rochester Conference Series on Public Policy* 39:195–214.

Williams, John. 2006. "Monetary Policy in a Low Inflation Economy with Learning." In *Monetary Policy in an Environment of Low Inflation: Proceedings of the Bank of Korea International Conference 2006*, 199–228. Seoul: Bank of Korea.

Wolman, Alexander. 2005. "Real Implications of the Zero Bound on Nominal Interest Rates." *Journal of Money, Credit, and Banking* 37, no. 2:273–96.

Woodford, Michael. 2003. *Interest and Prices: Foundations of a Theory of Monetary Policy*. Princeton, NJ: Princeton University Press.

Comment

Lawrence J. Christiano, *Northwestern University*

I. Introduction

Eggertsson's paper represents an important contribution to the analysis of fiscal policy in the New Keynesian model when the zero lower bound on the nominal interest rate is binding. The paper accomplishes a lot. It analyzes two types of taxes on capital and labor, the investment tax credit, a sales tax, and two types of government spending. It deserves to be an important reference on fiscal policy in a binding zero lower bound. In my discussion, I focus on the subset of Eggertsson's results that initially surprised me and that I think will surprise many other readers too.

Eggertsson shows that if output collapses because of a binding zero lower bound, then a cut in the household labor income tax is likely to simply aggravate the collapse. A binding zero bound causes a recession by triggering a fall in the demand for goods. Eggertsson's result is surprising because it seems to contradict a long-standing centerpiece of Keynesian orthodoxy. According to that orthodoxy, cutting taxes in a recession—particularly one caused by inadequate aggregate demand—helps to stimulate the economy. As it turns out, there is no contradiction between Eggertsson's analysis and the Keynesian orthodoxy. The New Keynesian model replaces the orthodox Keynesian transmission mechanism for taxes with a different mechanism. In the orthodox analysis—featured in standard undergraduate macroeconomics textbooks—consumption is principally determined by current disposable income, and a tax cut stimulates spending by raising disposable income. In the standard New Keynesian environment adopted by Eggertsson, households are Ricardian. They set consumption as a function of lifetime wealth, and this is unaffected by a tax cut.

But Eggertsson's result is nevertheless still surprising. In his environment, an income tax cut affects the economy by stimulating labor supply. Conventional economic reasoning suggests that something which stimulates labor supply will increase output, not accelerate its collapse. But conventional reasoning is not a good guide about what happens in a binding zero lower bound. The increased labor supply induced by a labor

978-0-226-00212-5/2011/2010-0202$10.00

income tax cut leads to a drop in marginal cost and, hence, in the price level. When there are price-setting frictions, a drop in the price level is accomplished by a period of falling prices. With the nominal interest rate unable to fall, the price deflation necessarily corresponds to a rise in the real interest rate. The increased real rate reduces aggregate demand and, hence, output. This is the mechanism whereby a cut in the labor tax rate magnifies a zero-bound output collapse in Eggertsson's model.

The following section summarizes the intuition behind the output collapse occasioned by a binding zero bound and elaborates on the intuition behind Eggertsson's tax result. I initially describe the result in an environment with price-setting frictions but no wage-setting frictions. As emphasized in Christiano, Eichenbaum, and Evans (2005) and Smets and Wouters (2007), to successfully match aggregate data it is essential to also include wage-setting frictions. The presence of wage-setting frictions has important implications for the magnitude of the impact of a change in the labor tax rate. Without wage-setting frictions, the impact can be enormous, and with these frictions the impact on employment and output may be very small. The intuition for this sensitivity is—as explained by Eggertsson—straightforward. A change in the labor tax rate affects the economy by shifting labor supply, and labor supply is largely irrelevant in the New Keynesian model with wage frictions.

The sensitivity of the quantitative impact of a tax change to the presence of wage-setting frictions goes away if the tax on labor is instead paid by the employer. This is because a labor tax rate levied on the employer hits firm marginal cost directly, without having to work its way through a potentially irrelevant labor supply curve.

That a cut in the labor tax rate paid by employers may exacerbate a recession is at least as surprising as Eggertsson's result for the household labor income tax rate. For example, a component of the American Recovery and Reinvestment Act of 2009 provides subsidies to firms to help pay the wages of qualified workers. Congress included this provision on the expectation that employment subsidies will stimulate employment. Eggertsson's argument suggests that the subsidies will instead exacerbate the recession by raising the real interest rate.

The comment closes with some concluding remarks. There I draw attention to empirical questions whose answer would help to fully assess the practical relevance of Eggertsson's findings.

II. Zero Bound, Output Collapse, and Marginal Cost

To explain Eggertsson's result, it is useful to briefly review the intuition underlying the economic collapse that can occur when the zero lower bound on the nominal rate of interest binds. Consider figure 1, which displays the demand and supply of saving. The supply of saving is represented as an increasing function of the real interest rate,

$$\text{real interest rate} = \frac{1 + R_t}{1 + \pi^e_{t+1}}.$$

Here R_t denotes the nominal return on household saving from t to $t + 1$, and π^e_{t+1} denotes the expectations of inflation over the same period. The vertical line represents the demand for funds. In Eggertsson's model the demand for funds is inelastic at zero. This is because there is nothing to do with savings in his environment. For example, there is no capital in the model. Nothing qualitative depends on this assumption about the demand for saving.

So far, there is no reason to suppose that the zero lower bound on R_t matters. It is the real interest rate that enters the demand and supply of saving, not the nominal interest rate. In principle, π^e_{t+1} could be any positive or negative number, so that nonnegativity of R_t does not imply any restriction on the real rate. The zero lower bound matters when we suppose that the public does not expect positive inflation, that is,

$$\pi^e_{t+1} \leq 0. \tag{1}$$

In his dissertation, Eggertsson proposed a formal rationale for (1). He posited that the monetary authority lacks the ability to commit to its future actions. In addition, households understand at time t that when the monetary authority sets the realized value of π_{t+1} in $t + 1$, it has both the incentive and ability (because it can always tighten monetary policy) to prevent $\pi_{t+1} > 0$. At the same time, it is not always feasible for the monetary

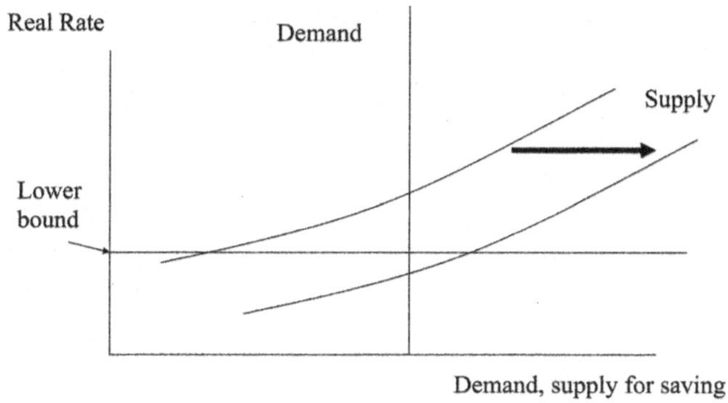

Fig. 1. Consequence of increase in saving when there is lower bound on real interest rate

authority to prevent deflation, $\pi_{t+1} < 0$. These are the elements of Eggertsson's model that rationalize (1). From a more pragmatic perspective, it may be hard for the Federal Reserve to persuade the U.S. public to raise π^e_{t+1} after having spent decades insisting that it will never tolerate a significant increase in inflation. Regardless of how (1) is interpreted, it is clear that under (1) the nonnegativity constraint on the nominal rate of interest implies a nonnegativity constraint on the real rate of interest.

Imagine the supply of saving in figure 1 shifting back and forth, say in response to disturbances in the rate at which households discount future utility. As long as the intersection between supply and demand occurs above the real interest rate lower bound, movements in the real rate can bring about equilibrium without output, consumption, and other variables being unduly disturbed.[1] However, suppose that at some point there is a very large jump in the supply of saving, so that loan market clearing cannot be accomplished by a move in the real interest rate. In this case, something else must happen to bring loan supply into line with demand.

In the New Keynesian model, a decline in output helps to shift the supply of funds back to the left for consumption-smoothing reasons. If this were all there was to it, then there would be a relatively modest recession whose dynamics correspond to the Keynesian "paradox of thrift" emphasized in undergraduate macroeconomics textbooks. However, in the New Keynesian model this is only part of the story of what happens when the lower bound on the interest rate starts to bind. The rest of the story can be a real disaster.

The problem is that while a drop in income is helping to restore equality between the demand and supply of saving, other forces come into play that increase how much income must fall to maintain equilibrium. In particular, the fall in income sets off a vicious deflation cycle that perversely raises the real rate of interest and thus increases the desire to save. The logic of the deflation cycle is depicted in figure 2. At the top of the figure we have the decline in spending associated with the rise in saving. The decline in spending produces a fall in output and, hence, in marginal cost. What happens next to expected inflation is crucial. The decline in marginal cost motivates firms to reduce prices. But what would be an instantaneous drop in the price level in a flexible price environment becomes a period of falling prices when there are Calvo-type price frictions. This happens because only a subset of firms adjust their prices in the period of the fall in marginal cost. The price level falls more in future periods as the other firms also adjust prices. That is, with price-setting frictions the drop in marginal cost produces a drop in π^e_{t+1}. With R_t at its lower

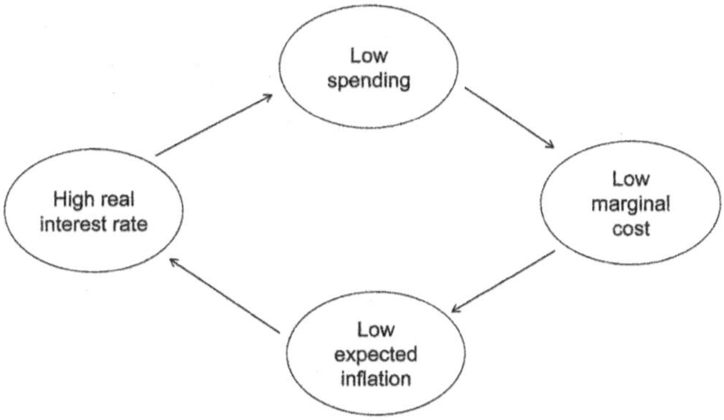

Fig. 2. Deflation spiral in zero bound

bound, the drop in π_{t+1}^{e} necessarily raises the real interest rate. This encourages households to further increase saving and cut back spending, initiating another cycle in figure 2. This deflation spiral idea is not new to the recent zero lower bound literature. For example, it is the focus of the analysis in DeLong and Summers (1986a, 1986b) and in the earlier literature that they cite.

The deflation spiral idea can be used to evaluate the likely effectiveness of policies designed to address the fall in output associated with a binding zero lower bound. For example, policies that reduce marginal cost are like throwing gasoline on a fire: they only accelerate the deflation spiral that sends the economy into output collapse. On the flip side, anything that raises marginal cost interrupts the deflation spiral and slows or even reverses the collapse in output.

Eggertsson's point is that a cut in household labor income taxes is counterproductive in the zero lower bound because it increases household labor supply and so reduces equilibrium wages. The fall in wages reduces marginal cost and accelerates output collapse, in his model.

III. Impact of Wage-Setting Frictions

I show that introducing wage-setting frictions into Eggertsson's model can have a substantial quantitative impact on the quantitative nature of his result. To understand why wage-setting frictions might make a difference, consider the supply and demand for labor in figure 3. Consider the extreme case in which the nominal wage rate (see the horizontal axis) is completely fixed. The assumption is that the quantity of labor is demand determined, so that employment is E. Suppose that initially

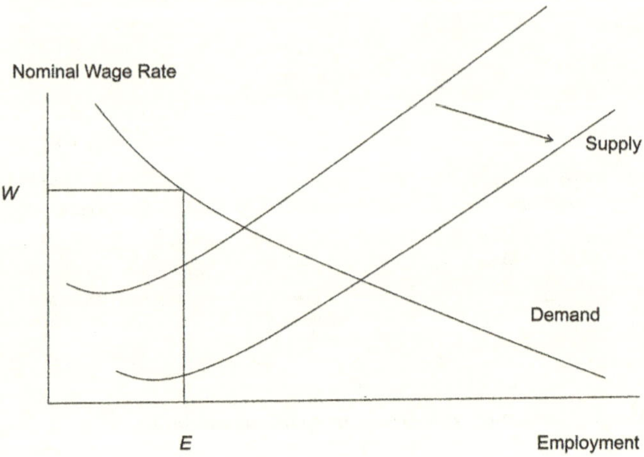

Fig. 3. Sticky wages and labor supply

labor supply is the upward sloped curve to the left. With this curve, the level of employment corresponding to the intersection of demand and supply lies to the right of E. A cut in the labor tax rate has the effect of shifting labor supply to the right. Note that the shift has no impact on employment or the wage rate. In the extreme example in figure 3, labor supply is irrelevant for price, wage, and employment determination. As a result, the impact on labor supply of a change in taxes has no effect at all on the equilibrium. This result is far more extreme than what we find in dynamic models with wage-setting frictions, but we now show that figure 3 does convey the qualitative impact of wage frictions.

A. Bringing Wage-Setting Frictions into the Model

I follow the currently standard Erceg, Henderson, and Levin (2000) approach to introducing wage-setting frictions into the model studied by Eggertsson. In the model, a homogeneous final good is produced by a representative, competitive firm using the following technology:

$$Y_t = \left(\int_0^1 Y_{t,i}^{1/\lambda_f} \, di \right)^{\lambda_f}, \quad 1 \leq \lambda_f < \infty. \tag{2}$$

The ith intermediate good is produced by a monopolist using the following production function:

$$Y_{t,i} = H_{t,i},$$

where $H_{t,i}$ denotes the quantity of a homogeneous labor input hired by the ith monopolist in a competitive market. The monopolist maximizes profits subject to the demand for its product, its production function, the wage rate, W_t, and Calvo price-setting frictions. The latter are characterized as follows:

$$P_{t,i} = \begin{cases} P_{t-1,i} & \text{with probability } \xi_p \\ \text{chosen optimally} & \text{with probability } 1 - \xi_p, \end{cases}$$

where $P_{t,i}$ denotes the ith monopolist's time t price.

Homogeneous labor is produced using the following aggregator function by a representative, competitive labor contractor:

$$H_t = \left[\int_0^1 (h_{t,j})^{1/\lambda_w} dj \right]^{\lambda_w}, \quad 1 \leq \lambda_w < \infty.$$

Here, $h_{t,j}$ represents the quantity of a j-type differentiated labor service hired by the labor contractor at a wage rate, $W_{t,j}$, that it takes as given. The jth type of labor, $h_{t,j}$, is supplied by a monopoly household with the following preferences:

$$E_0 \sum_{t=0}^{\infty} \beta^t \left(\log C_t - A \frac{h_{t,j}^{1+\phi}}{1+\phi} \right), \quad \beta \in (0,1), A, \phi > 0.$$

The budget constraint is

$$P_t C_t + B_{t+1} \leq R_{t-1} B_t + (1 - \tau_t) W_{t,j} h_{t,j} + \Pi_{t,j},$$

where τ_t is the tax rate on labor income and the wage rate is set subject to Calvo-style frictions:

$$W_{t,j} = \begin{cases} W_{t-1,j} & \text{with probability } \xi_w \\ \text{chosen optimally} & \text{with probability } 1 - \xi_w. \end{cases}$$

Here B_{t+1} represents the household's time t purchase of a nominal bond. Finally, the object, $\Pi_{t,j}$, denotes profits, lump-sum taxes, and net transfers from an insurance arrangement against the Calvo wage-setting uncertainty. The operation of this insurance market ensures that equilibrium household consumption and saving are independent of j.

The resource constraint for this economy is

$$C_t = Y_t.$$

I close the model with a characterization of monetary policy. Let Z_t denote the net "shadow interest rate." It is set as follows:

$$Z_t = \frac{1}{\beta} - 1 + 1.5\pi_t, \quad \beta \in (0,1),$$

where, as before, π_t denotes the net rate of inflation. The actual rate of interest, R_t, is set as follows:

$$R_t = \begin{cases} Z_t & Z_t \geq 0 & \text{zero bound not binding} \\ 0 & \text{otherwise} & \text{zero bound binding.} \end{cases}$$

That is, the actual interest rate coincides with the shadow rate if the shadow interest rate is nonnegative. Otherwise, the actual interest rate is zero.

B. *Computational Experiment*

In my benchmark parameterization, I set

$$\xi_p = \xi_w = 0.75, \ \beta = \frac{1}{1+r} = 0.99, \ r = 0.01, \ \lambda_w = \lambda_f = 1.20, \ \phi = 1,$$

so that the average amount of time between price and wage reoptimization is 1 year. In addition, households discount future utility at an annual rate of 4%. The object, $1/\phi$, is often interpreted as a Frisch elasticity, and it is set here at unity.[2] The steady state price and wage markups are 20%.[3]

I conduct the zero bound experiment as follows. The model is in a deterministic steady state until $t = 1$. At $t = 1$, the rate at which period·2 utility is discounted drops from its steady state value of 0.01 (per quarter) to $r = -0.01$. The discount rate remains low for 15 quarters, after which it rises back to its steady state value. The experiment from $t = 1$ and on is fully deterministic. I do not implement Eggertsson's stochastic experiment because the simultaneous presence of both sticky wages and prices appears to inject an endogenous state variable into the system, making Eggertsson's stochastic experiment difficult to implement.[4] For an explanation of this point and for other technical details associated with the computational experiment reported here, see Christiano (2010).

I set the labor tax rate, τ, to 0.30 in the steady state. In the "no policy response" simulation, the labor tax rate is held at its steady state value throughout the simulation. In the alternative simulation, the labor tax rate is increased to $\tau = 0.40$ for as long as the zero lower bound on the interest rate is binding (the period over which the lower bound binds is endogenously determined). In the periods of the alternative simulation when the lower bound is not binding, the labor tax rate is held at its steady state value. Note that in the experiment, it is an increase, not a decrease, in the labor tax rate that I consider. The logic of Eggertsson's analysis implies that this policy intervention should stimulate the economy.

Figure 4 displays the simulation results. In the no policy response simulation the zero bound is binding in periods 1–11 and ceases to bind in periods 12 and later. In the alternative simulation with the policy response, the zero bound ceases to bind one period earlier, in period 11 (see fig. 4*A* and *E*). Note that wage and price deflation are –20% and –13% per annum, respectively, at the beginning of the simulation. Evidently, the real rate of interest is very high. This helps explain the large drop in output. In the no policy response simulation, output drops a little over 35% in the first period and does not return to steady state until 15 quarters have elapsed. The impact of the increase in the labor tax rate on the shadow interest rate, Z_t, and on wage and price inflation is substantial. However, the impact on the drop in output and employment is only modest. With the rise in the labor tax rate, the output drop is reduced from a little over 35% to 30%.

The impact of the degree of wage stickiness on the output drop in the zero bound can be seen in figure 5. Figure 5*A* repeats figure 4*D* for convenience. Figure 5*B* repeats the simulations for the case, $\xi_w = 0.2$,

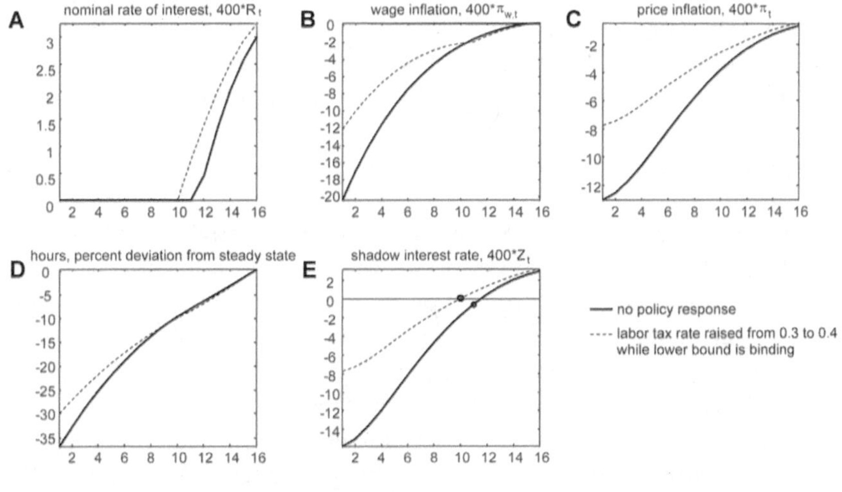

Fig. 4. Baseline simulation

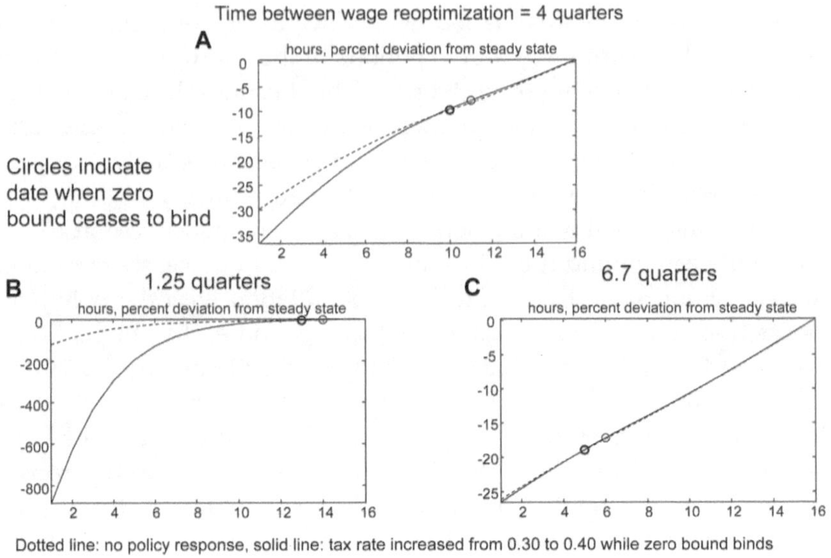

Fig. 5. Different degrees of wage stickiness

which correspond to an average wage duration of 1.25 quarters. In this case, there is relatively little stickiness in wages. Two results are evident in figure 5. First, consistent with findings reported elsewhere, the increased wage flexibility makes the zero bound far more severe.[5] Second, and more relevant to my present objective, the impact of the tax rise is enormous. The tax increase reduces the fall in output in the zero bound by a factor exceeding 4. Figure 5C displays the results when wages are more sticky than in the baseline. Consistent with the intuition in this comment, the impact of the tax hike is now virtually nil.

IV. Concluding Remarks

Eggertsson's paper represents an eloquent and thoughtful analysis of fiscal policy when the zero bound on the nominal interest rate binds. In principle, this is a very difficult problem to analyze technically. However, Eggertsson's judiciously chosen simplifications enable him to conduct an analysis that is both transparent and interesting.

A full evaluation of Eggertsson's suggestion that a labor income tax cut may be counterproductive when the zero bound binds requires investigating at least two issues. First, in the introduction I mentioned the "orthodox Keynesian analysis," in which households are non-Ricardian and the primary mechanism by which a change in taxes on household labor income affects the economy operates through changes in household disposable income. If this is in fact the way tax changes operate on the economy, then a labor income tax cut would have the traditional expansionary effect after all, even in a recession caused by a binding zero lower bound. This possibility deserves exploration.[6]

Second, the reason a tax cut on labor—whether paid by the employer or the household—in Eggertsson's analysis causes a drop in output when the zero bound binds is that it accelerates the destructive deflation cycle. As the intuition in the previous section emphasized, two ingredients are necessary for the existence of such a cycle: (i) that downward pressure on the price level produces deflation over time rather than an instantaneous price drop and (ii) that spending on goods displays substantial sensitivity to the real interest rate. An empirical assessment of the importance of i and ii would be very useful for assessing the relevance to a modern economy of the deflation cycle.

Endnotes

In preparing this comment, I have benefited from conversations with Martin Eichenbaum and Daisuke Ikeda.

1. In the Ramsey-optimal equilibrium of a model like Eggertsson's (in which there is no capital), a shock to households' discount rate has no impact on consumption and employment. This is because the equilibrium values of these variables are determined by the resource constraint and the intratemporal efficiency condition. Neither of these equations involves the discount rate. In this equilibrium, the real interest rate simply adjusts recursively to ensure that the intertemporal saving decision is consistent with the Ramsey-optimal level of output and employment. For a recent review of this well-known result, see Christiano, Trabandt, and Walentin (2011).

2. Christiano et al. (2011) argue that there is no particular reason to think of $1/\phi$ as a Frisch elasticity. As a result, it is difficult to use empirical evidence on the Frisch elasticity to evaluate the value assigned to ϕ.

3. Actually, λ_f plays no role in the linearized dynamics of the model when firm marginal cost is constant, as it is here. The wage markup does play a role because households have an upward-sloped marginal cost of working. For the reasons outlined in the literature on firm-specific capital, a smaller value of λ_w has the effect of flattening the wage Phillips curve (see Christiano et al. 2011).

4. I say "appears to inject" because I did not rule out the possibility that there is a way to rewrite the system so that it has no state variable.

5. This is consistent with DeLong and Summers (1986b), who find that, given the degree of wage stickiness in U.S. data, an increase in wage flexibility leads to greater volatility. This is also consistent with the results in Christiano, Eichenbaum, and Rebelo (2009), who consider an experiment like the one reported here. Holding fixed the size of the shock, they find that the magnitude of the output drop in the zero bound is greater when price flexibility is increased above the value calibrated to the U.S. economy. As we find here, they find that the increase in the amount by which output drops is very large. The drop in hours worked in fig. 5*B* is so large that there must surely be substantial error in the linear approximation. I assume that while the precise magnitudes may be off, the qualitative result that the impact of the tax hike is bigger with greater wage flexibility is correct.

6. Johnson, Parker, and Souleles (2009) is an example of the kind of empirical research that is relevant. For an extension of the New Keynesian model to allow for non-Ricardian consumers, see Gali, Lopez-Salido, and Valles (2007).

References

Christiano, Lawrence J. 2010. "Technical Notes for Discussion of Eggertsson, 'What Fiscal Policy Is Effective at Zero Interest Rates?'" Manuscript, http://faculty.wcas.northwestern.edu/126lchrist/research/Eggertsson_comment/temp.pdf.

Christiano, Lawrence J., Martin Eichenbaum, and Charles L. Evans. 2005. "Nominal Rigidities and the Dynamic Effects of a Shock to Monetary Policy." *Journal of Political Economy* 113, no. 1:1–45.

Christiano, Lawrence J., Martin Eichenbaum, and Sergio Rebelo. 2009. "When Is the Government Spending Multiplier Large?" Working paper no. w15394, NBER, Cambridge, MA.

Christiano, Lawrence J., Mathias Trabandt, and Karl Walentin. 2011. "DSGE Models for Monetary Policy Analysis." In *Handbook of Monetary Economics*, ed. Benjamin Friedman and Michael Woodford, 285–367. Amsterdam: North-Holland.

DeLong, J. Bradford, and Lawrence H. Summers. 1986a. "The Changing Cyclical Variability of Economic Activity in the United States." In *The American Business Cycle: Continuity and Change*, ed. R. J. Gordon. Chicago: University of Chicago Press (for NBER).

———. 1986b. "Is Increased Price Flexibility Stabilizing?" *American Economic Review* 76, no. 5 (December): 1031–44.

Erceg, Christopher J., Dale W. Henderson, and Andrew T. Levin. 2000. "Optimal Monetary Policy with Staggered Wage and Price Contracts." *Journal of Monetary Economics* 46:281–313.

Gali, Jordi, J. David Lopez-Salido, and Javier Valles. 2007. "Understanding the Effects of Government Spending on Consumption." *Journal of the European Economic Association* 5, no. 1 (March): 227–70.

Johnson, David S., Jonathan Parker, and Nicholas S. Souleles. 2009. "The Response of Consumer Spending to Rebates during an Expansion: Evidence from the 2003 Child Tax Credit." Manuscript, Northwestern University.

Smets, Frank, and Raf Wouters. 2007. "Shocks and Frictions in US Business Cycles: A Bayesian DSGE Approach." *American Economic Review* 97, no. 3:586–606.

Comment

Lee E. Ohanian, *University of California, Los Angeles*

I. Introduction

Gauti Eggertsson's paper, "What Fiscal Policy Is Effective at Zero Interest Rates?" addresses one of the classic questions in macroeconomics: what government policies should be used to fight deflation and depression? And over the years, there have been many proposed answers, including monetary easing (Friedman and Schwartz 1963; Lucas and Rapping 1969), increasing government spending (Keynes 1936), and increasing competition and efficiency (Prescott 1999; Kehoe and Prescott 2007).

Eggertsson's very creative and provocative paper discusses various proposals for exiting deflationary depressions, with a focus on what at first glance seems counterintuitive. He argues that when nominal interest rates cannot fall due to the bound at zero, then policies that otherwise would be considered contractionary, such as tax increases, increasing firm's monopoly power, wage and price controls, or expanding trade barriers that raise the prices of imported intermediate goods, can increase employment, output, and welfare, despite the fact that these policies depress the economy in normal times. He also argues that policies that increase nominal demand, such as increasing government spending, can have an order of magnitude larger effect at the zero bound than during normal times.

My comment is organized as follows. I will discuss the mechanics for these paradoxical results in a simple cash-in-advance (CIA) economy. I will then discuss issues related to the quantitative importance of the zero bound mechanism in terms of how tight the zero bound constraint was during the 2008 recession. I will also discuss the extent that the interest rates that actually have been near zero during the 2008 recession reflect institutional features that are not captured in models like the one in this paper and thus may have important implications for interpreting the zero bound and quantifying the impact of policies on real activity.

I will then discuss evidence on this mechanism from three episodes that have been described as being relevant for the zero bound: the Great

978-0-226-00212-5/2011/2010-0203$10.00

Depression, Japan's lost decade of the 1990s, and the 2008 U.S. recession. I will conclude from these episodes that the zero bound, in conjunction with variation in nominal demand, does not appear to have nearly as large an impact on actual economies as predicted by the zero bound theory.

II. The Zero Bound Mechanism in a Simple Economy

Eggertsson finds that, in a model with Calvo pricing and in which there are no other monetary frictions, the zero lower bound turns standard economic logic on its head. Specifically, he finds that expanding the supply side of the economy during a deflationary depression, such as cutting labor income taxes, will further reduce employment. Instead, promoting economic recovery in this model requires expanding nominal demand, such as an unexpected increase in government spending. Moreover, demand-side factors may have an order of magnitude larger effect when nominal rates are zero than when they are not.

I now illustrate this in a cash-credit good model along the lines of Lucas and Stokey (1987). Lowercase letters denote household choices, and uppercase letters denote aggregate (per capita) variables. There is a representative household with one unit of time endowment each period. Preferences over consumption of a single final good (c) and nonmarket time $(1-h)$, and in which preferences over consumption are perturbed by the taste shifter ξ, are given by

$$\max E \sum_{t=0}^{\infty} \beta^t \{\xi_t U(c_t) + V(1-h_t)\}.$$

The household budget constraint is given by

$$m_t + b_t = (1-\tau)W_t h_t + R_t b_{t-1} + \pi_t + (m_{t-1} - P_{t-1}c_{t-1}) + T_t. \tag{1}$$

The constraint requires that the sum of after-tax wage income, income from holding one-period bonds, profits, cash from the previous period, and government transfers is sufficient to finance new bond holdings and money. The cash-in-advance constraint (CIA) is given by

$$P_t c_t \leq m_t. \tag{2}$$

The technology and resource constraints in the economy are given by

$$Y_t = A_t H_t, \tag{3}$$

$$Y_t = C_t + G_t. \tag{4}$$

To first see how a taste shock affects the economy, suppose as in Eggertsson that there is a decline in the marginal utility of consuming at date t, such that $\xi_t < 1$. Moreover, I assume for heuristic purposes that $\xi_{t+i} = 1$ for all future dates. Equation (5) shows the Euler equation for this economy:

$$\xi_t U'(c_t) = \beta E_t \left\{ \frac{P_t}{P_{t+1}} U'(c_{t+1}) R_{t+1} \right\}. \tag{5}$$

Now suppose that the right-hand side of the Euler equation is fixed. This assumption is central for understanding the mechanics of Eggertsson's argument. Under this assumption, note that the decline in ξ_t must reduce consumption today if the Euler equation is to be satisfied. Moreover, note that with G fixed, the decline in consumption also drives down output and employment one for one given the additive resource constraint and constant returns to scale production in the single input labor. Thus, assuming that the right-hand side of equation (5) cannot decline guarantees that income, output, and employment all fall.

Next I will show how a tax cut will result in even lower employment and output. To see this, consider the household's intratemporal condition that equates the marginal rate of substitution between consumption and leisure to the after-tax real wage:

$$\xi_t U'(c) = \frac{v'(1-h)}{(1-\tau)W}.$$

With the right-hand side of the Euler equation fixed, cutting the labor income tax rate puts additional downward pressure on the left-hand side of the Euler equation, as the tax cut reduces the denominator in the equation. This means that employment, consumption, and labor must fall more than the case of a decline in ξ and no tax cut. This simple example shows that the key to generating the paradoxical result that expanding the supply side further depresses the economy is preventing the right-hand side of the Euler equation from falling in response to the decline in ξ_t.

III. Effective Policies in the Presence of the Zero Bound

In Eggertsson's model, the right-hand side of the Euler equation cannot fall because of sufficiently inflexible Calvo pricing and the assumption that the interest rate cannot fall. Thus, a taste shock in Eggertsson's model actually raises the right-hand side of the Euler equation through expected deflation and the inability of the interest rate to fall. I next show what policies are expansionary in my simple example economy. The policies that can raise employment and output are those that reduce the right-hand side of the Euler equation:

$$\beta \frac{P_t}{P_{t+1}} U'(c_{t+1}) R_{t+1}.$$

The most direct approach to reducing the right-hand side of the Euler equation is by raising expected inflation. This could be accomplished with a credible announcement by the central bank that it will increase the growth rate of base money, which would then increase inflation expectations through the standard quantity theoretic channel. However, Eggertsson argues that this approach will not be effective because of his view that households would not believe such an announcement. This is because households in his model understand that inflation reduces welfare, and thus these households would view an announcement of inflationary money growth as being noncredible, which would not lead to an increase in inflation expectations and thus not reduce the right-hand side of the Euler equation.

Eggertsson's argument that households would not believe a central bank's promise to inflate stands in contrast to the historical record. Specifically, virtually all of the credibility problems that central banks historically have faced is convincing households that they will reduce inflation, not raise inflation. Households seldom have had trouble understanding the incentives for governments to create inflation, even anticipated inflation. Moreover, in terms of Eggertsson's argument that inflation reduces welfare, inflation can be welfare enhancing in an economy with a large amount of nonindexed nominal debt, particularly if a significant amount of nominal debt is held by individuals outside the country. Thus my own view is that if policy makers are concerned about the zero bound, then monetary policy is a direct and quick protocol.

In addition to monetary policy, there are a number of other approaches to increasing the right-hand side of the Euler equation. One approach is adopting wage and price controls to raise expected inflation. This is an interesting approach, because the goal of boosting prices and wages to foster economic recovery was specifically the goal of much of Roosevelt's New Deal (see Cole and Ohanian 2004). I will return to the impact of these policies in Section VI.

Another approach to reduce the right-hand side of the Euler equation is by constructing a sequence of intertemporal consumption taxes that make date t consumption relatively inexpensive by promising to raise consumption taxes in the future as follows:

$$\beta \frac{P_t}{P_{t+1}} \frac{1+\tau_{ct}}{1+\tau_{ct+1}} U'(c_{t+1}) R_{t+1}.$$

Government spending is also a possible approach. Note first that if the right hand of equation (5) is fixed, then the government spending "multiplier" is necessarily one, which follows from the fact that production is constant to returns to scale and government spending and consumption are additive in the economy's resource constraint. But note that government spending can have a large "multiplier"—or more broadly, the impact of any policy change can raise employment substantially—if in the absence of a policy intervention the taste shock ξ results in a large expected deflation in which R is driven to 0, and the policy change can reverse this. In Eggertsson's model, government spending has this impact because it raises anticipated inflation.

IV. Importance of Calvo Pricing Plus Long-Lived Price Rigidity

Given the mechanics of how supply side and demand side policy work under the zero bound, I now discuss some technical issues related to Eggertsson's model, with a focus on the importance of Calvo pricing and on why long-lived price rigidity is important. Deriving a unique solution in Eggertsson's model, as well as generating a large impact from nominal demand shifts, depends on parameter values, particularly those that govern the duration of price rigidity in the Calvo model (α), consumption and labor supply elasticities (σ, ω), the expected duration of the low demand state (μ), and the elasticity of demand across intermediate good producers (θ).

A unique solution requires that the following inequality holds in which κ is a nonlinear function of other model parameters:

$$(1-\mu)(1-\beta\mu) > \kappa(\alpha, \sigma, \omega, \theta)\mu\sigma.$$

I now make assumptions on some of the parameters in order to understand the implications of this inequality. I assume that the household discount factor, β, is close to one, and I also assume a Rogerson-Hansen utility function for the representative household in which preferences are logarithmic over consumption and linear in leisure. Under these assumptions, the inequality becomes

$$\frac{(1-\mu)^2}{\mu} > \frac{(1-\alpha)^2}{\alpha}.$$

This states that the odds that the economy exits the low demand state, $(1-\mu)/\mu$ scaled by that probability $(1-\mu)$, must exceed the odds of changing prices, scaled by that probability $(1-\alpha)$. Note that this inequality is difficult to satisfy as prices change frequently: $\alpha \rightarrow 0$ and thus implies that the model solution may not be well defined, as prices change frequently. In contrast, Eggertsson chooses $\alpha = 0.77$. This is important because it is reasonable that the incentive to change prices rises during turbulent periods, such as the crises that are central for this issue. Addressing this issue requires departing from the simplicity of Calvo price setting.

V. How Binding Is the Zero Bound, and Is Zero the Bound?

The quantitative importance of the zero bound depends on the deflation rate, which in turn affects how binding the zero bound constraint is through deflation-induced increases in the real interest rate. Eggertsson's analysis is based on a 10% deflation rate, which yields a very binding zero bound constraint by generating a real interest rate of 10%.

While the zero bound is very binding in Eggertsson's analysis, it is unclear how binding it is in recent episodes in which this mechanism is presumed to be important, including the U.S. 2008 recession and Japan in the 1990s. This is important because the quantitative impact of the nominal demand policies stressed by Eggertsson hinge on a very binding zero bound. One reason why the tightness of the constraint in these recent episodes is an open question is because there was very little deflation. For example, the consumer price index (CPI) in the United States increased on average –0.03% between September 2008 and April 2010 in the United States, and averaged 0.02% in Japan between January 1992 and December 2002. This means that real interest rates on many securities, particularly those with nominal rates that are near zero, are not nearly as high as in Eggertsson's analysis.

Another reason why the tightness of the constraint is an open question is because of the actual pattern of nominal interest rates during the 2008 U.S. recession and whether Eggertsson's model is equipped to plausibly capture that pattern. Specifically, the model implicitly has a single asset in which the nominal interest rate is zero. But many securities during the

2008 recession have returns well above zero. Moreover, the securities with rates that are near zero are primarily very short-term money market instruments, and according to market participants, the economic forces that are driving these rates to near zero are unique. Specifically, a view among those who trade money market securities is that the near zero behavior of interest rates is due to government policies that have flooded those markets with cash from various government programs, including TARP, as evidenced by the following statement:[1]

> There is a massive wall of liquidity, a pile of cash which needs a home driving yields lower, as institutions need to show cash in something other than a mattress. Whatever the case, I am certain that present circumstance is not an indicator of financial stress as plunging bill rates have been in the past.
>
> Those who have access to Fed Funds market (banks and other financial institutions) are flooding that market with cash. Those who don't have access to that inter-bank market (hedge funds, mutual funds, etc.) are flooding T-Bill market with cash. ... Money market rates are at ridiculously low levels, from cash from government programs like TARP.

Moreover, there are institutional features at work in money markets such that the nominal bound on some money market rates is sometimes less than zero. Some treasuries have yielded –300 basis points, reflecting penalties on failure to deliver securities related to short sales. This was particularly important between 2003 and 2004, and during the current recession in 2009. This indicates that cash and bonds are not always perfect substitutes at interest rates of zero and that negative rates are possible. This raises questions about what the bound is on money market securities and indicates that the bound may fluctuate considerably over time.

Taken together, this suggests that models with standard Euler equations, such as in this paper, could address these issues along two dimensions. One approach is to abstract from money market complications, and focus on non–money market securities, but nominal rates on these securities are greater than zero. And note that securities with rates above zero may provide another interest rate channel for central bank policy to possibly operate. Alternatively, models could be developed with money market institutional detail to study those securities with near zero nominal rates, but this would result in a nonstandard Euler equation. In the absence of models like this, it is hard to know what the implications of interest rate bounds on money market assets are for the issues that are the focus of this paper.

VI. Economic Activity during Assumed Zero Bound Episodes

This section presents data during three episodes in which the zero bound is presumed by some economists to be important: the U.S. Great Depression, Japan in the 1990s, and the 2008 U.S. recession. In each of these cases I find little support that the zero bound had a strong impact on economic activity.

I begin with the U.S. Great Depression. In other research, Eggertsson (2008) has argued that Roosevelt's New Deal wage and price controls from the National Industrial Recovery Act was key for generating recovery from the depression by raising inflationary expectations. Table 1 shows data between 1932 and 1938 for the GDP deflator, consumption, hours worked, real GNP, and the right-hand side of the Euler equation in the model described above, which is $(P_t/P_{t+1})(1/C_{t+1})R_{t+1}$, in which the price level is the GDP deflator, consumption is nondurables plus services, and the interest rate is the 3-month Treasury rate. All data except the Euler equation are relative to 1929 levels. The Euler equation is measured relative to its average calculated between 1929 and 1931.

Table 1 shows that there was substantial deflation through 1932, resulting in a right-hand side of the Euler equation that was high during the Depression. But prices stabilized by 1933, and there was some inflation afterward. This led to a significant decline in the right-hand side of the Euler equation after 1932, but note that there was not much economic recovery. Per capita hours worked remained far below trend throughout the period, with virtually no recovery through 1935. There was also very little recovery in consumption, and the recovery that did occur in GDP was largely the result of productivity growth. This weak recovery contrasts with the prediction of the zero bound argument, which predicts a strong recovery based on rising inflation that induces a fall in the right-hand side of the Euler equation.

Table 1
U.S. Great Depression

	Price Level	Consumption	Hours	Real GNP	Euler Right-Hand Side
1932	78.2	76.0	73.5	65.2	70.0
1933	76.5	72.2	72.7	61.9	52.4
1934	83.0	72.1	71.8	64.6	49.7
1935	84.6	73.1	74.8	68.1	47.9
1936	85.0	77.0	80.7	74.9	58.2
1937	89.1	77.2	83.1	76.0	47.1
1938	87.0	74.3	76.4	70.6	44.5

I next consider Japan in the 1990s. Figure 1 shows per capita real GDP relative to trend. Real output per person peaks in 1991 and then declines steadily over the next 10 years or so, cumulatively falling about 12%. Some have argued that Japan's prolonged slump was the consequence of anticipated deflation and a zero bound constraint that raised real interest rates (see, e.g., Krugman 1998; Auerbach and Obstfeld 2005). Figure 2 shows Japanese inflation, which is primarily positive through most of the slump, suggesting that real rates were not high as a consequence of deflation. Rather, real interest rates were quite low, which is inconsistent with the view that Japan's slump was not due to the zero bound and deflation.

Another reason that I am skeptical that Japan's slump was primarily due to the zero bound is because of large increases in government spending. Figure 3 shows government consumption, which was about 14% of GDP in 1991 and which rose to 18% over the next 10 years. According to the zero bound argument, this increase in government spending, which contributed to an increase in the primary deficit from around 50% of GDP in 1991 to about 160% by 2007, should have expanded employment and output. In contrast to this prediction, higher government spending appears to have had little effect on GDP, which fell steadily while government spending was rising.

So what then is responsible for Japan's slump if not the zero bound and deflationary expectations? Hayashi and Prescott (2002) conclude

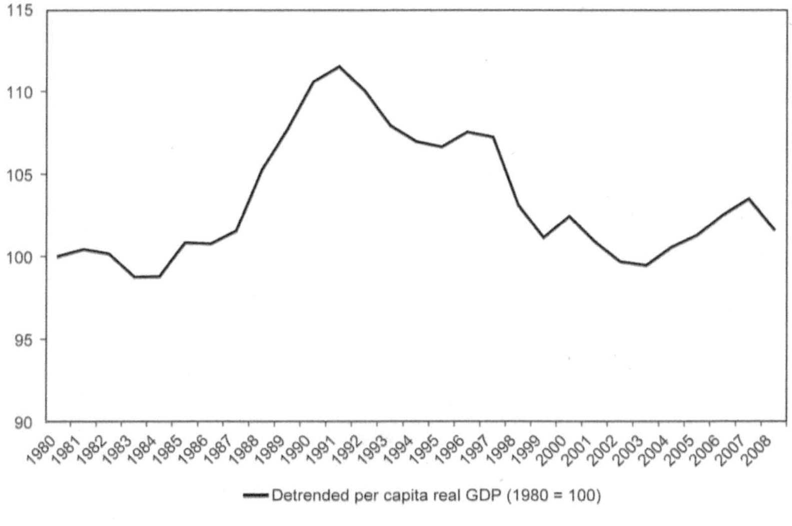

Fig. 1. Real output, Japan

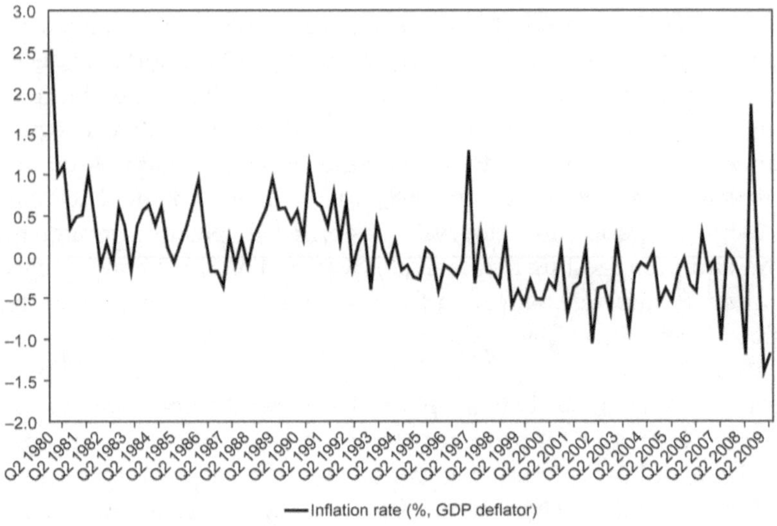

Fig. 2. Inflation, Japan

that Japan's slump was due to a decline in the growth rate of productivity. Figure 4 shows that total factor productivity declined by about 20% relative to trend after its 1991 peak. Hayashi and Prescott show how this change can quantitatively account for Japan's depression and also low real interest rates. Moreover, note that productivity stopped falling

Fig. 3. Government consumption, Japan

Fig. 4. Total factor productivity, Japan

around 2000, which is around the time when Japan's GDP began to stabilize.

The third episode I consider is the 2008 U.S. recession. I exploit the fact that there are large seasonal changes in nominal demand, which according to the zero bound argument should have a much larger impact on the economy during 2009 than during other times. Specifically, economic activity seasonally peaks in the fourth quarter and is at its lowest point in the first quarter. Table 2 compares nonseasonally adjusted per capita hours worked between the fourth and third quarters and between the fourth and first quarters during the 2009 recession to their postwar averages. However, I find very little difference between the size of the seasonal movements across quarters in 2009 compared to their average movements. This finding is similar in spirit to that in Mulligan (2009), who found that the large seasonal increase in the labor force at the start of the summer in 2009 was largely absorbed into employment, and which is inconsistent with the zero bound argument. These data indicate

Table 2
Nonseasonally Adjusted Hours

	Q4–Q3 Change	Q4–Q1 Change
Postwar average	2.2%	3.3%
Current recession (2009)	3.0%	4.2%

that seasonal changes in nominal demand did not have the large impact predicted by a strongly binding zero bound.

VII. Conclusion

This is an intriguing and provocative paper that is a significant contribution to the literature on policy analysis in economies with nominal interest rates that are near zero. This paper argues that with substantial price rigidity and with nominal rates that cannot fall, government spending can have very powerful expansionary effects and that supply side factors that are usually considered to be expansionary actually deepened a depression. The central mechanism that delivers these results is that the right-hand side of the Euler equation in the model cannot fall.

I conclude from analyzing data from three episodes for which the zero bound is presumed to be important—the Great Depression, Japan's lost decade, and the 2008 recession—that the zero bound does not have nearly as large of an impact as suggested in these models. These empirical challenges from the perspective of the zero bound literature are interesting future avenues for research.

Endnotes

I thank Paco Buera, Ariel Burstein, Hal Cole, Ellen McGrattan, and, in particular, V. V. Chari for discussions. I thank Giang Ho for superb research assistance.

1. Tyler Durden, "Post-Lehman Deja Vu as T-Bill Yields Turn Negative," *Zero Hedge* (blog), http://www.zerohedge.com/article/post-lehman-deja-vu-t-bill-yields-turn-negative.

References

Auerbach, A. J., and M. Obstfeld. 2005. "The Case for Open-Market Purchases in a Liquidity Trap." *American Economic Review* 95, no. 1:110–37.

Cole, H. L., and L. E. Ohanian. 2004. "New Deal Policies and the Persistence of the Great Depression: A General Equilibrium Analysis." *Journal of Political Economy* 112, no. 4:779–816.

Eggertsson, G. 2008. "Was the New Deal Contractionary?" Working paper (June), Federal Reserve Bank of New York.

Friedman, M., and A. J. Schwartz. 1963. *A Monetary History of the United States, 1867–1960*. Princeton, NJ: Princeton University Press.

Hayashi, F., and E. C. Prescott. 2002. "The 1990s in Japan: A Lost Decade." *Review of Economic Dynamics* 5, no. 1:206–35.

Kehoe, T. J., and E. C. Prescott. 2007. *Great Depressions of the Twentieth Century*. Minneapolis: Federal Reserve Bank of Minneapolis.

Keynes, J. M. 1936. *The General Theory of Employment, Interest and Money*. London: Macmillan.

Krugman, P. 1998. "Japan's Trap." Manuscript (May), Princeton University, http://web.mit.edu/krugman/www/japtrap.html.
Lucas, Robert E., Jr., and L. A. Rapping. 1969. "Real Wages, Employment, and Inflation." *Journal of Political Economy* 77, no. 5:721–54.
Lucas, Robert E., Jr., and N. L. Stokey. 1987. "Money and Interest in a Cash-in-Advance Economy." *Econometrica* 55, no. 3:491–513.
Mulligan, C. B. 2009. "School Is Out for Summer: A Gem in the Jobs Report." *Economix* (blog), *New York Times* (August 11), http://economix.blogs.nytimes.com/2009/08/11/schools-out-for-summer-a-gem-in-the-jobs-report/.
Prescott, E. C. 1999. "Some Observations on the Great Depression." *Federal Reserve Bank of Minneapolis Quarterly Review* 23 (Winter): 25–29.

Discussion

Gauti Eggertsson began by responding to Lawrence Christiano's discussion on the quantitative significance of changes to the labor wedge. Eggertsson agreed that the aggregate supply effects of tax changes may not be very large and noted that tax cuts may increase aggregate demand (by, e.g., boosting income for liquidity-constrained consumers), pushing up prices and output. He clarified that his primary aim is to highlight the importance of policies that stimulate aggregate demand as opposed to aggregate supply.

Eggertsson also responded to several points made in Lee Ohanian's presentation. With respect to a slightly negative policy rate achieved by the Swedish Riksbank, Eggertsson noted that the level of the constraint is not central to his results and that central banks around the world were constrained in their ability to cut interest rates. As to the empirical importance of the zero lower bound, Eggertsson argued that the answer to that question depends on the sensitivity of aggregate demand to the interest rate. He noted that the absence of a deflationary spiral should be understood in the context of large increases in the Fed balance sheet and government spending. Eggertsson emphasized that a key question about the current crisis and previous lower bound episodes is what one should expect would have been the counterfactual path of output and prices under a different set of policies. He referenced a related paper in which he argues that policy mistakes by the Roosevelt administration in 1937 cut short an incipient recovery (Gauti B. Eggertsson and Benjamin Pugsley, "The Mistake of 1937: A General Equilibrium Analysis," *Monetary and Economic Studies* [Bank of Japan] 24, no. S-1 [2006]: 1–40).

Daron Acemoglu and others wondered whether the counterintuitive result that an increase in the income tax could be expansionary was, in fact, too surprising. In particular, Acemoglu asked whether the monetary policy rule might be too rigid and whether the monetary authority might

978-0-226-00212-5/2011/2010-0204$10.00

respond very differently to an event where the zero lower bound binds. Eggertsson indicated the importance of central bank credibility, noting that he considers alternative policies and abstracts from unconventional monetary policies. Acemoglu asked what monetary policy would be needed to overturn the main result. Eggertsson noted that his results simply require a constant nominal interest rate in response to a fiscal expansion, adding that debt dynamics or demand-side effect of tax cuts could affect inflation expectations and the interest rate.

Michael Woodford, reiterating Eggertsson, disagreed with Ohanian as to whether the Riksbank was unconstrained by the zero lower bound. He noted that the projections for the policy rate published by the Riksbank showed a period of no change in the interest rate followed by a sharp jump in the future indicating that monetary policy faced a constraint. Ohanian asked how low the Riksbank thought it could lower the policy rate. Woodford responded that officials at the bank were concerned that lowering the repo rate below 25 basis points could have adverse effects on trading in the money market. Also, responding to Ohanian, Woodford emphasized that Eggertsson's qualitative results were robust to more complex mechanisms of price setting beyond Calvo pricing—the key is some degree of price rigidity. Woodford added that if prices were flexible, prices should have fallen sharply during the credit crisis to generate positive inflation expectations and a sufficient fall in real interest rates to maintain full employment.

Valerie Ramey identified the late 1930s and early 1940s as a good empirical test for the fiscal multiplier at the zero lower bound. At that point, the interest rate on 3-month Treasury bills was lower than today and government spending multipliers did not exceed one—well below the multipliers implied by the Eggertsson analysis. Eggertsson responded that his calibration attempted to capture the economic conditions in 1933 rather than 1940, when the United States was much closer to full employment. But he agreed that the model-based multiplier would still exceed one. On this issue, Robert Gordon added that using quarterly government spending and GDP data, his work found multipliers of up to 2.2 through the second quarter of 1941. The multiplier dropped near the end of that year due to wartime supply constraints.

However, Gordon took issue with aspects of Eggertsson's model. He noted that prices rose from 1933 to 1940 while output remained far below potential. Likewise, over the last decade, Japan experienced flat prices or a slight decline while output remained well below potential. Eggertsson responded that outright deflation is not needed in these models as the shocks that cause the recession may have some cost-push element. He cited the work of Curdia and Woodford (2009) examining the effect of intermediation shocks that increase credit spreads. The key issue is that further monetary easing is not possible. Gordon also expressed skepticism over the sharp movements of the real wage in Eggertsson's simulations.

Frederic Mishkin commented that, while deflation has not been very large, the credit crisis in 2008 required very low real interest rates (on the order of –5%) which could not be attained regardless of the precise bound on the policy rate or the level of inflation. He also called for greater analysis of unconventional monetary policy and its effect on central bank credibility and independence. Eggertsson briefly noted that he is working on research in this direction.

Susanto Basu commented on how positive productivity shocks can be contractionary in New Keynesian models by lowering expected inflation and raising real interest rates in the short run. He also encouraged Eggertsson to frame the results in terms of accommodative versus restrictive monetary policy rather than the zero lower bound. He noted that Eggertsson's qualitative results would continue to hold assuming monetary policy accommodated a fiscal expansion regardless of the level of the interest rate. Basu also asked, as an empirical matter, whether aggregate spending was really as responsive to changes in the real interest rate as implied in the Eggertsson simulations.

John Taylor took issue with Eggertsson's comment that the small fiscal multipliers found in his work with Cogan, Cwik, and Wieland were the result of assuming a permanent increase in government spending. While one simulation in their model assumed a permanent increase, the primary experiment of interest was a simulation of the effect of the Recovery Act as written. Taylor noted that this experiment found a much more modest impact of government spending on output than studies by the Obama administration in early 2009. He also noted that, while the zero lower bound was binding, it was not clear that the policy rate should have been very negative; the Taylor rule called for a funds rate of –1% (rather than –5%) over a fairly short period. Eggertsson responded that determining the proper real interest rate target is a key empirical issue that deserves greater attention.

While recognizing the theoretical contribution, Greg Mankiw questioned the policy recommendations. If tax cuts could deepen a recession, would it make sense to pursue policies that reduced aggregate supply like imposing regulations and discouraging job search? He emphasized the need to think about the effect of such policies on investment demand and noted that policies designed to boost aggregate supply would also bolster business confidence and investment. Eggertsson responded by emphasizing that policies must be recognized as temporary and cited extensions of his model that include endogenous capital formation. He also reiterated that the demand-side effects must be understood for any fiscal policy under consideration.

Jordi Galí provided further comments on the realism of the model. He noted that the government spending multiplier could be strengthened at the lower bound by using Jaimovich-Rebelo type preferences, which would weaken the wealth effects and limit the shift in aggregate supply. Moreover, such preferences would also weaken the effect of government spending shocks in non-zero-lower-bound circumstances. He also added that he could not think of a single government that pursued tax cuts in the current credit crisis for supply-side effects; the stated purpose was to increase disposable income. Eggertsson responded that because of possible demand-side effects, he was unwilling to push his headline conclusion too strongly.

Deborah Lucas asked about the degree to which Eggertsson's results depended on a single economy-wide interest rate. She noted a large disconnect between the Fed funds rate and the decision-relevant interest rates facing consumers. She added that the Fed purposed credit-easing policies, in addition to standard monetary easing, in order to try to influence borrowing rates. Eggertsson cited the Curdia and Woodford model with multiple interest rates, noting that their model can be reduced to a similar set of equations as a standard New Keynesian model.

3

Two Monetary Tools: Interest Rates and Haircuts

Adam Ashcraft, *Federal Reserve Bank of New York*
Nicolae Gârleanu, *University of California at Berkeley, NBER, and CEPR*
Lasse Heje Pedersen, *New York University, NBER, and CEPR*

If it is known that the Bank of England is freely advancing on what in ordinary times is reckoned a good security—on what is then commonly pledged and easily convertible—the alarm of the solvent merchants and bankers will be stayed.
—Walter Bagehot (1873, 198)

Financial institutions play a key role as credit providers in the economy, and liquidity crises arise when they become credit constrained themselves. In such liquidity crises, financial institutions' ability to borrow against their securities plays a key role, as Bagehot points out. In the private markets, it can become virtually impossible to borrow against certain illiquid securities, and, more broadly, the "haircuts" (also called margin requirements) on many securities increase in crises.[1] Furthermore, security prices may drop significantly, especially for securities with high haircuts. To alleviate the financial institutions' funding problems, and their repercussions on the real economy, central banks have a number of monetary policy tools available, such as interest rate cuts and lending facilities with low haircuts.

This paper studies the links between haircuts, required returns, and real activity, and evaluates the different monetary policy tools theoretically and empirically. In a production economy with multiple sectors financed by agents facing margin constraints, we show that binding constraints increase required returns and propagate business cycles. The central bank policy of reducing the interest rate decreases the required returns of low-haircut assets but may increase those of high-haircut assets, since it may increase the shadow cost of capital for constrained agents. A reduction in the haircut of an asset unambiguously lowers its required return and can ease the funding constraints on all assets.

978-0-226-00212-5/2011/2010-0301$10.00

Empirically, we estimate that lowering haircuts through lending facilities significantly decreased the required return during the recent crisis, and we provide unique survey evidence suggesting a strong demand sensitivity to haircuts.

Our model features heterogeneous-risk-aversion agents who are limited to holding positions with total haircuts not exceeding the agents' capital. While this is a single funding constraint, it affects securities differently, depending on their haircuts. This is the key funding constraint for real-world financial institutions; for instance, Bear Stearns, Lehman, and AIG collapsed when they could not meet their margin constraints.

In the model, risk-tolerant agents take leveraged positions in equilibrium, and, as we will see, play a role that resembles that of the real-world financial institutions described above. When these leveraged agents' margin requirements become binding, their shadow cost of capital increases, driving up equilibrium required returns, especially for high-haircut assets, which use more of the now expensive capital. This mechanism lowers investment and output, and leads to persistent effects of i.i.d. (independently and identically distributed) productivity shocks, thus exacerbating business cycle swings, especially in high-haircut sectors. The margin-constraint business cycle is driven by risk-tolerant agents' wealth as the key state variable, which falls whenever asset values and labor income do. The consequences are disproportionately severe for the high-haircut sectors because constrained investors reallocate capital toward assets that can be financed (i.e., leveraged) more easily.

Central banks often fight low real activity by reducing the interest rate to lower the required return on capital. This policy, however, makes leveraged investing more attractive, thus possibly increasing the shadow cost of capital, which in turn may actually increase the required return on high-haircut assets. Low-haircut assets' returns, on the other hand, depend only weakly on the shadow cost of capital—the extreme case is that of an asset with zero haircut, whose required return is driven purely by the interest rate and riskiness, and independent of the state of the constraint—and therefore are brought down by reducing interest rates. Naturally, decreases in required returns are accompanied by increased investment and production, and vice versa.

This observation motivates a natural policy question: What can be done when lowering the interest rate does not help high-haircut sectors (or when the nominal interest rate is already zero)? As Bagehot points out, the central bank can lend against a wide range of securities and, we might add, at a modest yet prudent haircut. We show that if the central bank decides to accept a particular security as collateral at a lower haircut than otherwise available, this always lowers its required return. The required returns of other securities either all increase or all decrease, depending on what happens to the shadow cost of capital. The most intuitive case is that the shadow cost of capital decreases due to the new source of funding, thus helping other securities as well, and we show that this happens when the haircut is reduced sufficiently.

Further, the shadow cost of capital decreases if the haircut on enough securities can be lowered. This observation is relevant for the debate about whether central banks should extend their lending facilities to legacy securities or restrict attention to new issues. The Term Asset-Backed Securities Loan Facility (TALF) program was initially focused on newly issued securities, since these imply new credit provided to the real economy. Lowering the haircut on these securities helps reduce their required returns but does little to ease the overall funding constraints in the financial sector. The legacy TALF program applied to existing securities and therefore had the potential to alleviate the funding problems more broadly—and flatten the haircut-return curve as a result.

As a final theoretical result, we show that the shadow cost of capital can be reduced through asset purchases or capital injections. Hence, these policy tools also lower required returns and stimulate real activity, but they may be associated with significant costs and risks.

Empirically, we find that central bank provided loans at modest haircuts can be a powerful tool for lowering yields and stimulating economic activity. We arrive at this conclusion by studying the introduction of the legacy TALF that provided loans with lower haircuts and longer maturity than otherwise available. Yields went down significantly when the TALF program was announced, increased when Standard and Poor's (S&P) changed its ratings methodology in a way that would make a number of securities ineligible for TALF, and finally went down again, and further than before, when TALF was implemented. We note that the yield of both TALF eligible and ineligible securities reacted to the news, consistent with the idea that the common shadow cost of capital was affected.

While suggestive, this string of yield reactions does not provide conclusive evidence, since so many other things went on at the same time. We use two approaches to isolate the effect of TALF: (1) we study evidence from a survey conducted in March 2009 (before the legacy TALF was introduced) asking market participants the prices they would bid for certain securities without TALF, with access to high-haircut term funding, and with access to low-haircut term funding; and (2) we study the reaction of market prices, adjusting for non-TALF effects by considering the price response to unpredictable bond rejections from the TALF program.

The survey indicated that participants would pay 6% more for a super senior CMBS (commercial mortgage-backed securities) bond if they had access to a 3-year loan with a high haircut than they would pay if they had no access to term leverage. The bid price was higher for lower haircuts and longer maturities, reaching 50% above the no-TALF bid for the longest term loan with a low haircut. The significance of the effect is also apparent in terms of yields: participants required a 15% yield without access to term leverage (which was the yield prevailing in the market), but their required bond yields dropped to 12% with access to 3-year loans with a low haircut (similar to what was actually implemented in TALF), and to 9.5% for 5-year loans. Hence, according to this survey, low-haircut term leverage similar to TALF had the potential to lower yields by 3%–5% for super senior bonds.

These results are evidence of significant demand sensitivity to haircuts. To make sure that the higher bid reflects the value of financing, not the value of being able to default on the loan, we focus on super senior CMBS, as these are the safest bonds. The participants in the survey were asked to estimate the losses on the pool in a stress scenario, and, even in the stress scenario, the estimated losses on the pool imply no losses on the safest super senior tranches.

The survey evidence is corroborated by transaction-price data showing the effect of TALF on actual bond yields, controlling for other effects. Indeed, we find a statistically significant rise in the yield spread of bonds that are unexpectedly rejected from the TALF program by the Fed, over and above the yield change of other bonds in the same security class during the same week. In other words, the required return rises for bonds that fail to benefit from TALF's lower haircuts. As further evidence consistent with the model, we find that this rise in yield is greater during the early part of the program (July–September 2009), when capital constraints were more binding, than in the later period (October 2009–March 2010). During the early period, we estimate that the TALF rejection led to an immediate 80 bps rise in yield, with the effect eventually falling to 40 bps.

The effect of lowering haircuts during crises can likely far exceed the estimated 40 bps long-term effect, for a couple of reasons. First, the economy and capital constraints had already improved substantially during this early legacy TALF period relative to the height of the crisis (e.g., March 2009, when the survey was conducted). Thus, the haircut effect during the height of the crisis would likely have been significantly larger. Second, we are only measuring the effect of a bond's haircut on its own yield, not that of the lending program on the liquidity in the system more broadly. In the language of our theory, we estimate only the effect of moving a bond along the haircut-return curve, not the flattening of the curve itself.

Our overall evidence suggests that the haircut tool is a powerful one, consistent with our model. To put the magnitude in perspective, recall that the Fed lowered the Fed funds rate from 5.25% in early 2007 all the way to the zero lower bound (0%–0.25%), a 5% reduction. Since we estimate that the haircut tool implemented with a program such as TALF can lower yields by well in excess of 0.40%, perhaps up to 3%–5% as our survey suggests, its effectiveness appears economically significant.

The estimated economic magnitude can be understood in the context of the model as follows: lowering the haircut by 80% lowers the required return by approximately 10% × 80% × 40% = 3% if the shadow cost of capital was around 10% for the 40% of risk-bearing capacity that was constrained during the crisis. With standard production functions, this leads to large effects on investment, capital, and output in the affected sectors.

Our paper is related to several large literatures. Borrowing constraints of entrepreneurs and firms affect business cycles and collateral values (Bernanke and Gertler 1989; Detemple and Murthy 1997; Geanakoplos 1997, 2003; Kiyotaki and Moore 1997; Bernanke, Gertler, and Gilchrist 1998; Caballero and Krishnamurthy 2001; Coen-Pirani 2005; Lustig and Van Nieuwerburgh 2005; Fostel and Geanakoplos 2008).[2]

Rather than focusing on borrowers' balance sheet effects (or credit-demand frictions), we consider the lending channel (or credit-supply frictions), as Holmström and Tirole (1997), Repullo and Suarez (2000), and Ashcraft (2005) have. The impact on the macroeconomy of financial frictions has been further studied recently by Kiyotaki and Moore (2008), Adrian, Moench, and Shin (2009), Cúrdia and Woodford (2009), Gertler and Karadi (2009), Gertler and Kiyotaki (2009), Reis (2009), and Adrian and Shin (2010). Also, Lorenzoni (2008) shows that there can be inefficient credit booms due to fire-sale externalities with credit constraints.

Our asset-pricing implications are related to Hindy (1995), Cuoco (1997), Aiyagari and Gertler (1999), and especially Gârleanu and Pedersen (forthcoming). Required returns are also increased by transaction costs and market-liquidity risk (Amihud and Mendelson 1986; Longstaff 2004; Acharya and Pedersen 2005; Duffie, Gârleanu, and Pedersen 2005, 2007; Mitchell, Pedersen, and Pulvino 2007; He and Krishnamurthy 2008). Market liquidity interacts with margin requirements as shown by Brunnermeier and Pedersen (2009), who also explain why margin requirements tend to increase during crises because of liquidity spirals, a phenomenon documented empirically by Adrian and Shin (2008) and Gorton and Metrick (2009a, 2009b).

We complement the literature by generating cross-sectional predictions in a multisector model with credit supply frictions due to margin constraints, by showing how interest rate cuts may be ineffective for high-haircut assets during crises, and by evaluating the effect of another monetary tool—haircuts—theoretically and empirically.

Haircuts play a central role in the paper. One may wonder, however, whether this institutional feature is of passing importance. To the contrary, we would argue that loans secured by collateral with a haircut have played an important role in facilitating economic activity for thousands of years. For instance, the first written compendium of Judaism's Oral Law, the Mishnah, states: "One lends money with a mortgage on land which is worth more than the value of the loan. The lender says to the borrower, 'If you do not repay the loan within three years, this land is mine'" (Mishnah Bava Metzia 5:3, circa 200 AD).[3]

The rest of the paper is organized as follows. Section I lays out the model, Section II derives the economic dynamics and effects of haircuts and interest rate cuts, Section III presents the empirical evidence, and Section IV concludes.

I. Model

We consider a simple overlapping-generations (OLG) economy in which firms and agents interact at times $\{\ldots, -1, 0, 1, 2, \ldots\}$. At each time t, J new young (representative) firms are started, and there are J old firms that were started during the previous period $t-1$. Old firm j produces output Y_t^j depending on its capital K_t^j, labor use L_t^j, and productivity A_t^j, which is a random variable. The output is

$$Y_t^j = A_t^j F(K_t^j, L_t^j), \tag{1}$$

where $F(K_t^j, L_t^j) = (K_t^j)^\alpha (L_t^j)^\beta$ is a Cobb-Douglas production function with $\alpha + \beta \le 1$. The productivity shocks A_t^j have mean $\bar{A}^j$ and variance-covariance matrix Σ_A, assumed invertible. Each type of firm uses its own specialized labor with wage w_t^j. Given the wage, firm j chooses its labor demand to maximize its profit $\bar{P}$:

$$\bar{P}(K_t^j, A_t^j, w_t^j) = \max_{L_t^j} A_t^j F(K_t^j, L_t^j) - w_t^j L_t^j. \tag{2}$$

Each young firm invests I_t^j units of output goods, which become as many units of capital the following period: $K_{t+1}^j = I_t^j$. Capital cannot be redeployed once productivity shocks are realized—in effect, it is specific to a type of firm (and depreciates fully each period as in Bernanke and Gertler 1989).[4]

The firm chooses investment to maximize its present value, which is computed using the pricing kernel ξ_{t+1}:[5]

$$\max_{I_t^j} E_t\Big[\xi_{t+1}\bar{P}(I_t^j, A_{t+1}^j, w_{t+1}^j)\Big] - I_t^j. \tag{3}$$

Each young firm j issues shares in supply θ^j, which we normalize to $\theta^j = 1$. These shares represent a claim to the firm's profit $\bar{P}_{t+1}^j$ next period, $t+1$. The shares are issued at a price of $P_t^j = E_t[\xi_{t+1}\bar{P}(I_t^j, A_{t+1}^j, w_{t+1}^j)]$. (Note that we use the notation P_t^j for the price of a young firm at time t and $\bar{P}_{t+1}^j$ for the price of the same firm when old.) The firm uses the proceeds from the sale to invest the I_t^j units of capital. The balance $P_t^j - I_t^j$ (which we show to always be nonnegative) represents a profit to the initial owners of the technology.

Each time period, young agents are born who live two periods. Hence, at any time, the economy is populated by young and old agents. Agents differ in their risk aversion; in particular, a agents have a high risk aversion, γ^a, while b agents have a lower risk aversion, γ^b.

All agents are endowed with a fixed number of units of labor for each technology and part of the technology for new firms. Specifically, a young agent (or "family") of type $n \in \{a, b\}$ inelastically supplies η^n units of labor to each type of firm, where the total supply of labor is normalized to one, $\eta^a + \eta^b = 1$, and owns a fraction ω^n of each of the young firms. At time t, a young agent $n \in \{a, b\}$ therefore has a wealth W_t^n that is the sum of his labor income and the value of his endowment in technologies,

$$W_t^n = \sum_j w_t^j \eta^n + \sum_j (P_t^j - I_t^j)\omega^n. \tag{4}$$

Agents have access to a linear (risk-free) saving technology with net rate of return r^f and choose how many shares θ to buy in each young firm. Depending on an agent's portfolio choice, his wealth evolves according to

$$W_{t+1} = W_t(1 + r^f) + \theta^\top\left[\bar{P}_{t+1} - P_t(1 + r^f)\right]. \tag{5}$$

Shares in asset j are subject to a haircut or margin requirement m_t^j, which limits the amount that can be borrowed using one share of asset j as a collateral to $P^j(1 - m_t^j)$. We can think of haircuts/margin requirements as exogenous or as set as in Geanakoplos (2003). Hence, each agent must use capital to buy assets and is subject to the margin requirement

$$\sum_j m_t^j |\theta^j| P_t^j \leq W_t^n. \tag{6}$$

The agents derive utility from consumption when old and seek to maximize their expected quadratic utility:[6]

$$\max_\theta E_t(W_{t+1}) - \frac{\gamma^n}{2}\mathrm{Var}_t(W_{t+1}). \tag{7}$$

An equilibrium is a collection of processes for wages w_t, investments I_t, stock prices P_t, and pricing kernels ξ_t so that markets clear.

A. *Haircuts, Credit Supply, and the Required Return*

To solve for the equilibrium, we first take the firms' investments as given and solve for the agents' optimal portfolio choice and the equilibrium required return. Agent n's portfolio choice problem can be stated as

$$\max_\theta W_t(1+r^f) + \theta^\top \left[E_t(\bar{P}_{t+1}) - P_t(1+r^f)\right] - \frac{\gamma^n}{2}\theta^\top \Sigma_t \theta, \tag{8}$$

where the variance-covariance matrix $\Sigma_t = \mathrm{Var}_t(\bar{P}_{t+1})$ is invertible in equilibrium (as shown by eq. [26] below). The first-order condition is

$$0 = E_t(\bar{P}_{t+1}) - P_t(1+r^f) - \gamma^n \Sigma_t \theta - \psi_t^n D(m_t) P_t, \tag{9}$$

where ψ_t^n is a Lagrange multiplier for the margin constraint,[7] and $D(\cdot)$ makes a vector into a diagonal matrix.[8]

Hence, the optimal portfolio is

$$\theta_t^n = \frac{1}{\gamma^n}\Sigma_t^{-1}[E_t(\bar{P}_{t+1}) - P_t(1+r^f) - \psi_t^n D(m_t) P_t]. \tag{10}$$

We assume that we are in the natural case in which the risk-averse agent is unleveraged and therefore has a zero Lagrange multiplier; that is, $\psi^a = 0$. (This outcome arises naturally with endogenous interest rates; see Gârleanu and Pedersen [forthcoming].) Let $\psi = \psi^b$. The market-clearing condition, namely

$$\bar{\theta} = \theta_t^a + \theta_t^b, \tag{11}$$

then implies that

$$\bar{\theta} = \frac{1}{\gamma}\Sigma_t^{-1}\left[E_t(\bar{P}_{t+1}) - P_t(1+r^f)\right] - \psi_t \frac{1}{\gamma^b}\Sigma_t^{-1}D(m_t)P_t, \tag{12}$$

where we use the notation γ as the representative agent's risk aversion,

$$\frac{1}{\gamma} = \frac{1}{\gamma^a} + \frac{1}{\gamma^b}. \tag{13}$$

Letting $x = \gamma/\gamma^b$, these calculations yield the equilibrium price

$$P_t = D(1 + r^f + \psi_t x m_t)^{-1}\left[E_t(\bar{P}_{t+1}) - \gamma\Sigma\bar{\theta}\right]. \tag{14}$$

Prices can be translated into returns $r_{t+1}^j = \bar{P}_{t+1}^j/P_t^j - 1$, giving rise to a modified capital asset pricing model (CAPM). To state such a result, we let $r_{t+1}^{\text{mkt}} = q_t^\top r_{t+1}$ be the market return, where $q_t^i = (\sum_j \theta^j P_t^j)^{-1}\theta^i P_t^i$ is the market capitalization weight of asset i, and define the market beta in the usual way; that is, $\beta_t^j = \text{Cov}_t(r_{t+1}^j, r_{t+1}^{\text{mkt}})/\,\text{Var}_t(r_{t+1}^{\text{mkt}})$.

Proposition 1 (Margin CAPM). The required return on security j depends on its market beta and its margin requirement:

$$E_t(r_{t+1}^j) - r^f = \lambda_t\beta_t^j + m_t^j\psi_t x, \tag{15}$$

where the market risk premium is $\lambda_t = E_t(r_{t+1}^{\text{mkt}}) - r^f - (\sum_j m_t^j q_t^j)\psi_t x$, m_t^j is the margin requirement on asset j, and ψ_t is the shadow cost of agent b's margin constraint.

The positive relation between the required return and beta is a central principle in finance (called the security market line). With margin constraints, the required return also depends on the margin requirement when constraints are binding, since the risk-tolerant agents cannot hold as many securities as they would otherwise. It is important to note that the effect of the constraint differs in the cross section of assets: assets that have high haircuts/margins use a lot of the investors' capital and, therefore, are associated with higher required returns.

Figure 1 illustrates graphically the dependence of the required return on haircuts (the "haircut-return line") when the constraint is slack, as well as when it binds. In the former case, the haircut levels do not affect the required returns, but when the constraint binds, that is, during crises, the required return increases with the haircut.

In the following sections, we consider a number of other economic properties of the model solved with the same parameters as those this figure is based on. The parameters are as follows. All firms have production

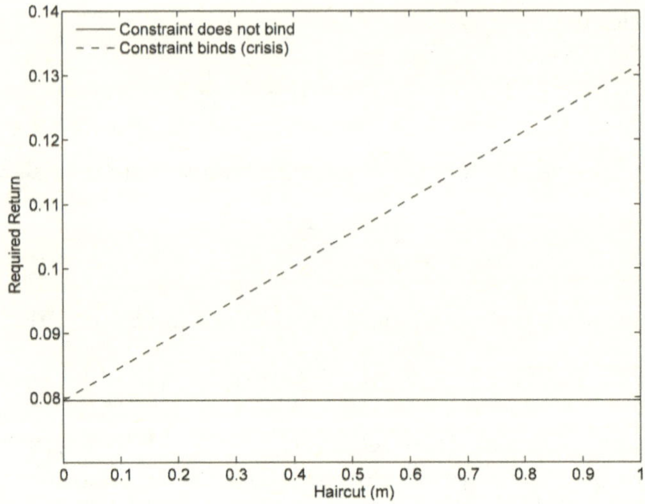

Fig. 1. Required return increases in the margin requirement (or haircut)

function parameters $\alpha = 0.3$ and $\beta = 1 - \alpha = 0.7$, and productivity shocks are identically distributed and independent with mean $\bar{A} = 3.3$ and standard deviation 0.67. There are 40 firms with relatively low haircut levels ($m = 0.1$), and 10 more firms with evenly spaced haircuts $m \in \{0.1, 0.2, \ldots, 1\}$. We assume that the absolute risk-aversion coefficients of the two agents are $\gamma^a = 28.5$ and $\gamma^b = 1.5$. In the "crisis" state, when b is constrained, his wealth is $W^b = 7.7$, and the "noncrisis" state captures any wealth level $W^b > 8.1$. Finally, the base-case interest rate is $r^f = 0.02$.

B. *Investment, Income, and Output*

Now we turn to the firm's optimal labor choice and investment. First, when the old firm j optimizes over its labor choice L_t^j, we get the first-order condition

$$\beta A_t^j (K_t^j)^{\alpha} (L_t^j)^{\beta - 1} = w_t^j. \tag{16}$$

Given that one unit of labor is supplied inelastically, the equilibrium wage is

$$w_t^j = \beta A_t^j (K_t^j)^{\alpha}, \tag{17}$$

since it gives rise to a labor demand of $L_t^j = 1$. It is important to note that a lower capital stock K—due to a lower investment in the previous period—results in lower wages, a phenomenon that plays an important role in the later analysis.

When young, the firm chooses its optimal investment I_{t-1}^j in a competitive environment and hence takes the wage at time t as given. Hence, to solve the young firm's investment problem at time $t-1$, consider first the optimal labor choice when the firm arrives at time t with a capital of I_{t-1}^j, while wages are set based on capital at time K_t^j (due to the "other" firms of this type, so not necessarily equal to investment, although $I_{t-1}^j = K_t^j$ in equilibrium):

$$L_t^j = \left[\frac{\beta A_t^j (I_{t-1}^j)^\alpha}{w_t^j}\right]^{1/(1-\beta)} \tag{18}$$

$$= \left[\frac{\beta A_t^j (I_{t-1}^j)^\alpha}{\beta A_t^j (K_t^j)^\alpha}\right]^{1/(1-\beta)} \tag{19}$$

$$= (I_{t-1}^j)^{\alpha/(1-\beta)} (K_t^j)^{-[\alpha/(1-\beta)]}. \tag{20}$$

Equation (16) shows that the profit is a fraction $1-\beta$ of the output (due to the Cobb-Douglas production function), so the profit is

$$(1-\beta)A_t^j (I_{t-1}^j)^\alpha (L_t^j)^\beta = (1-\beta)A_t^j (I_{t-1}^j)^{\alpha/(1-\beta)} (K_t^j)^{-[\alpha\beta/(1-\beta)]}, \tag{21}$$

which gives the young firm's investment problem as

$$\max_{I_t^j} \left\{(1-\beta) E_t\left[\xi_{t+1} \bar{A}_{t+1}^j (I_t^j)^{\alpha_j/(1-\beta)} (K_{t+1}^j)^{-\alpha_j\beta/(1-\beta)}\right] - I_t^j\right\}. \tag{22}$$

The maximum value attained by equation (22) is $P_t^j - I_t^j$. The first-order condition is

$$\frac{\alpha_j}{1-\beta}(1-\beta) E_t\left[\xi_{t+1} A_{t+1}^j (I_t^j)^{\alpha_j/(1-\beta)-1} (K_{t+1}^j)^{-\alpha_j\beta/(1-\beta)}\right] = 1, \tag{23}$$

which implies

$$P_t^j = \frac{1-\beta}{\alpha_i} I_t^j \; I_t^j. \tag{24}$$

A direct implication of equation (24) is that the firm's initial value (before the shares are issued) is nonnegative.

Investment decisions determine profits (i.e., the value of old firms), whose moments can be calculated explicitly given that $\bar{P}^j_{t+1} = (1-\beta)A^j_{t+1}(I^j_t)^\alpha$:

$$E_t(\bar{P}^j_{t+1}) = (1-\beta)\bar{A}^j(I^j_t)^\alpha, \tag{25}$$

$$\Sigma_t = (1-\beta)^2 D(I^\alpha_t)\Sigma_A D(I^\alpha_t). \tag{26}$$

In turn, these moments determine the required return as discussed in Section I.A. Hence, combining equations (25) and (26) with (14) gives the equation that determines investment:

$$(1 + r^f + \psi_t x m_t)\frac{1}{\alpha} = D(I^{\alpha-1}_t)E_t(A_{t+1}) - \gamma(1-\beta)D(I^{\alpha-1}_t)\Sigma_A I^\alpha_t. \tag{27}$$

To see the intuition behind this formula, consider as an example the case when productivity shocks are independent across firms and $\alpha = 1/2$. Under these assumptions,

$$(I^j_t)^{1/2} = \frac{\frac{1}{2}E_t(A^j_{t+1})}{1 + r^f + \gamma\frac{1-\beta}{2}\mathrm{Var}_t(A^j_{t+1}) + \psi_t x m^j_t}. \tag{28}$$

Naturally, investment increases with the expected productivity $E_t(A^j_{t+1})$ and decreases with productivity risk $\mathrm{Var}_t(A^j_{t+1})$. Further, investment decreases when the required return is elevated by ψ due to investors' binding margin constraint, especially for assets with high margin requirements m^j_t. This cross-sectional effect is illustrated in figure 2.

II. Haircuts, Business Cycles, and Monetary Policy

We now turn to the equilibrium properties of the economy and the effects of monetary policy. The model is set up to generate no business cycles in the absence of the credit frictions. However, when the margin constraints of the risk-tolerant agents become binding, required returns increase and business cycles arise.

Proposition 2 (Margin Constraint Accelerator). Absent margin constraints, output is independent over time. With margin constraints, output, income, investment, consumption, wages, and required returns are correlated over time, due to the propagation of a productivity shock sufficiently severe to make the risk-tolerant investors' margin requirement bind.

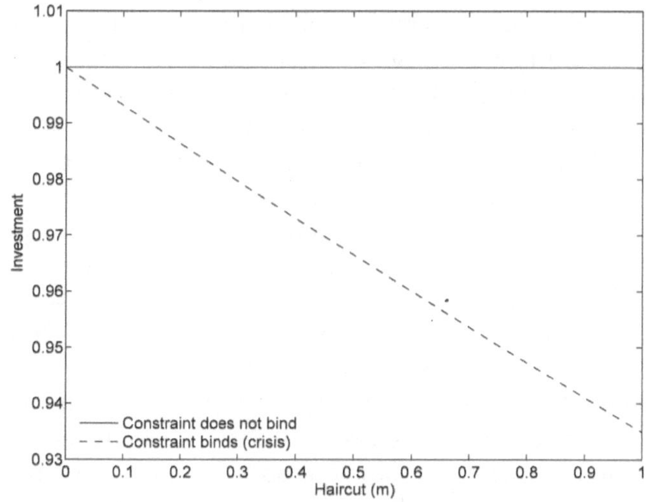

Fig. 2. Less real investment in high-haircut sectors when constraints bind

Margin-constraint-driven business cycles are propagated through the persistent effect on the wealth of the risk-tolerant agents. The basic mechanism is that binding constraints raise the required return, reducing real investment, which reduces the following period's expected output and income, which in turn makes the financing constraint harder to satisfy, and so on. As seen in figure 3, lower real investment reduces labor

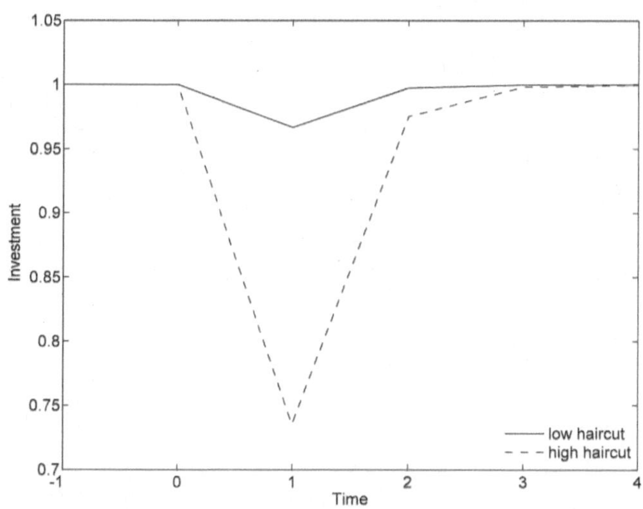

Fig. 3. Real investment following a shock that makes margin requirements bind

income and the value of technologies, leading to lower real investment in the future, until the risk-tolerant agents are recapitalized.

Next, we consider the effect of a reduction in interest rates. While, in New Keyensian models, monetary policy acts through a reduction in the nominal interest rate, which in turn reduces the real rate because of sticky prices, we take a shortcut and consider the effect of reducing the real rate directly. To concentrate on the margin constraint as the only channel through which different assets interact, we assume throughout this section that productivity shocks are independent in the cross section and that the constraint is binding at time t. In the interest of simplicity, we also make the usual assumption $\alpha + \beta = 1$.

Proposition 3 (Interest Rate Cuts). If type a agents are sufficiently risk averse, then a cut in the current interest rate increases the shadow cost of capital ψ_t, increases the required return of high-haircut assets, and lowers the real investment in high-haircut assets. More precisely, there exists a cutoff $\bar{m}_t$ with $\min_i m_t^i < \bar{m}_t < \max m_t^i$ such that the required return on asset i increases and the real investment I^i decreases if and only if $m_t^i > \bar{m}_t$.[9]

The effect of an interest rate cut is illustrated in figure 4. A reduction in the interest rate lowers the required return for assets with low haircuts, but it increases the required return for high-haircut assets. This outcome obtains because risk-tolerant investors' desire for leverage increases with the lower interest rate, elevating the shadow cost of capital. The higher

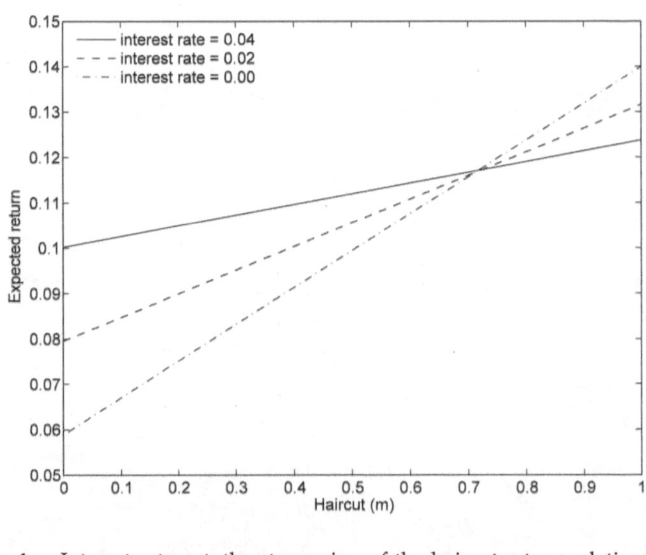

Fig. 4. Interest rate cut: the steepening of the haircut-return relationship

shadow cost of capital increases the required return, and this effect overwhelms the direct effect of the interest rate cut for high-haircut assets. As a result, the real investment and output decrease in high-margin sectors.

Hence, to increase investment and output in illiquid (i.e., high-haircut) sectors, a central bank needs to either move them down the haircut-return curve or flatten the entire curve. Said differently, it needs to either (*a*) target these assets to make them more liquid, or (*b*) improve the overall liquidity of the system:

Proposition 4 (Haircut Cuts). (*a*) If the margin requirement on asset *j* is reduced, then the required return for that asset decreases, and real investment in the asset increases. The real investments in the other assets either all increase or all decrease. (*b*) The required returns decrease, and real investments increase for all assets if m_t^j is decreased sufficiently or if the haircuts on sufficiently many assets are decreased by a given fraction.

Figure 5 illustrates the statement of this proposition. The margin constraint on one of the assets is reduced from $m^j = 0.7$ to $m^j = 0.5$, which has two effects. First, if asset *j* is infinitesimal, aggregate quantities remain the same, but the required return on asset *j* decreases (and investment increases) as it is moved down the haircut-return curve. Second, the reduction in haircut relaxes—this is the typical outcome, although the converse is theoretically possible—the margin constraint of agent *b*, that is, reduces his shadow cost of capital ψ, which flattens the haircut-return

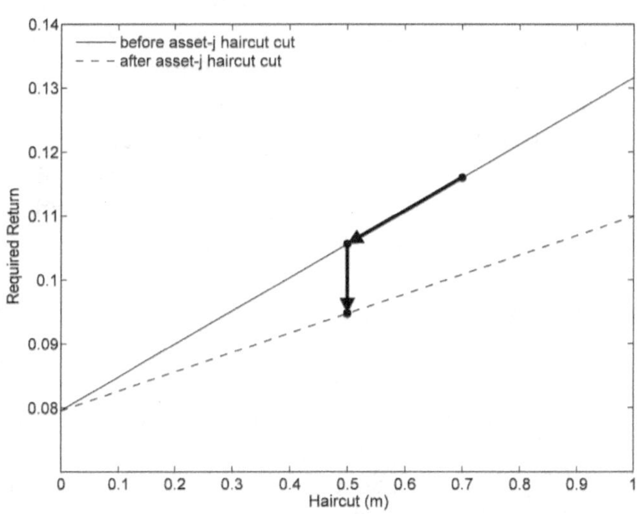

Fig. 5. Haircut cut for one asset

line, further reducing the required return for asset j as well as that of other assets.

Proposition 4 is the central result that underlies our empirical tests. In the next section, we find that the haircut-return curve indeed flattens when the central bank lending facilities are announced, which is consistent with part *b*, and that a security's yield responds to news about its central bank provided haircut, consistent with part *a*.

It is worth discussing why the central bank can provide loans at lower haircuts than otherwise available in the market. This assumed ability rests on two premises. First, the central bank is special in that it does not have a margin constraint—in contrast, it has a unique access to money that it can lend during crises. Second, while haircuts must be large enough to protect lenders from credit risk, the funding markets can be broken so badly in crises—with market haircuts rising as high as 100%—and, therefore, the central bank can offer lower haircuts while taking little credit risk.

Just as is the case with productivity shocks covered by proposition 2, the effects of policy intervention are persistent. For instance, reductions in the interest rate or in haircuts change the real investment and therefore future labor income and investment. Indeed, lowering haircuts sufficiently or for sufficiently many assets increases output in both the current and future time periods. These dynamic effects follow intuitively from the previous propositions, so let us instead end this section by considering the effects of capital injections in the institutions whose investment ability is constrained by margin requirements, or purchases of assets in sectors in which the government wants to promote real investment.

Proposition 5 (Capital Injection and Asset Purchases). (*a*) If agent *b*'s wealth is increased, required returns go down, and real investment increases for all assets. (*b*) If the government buys shares in asset i, then the real investment in that asset increases, and the investments in all other assets all either increase or decrease. If the government purchase is sufficiently large, then all real investments increase.

III. Haircuts and Prices: The Effect of TALF

Our theory suggests that the ability to borrow against securities plays an important role in liquidity crises and their resolution. Consistent with this implication, central banks around the world created a number of lending facilities to provide collateralized loans at lower haircuts than otherwise available during a crisis (but often higher than the market-provided haircut during good times).

The main lending facility in the United States is the Federal Reserve's Discount Window, which is available only to banks with reserve accounts. The discount window can be used to supply liquidity to banks in times of stress, enabling them to increase lending to the rest of the economy. However, during the crisis of 2007–9, banks' own balance sheet problems impaired this transmission mechanism, and therefore the Fed introduced additional lending facilities, including, for the first time ever, facilities that were available more broadly to nonbanks. The TALF is a good example: it was put in place in 2008 to provide loans against asset-backed securities (ABS) at a haircut, available to any U.S. company or investment fund. The program was motivated by the credit-supply frictions that we model:

> New issuance of ABS declined precipitously in September and came to a halt in October. At the same time, interest rate spreads on AAA-rated tranches of ABS soared to levels well outside the range of historical experience, reflecting unusually high risk premiums. The ABS markets historically have funded a substantial share of consumer credit and SBA-guaranteed small business loans. Continued disruption of these markets could significantly limit the availability of credit to households and small businesses and thereby contribute to further weakening of U.S. economic activity. The TALF is designed to increase credit availability and support economic activity by facilitating renewed issuance of consumer and small business ABS at more normal interest rate spreads. (Board of Governors of the Federal Reserve System, press release, November 25, 2008)

The original TALF was directed at lowering the haircut only on newly issued securities, because these securities are related to the new loans provided to the real sector of the economy. This makes it difficult to assess the price effect of the program since these yet-to-be-issued securities were naturally not traded when the program was announced.

TALF was later extended to legacy securities, that is, securities that had been issued before 2009. The extension of TALF to legacy securities sought to reduce the liquidity discount for these securities, improving the balance sheet of financial institutions that held them, and to lower the opportunity cost of making new loans. In the language of our model, the new-issue TALF sought to move newly issued securities down the haircut-return curve, while the legacy TALF sought to flatten the curve itself (proposition 4). We next describe the events surrounding the introduction of the legacy TALF, and then we test empirically its effect.

A. *The Introduction of the Legacy TALF*

The first indication that the Federal Reserve would attempt to support the legacy CMBS market was made in a joint announcement by the Federal Reserve and Treasury on March 19, 2009, suggesting that legacy CMBS with a current AAA rating and legacy RMBS (residential mortgage-backed securities) with an original AAA credit rating were being studied for inclusion in the TALF program. The new-issue TALF program had its first subscription on the same date and provided investors with term nonrecourse leverage against eligible collateral in order to stabilize funding for nonbanks that relied on the term ABS market. The U.S. Treasury also announced details around the securities public-private investment program (PPIP), where the taxpayer would take an equity stake in a joint venture with selected asset managers in order to purchase legacy securities. As illustrated in figure 6, CMBS prices rallied significantly across the capital structure, consistent with a flattening of the haircut return curve (proposition 4). The vertical lines in the graph correspond to this key date as well as four others, summarized below the graph.

On May 19, 2009, the Federal Reserve Bank of New York confirmed that the legacy TALF program would move forward for CMBS and released preliminary terms. In particular, eligible collateral was limited

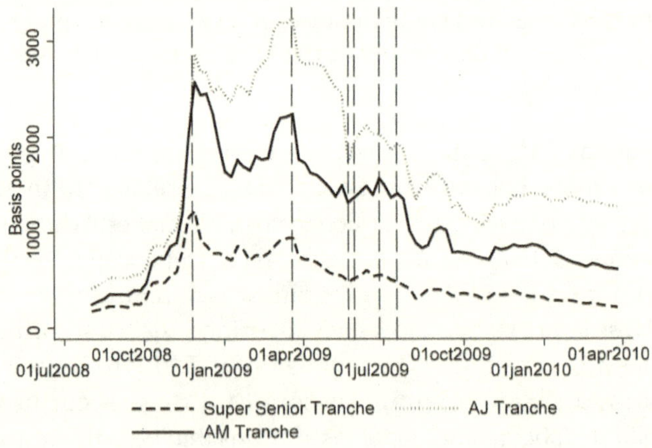

Fig. 6. The yield spread on super senior CMBS bonds, riskier mezzanine AM bonds, and even more junior AJ bonds. The vertical lines represent the key announcement dates, as follows: 11/25/2008, initial TALF for ABS, suggesting possible expansion for CMBS; 3/19/2009, Legacy securities will be part of TALF; 5/19/2009, super senior legacy fixed rate conduit CMBS eligible for TALF; 5/26/2009, S&P considers methodology change for fixed rate conduit CMBS; 6/26/2009, S&P implements new methodology; 7/16/2009, first subscription for legacy TALF.

to super senior fixed-rate conduit CMBS bonds with a AAA credit rating from at least two rating agencies and no lower rating. Despite the fact that the program did not make junior AAA bonds eligible collateral, figure 6 illustrates that spreads for all original AAA bonds continued their rally following the announcement. This broad effect is consistent with the TALF lowering the shadow cost of capital (ψ in our model) by relieving financial institutions' capital constraints as intended by the Fed.

On May 26, 2009, however, S&P released a Request for Comment on proposed changes to their rating criteria for fixed-rate conduits. In the release, the rating agency suggested that these changes would put not only junior AAA-rated bonds on negative downgrade watch, but also a significant fraction of super senior bonds just made eligible for the TALF program. While the statement contained no new information about the credit risk of the bonds (it was simply a change in ratings methodology), AAA CMBS spreads retreated broadly following the announcement, since such a rating action would make the bonds ineligible for TALF. Research groups affiliated with CMBS dealers complained in their weekly reports about the action and encouraged the Federal Reserve Bank of New York to drop S&P as a rating agency for the program.

On June 26, 2009, the rating agency went forward with its proposed changes to criteria and put much of the fixed-rate conduit universe on rating watch negative. Over 90% of junior AAA bonds were placed on watch, and more than 20% of super senior bonds were also placed on watch.

One week later, on July 2, the Federal Reserve announced the final program details for the legacy program, which had its first subscription on July 16, 2009. These details clarified that investors would have to have acquired the bond in an arm's-length transaction in the 30 days before the subscription date, a requirement meant to facilitate price discovery. In addition to a standard 3-year TALF loan maturity, the program permitted investors to take out a 5-year loan, which was better suited to the longer dated CMBS collateral. However, the loans came with a carry cap that limited the amount of income that an investor could receive immediately to ensure that the Federal Reserve was paid in full before investors received one dollar of upside.

B. *Price Sensitivity to Haircuts: New Survey Evidence*

Figure 6 already provides suggestive evidence on the effect of TALF on market prices, but we need a more rigorous approach to answering the central questions of whether TALF caused yields to narrow and, if so, by how much. We first examine unique survey data on these specific questions, and next examine market prices.

In March 2009, a survey was conducted among market participants, including both investors and dealers, about how they would value term nonrecourse collateralized loans provided for the purchase of certain CMBS securities. The respondents indicated that lowering haircuts could have a large effect on price and liquidity in the CMBS market. The price effect could be driven by both the value of access to capital, consistent with our model, and the participants' option to walk away from the loan. Since we are interested in the value of access to capital, we focus on the safest securities, which, according to our estimates, had very small risk on a hold-to-maturity basis.

These CMBS bonds are securities backed by a pool of commercial real estate loans. The cash flows from the securities are split into various tranches. We focus on the most senior tranches, those that have priority in case there is not enough money to pay all the tranches. In particular, we focus on the tranches that were rated AAA. Even within the AAA securities, there are differences in seniority, however. The most senior ones—the so-called super senior ones—are called A1, A2, A3, A4, A5, and A1A; the next most senior are called AM (mezzanine within those originally rated AAA, but relatively senior more broadly); and the least senior ones are called AJ (junior within AAA). The A1 and A2 receive cash flows earlier than A3, A4, and A5, but have the same seniority, while A1A receive payments from a different part of the pool as explained in more detail in appendix A.

1. Losses in Stress Scenarios

Market participants were asked about their expectations for credit loss in both a "base case" and "stress scenario," each defined by the respondent. Figure 7 shows the distribution of the participants' stress losses for each pool, illustrated using a box plot. The top of each box is the 75th percentile, the bottom of the box is the 25th percentile, the middle line is the median, and the largest and smallest observations are indicated with whiskers.

The figure shows that the median market participants generally thought that pool stress losses would be around 20%, and less than 10% for the MLMT pool. These overall pool stress loses are small enough that the super senior CMBS bonds would avoid any losses. Indeed, for the super senior bonds to incur losses, each pool must lose more than 30% of its value, except the 2004 MLMT pool, which was only subordinated at a 20% rate. (Given that these loans often have recoveries of at least 50%, a 30% loss requires that more than 60% of the pool ultimately default.) Focusing on the most pessimistic market participants, only super senior bonds from the 2007 vintage seemed vulnerable to loss.

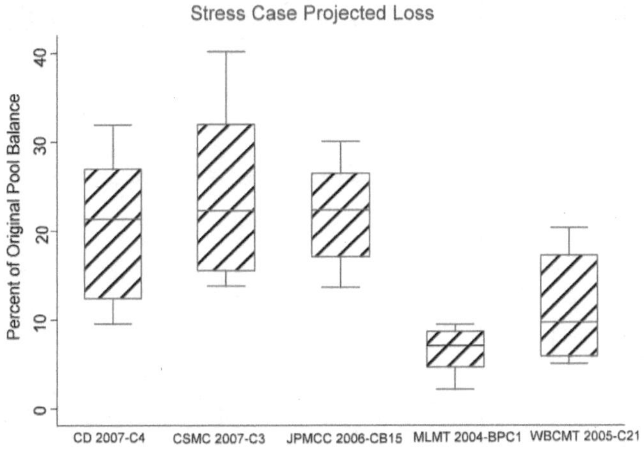

Fig. 7. Distribution of survey responses regarding the potential stress loss of each CMBS pool. In this box plot, the top of each box is the 75% percentile, the bottom of the box is the 25% percentile, the middle line is the median, and the largest and smallest observations are indicated with whiskers.

(However, the figure also illustrates that several of the AJ and AM bonds were at risk of loss in a stress scenario.)

2. Prices and Haircuts

The key part of the survey asked market participants the amount they would bid for the bond without a Fed facility (their "cash bid"), the amount they would bid under a number of alternative financing arrangements, and their guess at the seller's ask price. In particular, the possible financing arrangements in the survey were Fed-provided collateralized loans with either a low or a high haircut (15% and 25% for super senior bonds; 33% and 50% for other bonds) using a loan rate of swaps plus 100 basis points, and loan maturity of 3 years, of 5 years, or matching the maturity of the bond.

Table 1 details the mean survey responses for each bond, and our main finding is illustrated more simply in figures 8–11. In particular, figure 8 shows the price of the super senior (A4) bonds. The x-axis has three different haircut options, from low to high: the low haircut proposed in the survey, the high haircut in the survey, and the case of no TALF program (i.e., the market-provided haircut, which is higher than the high survey haircut, often 100% at that time, meaning that the collateral was not accepted, certainly at those maturities). For simplicity, we normalize the prices by dividing by the no-TALF price (i.e., the cash bid). This is

Table 1
Mean Survey Response across Participants for Each Security in the Survey

Deal	Issue Date	Class	Ask Price	Cash Bid	3-Year Loan High Haircut	3-Year Loan Low Haircut	5-Year Loan High Haircut	5-Year Loan Low Haircut	Maturity-Matched Loan High Haircut	Maturity-Matched Loan Low Haircut
JPMCC 2006-CB15	6/1/2006	A-4	61.97	56.96	62.75	70.84	74.43	82.23	84.79	92.51
		AM	42.14	33.69	34.12	45.39	37.97	51.12	49.18	63.04
		AJ	25.07	21.03	24.72	30.40	27.32	39.12	31.44	44.79
WBCMT 2005-C21	10/1/2005	APB	86.33	84.81	88.60	92.14	88.51	93.14	90.55	95.15
		A-4	76.48	73.58	72.00	77.09	80.81	85.95	86.57	92.51
		AM	54.10	46.41	46.04	52.61	51.53	59.41	63.62	72.05
		AJ	40.42	34.82	33.94	43.31	38.06	48.33	47.27	60.42
CSMC 2007-C3	6/1/2007	A-2	77.45	73.83	84.57	89.40	85.35	90.08	88.04	92.56
		A-4	58.39	52.94	59.31	66.79	69.71	76.35	81.27	89.68
		AM	39.99	31.02	34.79	39.39	39.81	44.31	47.24	60.42
		AJ	22.03	17.77	22.90	28.14	26.04	31.07	29.70	43.40
CD 2007-CD4	3/1/2007	A-2B	78.75	76.63	85.30	88.56	85.55	89.11	88.52	93.32
		A-3	66.28	61.58	74.78	80.08	81.07	86.79	85.89	91.61
		A-4	62.55	57.40	62.37	68.74	70.26	75.88	80.89	88.37
		AMFX	41.47	33.20	35.03	39.81	41.37	44.94	49.38	59.05
		AJ	23.84	19.99	23.21	28.87	26.63	33.02	30.37	43.62
MLMT 2004-BPC1	11/1/2004	A-2	95.91	96.86	95.20	96.05	92.46	94.11	93.65	95.06
		A-3	84.31	84.27	87.35	90.68	86.39	89.27	88.84	92.35
		A-5	77.91	76.04	77.60	80.83	82.54	86.80	85.30	90.55
		AJ	46.23	43.56	48.27	53.47	53.21	61.47	61.81	72.33

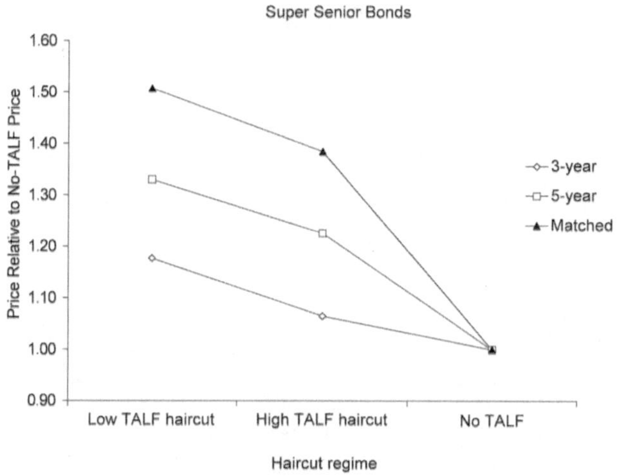

Fig. 8. The figure shows the average survey bid price of super senior CMBS A4 bonds by haircut group. The participants bid the highest price if they have access to a TALF loan with a low-haircut TALF, lower if the TALF loan has a high haircut, and lowest if they do not have access to TALF. All prices are normalized by the no-TALF price. The three lines correspond to a 3-year TALF loan, a 5-year TALF loan, or a maturity-matched TALF loan (longest).

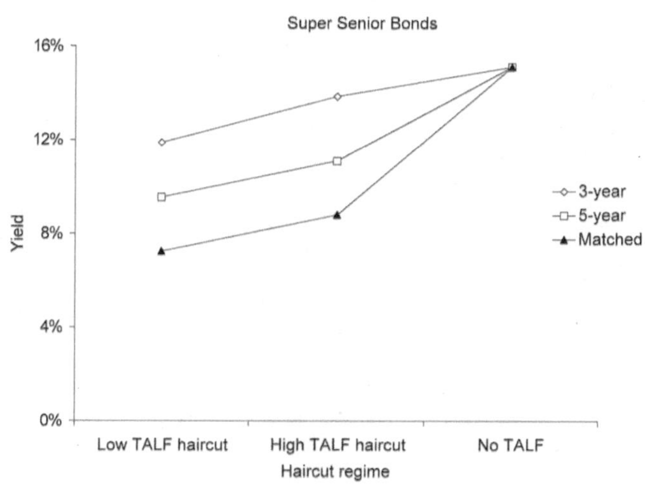

Fig. 9. The figure shows the annual yields corresponding to the average survey bid price of super senior CMBS A4 bonds by haircut group. The yield (i.e., the required return) is lowest with a TALF loan with a low-haircut TALF, higher if the TALF loan has a high haircut, and highest if there is no TALF. The three lines correspond to a 3-year TALF loan, a 5-year TALF loan, or a maturity-matched TALF loan (longest).

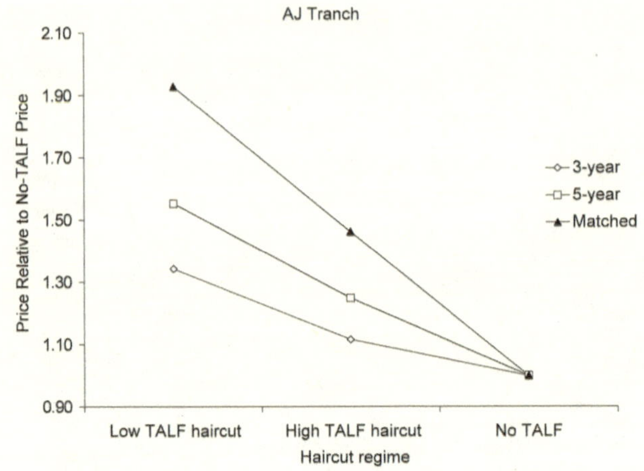

Fig. 10. The figure shows the average survey bid price of CMBS AJ bonds by haircut group. The participants bid the highest price if they have access to a TALF loan with a low-haircut TALF, lower if the TALF loan has a high haircut, and lowest if they do not have access to TALF. All prices are normalized by the no-TALF price. The three lines correspond to a 3-year TALF loan, a 5-year TALF loan, or a maturity-matched TALF loan (longest).

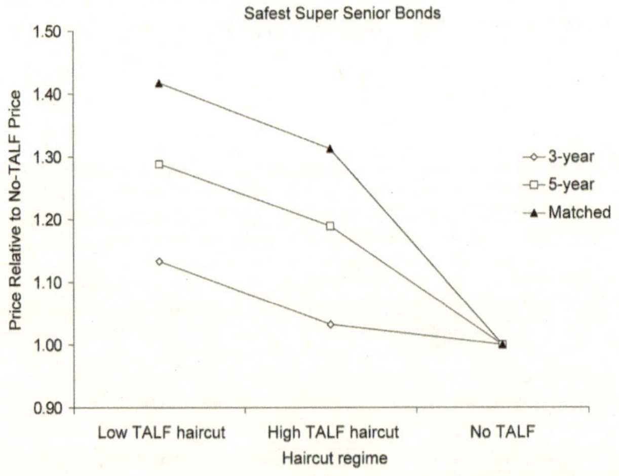

Fig. 11. The figure shows the average survey bid price of the safest super senior CMBS A4 bonds by haircut group. The participants bid the highest price if they have access to a TALF loan with a low-haircut TALF, lower if the TALF loan has a high haircut, and lowest if they do not have access to TALF. All prices are normalized by the no-TALF price. The three lines correspond to a 3-year TALF loan, a 5-year TALF loan, or a maturity-matched TALF loan (longest).

illustrated for 3-year loans, 5-year loans, and maturity-matched loans (approximately 10-year loans).

We see that lower haircuts are associated with substantially higher prices, and, the longer the loan, the larger the effect. With a 3-year loan with a high haircut, respondents say they are willing to pay 6% more for these securities. If the haircut is lowered, their bid increases to 18% over their cash bid, a strikingly large effect. If the loan is extended to 5 years, the price premium increases to 33%, and a maturity-matched loan has a 51% premium. This strong price sensitivity to the maturity of the loan is consistent with a fear of having to refinance the collateral in a bad market, which was expressed by the investors in follow-up discussions.

These prices can also be expressed in terms of annualized yield to maturity as we do in figure 9. The average yield of these bonds was around 15% at the time of the survey (about 12% above the swap rate at that maturity). Having access to a 5-year term loan lowers the yield to 11% with a high haircut, and to 9.5% at a low haircut. To put these numbers in perspective, recall that during the crisis, the Fed lowered the Fed funds rate from 5.25% in early 2007 all the way to the zero lower bound (0%–0.25%). If the TALF could lower the yields by several percentage points as our survey suggests, then it is a powerful tool.

Figure 10 shows that the effect of access to leverage is much stronger on the lower priced AJ bonds. In some extreme cases, the bid price more than doubles with the TALF program, relative to the bid price without it. This stronger effect could be due to the fact that these bonds were even more difficult to finance in the market, or because of the value of walking away from the loan.

To really focus on the shadow value of capital, figure 11 plots the results for only the safest super senior bonds, namely those that were significantly overcollateralized, even beyond the most pessimistic respondent's stress scenario. Taking the responses at face value, this means that any losses on these bonds would be unlikely, and in the unlikely event of a loss, recovery rates would likely be high.

We see that the price effect of lowering haircuts is large even in the case of the safest super senior bonds, consistent with the program relieving a binding margin requirement for financial institutions. This interpretation is consistent with follow-up discussions with market participants in which they described their methodologies. The typical firm used discount rates over 20% even for risk-free cash flows that had to be completely funded with the firm's own capital. Finally, table 1 also shows that survey-based ask prices were significantly above cash bid prices, illustrating market illiquidity.

C. *Do Haircuts Affect Market Prices?*

Having established a strong link between haircuts and prices in survey data, we next consider how market prices reacted to the program. As discussed above, yields narrowed significantly around the introduction of the program, but many other events occurred at the same time. Hence, to assess the causality of haircuts on market prices, we apply a finer statistical tool. Specifically, we consider the market response to news that a bond is rejected from use in the TALF program.

This strategy is based on the fact that TALF was available only for AAA-rated super senior bonds accepted by the Fed after a review of the credit risk of the loan. When a bond was rejected, it would not benefit from the program's low haircuts, and, therefore, our model predicts that its yield should rise by an amount that is increasing in the shadow cost of capital.

We note that the Fed's decision is unlikely to have conveyed private information about the bonds. While the Fed employed outside vendors with expertise in commercial real estate, the risk assessment process used only information available from publicly available prices, offering documents, and servicing reports.

The decision to reject bonds was nevertheless news to the market, as market participants were generally confounded by which bonds were rejected. For example, investment bank research that discussed the efficacy of the risk assessment procedures denoted the process as a "black box" and, following the November 2009 subscription, Citi wrote, "So once again we come up short in trying to understand the Fed's rejection process" (Berenbaum, Gaon, and Mather 2009, 3).

To assess the impact of TALF eligibility, we run the following regression using weekly data on yield spreads of approximately 1,600 super senior fixed-rate conduit bonds from August 2008 through March 2010, with standard errors corrected for heteroskedasticity and clustered at the security level:

$$\Delta \text{spread}_{j,t} = \sum_{k=0}^{4} c_k^r 1(\text{reject})_{j,t-k} + \sum_{k=0}^{4} c_k^a 1(\text{accept})_{j,t-k} + \sum_{k=1}^{4} c_k^\Delta \Delta \text{spread}_{j,t-k} + fe_{j,t} + \varepsilon_{j,t}. \tag{29}$$

The dependent variable is each bond j's change in yield spread during week t, the c's are regression coefficients, and the explanatory variables are indicator functions for whether this bond was rejected during the current week or any of the previous four weeks, indicator functions for whether the bond was accepted during the same time periods, lagged yield changes, and fixed effects ($fe_{j,t}$) for each combination of week, vintage, and security class. The interpretation of the coefficients on the rejection dummies is the effect of rejection on the change in yield spread, over and above the general market yield changes for nonsubmitted bonds of that security class and vintage during that week (captured by the fixed effects), and similarly for the acceptance dummies.

Figure 12 shows the estimated response of spreads to being rejected or accepted from the TALF program. We construct this graph by setting the initial yield spread to 300 bps and then tracing the response to a TALF decision by iterating equation (29) using the estimated coefficients. The initial response to a rejection is a statistically significant rise in the yield spread by over 20 bps, and this effect is reduced to 3 bps over time. The larger initial effect could be due to price pressure associated with selling by agents who will only hold the bonds if they can get access to leverage. In contrast, the effect of TALF acceptance is only about 5 bps and appears mostly temporary. The larger effect of rejection can be explained by the fact that only a small fraction of bonds was rejected (between 1% and 10%, except in the last weeks of the program), so a rejection is more surprising.

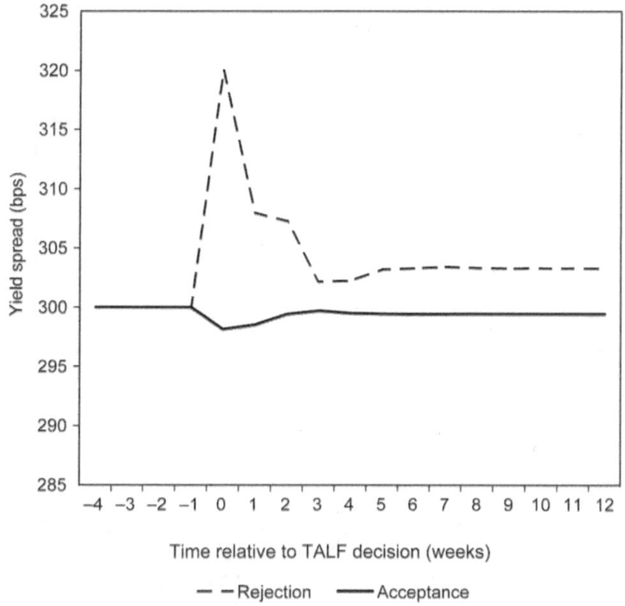

Fig. 12. The price effect of TALF rejections. This figure shows the yield-spread response of CMBS bonds that are accepted or rejected from the TALF program. The yield spread of rejected bonds rises after the decision, as these bonds will not benefit from the low haircuts provided by TALF.

The model implies that financing terms (i.e., access to low haircuts) are more important when the shadow cost of capital is high, that is, during times of binding capital constraints. To investigate this implication, figure 13 considers the effect of TALF rejections separately for the early subsample (July 2009 through September 2009) and the late subsample (October 2009 through March 2010) by estimating equation (29) separately for each period. The early period includes what appeared to be the end of the 2007–9 U.S. banking crisis, while banks and the economy were doing better in many respects during the later period (e.g., lower TED spreads, rising stock market).

Figure 13 shows that the effect of TALF rejections was much larger in the early period. During the early period, a rejection was followed by a statistically significant 80 bps increase in yield spreads, and the effect eventually went down to about 40 bps. During the later sample, the impact of a rejection was smaller and more transitory, with an immediate impact of only 15 bps. Hence, it appears that the legacy TALF program

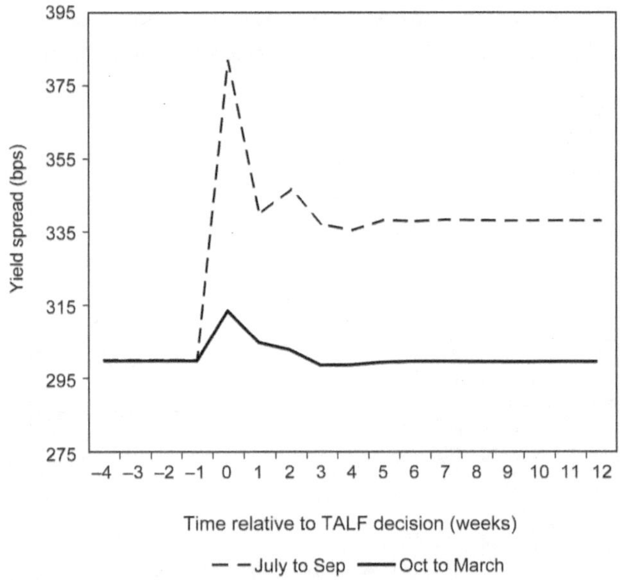

Fig. 13. The price effect of TALF rejections by subsample. This figure shows the yield-spread response of CMBS bonds that are rejected from the TALF program for, respectively, the period from July to September 2009 (the ending of the financial crisis) and from October 2009 to March 2010 (when the banking crisis was mostly over). The effect of rejections is significantly larger in the former period, consistent with the model's prediction that haircuts have a larger effect on prices when capital constraints are tight and the shadow cost of capital is high.

had a significant impact on CMBS spreads, at least for the first 3 months of the program, when capital constraints were still tight. As liquidity returned to the markets, the liquidity provided by the program became less important. The dependence of the rejection effect on liquidity provides another argument against the rejection effect being driven by information.

IV. Conclusion: Two Monetary Tools

We model how required returns increase when credit suppliers hit their margin constraints, reducing economic activity and propagating business cycles. The effect is largest for illiquid assets that are difficult to finance in a crisis, that is, assets with high haircuts.

Surprisingly, while an interest rate cut reduces the required return for liquid low-margin assets, it can increase the required return for illiquid high-margin assets. This is because the lower interest rate increases the desire for leverage and, as a result, increases the shadow cost of capital. This effect increases the required return for high-margin assets, countervailing the direct effect of the interest rate cut.

A haircut cut, however, always reduces the required return on the affected asset and stimulates real activity in that sector. This can be achieved if the central bank accepts such securities as collateral in exchange for loans. Hence, haircuts provide a second monetary policy tool in addition to the standard interest rate tool.

While haircuts can be decreased in crises by offering loans at moderate haircuts, they cannot be similarly increased in good times when credit might be excessive. Indeed, if a central bank offers collateralized loans at high haircuts, borrowers can simply get their loans elsewhere. However, in addition to the market-imposed margin constraints, financial institutions also face regulatory capital requirements that can be captured in our framework in a straightforward way.[10] Hence, to reduce business cycles, a central bank may need capital requirements in good times and lending facilities that stand ready in periods of liquidity crisis.

We examine empirically the effectiveness of the second monetary tool, studying the natural experiment of the introduction of the TALF lending facility. We find strong effects of providing collateralized loans at low haircuts. Survey evidence shows that yields on affected securities might drop as much as 5% at the height of the crisis, illustrating a significant demand sensitivity to haircuts.

We also consider the effect on actual market prices of TALF. To isolate the effect of TALF, we estimate the change in yield following the Fed's unpredictable announcement of a bond's acceptance or rejection from the program. The yield spread of rejected bonds rises significantly relative to other bonds, and the rejection effect is largest during crisis times when the shadow cost of capital is high.

This approach estimates the effect of moving certain securities down the haircut-return curve (fig. 5) by reducing their haircuts. Another important potential benefit of lending programs is that they can reduce the required compensation for tying up capital more broadly, that is, flattening the haircut-return curve (fig. 5 and proposition 4) because the program improves the funding conditions of constrained agents. Consistent with this consideration, the yields on both affected and unaffected securities went down when it was announced that legacy TALF was being considered, down when legacy TALF was confirmed, up when a rating-methodology change made TALF less applicable, and finally down when TALF was actually implemented.

The total effect of the haircut tool is thus to move securities down the haircut-return curve and to flatten the curve itself, reducing the yield on securities, which in turn improves the credit supply to the real economy. In the data, as in the model, this monetary tool appears to be effective during crises.

Appendix A

A Background on CMBS Securities

CMBS bonds are securities backed by a pool of commercial real estate loans. The cash flows from the securities are split into various tranches. We focus on the most senior tranches, those that have priority in case there is not enough money to pay all the tranches. In particular, we focus on the tranches that were originally rated AAA (and, as we will see, continued to be rated AAA for the most part). Even within the AAA securities, there are differences in seniority, however. The most senior ones—the so-called super senior ones—are called A1, A2, A3, A4, A5, and A1A; the next most senior are called AM (mezzanine within AAA, but relatively senior more broadly); and the least senior ones are called AJ (junior within AAA). The A1 and A2 receive cash flows earlier than A3 and A4, but have the same seniority, while A1A receive payments from a different part of the pool, as explained below.

The real estate loans in the pool underlying fixed-rate conduit CMBS have a fixed interest rate; a maturity of 5, 7, or 10 years; and amortization schedule over 30 years (implying a principal payment at maturity). The loan pool typically includes more than 100 loans, but the largest 10 loans can represent 40% of the overall balance. While the pool can be diversified by geography and property type, given the balloon nature of the loans there is correlated refinancing risk. The so-called super senior tranches generally had 30% subordination at issue in the most recent vintages (i.e., starting in 2005) but had as little as 20% subordination in earlier vintages. In contrast, the AM and AJ tranches, each which also had AAA ratings at issue, only had 20% and 12% subordination, respectively. These bonds have structural leverage given their subordination to the super senior class, which makes it possible for investors to incur losses of 100%.

The loan pool underlying fixed-rate conduit CMBS is often tranched into one pool of multifamily loans and another pool of all other loans. Principal payments from the multifamily loans are directed to the A1A tranche. Given the involvement of the government-sponsored enterprises in agency-sponsored multifamily CMBS issues, it should not be surprising that loans in this pool are generally adversely selected from the multifamily universe. Cash flows from other property types (office, retail, industrial, etc.) are directed to sequential-pay super senior classes, which generally included A1, A2, A3, and A4. Upon receipt, principal is first distributed to the A1 tranche until it paid in full, and then to the A2 tranche. This time tranching makes the A1 and A2 bonds have shorter average lives (5 years) and the A3 and A4 bonds longer average lives (10 years). Despite the time tranching, all of these bonds are structurally senior. In particular, if credit losses on the overall loan pool rise above 30%, the allocation of losses and principal from that point in time goes pro rata among the super senior tranches. The survey instrument focused on AAA-rated tranches from five fixed-rate conduit CMBS deals illustrated in table A1.

Table A1
Descriptive Statistics on the CMBS Securities Used in the Survey

Deal	Issue Date	Class	CUSIP	Maturity	Ave. Life	Coupon	Moody's	Fitch	S&P	Real Point	% 60+ Delinquencies	% Foreclosure	Orig. Subordination	Cur. Subordination	% Pool Loss Base	% Pool Loss Stress
JPMCC																
2006-CB15	6/1/2006	A-4	46627QBA5	6/12/2043	7.08	5.81	Aaa	AAA	NR	Perf	6.64	1.78	30.00	30.44		
		AM	46627QBC1	6/12/2043	7.23	5.86	Aaa	AAA	NR	Perf	6.64	1.78	20.00	20.30		
		AJ	46627QBD9	6/12/2043	7.24	5.89	A2	AAA	NR	Perf	6.64	1.78	12.25	12.43	10.72	21.97
WBCMT																
2005-C21	10/1/2005	APB	9297667F4	10/15/2044	2.89	5.17	Aaa	AAA	AAA	Outperf	1.36	0.00	30.00	35.14		
		A-4	9297667G2	10/15/2044	5.88	5.21	Aaa	AAA	AAA	Outperf	1.36	0.00	30.00	35.14		
		AM	9297667J6	10/15/2044	6.50	5.21	Aaa	AAA	AAA	Outperf	1.36	0.00	20.00	23.43		
		AJ	9297667K3	10/15/2044	6.56	5.21	Aaa	AAA	AAA	Outperf	1.36	0.00	13.38	15.67	4.67	11.43
CSMC																
2007-C3	6/1/2007	A-2	22544QAB5	6/15/2039	3.06	5.72	Aaa	NR	AAA	Perf	2.04	0.94	30.00	30.07		
		A-4	22544QAE9	6/15/2039	8.01	5.72	Aaa	NR	AAA	Perf	2.04	0.94	30.00	30.07		
		AM	22544QAG4	6/15/2039	8.16	5.72	Aaa	NR	AAA	Perf	2.04	0.94	20.00	20.05		
		AJ	22544QAH2	6/15/2039	8.16	5.72	A1	NR	AAA	Perf	2.04	0.94	12.50	12.53	13.47	24.24
CD																
2007-CD4	3/1/2007	A-2B	12513YAC4	12/11/2049	2.76	5.21	Aaa	AAA	AAA	Perf	3.69	3.42	30.00	30.10		
		A-3	12513YAD2	12/11/2049	4.82	5.29	Aaa	AAA	AAA	Perf	3.69	3.42	30.00	30.10		
		A-4	12513YAF7	12/11/2049	7.63	5.32	Aaa	AAA	AAA	Perf	3.69	3.42	30.00	30.10		
		AMFX	12513YAH3	12/11/2049	7.83	5.37	Aaa	AAA	AAA	Perf	3.69	3.42	20.00	20.06		
		AJ	12513YAJ9	12/11/2049	7.90	5.40	A1	AAA/*-	AAA	Perf	3.69	3.42	11.13	11.16	11.14	20.40
MLMT																
2004-BPC1	11/1/2004	A-2	59022HEU2	10/12/2041	0.46	4.07	NR	AAA	AAA	Outperf	0.44	0.00	20.00	21.00		
		A-3	59022HEV0	10/12/2041	2.47	4.47	NR	AAA	AAA	Outperf	0.44	0.00	20.00	21.00		
		A-5	59022HEX6	10/12/2041	5.40	4.86	NR	AAA	AAA	Outperf	0.44	0.00	20.00	21.00		
		AJ	59022HFT4	10/12/2041	5.57	4.92	NR	AAA	AAA	Outperf	0.44	0.00	12.38	13.00	3.16	6.58

Note: These statistics are as of the time of the survey in March 2009.

Appendix B

Proofs

Proof of Proposition 1. Given the constraint (eq. [6]), the first-order condition for the portfolio choice is

$$0 = E_t(\bar{P}_{t+1}) - P_t(1 + r^f) - \gamma^n \Sigma_t \theta - \psi_t^n D(y_t^n) D(m_t) P_t, \tag{B1}$$

where $y_t^{n,i} = 1$ if $\theta^i > 0$, $y_t^{n,i} = -1$ if $\theta^i < 0$, and $y_t^{n,i} \in [-1, 1]$ if $\theta_t^i = 0$. Under the assumption that W^a is sufficiently large, agent a is unconstrained; that is, $\psi_t^a = 0$, and equating aggregate supply and demand gives a more general version of equation (14) in the text:[11]

$$E_t[r_{t+1}] - [r^f + \psi_t x D(y_t) D(m_t)] = \gamma D(P_t)^{-1} \Sigma \bar{\theta} \tag{B2}$$

$$= \gamma P_t^{\text{mkt}} \operatorname{Cov}_t(r_{t+1}, r_{t+1}^{\text{mkt}}). \tag{B3}$$

Aggregating (B3), that is, premultiplying by $q^\top$, gives

$$E_t[r_{t+1}^{\text{mkt}} - (r^f + \psi_t x m_t^{\text{mkt}})] = \gamma P_t^{\text{mkt}} \operatorname{Var}_t(r_{t+1}^{\text{mkt}}), \tag{B4}$$

where m_t^{mkt} is the market value weighted haircut m, taking into account the sign y of the constrained agent's position:

$$m_t^{\text{mkt}} = q_t^\top D(y_t) m_t.$$

Combining (B3) and (B4) yields the result in the proposition, given that $y_t^i = 1 \; \forall \, i, t$.

Proof of Proposition 2. Let $\overline{W}^b$ denote the wealth invested by agent b in the risky assets when not constrained. If the realization of the productivity vector A_t is low enough, then $W_t^b < \overline{W}^b$; that is, agent b becomes constrained, and the investment level changes. (According to proposition 5, investment actually decreases, in all sectors, under the additional assumptions that Σ_A is diagonal and $\alpha + \beta = 1$.) Consequently, the reduced output due to the low productivity shock predicts a level of output different from the average output.

The proofs of propositions 3–5 are based on the following three equilibrium restrictions: the optimality of aggregate demand (eq. [12]), the first-order condition for agent a's demand (eq. [10]), and the binding margin constraint of agent b (eq. [6]):

$$0 = -(I_t^i)^{1-\alpha}(1 + r_t^f + \psi_t x m_t^i y_t^i) + \bar{A}^i - \gamma \Sigma_A^i (I_t^i)^\alpha \bar{\theta}^i, \tag{B5}$$

$$0 = -(I_t^i)^{1-\alpha}(1 + r_t^f) + \bar{A}^i - \gamma^a \Sigma_A^i (I_t^i)^\alpha \theta_t^{i,a}, \tag{B6}$$

$$0 = \sum_i m_t^i(\bar{\theta}^i - \theta_t^{i,a}) \frac{1-\beta}{\alpha} I_t^i - W_t^b. \tag{B7}$$

Equation (B5) is accompanied by the complementary slackness condition $(1 + y_t^i)(1 - y_t^i)\theta_t^{i,b} = 0$, in addition to the restriction $y_t^i \in [-1, 1]$. Comparing (B5) and (B6) shows that, since $\gamma^a > \gamma$, $y_t^i > 0$: otherwise $\theta_t^{i,a} < \bar{\theta}_t^i$, that is, $\theta_t^{i,b} > 0$, which means $y_t^i > 0$—this would be a contradiction. Note the implication that there is no shorting in equilibrium.

If $\theta^{i,b} > 0$ for all i, then we have a system of $J + J + 1$ equations, to be solved for the same number of unknowns, namely, agent a's security positions $(\theta^{1,a}, \ldots, \theta^{J,a})$, the firms' investments $(I^1, \ldots, I^J)$, and the shadow cost of capital ψ. We have eliminated agent b's security positions using the equilibrium relation $\theta^{i,a} + \theta^{i,b} = \bar{\theta}^i$, and we have eliminated share prices using $P_t^j = [(1 - \beta)/\alpha] I_t^j$ from equation (24). The same conclusion holds in general, noting that for every i such that $\theta^{b,i} = 0$, an unknown y^i is introduced.

Proof of Proposition 3. Suppose first $\gamma^a = \infty$; that is, agent b is the sole investor in risky assets. A decrease in r_t^f must be accompanied by increases in I_t^i for some i and decreases for other i, in order to preserve the satisfaction of the margin constraint (B7). I_t^i decreases, however, if and only if $r_t^f + \psi_t m_t^i$ increases. It follows that ψ_t increases, and that $r_t^f + \psi_t m_t^i$ increases if and only if m_t^i is large enough. Reasoning by continuity, we infer that the results hold also when the risk tolerance $(\gamma^a)^{-1}$ is close enough to zero.

A more general result can be derived. In particular, for any value γ^a, it holds that, if $\theta_t^{i,b} > 0$, then $\partial(r_t^f + \psi_t m_t^i)/\partial r_t^f > 0$, and therefore $\partial I_t^i/\partial r_t^f < 0$, for m_t^i below a certain threshold, possibly equal to 1. If $\theta_t^{i,b} = 0$, then $\partial I_t^i/\partial r_t^f < 0$.

Proof of Proposition 4. (*a*) Suppose first that $\theta_t^{j,b} > 0$. A decrease in m_t^j implies that $(1 - \theta_t^{i,a})I^i$ increases for some i, so that I^i increases. If $i \neq j$, equation (B5) then implies that ψ_t decreases, so that I_t^i increases for all i such that $\theta_t^{i,b} > 0$. In the case $\theta_t^{i,b} = 0$, I^i may only increase, since $\theta_t^{i,b}$ and I^i react in the same direction, and $\theta_t^{i,b}$ 0.

If I_t^i decreases for all $i \neq j$, $\theta_t^{i,b} > 0$, which implies that ψ_t increases, then it must be the case that either I_t^j increases (and therefore $\psi_t m_t^j$ decreases), or I_t^i with $\theta_t^{i,b} = 0$ increases. The latter is impossible, though, since it requires that $\psi_t m_t^i y_t^i$ decreases, while ψ_t increases, as does y_t^i (from some value in $[-1, 1]$ to 1, since $\theta_t^{i,a}$ decreases with a fall in I_t^i, and therefore $\theta_t^{i,b}$ becomes strictly positive).

Suppose now that $\theta_t^{j,b} = 0$. Then either the decrease in m_t^j has no impact, or $\theta_t^{j,b}$ becomes strictly positive, while I^j increases. The effect on I_t^i for $i \neq j$ is as above.

(*b*) Suppose first that $\theta^{j,b} > 0$. If m_t^j becomes 0, then $(1 - \theta_t^{j,a})I^i$ increases for some $i \neq j$, which, following the first steps above, leads to a decreased ψ_t and higher investment in all assets. If, on the other hand, $\theta_t^{j,b} = 0$, then I_t^j clearly increases, while all other investments are unaffected.

Finally, if all haircuts m_t^i are lowered by the same fraction $\varepsilon \in (0, 1)$, then some product $(1 - \theta_t^{i_0,a})I^{i_0}$ increases, so that $\psi_t m_t^{i_0}$ decreases, which implies that $\psi_t m_t^i$ decreases for all i.

Proof of Proposition 5. (*a*) Equation (B7) implies that an increase in W^b must be accompanied by a decrease in $\theta^{i,a}$ or an increase in I^i for some i. Equation (B6) implies that $\theta^{i,a}$ and I^i are negatively related to each other, so that, for some i, both $\theta^{i,a}$ decreases and I^i increases.

Finally, from (B5) it follows that the increase in I^i must be offset by a decrease in ψ. For all $j \neq i$ with $\theta^{j,b} > 0$, therefore, I^j must also increase. If $\theta^{j,b} = 0$, then I^j does not change as long as $\theta^{j,b}$ does not.

(*b*) If $\bar{\theta}^i$ goes down, then either $\theta^{i,a}$ or $\theta^{i,b}$ must decrease. If $\theta^{i,a}$ decreases, then I^i must increase (by [B6]). If $\theta^{i,b}$ decreases, then either I^i increases or $\theta^{j,b}I^j$ increases for some $j \neq i$. In this case, then, I^j increases, and therefore ψ decreases, which implies that $\theta^{i,b}$ increases, which is a contradiction. We conclude that I^i increases. Note that investments in the other technologies either all increase or all decrease. If $\bar{\theta}^i$ becomes 0, then $\theta^{j,b}I^j$ increases for some $j \neq i$, so that ψ must decrease, implying that I^j increases for all j with $\theta^{j,b} > 0$.

Appendix C

Data Sources

The survey was conducted by one of the authors in mid-March 2009 of eight market participants, including CMBS dealers as well as money managers who traded CMBS.

The econometric analysis exploits a proprietary data set on end-of-week prices for more than 2,000 originally rated AAA tranches of the outstanding fixed rate conduit universe for 2009, as well as credit ratings actions on those tranches for the same time period.

Endnotes

We are grateful for useful discussions with Tobias Adrian, Darrell Duffie, Livia Levine, Guido Lorenzoni, Andrei Shleifer, and Michael Woodford as well as from participants at the Liquidity Working Group at the Federal Reserve Bank of New York, the Conference on Financial Frictions and Macroeconomic Modeling, Cowles Foundation Conference in General Equilibrium and Its Applications, the annual meeting of the American Economic Association, the Money and Banking Workshop at the University of Chicago Department of Economics, New York University, the Stockholm School of Economics, and University of California at Berkeley.

1. To understand the meaning of a haircut, suppose that before the crisis, a financial institution could borrow \$98 with a \$100 bond as collateral. The \$2 difference is the lender's extra margin of safety and is called a 2% haircut. This allows the borrower up to 50-to-1 leverage. If the haircut went to 20%, the institution would need to finance \$20 of the position with its own capital and could only support a 5-to-1 leverage.

2. See also the related literatures in corporate finance and banking: Shleifer and Vishny (1992), Allen and Gale (1998, 2004, 2005), and Holmström and Tirole (1998, 2001).

3. The Talmud provides further detail on how the haircut should be treated in the event of default: "Rav Huna: If this condition was made when the money was given, then it is binding, even if the field is worth more than the loan. If the condition was made after the money was given, then the lender can only take the portion of the land equivalent to the value of the loan" (Babylonian Talmud Bava Metzia 66a–66b).

4. If depreciation is only partial, and disinvestment is costless following production, then the results are qualitatively the same.

5. Given that markets are incomplete, different types of agents may employ different pricing kernels, but the homogeneity of the production function means that, since they agree on the current price of the firm, they also agree on the optimal investment policy.

6. The results do not rely on this utility function. Indeed, preferences are mainly used below to derive the required return as a margin CAPM, and an almost identical margin CAPM relationship is derived with constant relative risk aversion in continuous time in Gârleanu and Pedersen (forthcoming). Further, Cuoco (1997) derives a modified CAPM for general convex constraints and general preferences.

7. Equation (9) holds if the optimal choice θ^n is strictly positive, which appears the most natural case. We state proposition 1 under this assumption. In appendix B, we provide the complete result.

8. For any vector $v \in \mathbb{R}^J$, $D(v)$ is a diagonal $J \times J$ matrix with (j, j) entry v_j.

9. More general results hold, but we omit them in the interest of simplicity.

10. Regulatory requirements are mathematically of a similar form: $\sum_i m_t^{\text{Reg},i} |\theta_t^i| P_t^i \leq W_t$, where $m_t^{\text{Reg},i}$ is the regulatory capital requirement for security i.

11. We use the notation $\psi^b = \psi$ and $y^b = y$.

References

Acharya, V. V., and L. H. Pedersen. 2005. "Asset Pricing with Liquidity Risk." *Journal of Financial Economics* 77:375–410.

Adrian, T., E. Moench, and H. Shin. 2010. "Financial Intermediation, Asset Prices and Macroeconomic Dynamics." Staff Report no. 422, Federal Reserve Bank of New York.

Adrian, T., and H. S. Shin. 2008. "Liquidity and Leverage." Staff Report no. 328, Federal Reserve Bank of New York.

———. 2010. "Financial Intermediaries and Monetary Economics." Staff Report no. 398, Federal Reserve Bank of New York.

Aiyagari, S., and M. Gertler. 1999. "Overreaction of Asset Prices in General Equilibrium." *Review of Economic Dynamics* 2, no. 1:3–35.

Allen, F., and D. Gale. 1998. "Optimal Financial Crisis." *Journal of Finance* 53, no. 4:1245–84.

———. 2004. "Financial Intermediaries and Markets." *Econometrica*, 72, no. 4:1023–61.

———. 2005. "Financial Fragility, Liquidity, and Asset Prices." *Journal of the European Economic Association* 2, no. 6:1015–48.

Amihud, Y., and H. Mendelson. 1986. "Asset Pricing and the Bid-Ask Spread." *Journal of Financial Economics* 17, no. 2: 223–49.

Ashcraft, A. 2005. "Are Banks Really Special? New Evidence from the FDIC-Induced Failure of Healthy Banks." *American Economic Review* 95, no. 5:1712–30.

Bagehot, W. 1873. *Lombard Street: A Description of the Money Market*. London: King.

Berenbaum, J., S. Gaon, and J. Mather. 2009. "November TALF Sees Three Rejections as Acceptance Criteria Remain Elusive." *Citi CMBS Weekly*, November 25.

Bernanke, B., and M. Gertler. 1989. "Agency Costs, Net Worth, and Business Fluctuations." *American Economic Review* 79, no. 1:14–31.

Bernanke, B., M. Gertler, and S. Gilchrist. 1998. "The Financial Accelerator in a Quantitative Business Cycle Framework." Working Paper no. 6455, NBER, Cambridge, MA.

Brunnermeier, M., and L. H. Pedersen. 2009. "Market Liquidity and Funding Liquidity." *Review of Financial Studies* 22:2201–38.

Caballero, R., and A. Krishnamurthy. 2001. "International and Domestic Collateral Constraints in a Model of Emerging Market Crises." *Journal of Monetary Economics* 48, no. 3:513–48.

Coen-Pirani, D. 2005. "Margin Requirements and Equilibrium Asset Prices." *Journal of Monetary Economics* 52, no. 2:449–75.

Cuoco, D. 1997. "Optimal Consumption and Equilibrium Prices with Portfolio Constraints and Stochastic Income." *Journal of Economic Theory* 72, no. 1:33–73.

Cúrdia, V., and M. Woodford. 2009. "Credit Frictions and Optimal Monetary Policy." Working paper, Columbia University.

Detemple, J., and S. Murthy. 1997. "Equilibrium Asset Prices and No-Arbitrage with Portfolio Constraints." *Review of Financial Studies* 10, no. 4:1133–74.

Duffie, D., N. Gârleanu, and L. H. Pedersen. 2005. "Over-the-Counter Markets." *Econometrica* 73:1815–47.

———. 2007. "Valuation in Over-the-Counter Markets." *Review of Financial Studies* 20:1865–1900.

Fostel, A., and J. Geanakoplos. 2008. "Leverage Cycles and the Anxious Economy." *American Economic Review* 98, no. 4:1211–44.

Gârleanu, N., and L. H. Pedersen. Forthcoming. "Margin-Based Asset Pricing and Deviations from the Law of One Price." *Review of Financial Studies*.

Geanakoplos, J. 1997. "Promises, Promises." In *The Economy as an Evolving Complex System II*, ed. W. B. Arthur, S. N. Durlauf, and D. A. Lane, 285–320. Reading, MA: Addison-Wesley/Longman.

———. 2003. "Liquidity, Default and Crashes: Endogenous Contracts in General Equilibrium." In *Advances in Economics and Econometrics: Theory and Applications II*, ed. M. Dewatripont, L. P. Hansen, and S. J. Turnovsky, 2:170–205. Cambridge: Cambridge University Press.

Gertler, M., and P. Karadi. 2009. "A Model of Unconventional Monetary Policy." Working paper, New York University.

Gertler, M., and N. Kiyotaki. Forthcoming. "Financial Intermediation and Credit Policy in Business Cycle Analysis." In *Handbook of Monetary Economics*, vol. 3A, ed. B. M. Friedman and M. Woodford. Amsterdam: Elsevier.
Gorton, G., and A. Metrick. 2009a. "Haircuts." Working paper, Yale University.
———. 2009b. "Securitized Banking and the Run on Repo." Working paper, Yale University.
He, Z., and A. Krishnamurthy. 2008. "Intermediated Asset Prices." Working paper, Northwestern University.
Hindy, A. 1995. "Viable Prices in Financial Markets with Solvency Constraints." *Journal of Mathematical Economics* 24, no. 2:105–35.
Holmström, B., and J. Tirole. 1997. "Financial Intermediation, Loanable Funds, and the Real Sector." *Quarterly Journal of Economics* 112, no. 1:35–52.
———. 1998. "Private and Public Supply of Liquidity." *Journal of Political Economy* 106, no. 1:1–39.
———. 2001. "LAPM: A Liquidity-Based Asset Pricing Model." *Journal of Finance* 56, no. 5:1837–67.
Kiyotaki, N., and J. Moore. 1997. "Credit Cycles." *Journal of Political Economy* 105, no. 2:211–48.
———. 2008. "Liquidity, Business Cycles and Monetary Policy." Working paper, Princeton University.
Longstaff, F. 2004. "The Flight-to-Liquidity Premium in U.S. Treasury Bond Prices." *Journal of Business* 77, no. 3:511–26.
Lorenzoni, G. 2008. "Inefficient Credit Booms." *Review of Economic Studies* 75, no. 3:809–33.
Lustig, H., and S. Van Nieuwerburgh. 2005. "Housing Collateral, Consumption Insurance, and Risk Premia: An Empirical Perspective." *Journal of Finance* 60, no. 3:1167–1219.
Mitchell, M., L. H. Pedersen, and T. Pulvino. 2007. "Slow Moving Capital." *American Economic Review* 97, no. 2:215–20.
Reis, R. 2009. "Interpreting the Unconventional U.S. Monetary Policy of 2007–09." *Brookings Papers on Economic Activity*, no. 2:119–82.
Repullo, R., and J. Suarez. 2000. "Entrepreneurial Moral Hazard and Bank Monitoring: A Model of the Credit Channel." *European Economic Review* 44, no. 10:1931–50.
Shleifer, A., and R. W. Vishny. 1992. "Liquidation Values and Debt Capacity: A Market Equilibrium Approach." *Journal of Finance* 47, no. 4:1343–66.

Comment

Tobias Adrian, *Federal Reserve Bank of New York*
Erkko Etula, *Federal Reserve Bank of New York*

I. Introduction

The Federal Reserve and other U.S. governmental bodies undertook a series of extraordinary policy interventions in 2008 to counter the severe financial market disruptions around the Bear Stearns crisis in March of 2008, and following the bankruptcy of Lehman Brothers in September of 2008. Among these interventions, the Federal Reserve introduced liquidity facilities aimed at restoring funding liquidity in various markets, including the commercial paper market via the Commercial Paper Funding Facility (CPFF), the repo market via Primary Dealer Credit Facility (PDFC) and the Term Securities Lending Facility (TSFL), and the asset-backed securities market via the Term Asset-Backed Securities Lending Facility (TALF).[1]

Ashcraft, Gârleanu, and Pedersen (henceforth Ashcraft et al.) offer a theory of haircut setting that presents a potential rationalization for the functioning of the TALF program. TALF was introduced by the Federal Reserve in response to a standstill in the issuance of asset-backed securities (ABS) in October 2008. This disruption in the ABS market had the potential to adversely affect the supply of credit to the real economy. It was also accompanied by an extraordinary surge in risk premia of ABS securities. The Federal Reserve provided funding for eligible AAA tranches of ABS securities via the TALF program. The TALF supplied term financing to ABS issuers by effectively providing investors with leverage that they were unable to obtain in the marketplace.

Financial institutions' ability to take on leverage depends on various constraints that include risk management, margin requirements, and haircuts. Such constraints can be imposed in two ways: either on the balance sheet of the entire financial institution, or on a security-by-security basis. The key assumption of Ashcraft et al. is that investors' leverage is constrained due to security-specific margins that prevail in

978-0-226-00212-5/2011/2010-0302$10.00

the marketplace. These margins are specific to each asset, and they are exogenous to the model.

In this discussion, we contrast the theory of Ashcraft et al. with an alternative theory of leverage based on Adrian, Etula, and Shin (2009; henceforth Adrian et al.).[2] The comparison of these two approaches allows us to work out in detail which implications of Ashcraft et al.'s theory are due to the security-specific constraints and which parts arise in a world where constraints are imposed on the balance sheets of financial institutions.

The policy experiment that is at the core of Ashcraft et al. is the comparison of haircut policy to interest rate policy. The key result of the paper is that in the economic setting of Ashcraft et al., cutting the risk-free rate can tighten the leverage constraints of some investors and thus induce greater risk premia on some assets. Margin policy—that is, central bank lending at margins below the margins prevailing in the marketplace—can directly influence the leverage available to investors in different assets and can more directly influence the supply of credit.

II. Intermediary Risk Appetite

A. *Leveraged Financial Intermediaries*

In order to understand the model of Ashcraft et al. in more detail, we contrast it with the closely related model by Adrian et al. Consider a leveraged financial intermediary (A) that manages its leverage actively. Denote the return to risky assets in excess of the risk-free rate at time $t+1$ by r^i_{t+1}, and the vector of excess returns by r_{t+1}. We suppose that intermediaries are risk neutral and maximize expected portfolio returns subject to a balance sheet constraint related to their value-at-risk (Var). Denoting by y^A_i the share of the active intermediary's wealth w^A_t in position i, the investment problem is

$$\max_{y^F_t} E_t\left(\boldsymbol{y}^{A\prime}_t \boldsymbol{r}_{t+1}\right) \qquad \text{s.t. } \mathrm{Var}_t \leq w^A_t. \tag{1}$$

If Var_t is a multiple κ of equity volatility, the risk constraint becomes $w^A_t \kappa \sqrt{\mathrm{Var}_t(\boldsymbol{y}^{A\prime}_t \boldsymbol{r}_{t+1})} \leq w^A_t$. By risk neutrality, this constraint binds with equality. It follows that the Lagrangian is

$$L_t = E_t\left(\boldsymbol{y}^{A\prime}_t \boldsymbol{r}_{t+1}\right) - \phi_t\left[\kappa\sqrt{\mathrm{Var}_t(\boldsymbol{y}^{A\prime}_t \boldsymbol{r}_{t+1})} - 1\right]. \tag{2}$$

The first-order condition for portfolio choice is

$$y_t^A = \frac{1}{\kappa\phi_t}[\mathrm{Var}_t(r_{t+1})]^{-1}E_t(r_{t+1}). \tag{3}$$

From equation (3), we see that the asset demands of the leveraged intermediaries are identical to the standard capital asset pricing model (CAPM) choices, but where the risk-aversion parameter is the scaled Lagrange multiplier $\kappa\phi_t$ associated with the balance sheet constraint. Even though the intermediary is risk-neutral, it effectively behaves as if it were risk-averse. In other words, the intermediary's "risk appetite" (the inverse of its effective risk aversion) fluctuates with shifts in $\kappa\phi_t$. As the balance sheet constraint binds harder, leverage must be reduced. Danielsson, Shin, and Zigrand (2009) solve for the rational expectations equilibrium of a continuous time dynamic model along these lines.

There are two key differences between the setup of Ashcraft et al. and Adrian et al. First, the leverage constraint imposed on intermediaries by Ashcraft et al. is asset specific, while the constraint imposed by Adrian et al. is institution specific.[3] Second, the constraint in Adrian et al. is proportional to the riskiness of the intermediaries' balance sheet, while it is a simple leverage constraint in the case of Ashcraft et al. A minor difference between the models is that Ashcraft et al. assume that both agents are risk averse, while Adrian et al. assume that financial intermediaries are risk neutral. As a result, the constraint is always binding in Adrian et al., but only sometimes binding in Ashcraft et al.

Because the constraint in Adrian et al. is proportional to the risk of the intermediaries' balance sheet, the Lagrange multiplier on the constraint plays the role of effective risk aversion. In contrast, in Ashcraft et al., the Lagrange multiplier on the constraint enters the asset demand additively, so it is more similar to a hedging demand (see eq. [10] of Ashcraft et al.). While changes in the tightness of the constraint shift the demand for risky assets in Adrian et al., they result in twists of the demand curve in Ashcraft et al.

B. *Equilibrium Returns*

Adrian et al. assume that passive (P) investors have constant relative risk aversion γ, so that their portfolio choice is[4]

$$y_t^P = \frac{1}{\gamma}[\mathrm{Var}_t(r_{t+1})]^{-1}E_t(r_{t+1}). \tag{4}$$

Market clearing then implies that the vector s_t of net supply of assets is $s_t = y_t^A w_t^A / (w_t^A + w_t^P) + y_t^P w_t^P / (w_t^A + w_t^P)$. Plugging the two asset demands (3) and (4) in the market-clearing condition and rearranging, Adrian et al. obtain an expression for the equilibrium expected returns:

$$E_t(r_{t+1}) = \mathrm{Cov}_t(r_{t+1}, r_{t+1}^W)\Gamma_t \tag{5}$$

$$= \beta_t \lambda_t, \tag{6}$$

where $r_{t+1}^W = s_t' r_{t+1}$ is the return on the aggregate wealth portfolio and $\Gamma_t = (w_t^A + w_t^P)/[w_t^A / (\kappa\phi_t) + w_t^P/\gamma]$ is the economy's effective risk aversion. The market risk premium per unit of exposure is $\lambda_t = \mathrm{Var}_t(r_{t+1}^W)\Gamma_t$.

Adrian et al.'s expression for equilibrium expected returns (eq. [5]) should be contrasted with equation (15) of proposition 1 in Ashcraft et al. There are two main differences. First, Ashcraft et al. do not explicitly solve for the price of market risk. Second, Ashcraft et al. have an additional term that determines expected returns. This additional term is proportional to the Lagrange multiplier of the constrained investors. While the theory of Adrian et al. is cast in terms of a CAPM with time-varying expected returns, the theory of Ashcraft et al. is cast as a deviation from CAPM.

C. *An Estimate of Effective Risk Aversion*

Adrian et al. demonstrate that the economy's effective risk aversion Γ_t has a reduced form representation that can be expressed as a function of the leverage of the active financial intermediaries and passive investors. Denoting the leverage of the active investors by $\mathrm{lev}_t^A \equiv 1 + \mathrm{debt}_t^A / w_t^A = \sum_i y_{i,t}^A$, and the leverage of the market by $\mathrm{lev}_t^{A\&P} \equiv 1 + (\mathrm{debt}_t^A + \mathrm{debt}_t^P)/(w_t^A + w_t^P) = \sum_i s_{i,t}$, Adrian et al. obtain

$$\Gamma_t = \gamma\left[1 + \frac{w_t^A}{w_t^P}\left(1 - \frac{\mathrm{lev}_t^A}{\mathrm{lev}_t^{A\&P}}\right)\right]. \tag{7}$$

Equation (7) states that the time variation in the effective risk aversion is represented by fluctuations in the leverage of active intermediaries relative to the leverage of the market, scaled by the wealth of active intermediaries relative to the wealth of passive investors. Specifically, an increase in active intermediaries' leverage is associated with a decrease in effective risk aversion. The greater the wealth share of the active intermediaries, the greater the impact of their leverage on Γ_t.

It is important to emphasize that the time variation in the effective risk aversion in Adrian et al. is not due to the specification of preferences but rather to the time variation in the tightness of the intermediaries' risk constraints.[5] As a result, the theory of Adrian et al. yields an expression for the effective risk aversion as a function of observable balance sheet components. Figure 1 displays an estimate of the effective risk aversion for the universe of U.S. investors between 1986Q1 and 2009Q4. Adrian et al. proxy the actively managed, leveraged financial intermediaries by the universe of U.S. primary dealers and let the rest of the Center for Research in Security Prices (CRSP) universe proxy for passive investors. The data are obtained from the CRSP/Compustat merged database.

The measure of effective risk aversion of Adrian et al. has a number of intuitive features. For instance, the series reaches its highest level during the latest financial crisis in the fall of 2008. It also exhibits a pronounced increase following the long-term capital management crisis, and following the savings and loans crisis prior to the recession of 1991.

D. *Impact on Investment*

Adrian et al.'s theory can be complemented with a real sector and real investment, following the setup presented by Ashcraft et al. In particular, assume that productivity shocks A^i_{t+1} are independently and identically distributed (i.i.d.), and that firms fully depreciate after one period, so that the one period return is pinned down by the liquidating

Fig. 1. Effective risk aversion of Adrian, Etula, and Shin (2009)

dividend. Under these assumptions, real investment directly inherits the persistence of the time-varying risk aversion; that is, investment is no longer i.i.d. Specifically, if we assume that the production technology is given by the Cobb-Douglas function $A^i_{t+1}K^{1/2}_{t+1}L^{1/2}_{t+1}$, the investment in Adrian et al. is

$$\left(I^i_t\right)^{1/2} = \frac{(1/2)E_t\left(A^i_{t+1}\right)}{1 + r_f + (1/4)\operatorname{Var}_t\left(A^i_{t+1}\right)\Gamma_t}. \tag{8}$$

In contrast, the equivalent equation in Ashcraft et al. is

$$\left(I^i_t\right)^{1/2} = \frac{(1/2)E_t\left(A^i_{t+1}\right)}{1 + r_f + (1/4)\operatorname{Var}_t\left(A^i_{t+1}\right)\gamma + \psi_t xm^i_t}.$$

The key difference is that in Adrian et al., the equilibrium investment is affected by systematic shifts in effective risk aversion Γ_t, whereas in Ashcraft et al. the equilibrium investment in project i fluctuates with the asset-specific term $\psi_t xm^i_t$. The shifts in effective risk aversion in Adrian et al. are amplified by the volatility of the productivity shock $\operatorname{Var}_t\left(A^i_{t+1}\right)$.

In both theories, investment is persistent, and a function of the tightness of financial constraints of the leveraged investors. Ashcraft et al. call this property the "margin-constraint accelerator" in their proposition 2.[6]

E. *Leverage-Return Trade-off*

In equilibrium, the theory of Adrian et al. implies a trade-off between returns and leverage. This can be most easily seen by plugging equation (7) into equation (5) for the case of the market return $r^i_{t+1} = r^W_{t+1}$:

$$E_t\left(r^W_{t+1}\right) = \operatorname{Var}_t\left(r^W_{t+1}\right)\gamma\left[1 + \frac{w^A_t}{w^P_t}\left(1 - \frac{\text{lev}^A_t}{\text{lev}^{A\&P}_t}\right)\right]. \tag{9}$$

In other words, the theory of Adrian et al. states that the expected market return is proportional to market variance (this is the usual risk-return trade-off), but this trade-off is magnified by the amount of intermediary leverage. Graphically, figure 2 shows this trade-off between returns and leverage for two different levels of market variance: higher leverage is associated with lower equilibrium returns; the impact of leverage on equilibrium returns is greater when the volatility of the market is higher.

Figure 2 should be compared with figures 2–4 of Ashcraft et al. Note that leverage is inversely proportional to haircuts, so the negative

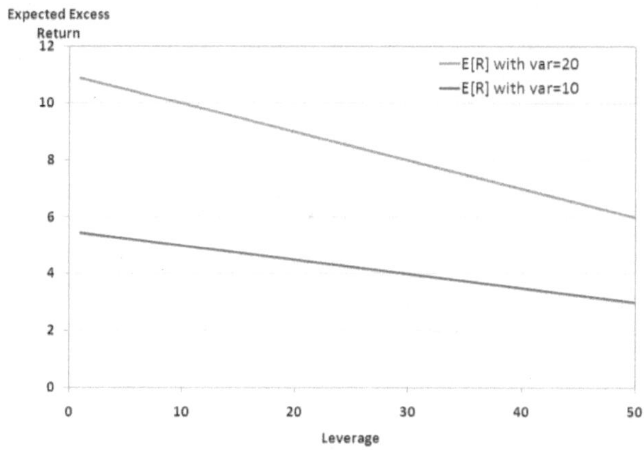

Fig. 2. Financial intermediary leverage and expected excess returns

leverage-return trade-off of Adrian et al. corresponds to the positive return-haircut trade-off of Ashcraft et al. The key difference between the theories can be summarized as follows: in Ashcraft et al., the product of exogenous margin and the Lagrange multiplier of the financial constraint determine the slope of each haircut-return curve, whereas in Adrian et al., the slope of the leverage-return trade-off is determined by the riskiness of each security. By implication, in Ashcraft et al., changes in the risk-free rate directly change the return-haircut trade-off for some securities (see proposition 3 and fig. 4 of Ashcraft et al.). In contrast, in Adrian et al., changes in the risk-free rate do not directly affect the leverage return trade-off. The leverage-return trade-off is affected only if the risk-free rate alters the equilibrium variance-covariance matrix of returns. The extent to which changes in the risk-free rate impact equilibrium second moments is a fruitful direction for future research.

Empirically, the trade-off between equilibrium expected returns and haircuts can be seen in figure 3, which is taken from Adrian and Shin (2009). During the financial crisis, the trade-off between haircuts and option-adjusted yield spreads steepened substantially. This is exactly what equation (9) predicts: as market volatility increased with the deepening of the financial crisis, the slope of the trade-off between required returns and the haircut (e.g., the inverse of leverage) was expected to increase.

III. Policy Implications

Ashcraft et al. assume that asset-specific haircuts are determined exogenously. As a result, Ashcraft et al. interpret TALF as an exogenous

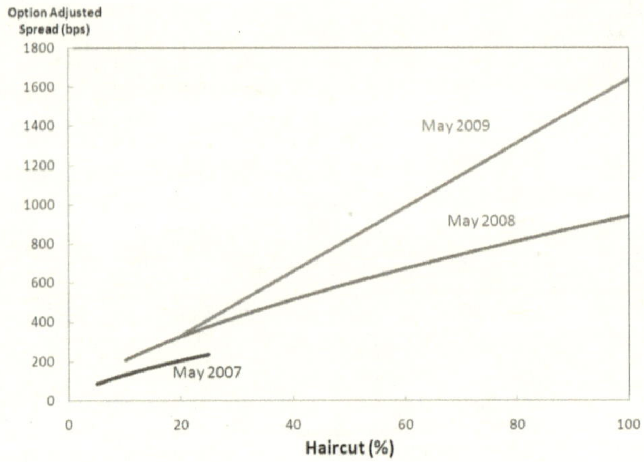

Fig. 3. The trade-off between credit spreads and haircuts

change in the haircut on ABS. The Federal Reserve offered lower haircuts than the ones that prevailed in the marketplace, thereby increasing the overall leverage of TALF investors and changing the leverage-return trade-off for eligible assets. This is paramount to a change in the equilibrium haircut-return trade-off, as figure 5 and proposition 4 of Ashcraft et al. show.

The assumptions in Adrian et al. are not sufficient to pin down the impact of TALF on equilibrium asset prices. Thus, additional assumptions are needed to determine the degree to which TALF changes equilibrium pricing in the model of Adrian et al. We will next discuss such assumptions.

At one extreme are assumptions that make TALF have no effect on equilibrium asset prices. If it is assumed that the proceeds from TALF are transferred from the central bank back to the economy in a manner that is not state contingent, then programs such as TALF (or asset purchases) will have no equilibrium asset pricing implications in the setting of Adrian et al. Cúrdia and Woodford (2010) provide a detailed discussion of the conditions under which quantity policies will have no effect on equilibrium risk premia.[7] However, there are two related assumptions underlying the Cúrdia-Woodford argument. First, the central bank is just a veil, a part of the government that serves as a channel for redistribution. Second, any distributive transfers that result from realized profits or losses made by the central bank are conducted in a non-state-contingent manner.

We emphasize that the Cúrdia-Woodford assumptions are quite restrictive, particularly in the midst of financial crises. The central bank is itself a player in the market with its own balance sheet. Via programs such as TALF, the Fed increases the size of its balance sheet to support prices in economically important parts of the market that suffer from disruptions. The Fed does this in a time frame that matters for investors—a period shorter than the long-run equilibrium in which the Fed's net profits have been redistributed to the economy. At an extreme, assuming that the central bank is just a channel for redistribution is equivalent to saying that when the Fed makes a profit on its holdings of agency mortgage-backed securities, financial intermediaries such as Citi and Bank of America get recapitalized immediately. Or, alternatively, why did the Treasury need TARP when the Fed's purchases would have automatically recapitalized all the banks? Relatedly, fiscal redistributions (via taxes and other means of transfer) are likely to depend not only on realized asset payoffs but also on a number of other considerations linked to the state of the economy. Hence, the non–state contingency of fiscal transfers is also a strong assumption that underlies the result that quantity policies have no equilibrium effects.

At the other extreme is the assumption that the central bank does not distribute the proceeds from TALF at all. In that case, the only effect of TALF will be to change the net supply of risky assets. The change in the net supply of risky assets, in turn, changes the market-clearing conditions and the effective risk aversion prevailing in the economy.

Under the assumption that the Federal Reserve does not redistribute the proceeds from TALF, or does so after a period that is beyond the investment horizon of investors, or does so in states that are irrelevant to investors' portfolio choice, variations in TALF lending can be interpreted as changes in the net supply of risky assets. In the setting of Adrian et al., such changes in s_t lead to changes in the relative leverage of active financial intermediaries (the term $\text{lev}_t^A/\text{lev}_t^{A\&P}$ in [7]). Since an increase in financial intermediaries' leverage results in a decrease in the economy's effective risk aversion, an increase in TALF lending is expected to result in a decline in risk premia (via [5]) and an increase in investment (via [8]).

A simple back-of-an-envelope calculation illustrates magnitudes for the securitized mortgage market. Suppose that active investors hold \$2*tr* assets (say, with equity \$0.1*tr*) and passive investors hold \$10*tr* assets (say, with equity \$2*tr*). Suppose that the government funds \$0.2*tr* in a way that it only transacts with active investors. The leverage of the active investors thus increases from $2/0.1 = 20$ to $2.2/0.1 = 22$. At the same time, the leverage of the overall financial sector increases from $12/2.1 = 5.7$

to $(12 + 0.2)/2.1 = 5.8$. The immediate change in effective risk aversion is then

$$\frac{\Gamma_1 - \Gamma_0}{\Gamma_0} = \frac{-(0.1/2)(22/5.8 - 20/5.7)}{[1 + (0.1/2)(1 - 20/5.7)]} = -1.63\%.$$

The government-induced releveraging of active investors results in a 1.63% reduction in the private sector's effective risk aversion. With a market beta for AAA credit returns of 0.8, the decline in required returns due to the government intervention is 1.3%. This is smaller than the 3% that Ashcraft et al. estimate, which might reflect that the TALF program targeted very specific assets, while our back-of-the-envelope calculation is aimed at the overall leveraged financial sector.

An alternative policy tool to the liquidity injections is changes in the capital requirements of financial institutions. This can be viewed as variation in κ. The parameter κ directly affects the risk appetite of the levered financial institution and hence equilibrium risk premia. Systematic changes in κ as a function of macroeconomic state variables can be interpreted as macroprudential policy, which is a primary topic of ongoing research.

Endnotes

The views expressed here are those of the authors and do not necessarily reflect those of the Federal Reserve Bank of New York or the Federal Reserve System.

1. Details on the Federal Reserve's liquidity facilities are provided by Adrian, Marchioni, and Kimbrough (2010) for the CPFF; Adrian, Burke, and McAndrews (2009) for the PDCF; Fleming, Hrung, and Keane (2009) for the TSLF; and Ashcraft, Malz, and Pozsar (forthcoming) for TALF.
2. Adrian et al. was first circulated publicly as a Federal Reserve Bank of New York Staff Report in January 2009; Ashcraft et al. rely on Gârleanu and Pedersen (2009), which was first circulated in September 2009. Adrian and Etula (2010) solve an intertemporal extension of Adrian et al. in continuous time.
3. Geanakoplos (1997, 2010) provides a theory of endogenous margin constraints.
4. The "passive" investors of Adrian et al. correspond to the risk-averse *a* investors in Ashcraft et al.
5. The time variation of effective risk aversion generated by institutional constraints can be contrasted to the time variation of effective risk aversion due to habit formation in preferences (see, e.g., Campbell and Cochrane 2000).
6. Empirically, the prediction that investment varies with risk premia fits nicely with the finding of Philippon (2009) that the invesment-to-capital ratio of nonfinancial corporations is closely correlated to risk premia in corporate bond markets.
7. The discussion in Cúrdia and Woodford (2010) is in turn based on Wallace (1981).

References

Adrian, T., C. Burke, and J. McAndrews. 2009. "The Federal Reserve's Primary Dealer Credit Facility." *Federal Reserve Bank of New York Current Issues in Economics and Finance* 15, no. 4:1–10.

Adrian, T., and E. Etula. 2010. "Funding Liquidity Risk and the Cross-Section of Stock Return." Staff Report no. 464, Federal Reserve Bank of New York.

Adrian, T., E. Etula, and H. S. Shin. 2009. "Risk Appetite and Exchange Rates." Staff Report no. 361, Federal Reserve Bank of New York.

Adrian, T., D. Marchioni, and K. Kimbrough. 2010. "The Federal Reserve's Commercial Paper Funding Facility." *Federal Reserve Bank of New York Economic Policy Review*, forthcoming.

Adrian, T., and H. S. Shin. 2009. "Prices and Quantities in the Monetary Policy Transmission Mechanism." *International Journal of Central Banking* 5, no. 4: 131–42.

———. Forthcoming. "Financial Intermediaries and Monetary Economics." In *Handbook of Monetary Economics*, vol. 3A, ed. B. M. Friedman and M. Woodford. Amsterdam: Elsevier.

Ashcraft, A., A. Malz, and Z. Pozsar. Forthcoming. "The Federal Reserve's Term Asset-Backed Securities Lending Facility." *Federal Reserve Bank of New York Economic Policy Review.*

Campbell, J. Y., and J. H. Cochrane. 2000. "Explaining the Poor Performance of Consumption-Based Asset Pricing Models." *Journal of Finance* 55, no. 6:2863–78.

Cúrdia, V., and M. Woodford. 2010. "The Central-Bank Balance Sheet as an Instrument of Monetary Policy." *Journal of Monetary Economics*, forthcoming.

Danielsson, J., H. S. Shin, and J.-P. Zigrand. 2008. "Endogenous Risk and Risk Appetite." Unpublished working paper, London School of Economics and Princeton University.

Fleming, M., W. Hrung, and F. Keane. 2009. "The Term Securities Lending Facility: Origin, Design, and Effects." *Federal Reserve Bank of New York Current Issues in Economics and Finance* 15, no. 2:1–10.

Gârleanu, Nicolae, and Lasse Heje Pedersen. 2009. "Margin-Based Asset Pricing and Deviations from the Law of One Price." Unpublished working paper, New York University and University of California, Berkeley.

Geanakoplos, J. 1997. "Promises, Promises." In *The Economy as an Evolving Complex System II*, ed. W. B. Arthur, S. N. Durlauf, and D. A. Lane, 285–320. Reading, MA: Addison-Wesley/Longman.

———. 2010. "The Leverage Cycle." *NBER Macroeconomics Annual* 24:1–65.

Philippon, T. 2009. "The Bond Market's Q." *Quarterly Journal of Economics* 124, no. 3:1011–56.

Wallace, N. 1981. "A Modigliani-Miller Theorem for Open-Market Operations." *American Economic Review* 71, no. 3:267–74.

Comment

Michael Woodford, *Columbia University and NBER*

It is common to consider monetary policy as a unidimensional problem, involving only the choice of an operating target for some short-term interest rate (the federal funds rate, in the case of the Federal Reserve). But other aspects of policy have been at center stage much of the time in the Fed's response to the recent financial crisis. In particular, whereas the Fed has traditionally adhered (at least to a large extent) to a policy of "Treasuries only" (Goodfriend 2011), under which the only asset on its balance sheet should be (mostly short-term) U.S. Treasury securities, the Fed has recently been involved in fairly large-scale extensions of credit to private institutions. These new programs have included "liquidity facilities" that extend (relatively short-term) credit to financial institutions of various types; facilities like the Term Asset-Backed Securities Loan Facility (TALF), discussed in this paper, that provide longer term financing for purchasers of privately issued financial assets, and thus effectively make the Fed a financial intermediary itself, rather than a mere supplier of liquidity to such intermediaries; and direct purchases of securities other than Treasuries, as in the case of the Commercial Paper Funding Facility (CPFF), which I discuss further below.[1]

It is therefore an important question for the theory of monetary policy to consider to what extent these additional dimensions of policy serve additional purposes that could not already be achieved through traditional interest rate policy. There are actually two questions that need to be considered: first, whether such policies should be effective at all, in changing financial conditions; and second, to the extent that they are effective and whether they are simply substitutes for more aggressive use of interest rate policy. The present paper is one of the first to directly address these important questions; it provides cogent theoretical and empirical analyses of the first question, and an interesting theoretical argument with regard to the second question as well.

978-0-226-00212-5/2011/2010-0303$10.00

Notably, the paper's argument for the relevance of central bank "haircut policy," even given the availability of traditional interest rate policy, does not turn on the observation that interest rate policy is sometimes (as in the United States since December 2008) constrained by the zero lower bound on nominal interest rates; this suggests the possibility of routine intervention along this dimension, rather than resorting to it only during especially severe crises (which are the only times that the zero lower bound is likely to be an issue).

I. Breaking the Modigliani-Miller Theorem for Central Bank Financial Policy

The authors' theoretical analysis of why central bank haircut policy—specifically, the willingness of the central bank to accept assets as collateral for loans under terms that are more generous than those prevailing in the market in the absence of central bank lending—can affect equilibrium asset prices, and hence the allocation of resources, is an important contribution. The approach that they take draws on earlier work by Gârleanu and Pedersen (2011) on the role of margin constraints in explaining violations of the law of one price in financial markets. I shall not undertake a general assessment of that theory here, but I want to comment on the importance of certain features of that theory for the conclusions reached. In fact, not all theories regarding the sources of observed spreads between the rates of return on alternative financial instruments lead to the same conclusions regarding the scope for additional dimensions of central bank policy; awareness of the differences may allow future work to focus more sharply on distinguishing the empirical relevance of these alternative theories, which will be important for further progress in the theory of monetary policy.

The most common argument for multiple dimensions of central bank policy with independent effects is based on portfolio-balance theory. According to this theory, changes in the portfolio held by the central bank change the aggregate portfolio that must be held in equilibrium by private investors; to the extent that the assets between which the central bank substitutes are not perfect substitutes, it is expected that a change in the relative prices of the different assets will be necessary to induce this portfolio substitution by private investors. In this view, the key to whether a given change in the central bank's portfolio should affect equilibrium rates of return is the degree to which the assets involved are perfect substitutes or not; and (in accordance with the modern theory of finance) it is often supposed that what determines whether different assets are substitutes is the respective contingencies under which they pay out a greater or lesser amount.[2]

But the mere fact that different assets have different state-contingent returns does not suffice to imply that the fact that the central bank purchases one of them rather than the other must have any effect on equilibrium asset prices, and hence on the allocation of resources. For example, in a representative-household asset-pricing theory, the equilibrium price of each asset should equal the present value of the income stream to which it is a claim, where the stochastic discount factor used to compute present values is based on the state-contingent consumption of the representative household. If a change in the portfolio of the central bank changes neither the state-contingent income stream associated with a single unit of a given asset nor the state-contingent aggregate supply of goods available for consumption, it should have no effect on the equilibrium price of the asset.[3]

Representative-agent asset-pricing theories have well-known difficulties accounting for the empirical behavior of asset prices; in particular, the size and variability of the spreads between the returns on different assets are difficult to account for without the hypothesis of time-varying risk premia, of a kind that are not easily explained by the relatively smooth variations observed in aggregate consumption. But the neutrality result just mentioned does not depend on the assumption of a representative household. The key to the result is the fact that, if the central bank shifts its portfolio among assets with different state-contingent payoffs, the state-contingent portfolio earnings of the central bank will be different as a result of the policy change, and these state-contingent portfolio earnings must be distributed to someone in the private sector (to the representative household, in a representative-household model).[4] This changes the degree to which the private investors demand particular assets in order to hedge against risks associated with its other sources of income.[5]

In the representative-agent model, the change in the hedging demand of the representative household precisely offsets the change in the central bank's portfolio, so that asset markets continue to clear at the same prices as before. But the argument is essentially a Modigliani-Miller theorem for changes in the net asset issuance of the government, as first pointed out by Wallace (1981), and doesn't depend at all on the existence of a representative agent. In fact, the only postulates needed to obtain the irrelevance result are (i) that all investors can buy or sell the same set of assets at the same market prices, and (ii) that each investor's objective, and the only relevant constraints on her portfolio choice, can be stated purely in terms of the state-contingent future value of her wealth.[6]

These postulates may well be satisfied, even a model that incorporates time-varying risk premia due to variation in the resources of the "natural buyers" of risky assets, and that allows for the amplification of disturbances by "leverage spirals." The model proposed by Adrian and Shin (forthcoming) provides a simple example. In this two-period model, investors are of two types, one of which funds the leveraged investment of the other (just as in the model proposed here). Letting the random variable W_2^h denote the second-period value of the investor h's wealth, "passive investors" are assumed to choose a portfolio to maximize

$$E[W_2^p] - \alpha \operatorname{Var}[W_2^p],$$

where $\alpha > 0$ parameterizes their degree of risk aversion; "active investors" instead choose a portfolio to maximize $E[W_2^a]$ subject to a "value-at-risk constraint," which requires that

$$W_2^a \geq 0,$$

with probability one. Both types choose arbitrary positions in two assets, a risky asset and a riskless asset, and are price takers in the markets for these assets.

Now suppose that, in the model of Adrian and Shin, we were to introduce a central bank that purchases a quantity x^{cb} of the risky asset at the market price in the first period and finances these open-market purchases by selling an equal quantity of the riskless asset. (Here I measure both quantities by the first-period market values of the assets purchased or sold.) This results in state-contingent second-period portfolio earnings for the central bank equal to $(R - r)x^{cb}$, where R is the (random) return on the risky asset and r is the (certain) return on the riskless asset. Suppose further that the additional income transferred to the Treasury as a result of these earnings by the central bank is distributed in fraction θ^p to the passive investors and in fraction $\theta^a = 1 - \theta^p$ to the active investors. The second-period wealth of investors of type h will then equal

$$W_2^h = (1 + r)W_1^h + (R - r)x^h + \theta^h(R - r)x^{cb},$$

where W_1^h is the first-period wealth of type h, and x^h is the quantity of the risky asset held by type h investors. Since both the objective and the constraints of type h investors depend only on $\tilde{x}^h \equiv x^h + \theta^h x^{cb}$, the optimal choice of $\tilde{x}^h$ will be independent of the central bank's choice of x^{cb}. Moreover, the condition for market clearing (that $\tilde{x}^p + \tilde{x}^a$ equals the total supply of the risky asset) can be expressed solely in terms of the two quantities $\tilde{x}^h$. Hence, the price for the risky asset that clears the market will be independent of the choice of x^{cb}.

This result implies that in a model satisfying the two postulates, like the one just sketched, direct (open-market) purchases of assets by the central bank should have no effect on the equilibrium structure of asset returns. But such a model implies that lending by the central bank to leveraged borrowers should accomplish little, either. Unless the central bank is willing to completely replace private sources of funding for the leveraged investors, they will still have to satisfy the VaR constraint. (It would not be enough that the central bank serve as the sole source of funding for their acquisitions of a particular category of risky assets, say mortgage-backed securities—because the VaR constraint relates to the global situation of a leveraged investor, it becomes irrelevant only if the central bank can supply all of the active investors' funding.) Hence, the decision problem of both types of investors would remain the same, and the market-clearing price vector for the various types of risky assets would remain the same.[7]

It is thus important to the conclusions of Ashcraft et al. that they do *not* assume a *global* leverage constraint, such as the VaR constraint proposed by Adrian and Shin, but rather an *asset-specific* margin constraint. Under this type of constraint, a central bank policy of lending to finance purchases of a particular kind of risky asset, with a lower margin requirement than the one imposed by the market, can substantially change the demand for that asset, even if the quantity of lending involved is only a small fraction of overall lending in the economy, or even of overall lending to leveraged intermediaries.

In fact, although it is not the main focus of their paper, the model proposed by Ashcraft, Gârleanu, and Pedersen is also one in which targeted asset purchases by the central bank are not, in general, predicted to be irrelevant for asset price determination. If the central bank acquires a risky asset with a positive margin requirement and redistributes the resulting increase in its state-contingent portfolio earnings at least partially to leveraged investors, then the optimal response of leveraged investors will not simply be to reduce their holdings of that asset by the amount $\theta^a x^{cb}$, in the case of no change in the prices of any assets. For while such a change in the portfolio choice of the leveraged investors would restore the same state-contingent value of W_2^a as would have existed in the absence of the central bank's asset purchases, these investors' leverage constraint will be relaxed by the change. In the case that the leverage constraint was previously binding (as in the equilibria discussed by Ashcraft et al.), relaxation of the constraint will allow the active investors to borrow more and purchase greater quantities of risky assets subject to margin requirements. The market for these assets will then no longer clear at the same vector of prices as before. The Modigliani-Miller theorem is broken by the assumption of asset-specific margin requirements, so that the leverage constraint of active investors cannot be expressed as a function solely of the random variable W_2^a.

It is therefore a matter of considerable importance for the theory of unconventional monetary policies, not simply whether there are binding constraints on the degree of leverage that is acceptable to those funding leveraged investors, but whether these leverage constraints involve only the total state-contingent wealth of leveraged investors (as in the case of a value-at-risk constraint), or whether they involve asset-specific margin constraints (as proposed here). While some implications of the two types of theories are broadly similar—for example, both imply that developments that redistribute wealth away from leveraged investors should raise equilibrium risk premia by tightening the leverage constraints on these investors, and that the resulting price movements should tend to further redistribute in the same direction, thus amplifying the direct effects of any such disturbance—they have quite different implications for the effects of central bank asset purchases and lending facilities.

II. Does This Theory Account for the Effects of the Fed's Programs?

To what extent does the proposed model succeed in accounting for the effects of the Fed's unusual lending programs? Ashcraft et al. present interesting evidence regarding the effects of Fed lending under the TALF. Their evidence indicates that TALF lending did affect the prices of assets that were eligible for use as collateral for borrowing under this program. It should be noted that the question addressed in their main empirical result (the regression results of Sec. III.C) is a fairly narrow one; in particular, they look only at the differential effect on commercial mortgage-backed securities that were eligible for the TALF program relative to the effect on similar securities that were not eligible. This means that their method "differences out" any effects of the TALF on asset prices that occur through relaxation of investors' capital constraints, as effects through this channel would affect the shadow value of relaxation of the margin constraints on all asset purchases, and hence would have similar effects on all assets subject to similar margin requirements, whether TALF-eligible or not.

But while the method is not suited to provide a quantitative estimate of the overall effects of the TALF on asset prices, their results do suffice to establish that the effects of the introduction of the TALF were not zero. This conclusion does allow one to exclude some potential theories; for example, unless one supposes that loans under the TALF were made at a subsidized rate of interest, it allows one to reject the hypothesis that the only constraint on leverage is a global constraint like the value-at-risk constraint discussed above. And the model proposed in this paper is at least one that can account for a nonzero differential effect of the kind that is measured.

Nonetheless, I am not convinced that this model alone can account for all of the relevant facts. Note that while the model of Ashcraft et al. can account for differential effects of central bank acceptance of particular assets as collateral, as under the TALF, the model predicts that there should be no differential effects of targeted asset purchases by the central bank. As explained in the previous section, this model, unlike the model of Adrian and Shin (forthcoming), does predict that open-market purchases of assets by the central bank will generally change equilibrium asset prices. But the effect on asset prices occurs purely as a consequence of the relaxation of the capital constraint of the leveraged investors; hence, the effect should be the same on all assets with similar margin requirements. This means that there should be no differential effect on the price of assets purchased by the central bank, relative to the prices of similar assets that happen not to be purchased by the central bank.

While the effects of these programs are only beginning to be studied, the available evidence is not obviously consistent with this prediction. For example, figure 1 shows the effects of Federal Reserve purchases of commercial paper under the CPFF, introduced in October 2008.[8] The heavy solid line plots the total value of the commercial paper purchased by the Fed under this program; the several lighter and/or dashed lines plot the spreads between the yields on various categories of commercial paper and the 1-month overnight interest rate swap rate (essentially a market forecast of the average level of the federal funds rate over the coming month). The explosion of the commercial paper spreads in September 2008 indicates the distress in these markets,

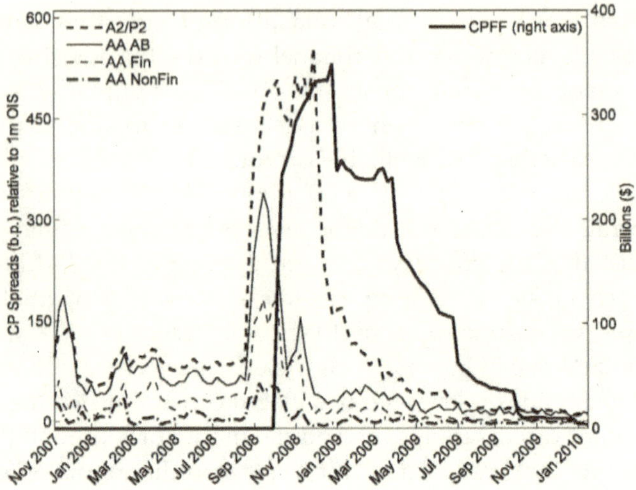

Fig. 1. Spreads between yields on four different classes of commercial paper and the 1-month OIS (overnight indexed swap) rate, together with the value of paper acquired by the Fed under its Commercial Paper Funding Facility. *Source*: Federal Reserve Board.

following the default of Lehman Brothers on its paper and the consequent runs on U.S. money-market mutual funds. The figure shows that in the case of the three types of AA-rated commercial paper (all of which were eligible for purchase by the Fed under the CPFF), spreads fell sharply as soon as purchases under the CPFF began. The figure also shows that in the case of A2/P2 commercial paper (lower rated, but still prime-grade paper issued by nonfinancial corporations, and not eligible for purchase under the CPFF), spreads remained very high for several more weeks.

While the evidence presented in this figure is much more casual than that offered by Ashcraft et al. in their study of the effects of the TALF, here too it seems that (i) the Fed's asset purchases affected asset prices, contrary to the Modigliani-Miller argument; and (ii) there was a particular effect on the prices of the specific securities purchased by the Fed, relative to those of other securities that were more similarly affected by market conditions in general. While observation i is consistent with the model proposed by Ashcraft et al., observation ii is not.[9] And there is an alternative way of breaking the Modigliani-Miller theorem, which is to deny the postulate that all investors can purchase the same spectrum of assets at the same market prices (and negligible transactions costs).

The implications of this alternative hypothesis of market segmentation for the effects of targeted asset purchases by the central bank are developed (in the context of a complete DSGE [dynamic stochastic general equilibrium] model of the monetary transmission mechanism) by Cúrdia and Woodford (2011). Under this view, certain assets are only purchased (or only purchased at low cost) by "specialists," who have an advantage over other investors in this particular activity. The Modigliani-Miller theorem no longer holds if the central bank purchases assets of this kind, if not all of the addition to the central bank's state-contingent portfolio earnings is distributed to the specialists; other investors will not reduce their holdings of the assets in question, even if the change in their state-contingent tax liabilities gives them a hedging motive for doing so, owing to their nonparticipation in that market. Moreover, under this mechanism, the central bank's purchases have a disproportionate effect on demand for the particular assets that it purchases (rather than increasing demand for all assets that are subject to margin requirements, by relaxing the capital constraints of leveraged investors), and the hypothesis of market segmentation makes it particularly likely that a substantial change in the price of those particular assets will be required for market clearing. The hypothesis of market segmentation also provides an alternative potential explanation for programs like the TALF. Targeted lending to the specialists who are able to purchase a particular kind of asset—and who have been forced to curtail their purchases owing to capital constraints, or some other disruption of the availability of funding for their activity—can similarly affect asset prices, and should similarly have a differential effect on the prices of the particular assets the purchases of which can be funded under the targeted lending program.

III. Is Credit Policy Equivalent to Interest Rate Policy?

Even granting the conclusion that programs like the TALF or the CPFF can influence financial market conditions, there remains the important question of whether such programs are nonetheless equivalent (or nearly equivalent) in their effects to some adjustment of the level of the federal funds rate, so that there is no need for a central bank to act on these other dimensions as well—or at least, no need for it to use them as long as further adjustments of the policy rate remain possible.

Ashcraft et al. show in the context of their model that central bank lending to finance purchases of risky assets that are subject to high margin requirements (or, for that matter, direct central bank purchases of such assets) are not equivalent to a reduction of the riskless rate of interest in their effects on investment spending. This is because in their model, an interest rate cut will increase the shadow value of relaxation of the capital constraint of leveraged investors, thus increasing the relative cost of investment in assets subject to high margin requirements. Central bank lending to finance purchases of such assets with less collateral, or direct purchases of such assets, will instead relax that constraint, lowering the relative cost of investment in assets subject to high margin requirements; hence, the effects of the two policies on the composition of aggregate expenditure are quite different.

It would be interesting to see evidence of this effect of monetary policy on relative asset demands. But the general conclusion is quite robust. Once one's model has multiple interest rates in it, and the possibility of variable spreads between them, there arises the possibility that different dimensions of financial conditions will be differentially affected by alternative central bank policies. Under the conditions discussed above that imply a Modigliani-Miller theorem, one can actually show that there is only one relevant dimension of central bank policy, namely, traditional interest rate policy,[10] but under almost any assumptions that break the Modigliani-Miller theorem, alternative central bank policies will be able to influence more than one dimension of financial conditions. Moreover, changes in the structure of relative yields on different kinds of financial claims will generally have consequences for the allocation of resources, so that there is no reason in general to suppose that interest rate policy alone will suffice to achieve desirable adjustments of financial conditions in response to the disturbances to which the economy may be subject. The possible welfare gains from active use of central bank credit policy alongside interest rate policy are illustrated in Cúrdia and Woodford (2011) in the context of one particular (fairly simple) model with endogenous credit spreads.

Yet despite this general observation, it is worth noting that the effectiveness of central bank credit policy does depend on binding financial constraints of one kind or another that break the Modigliani-Miller theorem. One can also reasonably expect that the effects of such policies are only substantial when the financial constraints are significant. This is surely true at some times; the kind of severe financial crisis that we have recently experienced provides a prime example. But it is less obvious whether the benefits of active credit policy should be large under more routine circumstances. Given the prudential arguments for preferring not to involve central banks in the allocation of credit (summarized, for example, by Goodfriend [2011]), it may be wise to reserve the use of these additional dimensions of policy for the unusual conditions associated with a financial crisis.

Endnotes

I would like to thank Tobias Adrian, Bill Brainard, and Vasco Cúrdia for helpful discussions, and the National Science Foundation for research support under grant SES-0820438.

1. See, e.g., Madigan (2009) for an overview of the new programs and Reis (2009) for an early discussion of the theoretical differences between programs of these different types.

2. Thus, Gagnon et al. (2010, 4) discuss the theoretical basis for the Fed's Large Scale Asset Purchase program by noting that "the LSAPs have removed a considerable amount of assets with high duration from the markets. ... In addition, the purchases of MBS reduce the amount of prepayment risk that investors have to hold in the aggregate."

3. This is the basis for the irrelevance result for unconventional monetary policies obtained in Eggertsson and Woodford (2003).

4. The direct consequence of a change in the state-contingent earnings of the central bank is a corresponding change in the state-contingent distribution that the central bank makes to the Treasury, but the change in the Treasury's state-contingent income from this source must ultimately change the net state-contingent tax obligations of parties in the private sector.

5. Hedging demands of this kind are frequently ignored in portfolio-balance models. When the securities demand functions in such models are explicitly derived from an analysis of investors' attitudes toward risk, as in Tobin (1997), a problem is typically considered in which investors have initial wealth to allocate and no future nonfinancial income or tax obligations at the time when the securities pay off. Macroeconomic models often simply postulate asset demands that are functions of the expected returns on the various available assets, without using any explicit choice problem to motivate them.

6. See Cúrdia and Woodford (2011) for further discussion.

7. This argument assumes that the central bank lends at the competitive market interest rate. If the bank lends at a below-market rate and ties the quantity lent at the subsidized rate to the quantity that an investor holds of a particular asset, by requiring that asset to be pledged as collateral for the subsidized loan, this is equivalent to paying investors a specified subsidy s per unit held of the asset. This should obviously be expected to change the equilibrium price of the asset in question and is potentially an alternative explanation for the findings of these authors about the effects on the prices of particular mortgage-backed securities of eligibility for funding under the TALF.

8. For further discussion of this program and its effects, see Adrian, Kimbrough, and Marchioni (2010) and Kacperczyk and Schnabl (2010).

9. Note that these observations are also inconsistent with the hypothesis that the effects of the TALF were due simply to the Fed's having made a certain kind of collateral a condition for obtaining a loan at a subsidized rate. Under that interpretation of the effects of lending under the TALF, one would not expect to see similar effects of direct asset purchases by the Fed, of the kind shown in fig. 1.

10. Again, see Cúrdia and Woodford (2011) for further development of this point.

References

Adrian, Tobias, Karin Kimbrough, and Dina Marchioni. 2010. "The Federal Reserve's Commercial Paper Funding Facility." Staff Report no. 423, Federal Reserve Bank of New York.

Adrian, Tobias, and Hyun Song Shin. Forthcoming. "Financial Intermediaries and Monetary Economics." In *Handbook of Monetary Economics*, vol. 3A, ed. B. M. Friedman and M. Woodford. Amsterdam: Elsevier.

Cúrdia, Vasco, and Michael Woodford. 2011. "The Central-Bank Balance Sheet as an Instrument of Monetary Policy." *Journal of Monetary Economics*, forthcoming.

Eggertsson, Gauti B., and Michael Woodford. 2003. "The Zero Bound on Interest Rates and Optimal Monetary Policy." *Brookings Papers on Economic Activity,* no. 1:139–211.

Gagnon, Joseph, Matthew Raskin, Julie Remache, and Brian Sack. 2010. "Large-Scale Asset Purchases by the Federal Reserve: Did They Work?" Staff Report no. 441, Federal Reserve Bank of New York.

Gârleanu, Nicolae, and Lasse Heje Pedersen. 2011. "Margin-Based Asset Pricing and Deviations from the Law of One Price." *Review of Financial Studies,* forthcoming.

Goodfriend, Marvin. 2011. "Central Banking in the Credit Turmoil: An Assessment of Federal Reserve Practice." *Journal of Monetary Economics,* forthcoming.

Kacperczyk, Marcin, and Philipp Schnabl. 2010. "When Safe Proved Risky: Commercial Paper during the Financial Crisis of 2007–2009." *Journal of Economic Perspectives* 24, no. 1:29–50.

Madigan, Brian. 2009. "Bagehot's Dictum in Practice: Formulating and Implementing Policies to Combat the Financial Crisis." In *Financial Stability and Macroeconomic Policy.* Kansas City: Federal Reserve Bank of Kansas City.

Reis, Ricardo. 2009. "Interpreting the Unconventional U.S. Monetary Policy of 2007–09." *Brookings Papers on Economic Activity,* no. 2:119–65.

Tobin, James. 1997. *Money, Credit and Capital.* New York: McGraw-Hill/Irwin.

Wallace, Neil. 1981. "A Modigliani-Miller Theorem for Open-Market Operations." *American Economic Review* 71:267–74.

Discussion

Lasse Pedersen opened by responding to issues raised by the discussants. Responding to Tobias Adrian's reference to asset-specific leverage constraints, he clarified that the agents face a single capital constraint on investment but that the haircuts are specific to the assets. On the implications of their model for macroprudential policy, Pedersen noted that the model could readily accommodate an additional constraint for regulatory capital, since leverage can be reduced in good times only through a different constraint. He also agreed with Adrian's comment that haircuts could be included as an explanatory variable in their regression analysis and argued that the Fed should collect more comprehensive data on haircuts as an important variable for study.

Responding to Michael Woodford's question about whether the Fed should directly purchase assets (such as mortgage-backed securities) or use lending programs to encourage private purchases, Pedersen offered his personal view that the lending facilities were less problematic. He argued that lending facilities exposed the Fed to less risk and could come off the Fed's balance sheet more easily, since loans were charged a penalty interest rate. Pedersen also argued that Woodford's market segmentation theory would be a useful extension of their existing model rather than an alternative. In his view, the asset-specific margins are a critical feature and could only be dispensed with given a very high degree of segmentation. Furthermore, Pedersen pointed to a companion paper that showed how differing haircuts could explain violations of the law of one price for assets that were otherwise very similar. Pedersen argued that a value-at-risk constraint, as opposed to asset-specific haircuts, could not explain these deviations from the law of one price.

Daron Acemoglu voiced concern that the asset-specific haircuts were fixed exogenously. He argued that these haircuts should respond endogenously to policy changes, and Pedersen conceded that more can be done to endogenize the haircuts.

978-0-226-00212-5/2011/2010-0304$10.00

Acemoglu also noted that their triple-differencing econometric approach may not capture the partial effect of changes in the haircut on asset prices. He noted that any change in the haircut of any individual security would change the Lagrange multiplier on the agent's constraint and operate through the other haircuts to change the price of all assets. Adam Ashcraft noted that differences in S&P ratings could control for the indirect effects of changes in haircuts. Acemoglu suggested adding additional terms capturing the interaction of ex post margins and time effects. However, Pedersen responded that their triple-differencing method is effectively doing this, since the type of security (A2 versus A1A) controls for the ex post margin. As Pedersen notes, A2 securities became eligible for TALF while the margins for other securities were unchanged (remaining at 100%), thus capturing the price effect of a change in just the margin for a particular security.

Nobuhiro Kiyotaki observed that asset-specific margin constraints emerge when borrowers' trading cannot be observed by the lender. He asked whether these margins might change due to concerns about the actions of borrowers. Pedersen responded that collateral should obviate the need of the lender to monitor the actions of the borrower. The size of the haircut depends on the underlying value and liquidity of the asset and should be independent of any borrower action.

Deborah Lucas echoed Kiyotaki's concerns, arguing that counterparty risk was a key factor in the credit crisis. She argued that the model presented makes the strong assumption of no credit risk, while, in reality, the Fed offered collateralized loans well below the market prices and therefore exposed itself to adverse selection. She also added that there appeared to be large pools of private liquidity on the sidelines that could have purchased assets cheaply. Ashcraft responded that the Fed had several restrictions on program participation and acceptable collateral that prevented any adverse selection. As an example, Ashcraft noted that TALF loans came with a carry cap that required repayment of the loan to the Fed before borrowers received any gains.

Lucas acknowledged that the Fed attempted to limit adverse selection but added that the Fed took on significant risk if the credit crisis worsened. Frederic Mishkin responded that, in performing its role as lender of last resort, the Fed always faces difficulty distinguishing between liquidity and solvency of assets, and Robert Hall described the Fed's actions as attempting to mitigate an externality.

Pedersen disagreed that the Fed faced substantial credit risk. He noted that their model shows that when the natural buyers are credit constrained, there is a role for a central bank to reduce haircuts and support investment. Taking commercial mortgage-backed securities as an example, Pedersen noted that the Fed was effectively lending $35 on $100 face value; such assets had never shown low enough recovery rates to expose the Fed to any credit risk. Similarly, he noted that some derivative securities backed by U.S. Treasuries were trading with yields in excess of 10%. In short, the credit risk in these examples appears negligible.

The discussion turned to the mechanics of the repo market when Hall asked what determines the interest rate and margin on repo transactions. Ashcraft and Pedersen responded that the interest rate is set quite close to the money market rates, with a haircut high enough to make the security essentially riskless. Acemoglu added that securities in the money market are not perfect substitutes, and Woodford cited work by John Geanakoplos that described how both the interest rate and leverage can be determined endogenously. Lucas added that collateral can be divided into standard and nonstandard collateral, with haircuts for the latter negotiated on a case-by-case basis, differing markedly among assets and counterparties. Adrian noted that there is no centralized market for repo transactions—reported rates are some average of a set of similar transactions.

Pedersen noted that, in principle, two parties will negotiate the haircut. However, after the failure of Lehman Brothers, several money market funds simply stopped accepting whole classes of collateral, effectively raising haircuts to 100%. For many funds, Treasuries and agency securities became the only acceptable form of collateral. Lucas also noted that their model abstracted from the two-sided risk seen in most repo markets, since collateral values can fall, though Adrian noted that such issues are addressed with triparty repo arrangements.

Julio Rotemberg asked how robust the model's conclusions are, given that the selling observed seemed to be mostly panicked and irrational. He noted that the model depended on two types of agents with differing levels of risk aversion. Pedersen responded that the margin capital asset pricing model holds in more general circumstances and can explain asset-pricing facts in both the time series and cross section.

Rotemberg noted that agents, in the model presented, have common knowledge of the risks determining asset prices and that an alternative view of the crisis might emphasize a high degree of disagreement about the quality of the underlying assets. If the optimistic agents are wiped out, then the Fed does well ex post in an intervention simply because only pessimistic agents are setting market prices. Lucas added that there seemed to be quite a few arbitrage opportunities, but hedge funds remained on the sidelines despite having the means to acquire these assets. Pedersen argued that the Rotemberg hypothesis is still consistent with his model, but the optimistic buyers need to be constrained in some way. However, he disagreed with Lucas's view that hedge funds could take advantage of these arbitrage opportunities. In Pedersen's view, hedge funds were clearly capital constrained and many went out of business.

Ashcraft wrapped up the discussion by noting that, while the Fed lending facilities appeared effective in this crisis, it remains an open question as to whether these instruments can be used prudently in the future.

4

Technology Diffusion and Postwar Growth

Diego Comin, *Harvard University and NBER*
Bart Hobijn, *Federal Reserve Bank of San Francisco and Free University Amsterdam*

Wars, and especially the Second World War (WWII), are extremely disruptive episodes that lead to a major destruction of productive resources. Glick and Taylor (2010) estimate that the total number of deaths in WWII is approximately 2% of the 1940 world population, while the wounded made up another 3%. Wolff (1991) reports that the war led to a destruction or dismantling of about a quarter of the capital stock in Germany and Japan. The arguably largely exogenous nature of these disruptions has made wars, and particularly the recoveries that follow them, episodes that are often studied to understand the transitional dynamics that drive economic growth.[1]

What is especially puzzling about postwar recoveries is that countries have recovered at very different speeds after wars. For example, it took Spain 15 years to reach the pre–Civil War level of per capita GDP. Conversely, Italy reached its pre-WWII GDP level just 6 years after the end of the war. One might be tempted to think that these different speeds of recovery are simply due to the different extent of war damage across countries. However, this turns out to be an oversimplified view of the dynamics that have driven postwar growth.

A common thread that emerged from the many studies of the postwar performance of Germany, Japan, and their industrialized counterparts is that the standard neoclassical growth model implies a much higher postwar convergence rate than observed during postwar growth recovery of these countries, especially that of Japan.[2] Furthermore, after growing at a substantially higher rate than their steady-state growth rates for several decades after WWII, many countries did not converge to their prewar growth trajectory. Instead, they converged to a growth path substantially higher than the one they were on before the war.

978-0-226-00212-5/2011/2010-0401$10.00

In our view, these failures of the neoclassical growth model to account for the postwar economic growth experiences suggest the importance of the path of technological progress. Eaton and Kortum (1997) emphasize the importance of endogenous technology adoption for matching the postwar productivity growth experiences of the manufacturing sectors in the world's five leading industrialized economies. Gilchrist and Williams (2004) argue that endogenous productivity growth due to the putty-clay nature of capital does a better job of matching the postwar growth experience of these economies than the standard putty-putty neoclassical growth model. Chen et al. (2006) claim that in the case of Japan, neoclassical transitional dynamics do just fine when one feeds the observed path of TFP growth into the standard growth model. However, they do not aim to explain how this TFP path came about.

Hence, just as cross-country differences in TFP *levels* account for the bulk of the enormous disparities in GDP per capita *levels* (see Klenow and Rodríguez-Clare 1997; Hall and Jones 1999), cross-country differences in TFP *dynamics* drive a large part of the differences in postwar growth experiences. It is thus important, as Prescott (1997) advocates, not only to have a theory of differences in TFP levels but also to understand the sources of differences in the dynamics of TFP.

In this paper we study the extent to which these differences in TFP dynamics across countries can be accounted for by observed differences in technology adoption patterns. In particular, we explore the idea that wars, in addition to destroying capital, affect the costs of adopting new technologies. This may occur for a variety of reasons. Our main focus here is on the reduction in adoption costs due to the postwar economic aid and technical assistance provided by the United States to Japan and Western Europe.

We argue that this reduction of adoption costs mainly reflects technology transfers from the United States to other countries and that such transfers disproportionately involved knowledge about state-of-the-art, modern, technologies. If this would be an important factor driving postwar productivity growth, then we would observe a disproportionate acceleration in the speed of adoption of new technologies in the countries that received economic aid and technical assistance from the United States during the postwar period. We then document that this is what we observe in the data.

We do so in three steps. First, we introduce a model of technology adoption and economic growth, similar to Comin and Hobijn (2010a), that allows us to estimate the speed of adoption of technologies, and changes in this speed, for many countries and technologies. We use data on direct measures of technology adoption from the Cross-Country Historical Adoption of Technology (CHAT) data set, described in Comin and Hobijn (2009a). These data cover major technologies related to transportation, communication, and electricity and have not been extensively used in the cross-country analysis of postwar growth dynamics. We complement these data with data on population, real GDP, and consumption from Maddison (2007) and Barro and Ursúa (2008). This allows us to consider a sample of 10 technologies and 39 countries with a varying degree of involvement in WWII.

We then show that U.S. economic aid and technology assistance are strongly associated with the adoption of new technologies during the postwar period. In particular, the average country that benefited from the program reduced the lags with which it adopted the new technologies in our sample by 4 years compared to other countries. For old technologies, instead, we find that the assistance programs led to an increase in the adoption lags after WWII. The differential effect of the technology assistance programs on new versus old technologies persists after including country fixed effects. This finding reinforces our prior that technology assistance reduces adoption lags through a reduction in the costs of adopting technologies rather than through an overall improvement in efficiency, since the increases in efficiency associated with the latter would have a more symmetric effect across technologies. Furthermore, the effect of technology assistance on adoption lags is robust to controlling for institutional measures such as polity (or its postwar change) as well as policies such as openness to trade.

The differential effect of U.S. assistance on the pace of adoption of new and old technologies as well as the robustness of the results to country fixed effects suggests that there were substantial forces beyond economy-wide effects, emphasized by, for example, De Long and Eichengreen (1991) and Eichengreen (2007), that drove the acceleration in technology adoption in the countries. In addition, we use the classification method of technologies applied in Comin and Hobijn (2009b) to show that this differential effect across technologies is not such that technologies subject to more lobbying saw a bigger decline in their adoption lags. Thus, we conclude that we find little evidence in support of Olson's (1982) hypothesis that WWII led to the decline in distributional coalitions that had slowed down technology adoption in Japan and Western Europe before the onset of the war.

Finally, we find that the reduction in the lags with which countries adopted new technologies explains a significant part of postwar growth differentials between countries, even when one controls for differences in institutions and openness to trade. Though this correlation is by no means a proof of causation, we do interpret it as indicative of the importance of U.S. technology transfers for postwar growth differentials across countries.

The paper is structured as follows. In Section I we document the main facts about the damage incurred by countries during WWII and the differences in their subsequent growth experiences. We augment the evidence on real GDP per capita with evidence on the impact of the war on technology usage and the subsequent recovery in the technology-specific measures for different countries. We also discuss the U.S. economic and technical assistance to Japan and Western Europe. In Section II we introduce the model, solve for the optimal decisions of firms and households, and define equilibrium. In Section III we explain how the model maps into predictions for the path of observable measures of technology adoption and use this mapping to derive reduced-form equations that allow us to estimate adoption lags. We discuss the resulting estimates of the changes in the adoption lags and their implications in Section IV. We present conclusions in Section V.[3]

I. WWII Damage and Subsequent Growth

A wide range of studies have documented the very strong growth experienced by many industrialized countries during the 3 decades that followed WWII.[4] In this section we give a brief review of economic growth in industrialized countries during these decades. Since our emphasis is on technology adoption, we augment the GDP-based analysis, which is very similar to that in other studies, with facts about the use of technologies. We first discuss the damage done during the war and then proceed by documenting postwar growth.

Figure 1 depicts the decline in real GDP per capita and technology usage per capita for three technologies. Since we focus on per capita measures, we implicitly correct for war deaths. Glick and Taylor (2010) tabulate estimated casualties for many countries. Their estimates suggest that the total number of deaths in WWII is approximately 2% of the 1940 world population, while the wounded made up another 3%.

Panel a of figure 1 shows pre- and postwar levels of log real GDP per capita for the countries in our sample. The horizontal axis is the 1938 log real GDP per capita level, in deviation from that in 1946 in the United States, while the vertical axis shows the minimum of the 1945 and 1946 levels of log real GDP per capita.[5] The dashed line is the 45-degree line.

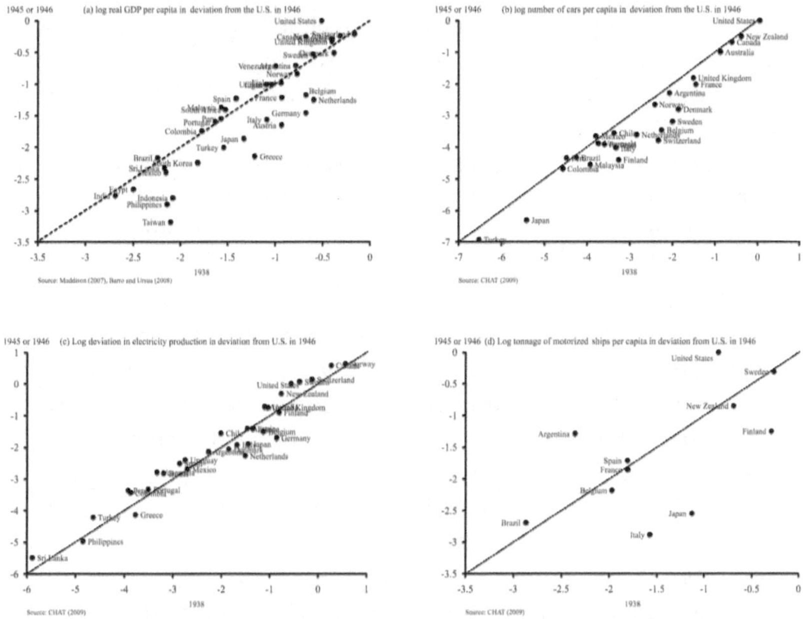

Fig. 1. Changes in real GDP and technology usage per capita during the WWII period. Sources: Panel a: Maddison (2007); Barro and Ursúa (2008); panels b–d: CHAT data set, as discussed in Comin and Hobijn (2009a).

Points below the 45-degree line depict countries that saw a GDP decline during the war. The vertical distance between the point and the 45-degree line approximately equals the percentage decline in real GDP per capita during the war. Germany, Japan, Austria, the Netherlands, and Greece as well as Indonesia, the Philippines, and Taiwan all saw real GDP per capita declines in excess of 40% during WWII. To put this in a historical perspective, the decline in U.S. real GDP per capita during the Great Depression was approximately 30%. The United States and Canada geared up their industrial complexes to produce military supplies during the war period and actually saw substantial increases in real GDP per capita during WWII.

These declines in real GDP in war-ravaged countries coincided with substantial declines in the usage of many technologies. In terms of aggregate capital stock measures, Wolff (1991) reports that WWII led to a destruction or dismantling of about a quarter of the capital stock in Germany and Japan. Panels b–d of figure 1 are the equivalent of panel a but for three technology usage measures rather than for real GDP. The three particular technologies depicted are cars, electricity, and steamships and motor ships, respectively.

The qualitative patterns in terms of declines in technology usage are very similar to those in real GDP. Countries that saw active combat on their soil during the war also saw very substantial declines in their technology usage. In fact, the merchant fleets of many countries were almost completely destroyed. Similarly, declines in cars per capita were much higher than those in real GDP per capita. Declines in electricity production, however, were less pronounced than those in overall economic activity.

The substantial declines in GDP and technology usage in war-ravaged countries were followed by a remarkable post-WWII rebound. This can be seen from figure 2. It shows the path of log real GDP and technology usage per capita for three technologies for four countries in our sample. The countries that we have chosen for illustrative purposes are the United States, Germany, Japan, and Argentina. We follow De Long (1988) and De Long and Eichengreen (1991) here and include Argentina as an example of a country that, in spite of being relatively rich at the onset of the war and almost unscathed by WWII, did not see the type of catch-up with the United States in the postwar period that many other industrialized economies saw.

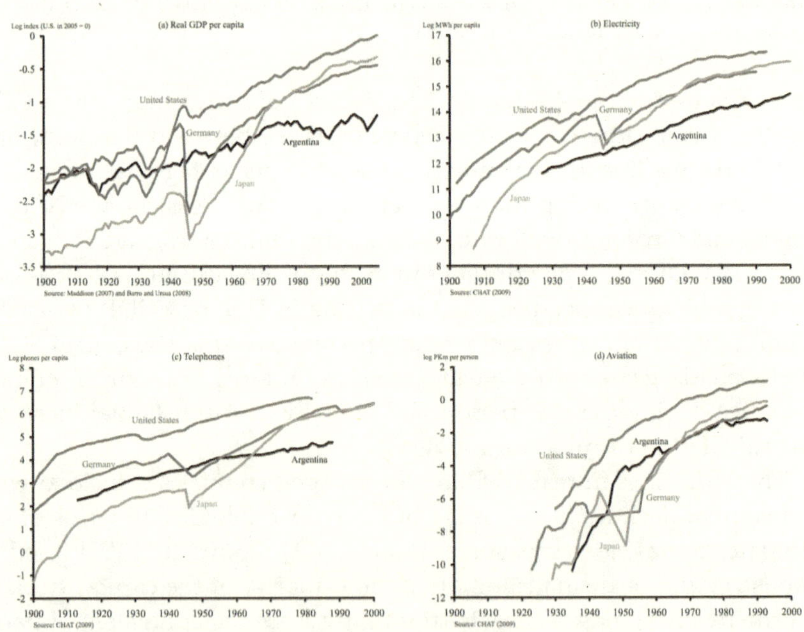

Fig. 2. Real GDP and technology usage per capita for four countries. Sources: Panel a: Maddison (2007); Barro and Ursúa (2008); panels b–d: CHAT data set, as discussed in Comin and Hobijn (2009a).

In terms of the paths of real GDP per capita (panel a), four things stand out from this figure. First, after all the turbulence of the Great Depression and WWII, the United States ended up on approximately the same growth path it was on before 1929. Second, Argentina starts to steadily fall behind the United States after WWII. Argentinian per capita GDP was 84% of that of the United States in 1938 and declined to 24% in the 1970s. The final two things to take away from panel a are the most important for the rest of the analysis in this paper.

The first is that it took Germany and Japan until between 1955 and 1960 to return to their prewar growth paths. The second is that, in contrast to the United States, both Germany and Japan did not converge to this prewar path but instead busted through it and converged to a growth path that was substantially higher than that in the prewar period.

Just as for the declines during WWII, the postwar experiences in terms of technology usage exhibit qualitative patterns very similar to those of real GDP per capita. The United States saw a relatively smooth path of technology usage for all of these technologies. Contrary to the path of log real GDP, however, these technology usage paths are inherently nonlinear. Argentina, while comparable in terms of technology usage at the beginning of the century, ends up trailing the other three countries by the end of it.

After the substantial declines in technology usage due to WWII we documented in figure 1, Germany and Japan returned to their prewar technology usage paths about as fast as or even slightly faster than they returned to their aggregate growth path. Moreover, just as for real GDP per capita, they did not converge back to this path but instead moved up to higher levels of technology usage. Of course, because of the nonlinear nature of the technology usage path, a more formal quantitative analysis of this claim requires taking a stance on the shape of this path, which is the reason that we introduce a theoretical model in Section II.

Germany and Japan are by no means the only two countries that, after the war, converged to a higher growth path than they were on before. Many Western European countries experienced this period of "supergrowth." As Dumke (1990) points out, the initial hypothesis was that most of the postwar experiences of these countries could be interpreted as driven by standard capital (re)accumulation after the destruction during the war. This is often referred to as the "reconstruction hypothesis" and is inspired by the standard neoclassical growth model with exogenous technological progress.

As better historical cross-country real GDP data became available in the 1980s, empirical studies (Abramovitz 1986; Baumol 1986) emphasized that the reconstruction hypothesis might be able to explain the return of these countries to their postwar growth paths, but it fails to explain the upward shifts in these paths. In order to understand these shifts, one has to understand the determinants of the productivity growth differentials that caused them. The observation that it is productivity growth differentials and not capital accumulation that account for most of the variation in postwar growth experiences across industrialized countries is known as the "productivity hypothesis."

We show in the remainder of this paper that the productivity growth that is at the heart of this hypothesis coincided with an acceleration in the rate at which the countries that caught up the most with the United States in the postwar decades adopted new technologies. The question is, What is the main driver of this joint acceleration in productivity growth and technology adoption? Was there a common factor that drove both of them, or did one lead to the other or vice versa?

Technology adoption decisions and other productivity enhancements are endogenous to many factors. For the purpose of our argument we distinguish two types of such factors. The first are those that lead to direct increases in the overall efficiency of the economy, which might then be amplified by an acceleration in the adoption of technologies. These include improvements in the capacity and quality of institutions (as in, e.g., Acemoglu, Johnson, and Robinson 2001). The second type of factors have small direct effects on productivity growth. Instead they affect productivity indirectly through the reduction of adoption costs and the associated increase in the rate of technology adoption. These factors include adoption history (see Comin, Easterly, and Gong 2010) and the international transfer of know-how about new technologies.

In principle, observed exogenous variation in these latter factors could be used for an instrumental variables analysis to quantify the causal effect of technology adoption on productivity and economic growth. Unfortunately, such a source of exogenous variation is not available, and thus, such an instrumental variables approach is not feasible.

Our approach here, instead, is to identify a factor that had large effects on adoption costs through technology transfers but the variation in which across countries was probably not exogenous. As an alternative to an instrumental variables approach, we then exploit the different cross-technology implications of a reduction in adoption costs as opposed to those of other types of factors. The particular factor we focus on is postwar U.S. economic aid and technical assistance to Western Europe and Japan.

A. *Technical Assistance and the Marshall Plan*

Following World War II, how did the United States go about providing technical assistance to Western Europe and Japan? The Marshall Plan, otherwise known as the European Recovery Program, was unveiled to the world in the summer of 1947 by U.S. Secretary of State George Marshall. As Eichengreen and Uzan (1992) describe, initially the aim of the program was to provide direct economic relief to Western Europe in the form of capital transfers as well as financing for investment and import purposes. While this initial effort was effective at alleviating the oppressive economic conditions in both the European commodities and capital markets, Boel (2003) argues that it failed to address the mounting productivity gap that had formed between the United States and Europe during WWII.

According to Boel (2003), Western Europe was experiencing "worsening trade and payment deficit[s]" that stemmed from the considerable productivity gap and its inability to compete economically. Owing to these conditions, the United States expanded and focused the Marshall Plan by instituting the Technical Assistance and Productivity Program in 1949 (Bjarnar and Kipping 1998). The main thrust of the Technical Assistance Program (TAP) was to increase productivity in Western Europe. The conventional wisdom surrounding the productivity gap was that Europe had technologically fallen behind the United States. To address these concerns, the United States used the TAP as a conduit through which to disseminate state-of-the-art technologies, technical knowledge, and managerial sciences.

The channels through which the technological transfer occurred inherently revolved around the lending of U.S. specialists to Europe and the allowance of their European counterparts to visit and observe processes in the United States. Additionally, U.S. government agencies played an important role in transferring technological advances. The Bureau of Labor Statistics, for example, contributed by providing statistical technical assistance that involved the exchange of specialists but also was focused on introducing a data- and statistics-rich approach to productive efficiency in Western Europe (Wasser and Dolfman 2005).

Europe was not the sole beneficiary of these productivity and technology exchanges. Tiratsoo (2000) documents how the United States in 1955 initiated its TAP in Japan. Like the TAP in Western Europe, the Japanese assistance plan focused on increasing technological and productive know-how.

Anecdotal evidence provided in several studies reveals the very significant impact these TAPs had on the productivity of individual companies and industries as a whole. For example, Tiratsoo (2000) recounts that after the Mitsubishi Company received technical assistance from the United States in building a new assembly plant, it was able to increase productive capacity by roughly 40%. The *International Directory of Company Histories* (2001) describes how, in 1950, two leading executives of Toyota Motor Company, "seeking new ideas for Toyota's anticipated growth, ... toured Ford Motor Company's factories and observed the latest automobile production technology. One especially useful idea they brought home from their visit to Ford resulted in Toyota's suggestion system, in which every employee was encouraged to make suggestions for improvements of any kind" (459).

Similar stories emerged about the U.S. technical assistance in Europe. Wasser and Dolfman (2005, 49) cite one source as saying that productivity within individual industries "commonly increased by 25 to 50 percent within a year with little or no investment" as a result of the TAP. Thus the TAP was not about stimulating productivity gains through capital spending as much as it was focused on the dissemination of technological and productive know-how about state-of-the-art technologies.

The extent of the knowledge transfers from the United States to Western Europe and Japan goes well beyond the formal TAP. U.S. efforts to boost productivity in its sphere of influence were part of a broader national security policy after 1953 and were in large part driven by the geopolitical realities of the Cold War.

What is important for the rest of our analysis is that the emphasis of these knowledge transfers was on modern, state-of-the-art, technologies. Because of this, if technical assistance–related knowledge spillovers were an important driving force of a postwar acceleration in technology adoption in Western Europe and Japan, then we would expect this to be especially the case for newer technologies.

B. *Other Factors Underlying Postwar Catch-up*

Most alternative explanations of the postwar supergrowth period have very different implications for the cross-technology variation in the changes in the speed of adoption from the old and new technology distinction emphasized above. Explanations that emphasize country-specific rather than technology-specific explanations imply that, to a first order, the effect of postwar changes on technology adoption should be symmetric across technologies. For example, Eichengreen (2007) emphasizes the reshuffling of the social contract between the government, employers, and workers after WWII in Western Europe. He argues that this led to a type of "coordinated capitalism" with high savings and subdued wage growth. Such a process can definitely explain many facts about the postwar growth experiences of leading industrialized nations. However, it applies as much to old as to new technologies.

Similarly, explanations based on country-specific factors such as changes in institutions and openness to trade do not explain the differential pattern of reduction in adoption lags between new and old technologies.[6] Besides country-specific factors, another factor often mentioned in relationship to the postwar productivity boost in Western Europe and Japan is Olson's (1982) theory of social rigidities. Olson argues that "the emasculation and abolishment of distributional coalitions" during postwar occupation and as part of the Marshall Plan reduced the special interest groups that had lobbied to slow down technology adoption before WWII.

If Olson's (1982) mechanism is an important factor driving the acceleration of technology adoption after WWII, then this acceleration would be particularly pronounced for technologies whose adoption impeded the interest of these lobbying groups. To distinguish between technologies for which this could be important or not, we follow Comin and Hobijn (2009b) and classify technologies in our data set into ones that are likely to be subject to lobbying and ones that are not. Since this classification is different from the "old" versus "new" distinction we discussed before, this means that Olson's (1982) hypothesis has cross-technology implications different from the technical assistance factor we focus on.

To set the stage for the rest of our analysis, consider figure 3. It depicts per capita GDP levels relative to those of the United States in 1950 and 1970 for the 39 countries in our sample. The further a country is above the 45-degree line, the faster it caught up with the United States during the 3 decades following the war. Black dots represent countries that received substantial postwar U.S. economic aid and technical assistance. As can be seen from the picture, countries that received U.S. support seem to have caught up faster than countries that did not receive U.S. support. What we show in the remainder of our analysis is that those countries that received U.S. support saw disproportionate declines in their technology gaps with the United States in terms of new technologies and that the change in this gap explains a significant part of the cross-country variation depicted in figure 3.

In order to relate postwar growth to an acceleration in the speed of technology adoption, we first need to quantify this speed. Because of

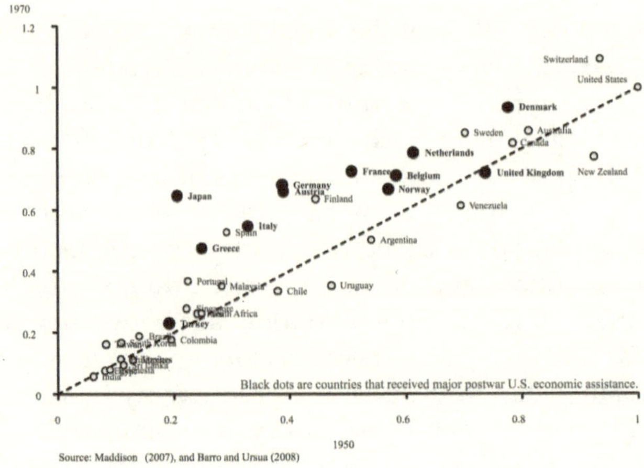

Fig. 3. Postwar catch-up in real GDP per capita. Sources: Maddison (2007); Barro and Ursúa (2008).

the inherent nonlinear nature of the technology usage measures depicted in panels b–d in figure 2, quantifying this speed involves relating these nonlinearities to an interpretable measure of the speed of technology adoption. For this purpose, we introduce a model of economic growth and technology adoption in the next section that relates cross-country growth dynamics to our measures of technology usage and allows us to interpret their observed curvature in terms of the amount of time that elapses between the invention of a technology and when it gets adopted in a country. This delay is the adoption lag.

II. Model with Endogenous TFP and Adoption Lags

We present a version of the model of technology adoption and growth introduced in Comin and Hobijn (2010a). The model that we present serves two main purposes. First, it allows us to illustrate how the endogenously determined path of the adoption of technologies determines the equilibrium level of aggregate TFP, thus relating the pattern of technology adoption to the path of productivity that is so crucial for understanding the postwar experiences of many industrialized economies. Second, we use the model to show how the endogenous technology adoption patterns yield curvature in the time path of measures of technology diffusion for which we have data. It is the curvature in these diffusion measures that we use to identify adoption lags in the data.

In contrast to Comin and Hobijn (2010a), the analysis in this paper focuses on the transitional dynamics of the model. This is important because of the emphasis on the postwar recovery in our analysis, which is inherently a realization of the transitional dynamics.[7]

Though our empirical analysis involves a cross section of different technologies, we present our theoretical model here in a one-sector framework to simplify the exposition and to allow for the study of aggregate dynamics that are comparable with available cross-country data.

A. *Preferences and Technology*

The unit measure of households in our model is assumed to have log preferences such that the optimal savings decision implies that the growth rate of consumption equals the difference between the real interest rate, $\tilde{r}$, and the discount rate ρ.[8] What is nonstandard is the technology side of our model. It is the focus of the rest of this subsection.

1. Capital Vintages and Adoption Lags

Our framework is one in which, as in Parente and Prescott (1994) and Eaton and Kortum (1997), the level of TFP is determined by the distance between a country's productivity level and the world technology frontier. Throughout, we take the evolution of the world technology frontier as exogenous.[9] Here we describe what, in particular, we mean by this distance. How this distance is the result of the technology adoption decisions of capital goods producers is explained later in this section.

The single good in this economy, which we use as the numeraire good such that it has a price of one, is produced using a constant elasticity of substitution (CES) technology that is used to combine a continuum of intermediate goods each produced with its own specific capital vintage, v. At each instant t, a new capital vintage is introduced such that the set of available intermediate goods is given by $v \in \overline{V} = (-\infty, t]$.

We distinguish two groups of intermediates, indexed by τ. The first, denoted by $\tau = o$, is the set of intermediates produced using old production methods, $v < \underline{v}$. The second, denoted by $\tau = n$, consists of intermediate goods produced using production methods that involve newer, more recently invented, capital vintages, $v \geq \underline{v}$. Hence, $\tau = o$ can be interpreted as the old technology and $\tau = n$ as the new one.

Aggregate output, Y,[10] is produced using

$$Y = (Y_o^{1/\mu} + Y_n^{1/\mu})^{\mu}, \tag{1}$$

where $\mu > 1$ and

$$Y_\tau = \left(\int_{V_\tau} Y_v^{1/\mu} dv \right)^\mu \tag{2}$$

for $\tau = o, n$. The set of vintages in use is thus given by $V = V_o \cup V_n$. However, not all available intermediates are necessarily used for the production of output, such that $V \subseteq \overline{V}$.

The use of a more expansive set of intermediates affects productivity in two ways. First of all, as already can be seen from (1) and (2), the use of more intermediates leads to a gain from variety. We call this type of productivity gain the *variety effect*.

The second effect occurs because technological progress is embodied in new capital vintages. Similarly to Solow (1960), newer capital vintages are more productive than their older counterparts. This difference in productivity levels is reflected in the technologies with which the intermediate goods are produced. Each intermediate, v, is produced by combining labor, L_v, and capital, K_v, using a Cobb-Douglas production function of the form

$$Y_v = Z_v L_v^{1-\alpha} K_v^\alpha, \tag{3}$$

where Z_v is the level of productivity embodied in the units of the capital vintage v; Z_v is constant over time and is increasing in v. Let γ be the growth rate of embodied technological change. Then

$$Z_v = Z_0 e^{\gamma v}, \tag{4}$$

where $\gamma > 0$. Hence, the world technology frontier consists of the productivity levels of the set of all available vintages $\overline{V}$. Moreover, if the set of technologies used, V, expands to include newer vintages, then this increases the overall productivity level. We refer to this as the *embodiment effect* of technology adoption.

If the most recent vintages are not used, then the embodied productivity level of the vintages in use falls short of that of the frontier. How much it falls short depends on the gap between the set of available and the set of used vintages.

Just as in Comin and Hobijn (2010a), we consider the case in which the set of vintages in use is of the form $V = (-\infty, t - D]$. Here $D \geq 0$ is the time that elapsed since the invention of the newest capital vintage that is being used in production. It is the *adoption lag*.

2. Capital Goods Production

Each capital vintage, v, is produced by a single monopolistic competitor. Capital goods production is fully reversible, and the unit production cost of a physical unit of capital is assumed to be constant across vintages and normalized to one unit of the final good.[11] Capital goods depreciate at the rate δ. Because the suppliers of these capital vintages have monopoly power, they can choose the rental rate R_v at which they rent out the capital stock. The monopoly profits that these suppliers make are then used to pay off the initial adoption costs that they incurred to become the sole supplier of the particular capital vintage.

3. Technology Adoption

In order to supply a particular capital vintage a firm has to incur a one-time adoption cost. These costs go up in the distance between the vintage adopted and the best vintage in place. In particular, let $\overline{v}_t = t - D_t$ denote the best vintage adopted at instant t. Then the adoption of $v = \overline{v}_t + dt$ at instant $t + dt$ costs

$$\Gamma_{v,t+dt} = e^{b\chi}\overline{\Psi}\left(\frac{\gamma}{\mu - 1}\right)\left[\frac{1}{\gamma}\frac{(Z_{\overline{v}_t+dt} - Z_{\overline{v}_t})/dt}{Z_{\overline{v}_t}}\right]\left(\frac{Z_{\overline{v}_t}}{Z_t}\right)^{\chi} Y_t, \tag{5}$$

where $b > 0$ and $\chi > 0$.

Hence, the adoption costs increase in the rate at which the set of adopted vintages expands. However, they are lower, the further away one is from the world technology frontier, as reflected by the productivity of the most recent vintage invented, Z_t. The parameter χ can be interpreted as the absorption rate. Discrete jumps in the set of adopted vintages, and thus in the adoption lag, are infinitely expensive and do not occur. Instead, the adoption lags evolve smoothly over time. The other parameter that determines the adoption costs is b, which is similar in interpretation to the barriers to adoption in Parente and Prescott (1994).[12]

The last term of the adjustment costs reflects that they are increasing in the size of the market. This is, on a theoretical level, important to assure the existence of a balanced growth path on which adoption lags are constant. Moreover, it is consistent with evidence that technology adoption involves a substantial use of resources beyond the installation of equipment.[13] The costs of these resources are generally increasing in the size of the market, that is, the marginal product of their use elsewhere in the economy.

B. *Factor Demands, Aggregation, and Productivity*

1. Factor Demands

The nested CES structure of the production function and the assumption that all factor inputs can adjust flexibly yields familiar expressions for the relative demands for intermediates and for prices. That is, the demand for the intermediate produced using vintage v equals

$$Y_v = Y(P_v)^{-\mu/(\mu-1)}, \tag{6}$$

where perfect competition in the production of intermediates yields that P_v equals the unit production cost:

$$P_v = \frac{1}{Z_v}\left(\frac{W}{1-\alpha}\right)^{1-\alpha}\left(\frac{R_v}{\alpha}\right)^{\alpha}. \tag{7}$$

Here, W is the real wage rate paid for the labor input L_v.

As in Comin and Hobijn (2010a), the monopolistic competitor that supplies capital goods of vintage v realizes that it faces a downward-sloping demand curve for its capital goods. This demand curve is downward sloping because an increase in the rental cost, R_v, raises the prices of the intermediates produced using capital vintage v. Such a price increase reduces demand for the intermediate good and thus for the capital goods used in their production. When this is taken into account, the profit-maximizing rental rate, R_v, that the supplier of capital good v chooses is equal to a gross markup times the user cost of capital. This rental rate is the same across capital vintages and equals

$$R_v = \frac{\epsilon}{\epsilon - 1}(\tilde{r} + \delta) = R, \tag{8}$$

where $\epsilon \equiv 1 + [\alpha/(\mu - 1)]$. This, combined with (7), implies that relative prices across intermediate inputs fully reflect relative embodied productivity levels for the capital vintages used to produce the intermediates.

2. Aggregation

The result is that we obtain very tractable aggregate production function representations. Because, for our empirical analysis, we use data at the technology level, that is, $\tau \in \{o, n\}$, we build the aggregation results up from that level. That is, we can write the level of intermediate output associated with technology τ as

$$Y_\tau = A_\tau K_\tau^\alpha L_\tau^{1-\alpha}, \tag{9}$$

where

$$K_\tau \equiv \int_{v \in V_\tau} K_v dv,$$
$$L_\tau \equiv \int_{v \in V_\tau} L_v dv,$$

and the technology-specific TFP level is given by

$$A_\tau = \left[\int_{V_\tau} Z_v^{1/(\mu-1)} dv \right]^{\mu-1}. \tag{10}$$

For results used for our empirical application, it is useful to realize that this aggregation result implies that the unit production cost, and thus the price, of Y_τ equals

$$P_\tau = \frac{1}{A_\tau} \left(\frac{W}{1-\alpha} \right)^{1-\alpha} \left(\frac{R_\tau}{\alpha} \right)^\alpha, \tag{11}$$

while the demand for output of technology τ is given by the iso-elastic demand function

$$Y_\tau = Y(P_\tau)^{-[\mu/(\mu-1)]}, \tag{12}$$

and the rental cost share of capital is equal to α, such that

$$R_\tau K_\tau = \alpha P_\tau Y_\tau. \tag{13}$$

In a similar way, the technology-specific production functions yield an aggregate production function representation, which reads

$$Y = AK^\alpha L^{1-\alpha}, \tag{14}$$

where $K \equiv K_o + K_n$, $L \equiv L_o + L_n$, and the aggregate level of TFP

$$A = [Z_o^{1/(\mu-1)} + Z_n^{1/(\mu-1)}]^{\mu-1} = \left[\int_{-\infty}^{t-Dt} Z_v^{1/(\mu-1)}\,dv\right]^{\mu-1}. \tag{15}$$

3. Productivity and Adoption Lags

These aggregation results allow us to relate the technology-specific and aggregate productivity levels, A_τ and A, to the set of vintages adopted, that is, to V, and thus to the adoption lags, D. Solving for the technology-specific TFP level for the new technology yields

$$A_n = \left(\frac{\mu-1}{\gamma}\right)^{\mu-1} Z_{\underline{v}} \underbrace{e^{\gamma(t-D-\underline{v})}}_{\text{embodiment effect}} \underbrace{\{1 - e^{-[\gamma/(\mu-1)](t-D-\underline{v})}\}^{\mu-1}}_{\text{variety effect}}. \tag{16}$$

Here $t - D - \underline{v}$ is the measure of vintages of the new technology that is in use, that is, of $V_n = (\underline{v}, t - D]$. This measure shows up in two ways. First, it shows up through the embodiment effect, which reflects that the average embodied productivity level is increasing in the number of vintages of the new technology in use. This is what drives long-run growth in the adoption of the new technology and in the economy as a whole. Second, the measure of vintages adopted also shows up because there are gains from variety in the CES production function. Since, in the long run, the growth rate of the number of varieties goes to zero, the variety effect is important during the early stages of adoption of the new technology and tapers off as the use of the technology becomes more widespread. It is this time-varying effect of the variety effect that drives curvature in the measured adoption of new technologies that we exploit in our empirical analysis.

The aggregate TFP level can be derived in a similar fashion. However, because aggregate TFP is driven by the whole set of vintages in use, that is, $V = (-\infty, t - D]$, which does not have an expanding measure of vintages adopted, the aggregate TFP level is not subject to the variety effect. As a result, it can be written as

$$A_t = A_0 e^{\gamma(t-D)}, \tag{17}$$

where

$$A_0 = Z_0 \left(\frac{\mu-1}{\gamma}\right)^{\mu-1}.$$

Hence, aggregate TFP in this model is endogenously determined by the adoption lags induced by the barriers to entry. The adoption lag, D, can be interpreted as the distance from the world technology frontier measured in years.

C. *Optimal Adoption*

So far, we have derived how the adoption lag affects the equilibrium level of productivity. We have not, however, solved for the optimal technology adoption decision that determines the lag. This is what we do here.

We denote the market value of a firm that supplies capital goods v at instant t, after entry into the market, as $M_{v,t}$. Any vintage gets adopted whenever, at time t, this market value exceeds the adoption cost, $\Gamma_{v,t}$, a firm needs to incur to enter the market. That is, for all vintages v that are being adopted at time t, it must be the case that

$$\Gamma_{v,t} \leq M_{v,t}. \tag{18}$$

If there is a positive adoption lag, then this holds with equality for the best vintage that is being adopted.

As we derive in appendix A, the market value of the firm that supplies capital vintage v equals

$$M_{v,t} = \int_t^{\infty} e^{-\int_t^s \tilde{r}_{s'} ds'} \pi_{vs} ds = \left(\frac{Z_v}{A_t}\right)^{1/(\mu-1)} \Psi_t Y_t. \tag{19}$$

Here Ψ_t is the total market value of all capital goods suppliers relative to GDP, which, if they are all publicly traded, can be interpreted as the stock market to GDP ratio.

Combining (5), (18), and (19) yields that the adoption lag satisfies the differential equation

$$\dot{D}_t = 1 - \left(\frac{\Psi_t}{\overline{\Psi}}\right) e^{\chi(\gamma D - b)}. \tag{20}$$

The intuition behind this equation is as follows. The higher the current adoption lag, the cheaper the adoption of technologies and the more quickly the adoption lag declines. The higher the stock market to GDP ratio, Ψ_t, the higher the ratio of future benefits from adoption relative to the current costs and the faster the adoption lag declines. Finally, the higher the barriers to entry, b, the more expensive technology adoption is and the adoption lag will decline less quickly. In fact, in steady state, where $\dot{D} = 0$, the adoption lag equals b/γ. In steady state, b is the percentage productivity loss due to the barriers to entry.

D. *Equilibrium*

Equilibrium is defined as in Comin and Hobijn (2010a). The details of this definition are relegated to the technical appendix. Two nonstandard features of the equilibrium are worth pointing out here.

First, for the aggregate equilibrium, it is important to know the amount of resources devoted to the adoption costs. The aggregate adoption costs in this economy turn out to equal

$$\Gamma = \left(\frac{\gamma}{\mu - 1}\right)\Psi Y. \tag{21}$$

Second, the aggregate resource constraint includes the aggregate adoption costs, such that

$$Y = C + I + \Gamma. \tag{22}$$

For our empirical analysis in Section III and beyond, we assume that adoption costs are measured as final demand. In particular, we assume that adjustment costs are measured as gross investment expenditures. This allows us to interpret Y as measured GDP, C as measured consumption, and $I + \Gamma$ as measured investment.[14]

The long-run growth rate of the economy depends only on the, exogenously given, growth rate of the world technology frontier. In particular, on the balanced growth path, this economy grows at rate $\gamma/(1 - \alpha)$.

III. Identification and Estimation of Adoption Lags

So far, our focus has been on the aggregate dynamics of our model. When we described the model, we specifically defined an old and a new technology. Moreover, we derived the equilibrium path of output and capital for the new technology as a function of the adoption lags. We did so to be able to map the equilibrium variables in our model into observed measures of technology usage, taken from Comin and Hobijn (2009a). In this section we describe this mapping and how it allows us to obtain estimates of technology adoption lags.

A. *Technology Measures*

The data we use from Comin and Hobijn (2009a) contain two types of measures of technology usage for a broad range of countries and a very long time span. First, the equivalent of Y_n is output produced with different technologies. Examples are megawatt-hours of electricity generated, the number of telegrams sent, and the number of ton-kilometers of freight transported by rail. The second type of measure, equivalent to K_n, consists of the number of the units of capital goods used to produce a particular intermediate like trucks that are used to provide road freight transportation services. Table 1 contains a list of the 10 technologies we use for our analysis. The choice of these technologies is mainly determined by the data requirements of the method applied. That is, we choose technologies for which we have a substantial number of observations for many years and countries both before and after WWII. The table also includes the classification of the technologies into "old" and "new." Technologies are classified as new if they were invented after 1850.

Our model has direct implications for the paths of these variables. This can be seen by combining (11), (12), and (13) and taking logarithms. With logs of variables denoted by small letters, for example, $y_\tau = \ln Y_\tau$, this yields that

$$y_\tau = y + \frac{\mu}{\mu - 1}[a_\tau - (1 - \alpha)(y - l) - \alpha r_\tau - \alpha \ln \alpha] \quad (23)$$

and

$$k_\tau = y + \ln \alpha + \frac{1}{\mu - 1}[a_\tau - (1 - \alpha)(y - l) - \alpha r_\tau - \alpha \ln \alpha] - r_\tau. \quad (24)$$

The main driving force behind the curvature in the technology usage measures is the productivity term a_τ. To understand how the adoption lags affect this curvature, consider figure 4. It plots the path of a_τ for five different cases. The first is the case in which vintages get adopted the instant they are invented, that is, the world technology frontier. The curvature in the world technology frontier is driven by the variety effect. That is, in the early stages of the adoption of a technology the increase in

Table 1
Technology Usage Measures

Technology	Description	New/Old
1. Aviation—passengers	Civil aviation passenger kilometers traveled on scheduled services by companies registered in the country concerned; not a measure of travel through a country's airports	New
2. Cars	Number of passenger cars (excluding tractors and similar vehicles) in use; numbers typically derived from registration and licensing records, meaning that vehicles out of use may occasionally be included	New
3. Electricity	Gross output of electric energy (inclusive of electricity consumed in power stations) in kilowatt-hours	New
4. Radios	Number of radios used in country	New
5. Railways—freight	Metric tons of freight carried on railways (excluding livestock and passenger baggage); freight for servicing of railroads is typically excluded but may be included for some countries	Old
6. Railways—passengers	Passenger journeys by railway in passenger kilometers; free passengers typically excluded but may be included for some countries	Old
7. Steamships and motor ships	Tonnage of steamships and motor ships (above a minimum weight) in use at midyear	Old
8. Telegrams	Number of telegrams sent in a year	Old
9. Telephones	Number of mainline telephone lines connecting a customer's equipment to the public switched telephone network as of year end	New
10. Trucks	Number of commercial vehicles, typically including buses and taxis (excluding tractors and similar vehicles), in use; numbers typically derived from registration and licensing records, meaning that vehicles out of use may occasionally be included	New

Source: All data taken from CHAT, described in Comin and Hobijn (2009a).

the number of vintages causes growth to exceed the long-run level of embodied technological change that sets in as the variety effect dissipates. The next two curves are those for constant adoption lags $D^* > D > 0$. These curves are horizontal shifts in the world technology frontier, where the size of the shift determines the technology adoption lag. Two of the paths are based on simulations in which there is an acceleration in technology adoption in the sense that at first adoption lags are constant

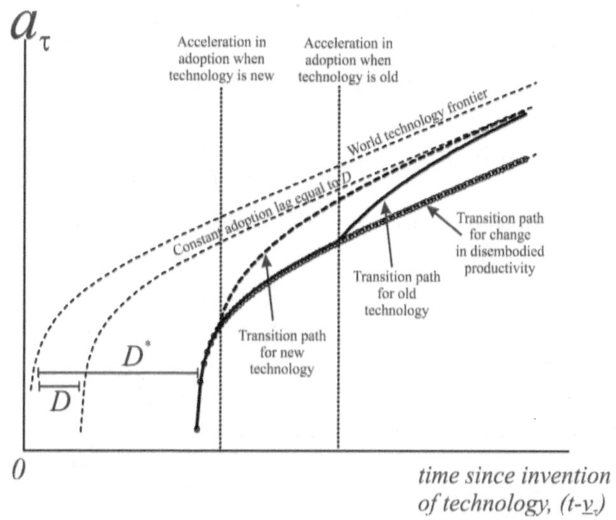

Fig. 4. Path of technology-specific TFP under different scenarios

at D^*.[15] However, at a certain point the adoption barriers are lowered and there is a transition toward shorter adoption lags of length D. What distinguishes these two paths is that for one the technology is relatively new while for the other it is older.

As can be seen from this figure, if the adoption lags are constant, then they are identified by the relative curvature of the path of a_τ at a particular point in time. This is the identification strategy used in Comin and Hobijn (2010a). However, our interest here is also in seeing whether we can identify changes in adoption lags over time for the same technology. The identification is a lot more complicated in that case. The initial adoption lag is determined by the curvature in the early part of the sample, and the change in the adoption lag is implied by the change in the intercept between the extrapolated initial path and the actual observed path for a_τ. The change in curvature in the middle part of the sample is due to the adjustment process. This change is what limits our analysis to technologies for which we have relatively long time-series evidence both before and after WWII.

B. *Reduced-Form Equation*

To get from equations (23) and (24) to the reduced-form equations we actually estimate, we take the steps described in this subsection.[16] It turns out that, to a first order, the productivity growth rate γ does not matter for the variety effect and thus for the curvature in a_τ. Therefore, as in Comin and Hobijn (2010a), we log-linearize a_τ around $\gamma = 0$. Both y_τ and k_τ depend on the rental rate r_τ. We use the optimal saving decision in the model to log-linearize the rental rate, which yields that r_τ is approximately proportional to the growth rate of consumption, Δc.[17]

The final steps have to do with that, using data for several technologies, we need to drop the one-sector assumption we used to derive the model and need to generalize our functional forms to accommodate the multitechnology nature of our data. As in Comin and Hobijn (2010a), to allow for multiple sectors, we use a nested CES aggregator, where $\theta/(\theta - 1)$ reflects the between-sector elasticity of demand and $\mu/(\mu - 1)$ is the within-sector elasticity of demand. In addition, the embodied technological change, γ_τ, and the invention date, $\underline{v}_\tau$, vary across technologies.

Finally, in Section I we documented very different rates of capital destruction during WWII across the different technologies in our data set. Since the model we considered has flexible capital mobility, it would imply an immediate replenishment of these capital losses and equate them across technologies. Hence, our model is not consistent with this varying impact. To match this feature of the data, we add a capital adjustment cost term to the equation.[18] The adjustment cost variable is denoted by X_τ below. It equals the investment to capital ratio for k_τ and output growth rate for y_τ.[19]

We make the following assumption about the adoption lag: before the war it is equal to D^*, and starting in 1945 it potentially converges to $D \neq D^*$. We study both the restricted case in which $D = D^*$ and the unrestricted case. We exclude the war years 1939–45 from our sample.

When we define the technology measures as $m_\tau \in \{y_\tau, k_\tau\}$, then the unrestricted reduced-form equation that we estimate can be written as

$$m_\tau = \beta_0 + y + \beta_1\{(\mu - 1)\ln[t - D - \mathbf{1}(t < 1939)\Delta D - \underline{v}_\tau] - (1 - \alpha)(y - l)\} + \beta_2[t - D - \mathbf{1}(t < 1939)\Delta D - \underline{v}_\tau] + \beta_3 \Delta c + \beta_4 X_\tau. \quad (25)$$

This equation is derived in detail in appendix A. Here $\mathbf{1}(\cdot)$ is an indicator function that is one if the condition holds and zero otherwise. The prewar adoption lag equals $D^* = D + \Delta D$. Finally, as we discussed above, we capture the transitional dynamics by the user cost term, β_3, and the adjustment cost term β_4.

C. Estimation

In principle, having data for many technologies and many countries, we can combine the country technology equations and obtain a very large system of nonlinear equations based on (25) to estimate. In practice, this turns out to be infeasible. Hence, instead of taking a system estimation approach, we estimate (25) for each country and technology separately. However, because (25) implies cross-country restrictions on the parameters, we do not do so in an unrestricted manner. We impose these cross-country restrictions by applying the U.S. estimates for all countries for the parameters that are assumed to be constant across countries. There are two parameters, μ and α, which we do not estimate but for which we simply impose the calibrated parameter values used in Comin and Hobijn (2010a), which are based on postwar U.S. evidence.

There is another advantage of this approach over a system estimation of the parameters. Because we apply this model to a very broad sample of countries, system estimation would be affected by serious misspecification of the model or measurement error in the data for each of these countries. Using this approach, we basically assume that the model is properly specified and the data are relatively reliably measured for the United States to identify the common parameters across countries.

The parameter restrictions we impose are based on the assumption that the technology parameters are the same across countries and that what potentially differ are adoption lags, preferences, and adjustment costs. This assumption means that β_1 and β_2 are the same across countries and that the other parameters can potentially vary. We estimate each equation using nonlinear least squares.

Note that the parameter β_2 captures the linear trend in the diffusion process of technology and that we estimate a different trend for each technology. This trend captures a variety of elements including embodied and disembodied productivity growth and the evolution of demand for the technology as countries develop (i.e., the Engel curve). Since the trend is specific to each technology, it captures the substitution away from old technologies that eventually are dominated by a superior technology (e.g., telegrams). These dynamics will not be reflected in the estimates of the adoption lags, either in the level (i.e., D) or on the postwar change (i.e., ΔD), which are identified through the curvature of the diffusion process.

It is also relevant for our analysis to discuss how variation in disembodied technological productivity, or in the size of the economy, affects our identified changes in the adoption lags. As can be seen from equations (20) and (25), changes in the disembodied part of TFP and the size of the economy do not affect the equilibrium adoption lags since they equally affect the costs and benefits of adoption.[20] In fact, persistent changes in disembodied productivity do not even affect adoption lags much along the transitional path. This can be seen from the simulated transition path for a permanent upward shift in disembodied productivity plotted in figure 4.

To induce some effects on our estimated adoption lags, we need to make the assumption that wages do not adjust temporarily to the increase in market size or in overall TFP. Incidentally, this assumption corresponds to the hypothesis presented by Eichengreen (2007), who argued that after WWII there was a change in the social contract in Europe that tempered unions' demands for wage increases despite the accelerating productivity. In that event, an increase in efficiency or market size will have a larger effect on the revenues than in the costs of adopting and using new technologies leading to a temporary increase in our technology usage measure, m_T, and to a reduction in the diffusion lags.[21] Note however, that this comparative dynamics would, to a first order, affect all the technologies symmetrically.

IV. Results

We present our results in three parts. In the first part, we summarize the estimated changes in adoption lags that we obtained using the method described above. In the second part, we estimate the association between the change in the speed of adoption and several measures of U.S. postwar involvement. In the final part, we study the association between technology adoption and postwar growth.

A. Estimated Changes in the Adoption Lags

The parameter estimates for the U.S. specification as well as for the level of the adoption lags, D, are very similar to those reported in Comin and Hobijn (2010a). That study also shows that a simplified version of specification (25) fits the diffusion curves for a sample of technologies and countries that contains those in our sample as well. Therefore, we focus our analysis on the estimated changes in the adoption lags.

Just as in (25) we use the convention that a positive change in the adoption lag reflects an increase in the speed of adoption. In this sense, we estimate the *reduction* in the adoption lag. In terms of the notation in (25), we estimate $\Delta D_{c\tau}$, where c denotes the country and τ the technology.

In practice, we obtain several estimates of $\Delta D_{c\tau}$ because we use various specifications nested in (25) that differ in terms of the inclusion of the adoption costs and the user cost and in whether the adjustment cost parameter is restricted to be equal to that for the United States. We do not need to take a stance on the right model specification. Instead, for each technology-country pair, we compute the average reduction in the adoption lag across the different specifications.[22]

Table 2 provides summary statistics for our estimates of the reduction in the adoption lags after WWII. On average, adoption lags decreased slightly after WWII in the sample of technologies and countries we analyze. There are significant differences across technologies. While new technologies experienced a reduction in adoption lags of almost 4 years, old technologies experienced an average increase in adoption lags of 4 years.

There is significant variation in the changes in adoption lags even within our groups of technologies. For example, across old technologies, the average reduction in adoption lags varies from 13 years for steamships and motor ships to an increase by 29 years for rail transportation of passengers. This might be problematic because of the unbalanced nature of our panel of estimated declines in adoption lags. In particular, if the countries that received U.S. help over the postwar period are overrepresented in our sample in technologies with increases in lags (e.g., railways) while countries that did not receive U.S. help are overrepresented in technologies that experienced declines in lags (e.g., steamships and motor ships), we could incorrectly conclude that U.S. help is associated with an increase in adoption lags.

This example is actually a good description of the unbalance in our sample of estimates. We take care of this problem by including technology fixed effects in the regressions in which we study the drivers or effects of adoption lags in new versus old technologies.

In addition to the distinction between old and new technologies, we distinguish between technologies with and without a close predecessor. As argued in Comin and Hobijn (2009b), this distinction allows us to explore Olson's (1982) hypothesis that interest groups associated with incumbent technologies may slow down the diffusion of a new superior technology. If this is the main driving force of the adoption lag reductions in our data, then these reductions should be especially large for those technologies that were substituting a predecessor technology.

Key to the implementation of this test is the classification of new technologies between those that have and those that do not have a competing

Table 2
U.S. Postwar Reduction in Adoption Lags

Technology	New/Old	Competing Predecessor	Relative Productivity	Mean Reduction	Standard Deviation	*N* Observations	*N* Countries
Cars	New	Yes	<1 (s)	–3.56	13.71		28
Trucks	New	Yes	<1 (s), 1.2 (c, in short distances)	–6.43	8.75		26
Telephones	New	No	3 (s)	–5.37	6.64		22
Steamships and motor ships	Old			13.21	20.2		25
Radios	New	Yes	<1 (r)	–5.97	10.32		19
Electricity	New	No	No predecessor	14.38	12.45		31
Rail freight	Old			–4.4	18.71		19
Rail passengers	Old			–29.44	38.81		28
Telegraphs	Old			7.85	24.26		24
Aviation	New	No	4 (s)	29.84	9.04		21
All new	...			3.9	16.9	147	36
New without competing predecessor	...			12.89	16.81	74	36
New with competing predecessor	...			–5.21	11.2	73	36
All old	...			–4.06	32.32	96	36
Total	...			.76	24.44	243	36

Note: Competing predecessor denotes whether we classify the (new) technology as having a predecessor technology with a productivity that is not too distant. The productivity is measured in terms of speed (s), recall rates (r), and cost of performing a task (c). Old technologies are those invented in a more distant past.

predecessor. Comin and Hobijn (2009b) use the relative productivity between new and incumbent technologies to conduct this classification. Table 2 reproduces the relative productivity of new technologies based on the micro studies surveyed in Comin and Hobijn (2009b). According to this classification, radios, trucks, and cars have a competing predecessor while electricity, planes, and telephones do not have a competing predecessor.

When classifying new technologies in these two groups, we find that technologies without a competing predecessor tended to experience larger reductions in adoption lags than those with one. In particular, the lags of the former declined by almost 13 years, while those of the latter increased on average by 5 years. Note that this is the opposite pattern one would expect if Olsonian incumbent dynamics were less prevalent after WWII.

B. *Effect of Postwar U.S. Assistance on Adoption*

The first stage of our analysis involves analyzing whether the U.S. postwar involvement changed the adoption dynamics and did so differently for old and new technologies. We consider three measures of U.S. involvement. The first is a dummy that is equal to one if the country received significant U.S. assistance. That basically corresponds to those countries that participated in the Marshall Plan and to Japan. Second, we consider the total expenditure in the U.S. TAP in the country. Finally, we consider the total U.S. aid expenditures between 1948 and 1953.

Table 3 reports the estimates of the effect of the U.S. postwar involvement measures on the reduction in the lags after WWII. The main finding from our estimates, reported in columns 1–3, is that a larger U.S. involvement is associated with a larger reduction in the adoption lags for new technologies. This effect is considerable. The average country that received significant postwar U.S. assistance experienced a reduction in the lags with which new technologies were adopted of about 4.5 years. Similarly, a one-standard-deviation increase in the U.S. expenditure in either the TAP or the Marshall Plan is associated with a decline in the adoption lags of new technologies of approximately 2.5 years. The effects for old technologies are even larger.

In contrast, for old technologies we find that a larger U.S. involvement is associated with an increase in the adoption lags. These effects seem even larger than for new technologies. The average country that received significant postwar U.S. assistance experienced an increase in the lags with which new technologies were adopted of about 14 years.

Table 3
U.S. Postwar Involvement and Reduction in Adoption Lags

	Dependent Variable: Postwar Reduction in Adoption Lags					
Independent Variable	(1)	(2)	(3)	(4)	(5)	(6)
Major postwar U.S. assistance	4.46* (2.28)					
Major postwar U.S. assistance × old technology	−14.06** (5.26)			−16.5*** (5.88)		
Technical assistance		.32*** (.093)				
Technical assistance × old technology		−.82*** (.283)			−.92** (.31)	
Total Marshall help			2.7*** (.74)			
Total Marshall help × old technology			−8.17*** (2.19)			−8.79*** (2.4)
Country fixed effects	No	No	No	Yes	Yes	Yes
n	243	243	243	243	243	243
R^2	.42	.42	.43	.50	.51	.51

Note: Major postwar U.S. assistance is a dummy that takes the value of one if the country participated in the Marshall Plan or it is Japan. Technical assistance in millions of U.S. dollars of U.S. funds commited (does not include matching funding from countries). Source: International Cooperation Administration (1958) and Tiratsoo (2000). Marshall help is U.S. dollars of U.S. aid between 1948 and 1953. Source: U.S. Agency for International Development. All regressions include a full set of technology dummies. Standard errors reported (in parentheses) are robust and are clustered at the country level.
*Significant at the 10% level.
**Significant at the 5% level.
***Significant at the 1% level.

One may wonder whether the effects of assistance on the adoption lags persist after controlling for any country-specific characteristic. To explore this, we rerun the regressions with country fixed effects. Since the assistance variables have only cross-country variation, this exercise allows us to identify only their differential effect on the reduction in the lags of new versus old technologies. The results, reported in columns 4–6, show that the effect of U.S. postwar assistance on adoption is very robust. Even after controlling for any possible country-specific factor, U.S. assistance is associated with a larger reduction in the adoption lags of new than of old technologies. The average country that received significant postwar U.S. assistance experienced a reduction in the adoption lags of new technologies 16.5 years larger than in the lags of old ones.

This finding is relevant since most of the omitted variables that could be driving the association between the assistance programs and the reduction in adoption lags should, a priori, affect all technologies more or less symmetrically. Take the power of unions, for example. If, as argued by Eichengreen (2007), the foreign intervention leads to a new social contract that reduces union demands, this should enhance investment in all forms of capital, those that embody new technologies and those that embody old technologies. So, to a first order, we should observe that the effects of such policies would be captured by the country fixed effect. The same is true for other changes that affect the size or efficiency of the economy such as the process of European integration or policies that lead to a more efficient bureaucracy, lower taxes, or less distorted markets. The fact that we are observing such a large and significant differential effect on the adoption lag of the new technologies leads us to believe that the driver of the effect of the assistance variables on the decline in adoption lags was not a general increase in efficiency.

Olson (1982) implies that the differential effect of the U.S. assistance in the diffusion of new technologies is due not to a transfer of technology but to a reduction of the power of incumbent producers. These producers might have used their power to raise barriers that slow down the diffusion of new technologies before WWII. As their power weakened, the diffusion of new technologies could have accelerated. Table 4 tests this hypothesis by estimating the differential effect of the U.S. assistance variables on the diffusion of new technologies with and without a close predecessor. Contrary to the Olsonian hypothesis, we find that technologies with a close predecessor did not experience a larger acceleration in diffusion than those without such close predecessors. This conclusion is robust to the inclusion of country fixed effects as shown in columns 4–6.

Hence, we conclude that a significant part of the postwar dynamics of technology diffusion we have uncovered can be explained by the U.S. assistance programs that resulted in a transfer of knowledge from the United States to other nations. This does not mean that the alternative driving forces we discussed did not contribute; it means that they do not match the cross-technology variation that we uncovered in the data.

C. *Effect of Adoption on Per Capita GDP*

We conclude our analysis by exploring whether postwar reductions in adoption lags are associated with faster growth. We do that by estimating the following specification:

$$y_{1970c} = \alpha + \rho \times y_{1950c} + \beta \times \overline{\Delta D_c} + \epsilon_c, \tag{26}$$

Table 4
U.S. Postwar Involvement and Diffusion of New Technologies With and Without Predecessor

	Dependent Variable: Postwar Reduction in Adoption Lags					
Independent Variable	(1)	(2)	(3)	(4)	(5)	(6)
Major postwar U.S. assistance	8.77***					
	(3.14)					
Major postwar U.S. assistance × has predecessor	−12.47***			−11.97**		
	(4.05)			(4.65)		
Technical assistance		.4**				
		(.176)				
Technical assistance × has predecessor		−.29			−.28	
		(.28)			(.33)	
Total Marshall help			3.94***			
			(1.34)			
Total Marshall help × has predecessor			−3.48***			−3.39
			(2.53)			(3.02)
Country fixed effects	No	No	No	Yes	Yes	Yes
n	147	147	147	147	147	147
R^2	.06	.026	.04	.27	.23	.24

Note: Has predecessor is a dummy variable that takes the value of one if the technology has a competing predecessor technology and zero otherwise. See the text for the definition of which technologies have competing predecessors. Major postwar U.S. assistance is a dummy that takes the value of one if the country participated in the Marshall Plan or it is Japan. Technical assistance is in millions of U.S. dollars of U.S. funds commited (does not include matching funding from countries). Source: International Cooperation Administration (1958) and Tiratsoo (2000). Marshall help is billions of U.S. dollars of U.S. aid between 1948 and 1953. Source: U.S. Agency for International Development. All regressions include a full set of technology dummies. Standard errors reported (in parentheses) are robust and are clustered at the country level.
*Significant at the 10% level.
**Significant at the 5% level.
***Significant at the 1% level.

where y_{Tc} denotes the log of per capita income in year T in country c, $\overline{\Delta D_c}$ is the average reduction in adoption lags across technologies for country c, and ϵ_c is an error term.

In column 1 of table 5, we estimate the effect of the reduction in the new technologies' adoption lags on (log) per capita income in 1970. We find that the reduction in the lag with which new technologies were adopted after WWII is significantly associated with faster postwar growth in per capita income.[23] In particular, the reduction of an additional year in the average lag with which new technologies were adopted led to a 1% increase in per capita income in 1970. This implies that a one-standard-deviation decline

Table 5
Acceleration in Technology Adoption and Postwar Economic Growth

	Dependent Variable: Log Real GDP per Capita in 1970					
Independent Variable	(1)	(2)	(3)	(4)	(5)	(6)
Log real GDP per capita in 1950	.935***	.95***	.938**	.931**	.966***	1.01***
	(.074)	(.11)	(.074)	(.09)	(.075)	(.058)
Reduction in lags, new technologies	.01**		.01**	.012*	.005***	.005**
	(.0046)		(.0046)	(.006)	(.002)	(.002)
Reduction in lags, old technologies		−.001	−.0012	−.0009	−.0015*	−.0012
		(.001)	(.001)	(.0007)	(.0008)	(.0009)
Openness 1950				−.0003		
				(.002)		
Polity 1950					.002	
					(.008)	
Polity 1970 − Polity 1950						−.016*
						(.009)
n	243	243	243	203	228	228
R^2	.84	.83	.85	.85	.89	.9

Note: Reduction in lags, new and old technologies, refers to the average decline in the adoption lags estimated according to eq. (25) across all new or old technologies in the country. Polity measures come from Polity IV. Openness is measured as the ratio of exports plus imports to GDP. Source: Heston, Summers, and Aten (2009).
*Significant at the 10% level.
**Significant at the 5% level.
***Significant at the 1% level.

in the adoption lags for new technologies is associated with an increase in the annual growth rate of per capita income of 0.65 percentage point between 1950 and 1970.

In column 2 we estimate the growth effects of a reduction in the adoption lags of the old technologies. For these technologies, we find no significant growth effect associated with an acceleration in their diffusion. Columns 3–6 show that these findings are robust to controlling for postwar institutions and policies. In particular, they are robust to controlling for the initial competition in the political system as measured by Polity and to the degree of trade openness in the economy openness as measured by the ratio of exports plus imports over GDP. The results are also robust to controlling for the change in these variables between 1950 and 1970. Hence, this suggests that the acceleration in the speed of diffusion of new technologies during the postwar period might have been a significant driver of the extraordinary growth performance of several Western European countries and Japan.

V. Conclusion

In this paper we revisited the remarkable postwar growth experiences of Western European countries and Japan. In addition to considering the oft-studied gains in real GDP per capita, we also considered technology usage measures for 10 technologies taken from Comin and Hobijn (2009a). The evidence we presented showed that, in terms of real GDP per capita, these countries did not return to their prewar growth path. Instead, they moved up to a higher path than they were on before the war. This boost in growth was mainly driven by growth in TFP. It was also accompanied by commensurate increases in technology usage.

We introduced a version of the model of technology adoption and economic growth from Comin and Hobijn (2010a) to translate these changes in the usage of these technologies into estimates of the acceleration in the speed of adoption of these technologies. We use this model to estimate changes in the time between the invention and adoption of 10 different technologies for 39 countries that occurred after WWII.

Our estimates reveal that good postwar growth performances relative to the United States happened in countries that also saw a relatively large pickup in the speed of adoption of technologies that had been invented less than a century before the end of the war. For older technologies, this positive correlation between postwar catch-up and changes in adoption lags is not present.

We document that a substantial part of the cross-country variation in these changes in adoption lags can be explained by differences in the amount of postwar U.S. economic aid and technical assistance across countries. We interpret this evidence of technology transfers from the United States to Western Europe and Japan as an important driving force of the impressive postwar growth performance by these recipients.

Of course, such technology transfers were probably not the sole driving force of the "supergrowth" that many countries experienced in the postwar period. Many studies, for example, Olson (1982), Eichengreen (2007), and Alvarez-Cuadrado and Pintea (2009), have proposed alternative explanations. None of these explanations, however, is consistent with the differential effect of the changes in the adoption of old and new technologies. This does not mean that they did not contribute to postwar catch-up in Western Europe and Japan, but it does mean that they cannot account for the variation in technology adoption patterns that we have uncovered in the data.

Endnotes

We would like to thank Daron Acemoglu, Chang-Tai Hsieh, James Robinson, Alan Taylor, and other participants of the NBER Macroeconomics Annual Conference for their many comments and suggestions. Furthermore, we are grateful to Colin Gardiner, Salifou Issoufou, and Hitesh Makhija for their excellent research assistance as well as Kan Kin for his assistance with the literature survey. We are indebted to the National Science Foundation (grants SES-0517910 and SBE-738101) for financial assistance. The views expressed in this paper solely reflect those of the authors and not necessarily those of the National Bureau of Economic Research, the Federal Reserve Bank of San Francisco, or the Federal Reserve System as a whole.

1. Some evidence, e.g., Hess and Orphanides (1995) and Miguel, Satyanath, and Sergenti (2004), suggests that the timing of wars might not be completely exogenous.

2. Van Ark and Pilat (1993) provide a detailed analysis of the performance of the manufacturing sectors. Cette, Kocoglu, and Mairesse (2009) study labor productivity and total factor productivity (TFP) measures for Japan, France, the United Kingdom, and the United States. Hayashi (1986, 1989), Christiano (1989), and Chen, Imrohoroğlu, and Imrohoroğlu (2006) focus on Japan in particular.

3. The details of the derivations of the equations in the main text are available in an online appendix that is part of the NBER Working Paper version of this article (Comin and Hobijn 2010b).

4. Among the many studies that touch on this topic are Abramovitz (1986), Baumol (1986), De Long (1988), Wolff (1991), and Van Ark and Pilat (1993).

5. We take the minimum of 1945 and 1946 because WWII ended at different times during 1945 in different countries. Hence, the 1945 data thus partially reflect economic activity during the war rather than right after it ended.

6. See Alvarez-Cuadrado and Pintea (2009) for a quantitative analysis of many of these factors in a theoretical growth model.

7. Christiano (1989) and Chen et al. (2006), e.g., emphasize the importance of transitional dynamics for understanding the behavior of the Japanese saving rate since 1945. Gilchrist and Williams (2004) do so for both Germany and Japan.

8. Throughout, we ignore population growth and just adjust for it in the calibration of our parameters.

9. Eaton and Kortum (1997) find, in a different theoretical framework, that endogenizing the path of the frontier does not improve the ability of their model to explain the postwar manufacturing productivity paths of Germany, Japan, France, the United Kingdom, and the United States.

10. Here and in the rest of this article, to save on notation we drop the time subscript, t, whenever its presence is self-evident.

11. Comin and Hobijn (2010a) are more specific about the distinction between investment-specific and embodied technological change. For the empirical methodology applied here, the distinction does not matter, however. Hence, we ignore it in the rest of our exposition.

12. The term $\overline{\Psi}$ is the steady-state stock market capitalization to GDP ratio, which is derived in the appendix. We include it and the other constant term to normalize the adoption costs to simplify the equilibrium expressions of the model.

13. See Brynjolfsson and Hitt (2000) for an analysis of the costs of adoption of information technologies.

14. Alternatively, one could define a GDP measure as

$$\tilde{Y} = Y - \Gamma = \left[1 - \left(\frac{\gamma}{\mu - 1}\right)\Psi\right] Y = C + I.$$

15. These paths are simulated using parameter values that are chosen to match U.S. balanced growth properties and the postwar catch-up in real GDP relative to the United

States by Japan. The basic shape of the paths plotted is not very sensitive to the parameter choice.

16. We limit ourselves to a short description and present the details behind these steps in the appendix.

17. Throughout, we have derived our results for log preferences, i.e., an intertemporal elasticity of substitution equal to one. This log-linear approximation actually holds for constant relative risk aversion preferences with any intertemporal elasticity of substitution.

18. The profit maximization problem subject to these adjustment costs that results in the inclusion of this term in our equations is described in the appendix.

19. We assume that these costs are present only during the postwar recovery.

20. This equal effect of disembodied productivity on these costs and benefits is necessary for the model to have a balanced growth path with constant adoption lags.

21. This argument can be formalized either by using the optimal adoption equation in the model (20) or by using the reduced-form expression for the demand for our technology measures (23) or (24).

22. As in Comin and Hobijn (2010a), we restrict attention to those estimates that are plausible and precise. We define these estimates in that article.

23. This is consistent with Dowrick and Rogers' (2002) finding that allowing for technology catch-up significantly enhances the fit of conventional cross-country growth regressions.

References

Abramovitz, Moses. 1986. "Catching Up, Forging Ahead, and Falling Behind." *Journal of Economic History* 46:388–406.

Acemoglu, Daron, Simon Johnson, and James A. Robinson. 2001. "The Colonial Origins of Comparative Development: An Empirical Investigation." *American Economic Review* 91:1369–1401.

Alvarez-Cuadrado, Francisco, and Mihaela I. Pintea. 2009. "A Quantitative Exploration of the Golden Age of European Growth." *Journal of Economic Dynamics and Control* 33:1437–50.

Barro, Robert J., and José F. Ursúa. 2008. "Macroeconomic Crises since 1870." *Brookings Papers on Economic Activity* (Spring), 255–350.

Baumol, William J. 1986. "Productivity Growth, Convergence, and Welfare: What the Long-Run Data Show." *American Economic Review* 76:1072–85.

Bjarnar, Ove, and Matthias Kipping. 1998. *The Americanisation of European Business: The Marshall Plan and the Transfer of US Management Models*. New York: Routledge.

Boel, Brent. 2003. *The European Productivity Agency and Transatlantic Relations, 1953–1961*. Copenhagen: Museum Tusculanum Press.

Brynjolfsson, Erik, and Lorin M. Hitt. 2000. "Beyond Computation: Information Technology, Organizational Transformation and Business Performance." *Journal of Economic Perspectives* 14:23–48.

Cette, Gilbert, Yusuf Kocoglu, and Jacques Mairesse. 2009. "Productivity Growth and Levels in France, Japan, the United Kingdom and the United States in the Twentieth Century." Working Paper no. 15577, NBER, Cambridge, MA.

Chen, Kaiji, Ayse Imrohoroğlu, and Selahattin Imrohoroğlu. 2006. "The Japanese Saving Rate." *American Economic Review* 96:1850–58.

Christiano, Lawrence J. 1989. "Understanding Japan's Saving Rate: The Reconstruction Hypothesis." *Federal Reserve Bank of Minneapolis Quarterly Review* 13:10–25.

Comin, Diego A., William Easterly, and Erick Gong. 2010. "Was the Wealth of Nations Determined in 1000 BC?" *American Economic Journal: Macroeconomics* 2, no. 3:65–97.

Comin, Diego A., and Bart Hobijn. 2009a. "The CHAT Dataset." Working Paper no. 15319, NBER, Cambridge, MA.

———. 2009b. "Lobbies and Technology Diffusion." *Review of Economics and Statistics* 91:229–44.

———. 2010a. "An Exploration of Technology Diffusion." *American Economic Review* 100:203–59.

———. 2010b. "Technology Diffusion and Postwar Growth." Working Paper no. 16378, NBER, Cambridge, MA.

De Long, J. Bradford. 1988. "Productivity Growth, Convergence, and Welfare: Comment." *American Economic Review* 78:1138–54.

De Long, J. Bradford, and Barry Eichengreen. 1991. "The Marshall Plan: History's Most Successful Structural Adjustment Program." Manuscript, University of California, Berkeley.

Dowrick, Steve, and Mark Rogers. 2002. "Classical and Technological Convergence: Beyond the Solow-Swan Growth Model." *Oxford Economic Papers* 54:369–85.

Dumke, Rolf H. 1990. "Reassessing the *Wirtshaftswunder*: Reconstruction and Postwar Growth in West Germany in an International Context." *Oxford Bulletin of Economics and Statistics* 52:451–92.

Eaton, Jonathan, and Samuel Kortum. 1997. "Engines of Growth: Domestic and Foreign Sources of Innovation." *Japan and the World Economy* 9:235–59.

Eichengreen, Barry J. 2007. *The European Economy since 1945: Coordinated Capitalism and Beyond*. Princeton, NJ: Princeton University Press.

Eichengreen, Barry J., and Marc Uzan. 1992. "The Marshall Plan: Economic Effects and Implications for Eastern Europe and the Former USSR." *Economic Policy* 7:14–75.

Gilchrist, Simon, and John C. Williams. 2004. "Transition Dynamics in Vintage Capital Models: Explaining the Postwar Catch-up of Germany and Japan." Working Paper no. 2004-14, Federal Reserve Bank of San Francisco.

Glick, Reuven, and Alan M. Taylor. 2010. "Collateral Damage: Trade Disruptions and the Economic Impact of War." *Review of Economics and Statistics* 92, no. 1:102–27.

Hall, Robert E., and Charles I. Jones. 1999. "Why Do Some Countries Produce So Much More Output per Worker than Others?" *Quarterly Journal of Economics* 114, no. 1:83–116.

Hayashi, Fumio. 1986. "Why Is Japan's Saving Rate So Apparently High?" *NBER Macroeconomics Annual* 1:147–234.

———. 1989. "Is Japan's Saving Rate High?" *Federal Reserve Bank of Minneapolis Quarterly Review* 13:3–9.

Hess, Gregory D., and Athanasios Orphanides. 1995. "War Politics: An Economic, Rational-Voter Framework." *American Economic Review* 85:828–46.

Heston, Alan, Robert Summers, and Bettina Aten. 2009. *Penn World Table Version 6.3*. Philadelphia: University of Pennsylvania, Center for International Comparisons of Production, Income, and Prices.

International Cooperation Administration. 1958. *European Productivity and Technical Assistance Programs: A Summing Up, 1948–1958*. Paris: International Cooperation Administration.

International Directory of Company Histories. 2001. London: Saint James Press.

Klenow, Peter J., and Andrés Rodríguez-Clare. 1997. "The Neoclassical Revival in Growth Economics: Has It Gone Too Far?" *NBER Macroeconomics Annual* 12:73–103.

Maddison, Angus. 2007. *Contours of the World Economy 1–2030 AD: Essays in Macro-economic History*. Oxford: Oxford University Press.

Miguel, Edward, Shanker Satyanath, and Ernest Sergenti. 2004. "Economic Shocks and Civil Conflict: An Instrumental Variables Approach." *Journal of Political Economy* 112:725–53.

Olson, Mancur. 1982. *The Rise and Decline of Nations*. New Haven, CT: Yale University Press.

Parente, Stephen L., and Edward C. Prescott. 1994. "Barriers to Technology Adoption and Development." *Journal of Political Economy* 102, no. 2:298–321.

Prescott, Edward C. 1997. "Needed: A Theory of Total Factor Productivity." *International Economic Review* 39:525–51.

Solow, Robert M. 1960. "Investment and Technical Progress." In *Mathematical Methods in the Social Sciences*, ed. Kenneth J. Arrow, Samuel Karlin, and Patrick Suppes. Stanford, CA: Stanford University Press.

Tiratsoo, Nick. 2000. "The United States Technical Assistance Programme in Japan, 1955–62." *Business History* 42, no. 4:117–36.

Van Ark, Bart, and Dirk Pilat. 1993. "Productivity Levels in Germany, Japan, and the United States: Differences and Causes." *Brookings Papers on Economic Activity: Microeconomics*, no. 2:1–69.

Wasser, Solidelle F., and Michael L. Dolfman. 2005. "BLS and the Marshall Plan: The Forgotten Story." *Monthly Labor Review* 128, no. 6:44–52.

Wolff, Edward N. 1991. "Capital Formation and Productivity Convergence over the Long-Term." *American Economic Review* 81:565–79.

Comment

Chang-Tai Hsieh, *University of Chicago and NBER*

Comin and Hobijn's paper looks at the role of technology diffusion and postwar growth in the OECD countries. The key idea is that differences in the barriers to technology diffusion may be behind the differential growth rates after the war. Conceptually, the model turns technology into another form of capital that can be accumulated. When technology is thought of in this manner, then frictions to technology adoption will have an effect on output per worker in the same way that a higher cost of capital lowers capital intensity and thus output per worker.

Let me illustrate this idea with a stripped-down version of the model in the paper. Suppose that output is given by

$$Y = Z_{\bar{v}_t} X,$$

where $X \equiv AK^{\alpha}L^{1-\alpha}$ and $Z_{\bar{v}_t}$ is an index of the country's technology vintage. The cost of having technology of this vintage is given by

$$C(Z_{\bar{v}_t}, Z_t) = \frac{b}{1+\chi}\frac{Z_{\bar{v}_t}^{1+\chi}}{Z_t^{\chi}},$$

where Z_t is the world technology frontier and $\chi > 0$ parameterizes the convex cost of technology adoption. The marginal cost of moving up the technology frontier is given by

$$C'(Z_{\bar{v}_t}, Z_t) = b\left(\frac{Z_{\bar{v}_t}}{Z_t}\right)^{\chi}.$$

The marginal cost is a function of b, which can be interpreted as the "friction" and the country's distance from the world technology frontier. Equating the marginal cost to the marginal benefit, we get the following expression for the country's technology gap relative to the world frontier:

$$\frac{Z_{\bar{v}_t}}{Z_t} = \left(\frac{X}{b}\right)^{1/\chi}.$$

978-0-226-00212-5/2011/2010-0402$10.00

In turn, aggregate output is

$$Y = Z_t \left(\frac{1}{b}\right)^{1/\chi} X^{(1+\chi)/\chi}.$$

Aggregate output is a function of the cost of technology adoption b with an elasticity of $1/\chi$. The diminishing returns to accumulating technology capital comes from the convex cost of technology capital. Thus, the importance of the differences in b will depend on the convexity of the technology cost adoption parameter χ. In effect, what the model does is to convert technology into another factor that can be accumulated.

What this paper does is to empirically measure b and to argue that differences in this parameter can explain the different growth performances after the war in the OECD countries. Specifically, the paper shows that output growth is associated with the adoption of "new" technologies such as airplanes, cars, electricity, radios, phones, and trucks and decreased use of "old" technologies such as railways, steamships, and telegrams. In terms of the model, the claim is that use of new technologies proxies for $Z_{\bar{v}_t}/Z_t$. The issue is that most of the "technologies" that are measured are consumption items, and not inputs into the production process. For example, why are expenditures on cars a measure of a country's technology gap? Why isn't it reasonable to think that expenditures shift toward cars and away from railroads (and horses) when incomes rise, regardless of the technology used in production?

The second claim is that the differences in technologies are driven in large part by differences in the cost of technology adoption (the parameter I have called b here). Conceptually, the technology gap is a function of b and a function of X, and what the paper is after is to isolate the role of b in explaining the technology gap. What the authors do is to use a postwar technical assistance program by the United States as a measure of "exogenous" variation in b. This program provided some money but mostly technical assistance to many countries after the war. As the paper shows, the amounts involved were quantitatively small. In Japan, for example, the program provided \$12 million of technical assistance aid and provided 165 engineers in the United States.

However, it is hard to believe that the exclusion restrictions necessary for this program to be used as an instrument for variation in technology adoption are satisfied. For example, the paper shows that the point estimate from a reduced-form regression of $\log(Y/L)$ on U.S. aid suggests that \$1 million in U.S. aid increases $\log(Y/L)$ by 0.018. If we take Japan again, Y/L in Japan in 1950 was about \$3,000 and population was

83 million. The point estimate thus suggests that $1 million in U.S. aid was responsible for increasing Japan's GDP by $4.5 billion. This rate of return seems wildly implausible and suggests that variation in the intensity of the U.S. technical assistance program was probably correlated with other factors that had an independent effect on output.

The paper suggests that we can solve the problem by regressing adoption lags on U.S. technical assistance as the first stage and then using the fitted adoption lags in the second stage of a regression of output on technology adoption. I do not see, however, how this solves the identification problem. The first-stage regression of adoption lags on U.S. technical assistance is unbiased only if U.S. technical assistance is uncorrelated with other variables that might have an independent effect on income. However, one would need to know more about the sources of variation in this program to know whether the exclusion restrictions hold. As it stands, the large point estimates of the reduced-form regression of output on the program indicate that the exclusion restrictions are not likely to be met.

In sum, the paper is ambitious and on a very important topic. The data the authors use are very interesting. The mechanism they have in mind is plausible. However, much more needs to be done to provide reliable estimates of the magnitude of the importance of technology adoption on growth and on the effect of barriers to technology adoption.

Comment

James A. Robinson, Harvard University

I. The Argument

The paper by Diego Comin and Bart Hobjin presents a very interesting and important analysis of the factors that put OECD countries onto a new growth path after 1945. The authors, building on previous work by others, are convincing that the rapid growth after the Second World War was driven not by simply neoclassical convergence but rather by total factor productivity increases and more specifically technology adoption. This argument is particularly important in explaining why countries such as Germany and Japan did not simply converge back to their old growth path but moved onto a new one with higher steady-state growth.

The authors present a model for this based on the idea that it was the technical assistance elements of the Marshall Plan introduced in 1949 (1955 for Japan) plus industrial trainees that visited the United States between 1949 and 1969 that explain this change in the pace of technology adoption. Their motivation for this is not to use this as "a" source of variation in technology adoption in order to estimate an instrumental variables model of the impact of technology adoption on growth. The reason is that they accept that it is impossible to exclude this technical assistance from the growth equation. Instead, they argue that this is "the" main explanation for the rapid increase in technology adoption. Their regressions show that assistance was particularly important for "new technologies" (aviation, cars, electricity, radios, telephones, and trucks) and not "old" (railways, steamships and motor ships, and telegrams) and argue that this makes some alternative institutional thesis untenable.

II. Questions

Though I found the paper very interesting, there are a number of issues that I find puzzling. First, I wondered what the data on assistance were

978-0-226-00212-5/2011/2010-0403$10.00

capturing. Consider Japan. After the Meiji Restoration in 1868 the Japanese government sent many students overseas and made a very sustained effort to adopt modern technology by visiting other countries and inviting foreigners to help them. The man who was to be Admiral Isoroku Yamamoto, for example, mastermind of the Japanese attack on Pearl Harbor in December 1941, even studied at Harvard University in the 1920s. Yet the paper codes 1955 as the date when the significant assistance to Japan begun. This tension even comes out in the paper since the authors discuss the 1950 visit of two leading executives of Toyota Motor Company to the Ford Motor factory. But this date is prior to when technical assistance began and obviously has nothing to do with it. Rather it represents part of the long post-1868 process of trying to adopt better technology. The year 1955 is too late to explain Japanese postwar growth. More important, given what was going on before the war, the authors need to compare, for example, the number of trainees in 1949–69 with the number before World War II to see if the change in the number of trainees can explain the change in the growth path.

Second, technical assistance from the United States did not start in 1949 either. For instance, the Princeton economist Edwin Kemmerer under the auspices of the U.S. government extensively toured Latin American countries in the 1920s and 1930s giving institutional advice. Among his many missions were two to Colombia in 1923 and 1930, which resulted in the foundation of the Central Bank and large changes in the structure of financial regulations (Drake 1988). Technology disseminated from the United States in other contexts as well, for example, during the military occupation of Haiti, the Dominican Republic, and Nicaragua. Indeed, the first direct-dialing telephone exchange in the Americas outside of the United States was built in Port au Prince by the Americans in the 1920s during their occupation of Haiti.

Third, there were a lot of things going on after 1945 other than the technical assistance on which the paper focuses that may have heavily influenced the growth of total factor productivity and the adoption of new technologies. For instance, in 1944 at the Bretton Woods conference, the World Bank was created. The first loan it made was $250 million to France in 1947, though the U.S. government allowed the money to be dispersed only after Communist legislators had been removed from the government. The second loan was $195 million for the Netherlands and the third was for Denmark. The striking thing about all these loans is that they are an order of magnitude larger than the sums of money involved in the Marshall Plan, and they were going to the same countries.

In addition to financial flows, the postwar world led to significant changes in the social contracts of the countries that experienced much higher economic growth. As Titmuss (1958) pointed out, there is a strong correlation between wars and changes in the social contracts of countries, for example, changes in the extent and form of income redistribution. Wars also have large consequences for political institutions, particularly democracy (Acemoglu and Robinson 2006). It is clear, therefore, that there are a lot of things going on after 1945 that might have had a positive effect on economic growth and that are highly correlated with Marshall Plan aid and technical assistance. This does not exhaust the extent of dramatic institutional changes at the same time, for example, the rise of socialist parties everywhere in Western Europe. The year 1945 was the first time the Labour Party had a majority in Britain, and this government introduced nationalization, large changes in labor market institutions, and compulsory secondary education for the first time. Indeed, some argue that this led to a new social contract between capital and labor: part of what Barry Eichengreen (2007) has called *Coordinated Capitalism*.

III. The Altruistic United States?

The paper implicitly presents a rather odd theory of technological dissemination. First, there is the United States, the world technology leader. Then there are the other countries that are inside the world technology frontier. Rather than maximize profits, national income, or anything else, the United States then gives away its technology. One might ask who gave it away? Was the Ford Motor Company happy to freely give away its technology to potential competitors? Or was it the U.S. government that forced it to do so? If so, what instruments did it use? Why did only some countries get this assistance, and what explains the timing? After all, General Douglas McArthur in his role as Supreme Commander of the Allied Powers attempted a massive reengineering of Japanese institutions in the 1940s that included rewriting the Constitution and agrarian reform, but technical assistance comes in 1955.

There is no discussion of why the United States so generously gave away its technological advantages. The obvious explanation is that this has something to do with the "Cold War" with the Soviet Union, but to recognize this introduces a whole series of important questions. After all, geopolitical competition and the threat of warfare have been argued to be important drivers behind technological change and the development strategy of Taiwan and South Korea, so why not Western Europe after the war as well? It seems that it would be useful to place the results of the paper within the broader context of the likely channels via which the Cold War might have influenced postwar growth.

The attitude of the British government during the first industrial revolution was very different. From 1780 until 1842, exports of textile machinery were illegal, and the state tried to stop skilled workers from emigrating (Daunton 1995, chap. 18). Like the United States during the Cold War, Britain was heavily involved in conflicts all over the world and cooperated with allies such as the Dutch to defeat the French. To my knowledge, however, the British never gave away their technology to the Dutch or anyone else. Quite the contrary.

Finally, the notion of the altruistic United States needs to be evaluated in the context of many other pieces of information. With regard to the U.S. occupation of Haiti, the Dominican Republic, and Nicaragua, it is clear that this was not motivated by altruism, but rather by the desire to collect debts and perhaps create pliant markets for U.S. goods. Indeed, the subsequent politics of the latter two nations was dominated by the dictatorships of two men, Rafael Trujillo and Anastazio Somosza, who rose to power thanks to the U.S. intervention, a situation the United States seems to have been perfectly happy with even if it did not actively create it. More generally, in the postwar period, the United States was quite content to overthrow democratic regimes and support authoritarian and coercive ones (Berger et al. 2009).

IV. An Alternative Hypothesis

All in all I find myself unpersuaded by the claim that technical assistance can have played such an important role in the postwar OECD growth miracles. I do not really see that the assistance offered by the United States after the war was so large or distinct from other types of similar assistance that it can have caused such a huge differential economic effect. Though it is possible that this assistance was qualitatively different because of the Cold War and the self-interested desire to rebuild Europe, there must be a significant concern about omitted variable bias in estimating the impact of measured assistance on technology adoption. The Cold War could have had many different effects on growth.

What might then explain them? A plausible alternative hypothesis was advanced by Mancur Olson in his book *The Rise and Decline of Nations* (1982). Olson argued that the rapid growth experienced by many Western European countries after World War II occurred because the war destroyed "distributional coalitions" that had previously blocked innovation and new technology adoption. I think that it is quite clear that this was the case in Germany and Japan. I also do not believe that the distinction between old and new technologies is evidence against the institutional view. It is those with specific investments in old technologies that would precisely attempt to block the development of new technologies.

Of course it is difficult to distinguish the technical assistance model proposed by the authors from an institutional one along the lines of Olson. To do so would require a more disaggregated analysis examining the extent of war damage to different sectors to investigate if sectors that experienced more war damage grew relatively faster. Though this would be a very imperfect proxy for the extent to which distributional coalitions were broken up, if this were true, it would certainly be consistent with Olson's model.

References

Acemoglu, Daron, and James A. Robinson. 2006. *Economic Origins of Dictatorship and Democracy.* New York: Cambridge University Press.

Berger, Daniel, William Easterly, Nathan Nunn, and Shanker Satyanath. 2009. "Commercial Imperialism? Political Influence and Trade during the Cold War." Working Paper no. 15981, NBER, Cambridge, MA.

Daunton, Martin J. 1995. *Progress and Poverty: An Economic and Social History of Britain, 1700–1850.* Oxford: Oxford University Press.

Drake, Paul W. 1988. *The Money Doctor in the Andes: U.S. Advisors, Investors, and Economic Reform in Latin America from World War I to the Great Depression.* Durham, NC: Duke University Press.

Eichengreen, Barry. 2007. *The European Economy since 1945: Coordinated Capitalism and Beyond.* Princeton, NJ: Princeton University Press.

Olson, Mancur C. 1982. *The Rise and Decline of Nations: Economic Growth, Stagflation, and Social Rigidities.* New Haven, CT: Yale University Press.

Titmuss, Richard M. 1958. *Essays on the Welfare State.* London: Allen & Unwin.

Discussion

Bart Hobijn opened the discussion by noting the inherent difficulties in any empirical study that attempts to distinguish among theories of long-run growth. He acknowledged the need for further consideration of some of the alternative hypotheses presented by the discussants, but he reiterated the value of explicitly articulating a channel of growth and presenting an empirical analysis using technical assistance as an instrumental variable. Responding to comments about the types of technologies tracked in their work, Hobijn noted that data availability restricted their options. They used both consumer and producer technologies to assemble sufficiently long time series. He also agreed with James Robinson that technical assistance expenditures were linked to broader mutual security efforts undertaken by the United States at the end of World War II.

Diego Comin responded to Chang-Tai Hsieh's concerns about simultaneity bias in the determination of GDP growth and technology adoption. He argued that using a structural model helps to deal with this issue by identifying restrictions for balanced growth and using the curvature of the path of TFP (rather than the level or trend) to identify adoption lags. With respect to Hsieh's concern that the reduction in utilization of old technologies may simply reflect higher incomes, Comin responded that initial income is included to control for this possibility. He acknowledged that technical assistance programs were quite small in magnitude but were representative of other types of technology transfer (such as Deming's work in Japan) that occurred at the same time and were likewise exogenous. He also liked Robinson's example of the Meiji Restoration in Japan as a historical instance of technology diffusion and growth acceleration. Comin argued that adding controls for polity and institutions did not affect their results but acknowledged that these controls may be insufficient if institutional changes had asymmetric effects on the adoption of new versus old technologies.

Daron Acemoglu criticized the instrumental variable approach used by the authors. He stated that, regardless of the structural model, the

978-0-226-00212-5/2011/2010-0404$10.00

instrumental variable did not satisfy the essential exogeneity requirements. The technical assistance program was part of the Marshall Plan and was tightly linked to political aspects and broader goals of reconstruction. He did not see how the distinction between old and new technologies helped their argument, and he noted that some European countries, such as Germany, were important leaders in many of the new technologies tracked in the paper. Acemoglu added that their mechanism of technological diffusion finds support in the historical record but that their econometric evidence was not credible. He cited a paper by William Kerr (2008) as a good example of an empirical strategy showing the causal effects of knowledge diffusion.

Comin responded that he could use Marshall Plan expenditures as an additional control and described the calculation of adoption lags based on the diffusion curves for each technology. Comin emphasized that the diffusion curves for different technologies are fitted to the available data for each technology. Acemoglu and Comin also disagreed on whether shocks orthogonal to technological adoption and diffusion would have differential effects on old and new technologies. Comin argued that a political or institutional change that improved efficiency would result in higher utilization of all technologies, which they do not see in the data.

Alan Taylor was supportive of the aims of the paper—particularly the effort to decompose neoclassical convergence (in capital) and technological convergence (in productivity). He cited a paper by Bosworth and Rogers (2003) that attempts to do this. However, he echoed concerns about technical assistance as an instrumental variable. Taylor noted that Germany, Japan, Italy, and France appear to be key drivers of their results, and two of these countries have their institutions essentially replaced at the end of World War II. Comin responded that these effects should be captured by polity controls and controls for initial conditions.

Taylor also expressed concerns about the modeling of investment, suggesting a putty-clay approach. He noted that Japan and Germany could rebuild their capital stock while Britain continued to operate with an older capital stock, perhaps accounting for growth differentials. Finally, Taylor also noted that these countries became part of the General Agreement on Tariffs and Trade, and lower trade barriers might have had important effects on growth. On the modeling assumptions, Hobijn responded that he was sympathetic to the putty-clay mechanism, but he noted that putty-clay models converge too quickly to steady state much like standard neoclassical models of reconstruction. Comin added that capital is subject to adjustment costs in the model, which are estimated in the data. Also, trade was explicitly controlled for in the regression analysis and had little effect on their results.

Samuel Pessoa asked whether adoption costs as a share of GDP were too high in their model along the transition path. Comin was unsure as to what data Pessoa had in mind and the corresponding measure in his model. Hobijn suggested discussing further offline.

Valerie Ramey also reiterated Acemoglu's view that the degree of technical assistance was strongly tied to political changes desired by the United States. She suggested looking at whether country total factor productivity growth can be tied to the number of students from a given country studying in the United States or Europe. Hobijn agreed with this suggestion, and Acemoglu noted that Kerr conducted this type of study, examining industry growth in China and the number of Chinese students studying in different areas. He agreed that the tacit knowledge mechanism identified by Kerr is consistent with Comin and Hobijn's hypothesis.

On putty-clay modeling, Simon Gilchrist noted that, if new technology was available with delay, then the speed of convergence in growth could be brought closer to the speed of convergence exhibited in the data. He also noted that Germany and Japan were excluded from many new industries developed in the 1930s and early 1940s, and this knowledge spread quickly after the end of the war. He agreed with the view that the Marshall Plan was primarily designed to induce political and economic changes and, as such, makes inferences based on technical assistance difficult. Comin added that the licensing program in 1950 in Japan mentioned by Gilchrist was not explicitly part of the technical assistance program, but the same mechanism of technology diffusion was at work.

Robinson noted that the German economy was heavily cartelized before occupation, and the United States sought to break up these monopolies. Acemoglu added that the United States tried something similar to break up the Japanese *zaibatsu*. These changes may have had effects on growth quite apart from technology diffusion. Lawrence Christiano wrapped up the discussion by asking whether a similar story would apply to other postwar economies such as France and the Netherlands.

5

In Search of Real Rigidities

Gita Gopinath, *Harvard University and NBER*
Oleg Itskhoki, *Princeton University and NBER*

I. Introduction

A large literature has recently emerged that documents patterns of nominal price stickiness at the very micro level—the good level. The documented nominal durations are significantly shorter than the estimated real effects of money on output.[1] The long-lasting real effects of monetary shocks can be reconciled with moderate price stickiness if real rigidities are an important phenomenon. Real rigidities are mechanisms that dampen price responses of firms because of factors such as strategic complementarities in price setting, real wage rigidity, and the dependence of costs on input prices that have yet to adjust, among other causes.[2] An important empirical literature has emerged recently that evaluates the question, are quantitatively important real rigidities present in the data? The answer appears to depend on which data one looks at.

In international economics there is a large and growing literature that estimates exchange rate pass-through from exchange rate shocks into prices. The estimated exchange rate pass-through is found to be incomplete; that is, if the dollar depreciates by 10% relative to the euro, dollar prices of goods imported from the euro area increase by less than 10% even in the long run. This incompleteness in pass-through is argued to be consistent with the presence of important real rigidities. Exchange rate changes generate relative price movements for the same good across markets despite costs being the same. This destination-specific markup is argued to be consistent with the presence of significant strategic complementarities in price setting.

The closed economy literature, however, uses indirect tests of real rigidities in the absence of well-identified and sizable shocks such as exchange rate shocks. The recent work based on micro evidence for

978-0-226-00212-5/2011/2010-0501$10.00

retail prices argues that real rigidities are not an empirically important phenomenon.

There are many developments in the measurement of real rigidities in the closed and open economy literatures, but these developments have taken place in parallel. In this paper we bring together the closed economy macro literature that focuses mainly on indirect tests of real rigidities with the international pricing literature that uses an observable and sizable shock, namely, the exchange rate shock, to evaluate the behavior of prices, particularly strategic complementarities in pricing. We first review the recent evidence on real rigidities to evaluate if there is a consensus emerging on the importance of these rigidities in the data. Second, since the two literatures use different metrics to evaluate the importance of real rigidities, we use unpublished international price data collected by the U.S. Bureau of Labor Statistics (BLS) to estimate both metrics using the same data. Third, we present new evidence on the dynamic response of international prices to exchange rate shocks and the response to competitor prices. Fourth, we calibrate sticky-price macro models (Calvo and menu cost) with a retail sector and a wholesale sector to the evidence on the variable markup channel of real rigidities. We evaluate the ability of our model to match the behavior of prices in the data and to measure the extent of monetary nonneutrality this channel generates.

In reviewing the literature, we group evidence based on whether the prices studied refer to retail (consumer) prices or wholesale prices. Wholesale prices can alternatively be viewed as intermediate-good prices in business-to-business transactions. The literature on exchange rate pass-through into at-the-dock prices of goods refers to wholesale prices. A review of the existing literature reveals one surprisingly consistent result across several studies, surprising since these studies use different methodologies and data sets. This result is that strategic complementarities, for example, operating through variable markups, play a small role for retail prices but appear to be quite important for wholesale prices.

We next use the BLS import price data to perform tests of real rigidity, in which we use measures employed in the closed economy literature, namely, the persistence of reset-price inflation (Bils, Klenow, and Malin 2009), and measures employed in the open economy literature, namely, the dynamic response of prices to exchange rate shocks. The actual import-price inflation series has a monthly persistence of 0.56, whereas the corresponding reset-price inflation series has a persistence of –0.04. In comparison, Bils et al. (2009) estimate for retail prices that the inflation series has persistence of –0.05 and the reset-price inflation series has a persistence of –0.41. In comparison to retail prices, import prices have greater persistence, but the magnitude of this persistence suggests that there is very little sluggishness in price adjustment.

However, when we project the aggregate import reset-price inflation on lags of the trade-weighted nominal exchange rate changes, we find that the autocorrelation of the fitted series is substantially higher as compared to that of unconditional reset-price inflation (0.33 vs. –0.04). We find similar evidence using micro-level price adjustments. We show that individual import prices, conditional on changing, respond to exchange rate shocks prior to the last time the price was adjusted and that these lagged effects are large and statistically significant. The pass-through conditional on a price change to the cumulative exchange rate change since the last price adjustment is 0.11, and the response to the cumulative exchange rate over the previous price duration is 0.08. Both these pieces of evidence that evaluate the response to a specific shock suggest a more important role for real rigidities as compared to the point estimate of the autocorrelation of reset prices.

Next, we evaluate the importance of strategic complementarities in price setting for incomplete pass-through, using some measures that capture the pricing behavior of competitors and measures that capture the extent of competition in sectors. These measures are not perfect, but they do provide useful information about pricing behavior. We use the prices set by other firms in the same 10-digit or four-digit harmonized code in the import price sample to control for the behavior of competitor prices, and we find that they have an important positive effect on firms' pricing, reducing the direct pass-through of exchange rate into prices. The point estimates are consistent with a markup elasticity of 1.5, which implies a 40% pass-through for purely idiosyncratic shocks. We also evaluate the sensitivity of firm pricing to shocks to competitors by measuring the response of prices to movements in the U.S. trade-weighted exchange rate that is orthogonal to the bilateral exchange rate for the country. We find the response to be sizable and significant. In a similar vein, we find that exchange rate pass-through is higher in response to a more aggregate shock as compared to more idiosyncratic shocks when comparing the response to bilateral exchange rate shocks versus trade-weighted exchange rate shocks.

We also relate the incompleteness in pass-through to certain sectoral features that proxy for the level of competition among importers. An important distinction between retail prices and wholesale prices is that the latter capture business-to-business transactions. Consequently, the strength of the bargaining power of the buyer can have an impact on the extent of pass-through. We use unpublished measures of concentration in the import sector provided to us by the BLS—specifically, the Herfindahl index and the number of importers that make up the top 50% of trade—to evaluate this hypothesis. While the point estimates in many cases suggest that sectors dominated by a few large importers have lower pass-through from foreign firms, the estimated standard errors are large.

Finally, we use estimates from the data to calibrate a closed economy model with different degrees of variable markup elasticity at the wholesale and retail level. In the existing monetary literature, there is typically no interesting distinction made between the retail and wholesale sectors. We calibrate the parameters for the wholesale sector using the evidence from international prices. In the benchmark model, we use Calvo price setting and later evaluate the case of menu cost pricing. First, we show that sluggishness in response to monetary shocks in wholesale prices feeds into slow adjustment of retail prices. However, the aggregate inflation and reset-price inflation series exhibit little persistence since their movement is dominated by more transitory shocks. However, conditional on monetary shocks or exchange rate–like shocks, the inflation series exhibit considerable persistence. Similarly, output series can exhibit significant monetary nonneutralities. Second, while calibrated real rigidities in the form of variable markups increase the size of the contract multiplier, their effects are limited unless they are coupled with exogenous sources of persistence. However, the model fails to match the slow dynamics in price adjustment that was documented in the empirical data, which suggests that additional sources of persistence are missing from the model.

Why does one observe differences in markup variability at the wholesale and retail levels? We do not provide a definitive answer here, but we conjecture that this can be consistent with differences in the competitive environment at the two levels. That is, the retail sector can be described as monopolistically competitive, whereas the wholesale sector is better described as a bargaining environment between a final-good producer and a limited number of intermediate-good suppliers. This can be formalized using a bargaining model of wholesale pricing; this can be found in the working paper version of this paper (Gopinath and Itskhoki 2010b). In this model, each final-good producer bargains with its intermediate-good suppliers regarding the price of intermediate goods. Given these bargained prices, the final-good producer is free to choose quantities of the intermediate inputs, as well as to set the price of its final good in the monopolistically competitive consumer market. This model results in constant markups at the retail stage but in variable markups at the wholesale level that depend, among other things, on the relative bargaining power of the final-good producer and on the market share of the intermediate-good supplier.

Important outstanding questions are whether wholesale prices are allocative and whether contracts specify fixed prices at fixed quantities. While there is no simple way to test this, Gopinath and Rigobon (2008) show that, in the case of contracts for international prices, contracts typically involve a fixed price with a quantity range specified as opposed to a fixed quantity. Moreover, firms export the same good at the same price to multiple destinations, and consequently prices behave in many cases like list prices. Further, the behavior of prices is consistent with models of monopolistic price setting, where prices are allocative, as is discussed in the papers of Neiman (2009), Gopinath and Itskhoki (2010a), and Gopinath, Itskhoki, and Rigobon (2010). Also, as we detail later, changes in intermediate-good prices effect final-good prices as they are fully passed through into retail consumer prices. These separate pieces of evidence are consistent with wholesale prices being allocative.

This paper is structured as follows. Section II provides a descriptive framework that spells out the sources of real rigidities that can result in sluggish price adjustment. Section III reviews the closed and open economy literatures on real rigidities that use micro price data. Section IV presents new empirical results on price adjustment, using international data. Section V presents the closed economy model with differential markup variability in the retail and wholesale sectors and sluggish price adjustment. All derivations and technical details are relegated to the appendices.

II. Real Rigidities: A Descriptive Framework

In this section, we set up some notation and spell out the sources of real rigidities that can result in sluggish price adjustment. This simple descriptive framework is used to organize the discussion of empirical evidence in the following two sections.

Define the *desired price* of a firm as the price it would set if it could adjust its prices flexibly in a given economic environment. With sticky prices, a forward-looking firm sets its price as a weighted average of future desired prices. The presence of real rigidities slows down the response of the desired price to a shock. Real rigidities, powered by nominal price stickiness and staggered price adjustment (Taylor 1980; Calvo

1983), can be either at the aggregate/industry level or at the micro/firm level. Real rigidities at the aggregate level include round-about production structure, as in Basu (1995); real wage rigidity, as in Blanchard and Gali (2007); and segmented input markets, as in Woodford (2003). Real rigidities at the firm level, or *strategic complementarities* in pricing, arise either from nonconstant marginal cost (i.e., decreasing returns to scale), as in Burstein and Hellwig (2007), or from variable markups. In turn, variable markups can be due to nonconstant elasticity of substitution (non-CES) demand, as in Kimball (1995) and Klenow and Willis (2006), or to strategic complementarities in price setting between large firms, as in Atkeson and Burstein (2008).

Empirical studies attempt to determine which of these channels of real rigidities, if any, are present in the data, as well as the plausible magnitudes of their effects. Since the empirical literature has examined evidence at both the retail and wholesale levels, we will maintain this distinction in our descriptive framework.

Retail (final-good) pricing. The log desired price for a final good i at time t can be written as a log desired markup over the marginal cost of the firm:

$$\tilde{p}_{it} = \mu_{it}^R + \alpha s_t + (1 - \alpha) w_t - z_{it},$$

where μ_{it}^R is the log desired markup, s_t is the log price of the intermediate input, w_t is the log price of other inputs (e.g., labor), and z_{it} represents the firm-specific marginal cost or markup shock, which may include an aggregate component common across a subset of firms; $\alpha \in [0, 1]$ is the share of intermediate inputs in the production cost of the final-good firms.

Throughout the paper we abstract from the nonconstant marginal cost channel of strategic complementarities in favor of the variable markup channel. For most purposes, the two mechanisms are largely substitutable; however, variable markups can additionally explain *pricing to market*, a phenomenon with strong empirical support, as discussed in the next section. We capture variable markups in the following reduced-form way:

$$\mu_{it}^R \approx \bar{\mu}^R - \Gamma_R (p_{it} - p_t),$$

where p_t is the industry price index and $\Gamma_R \geq 0$ is the elasticity of the firm's markup with respect to its relative price. That is, a higher relative price of the firm reduces its desired markup. As we discuss in more detail in Section V, this simple description of the desired markup is consistent with various models of variable markups cited above.

Combining the above two equations, we arrive at

$$\tilde{p}_{it} = \frac{1}{1+\Gamma_R}[\bar{\mu}^R + \alpha s_t + (1-\alpha)w_t - z_{it}] + \frac{\Gamma_R}{1+\Gamma_R}p_t. \tag{1}$$

When $\Gamma_R > 0$, the desired price of the firm increases in the prices set by the competitors of the firm, which we refer to as *strategic complementarities in price setting*. Under the same circumstances, a response to an idiosyncratic marginal cost/markup shock (such as z_{it}) is incomplete: the pass-through of an idiosyncratic shock into the desired price equals $1/(1+\Gamma_R) \in [0,1]$.

To summarize, sluggishness in the response of desired final-good prices may arise either due to staggered price adjustment when $\Gamma_R > 0$ or due to sluggish adjustment in the marginal cost, that is, due to a slow response of s_t and/or w_t to shocks.

Wholesale (intermediate-good) pricing. Let the log desired price of an intermediate variety j be

$$\tilde{s}_{jt} = \mu_{jt} + w_t + \phi_j e_t - a_{jt},$$

where μ_{jt} is the log desired markup, w_t is the price of inputs (e.g., labor), and a_{jt} is a firm-specific marginal cost or markup shock, which again may contain an aggregate component. Furthermore, we allow the cost of intermediate firms to respond directly to exchange rate fluctuations e_t with various elasticities ϕ_j. For example, some of the intermediate varieties may be produced abroad, so that their marginal cost in local currency fluctuates together with the exchange rate.[3] Finally, the log price of the intermediate good, s_t, is an aggregate of the prices of intermediate varieties, s_{jt}, which can be approximated by a geometric average: $s_t \approx \int_j s_{jt} dj$.

We similarly introduce the possibility of variable markups for the intermediate varieties:

$$\mu_{jt} \approx \bar{\mu} - \Gamma(s_{jt} - s_t),$$

where Γ is again the price elasticity of markup that may vary across varieties j. We can rewrite the desired price of the intermediate variety as

$$\tilde{s}_{jt} = \frac{1}{1+\Gamma}(\bar{\mu} + w_t + \phi_j e_t - a_{jt}) + \frac{\Gamma}{1+\Gamma}s_t. \tag{2}$$

Purely idiosyncratic shocks wash out in the aggregate and do not affect s_t. Therefore, they get passed through into desired prices immediately with a pass-through coefficient of $1/(1+\Gamma)$. More aggregate shocks have two channels through which they affect the desired price—directly (w_t or e_t) and via the prices of competitors (s_t). Coupled with nominal price stickiness and staggered price adjustment, variable markups ($\Gamma > 0$) may generate sluggish adjustment that lasts past the periods of nominal stickiness.

Aggregate real rigidities. Various aggregate sources of real rigidities enter through a sluggish adjustment to shocks of the marginal cost component, denoted by w_t. Specifically, real wage rigidities, Basu (1995) round-about production, and segmented input markets can all be captured by a slow adjustment of w_t to shocks. For concreteness, one can use the following structure to think about aggregate real rigidities (see Sec. V):

$$w_t = \gamma m_t + (1-\gamma)p_t, \tag{3}$$

where m_t is aggregate nominal spending, p_t is the consumer price level, and $\gamma > 0$ is the elasticity of the cost w_t with respect to monetary (nominal spending) shocks. The smaller is γ, the more sluggish is the response of aggregate costs to monetary shocks, that is, the stronger are aggregate real rigidities.

Equations (1)–(3) describe our simple framework to account for real rigidities.[4] Sluggish adjustment in the desired final-good prices $\tilde{p}_{it}$ can arise due to one of the three channels: (*a*) sluggish response of aggregate costs w_t (small γ), (*b*) sluggish adjustment of intermediate prices s_t ($\Gamma > 0$ provided $\alpha > 0$), and (*c*) gradual adjustment in final-good desired prices ($\Gamma_R > 0$). We now evaluate the evidence on these different sources of real rigidities.

III. Evidence on Real Rigidities: A Review

Although appealing at the intuitive level, real rigidities are hard to identify and measure in the data. Aggregate real rigidities imply a sluggish response of the marginal cost of firms to aggregate shocks. Firm-level real rigidities imply a muted response of the firms' prices conditional on price adjustment to the marginal cost shocks. Since data on marginal costs are usually unavailable, it is hard to test these mechanisms directly. Therefore, the literature relies either on calibrations or indirect empirical tests.

In parallel, the international literature has a long tradition of estimating exchange rate pass-through, namely, the response of international prices to changes in exchange rates.[5] A standard assumption in the empirical pass-through literature is that changes in the exchange rate represent a shock to the firm's costs that is orthogonal to other shocks that affect the firm's pricing decision and, in reverse, they are not affected by firm pricing. This assumption is motivated by the empirical finding that exchange rate movements are disconnected from most macro variables at the frequencies studied in the literature (1–2-year horizons).[6] While this assumption might be more problematic for commodities such as oil or metals and for some commodity-exporting countries such as Canada, it is far less restrictive for most differentiated goods and most developed countries. Alternatively, the exchange rate change can be viewed not as a pure exogenous cost shock but rather as an observable signal about the underlying fundamental macro shocks that differentially affect the costs of domestic and foreign firms. In this case, the coefficients on the exchange rate have less of a structural interpretation, but they can still provide useful information about the nature of firm pricing.

The estimated exchange rate pass-through has typically been found to be incomplete. This incompleteness in pass-through can be consistent with various sources of firm-level and aggregate real rigidities, as well as with rational inattention and sticky information. The fact that firms export the same good to multiple destinations provides a mechanism to distinguish the source of the real rigidity. The pervasive evidence on *pricing to market*, the practice of charging different prices for the same good in different locations, provides support for the variable markup channel of incomplete pass-through.

In Sections III.A and III.B, we review the empirical evidence on real rigidities in the closed and open economy literatures, respectively. We restrict attention to the most recent literature that uses micro-level price data.

A. *Closed Economy Literature*

In the closed economy literature the evidence on real rigidities typically arises from indirect identification strategies. Klenow and Willis (2006) evaluate the variable markup channel of real rigidities by calibrating a menu cost model with Kimball (1995) demand to match the BLS micro retail price evidence on the frequency and size of price adjustment. They conclude that the levels of real rigidity sufficient to generate significant monetary nonneutrality have implausible implications for the required size of menu costs and idiosyncratic productivity shocks. Intuitively, significant real rigidities compress price dispersion so that much larger idiosyncratic shocks are required to match the size of price adjustment. At the same time, large menu costs are required to match the average durations of price rigidity given large idiosyncratic shocks.

Burstein and Hellwig (2007) replace Kimball demand with increasing marginal costs at the firm level to generate strategic complementarity in price setting. They calibrate the extent of decreasing returns to scale (elasticity of the marginal cost with respect to output) in order to match scanner data from a large chain of supermarkets in the Chicago area (Dominick's) on the comovement between prices and market shares. This calibration implies a moderate role for strategic complementarities generated via curvature in marginal costs.

Bils et al. (2009) develop a test to assess a broad class of models with real rigidities. They examine the persistence of the actual inflation and reset-price inflation series. *Reset-price inflation* is defined as an average reset price change within the group of goods that adjusts prices in a given period, while reset prices for all other goods are indexed by reset-price inflation (for a formal definition, see Sec. IV.A). If real rigidities are important, there should be significant persistence both in the actual inflation and the reset-price inflation series. The paper finds low persistence for actual price inflation and negative persistence for reset-price inflation (in both cases persistence is measured as the monthly autoregressive coefficient), suggesting that the selection mechanism present in menu costs models (emphasized by Caplin and Spulber [1987]) offsets the effects of real rigidities and that the real effects of money last less time than nominal price durations.

In a different paper, Klenow and Willis (2007) find that micro price changes respond to old macro information, known prior to their previous price adjustment. They interpret this as evidence of sticky information, in the spirit of Mankiw and Reis (2002); nevertheless, this evidence is also consistent with the presence of real rigidities and pricing complementarities that lead to incomplete price adjustment at the micro level.

As previously mentioned, these tests for real rigidities are indirect, relying mainly on calibrations or statistical properties of observable prices, given that marginal costs and markups are not directly observable. The exception to this is a paper by Eichenbaum, Jaimovich, and Rebelo (2011), which uses scanner data for a large grocery store chain in the United States. Eichenbaum et al. observe both the wholesale price at which the store obtains the good (specific universal product code [UPC]) and the retail price at which the store sells it. At very short horizons the wholesale price can be viewed as the relevant marginal cost for the firm. They find that, conditional on changing reference prices, there is no evidence of variable markups; that is, all of the reference wholesale cost change is passed through into reference retail prices.[7]

B. *Open Economy Literature*

The open economy literature evaluates the response of retail prices and at-the-dock prices to exchange rate shocks. While pass-through is less than one in both cases, pass-through into retail prices is always much lower than into at-the-dock prices. This is not surprising given that distribution costs, which are mainly nontraded costs unaffected by the exchange rate, are an important component of retail prices (e.g., see Goldberg and Campa 2010). Goldberg and Knetter (1997) summarize a large body of the earlier empirical literature on pass-through.

A virtue of international price data is that one observes the prices at which the same firm sells its product in different destinations. There is considerable evidence of *pricing to market*; that is, firms sell the same product at different prices in different destinations. This concept, first proposed in Dornbusch (1987) and Krugman (1987), attributes an important role to strategic complementarities that generate variable markups. In a recent paper, Fitzgerald and Haller (2008) provide the most direct evidence of this phenomenon. They examine the pricing of Irish manufactures in domestic and export (UK) markets. They find a pronounced price differential response to exchange rate movements. Since the goods are manufactured in the same plant, the difference is attributable to variation in markups.[8] Similarly, Burstein and Jaimovich (2008) use supermarket scanner data for stores in the United States and Canada and find that products with the same UPC produced in the same country sell at different wholesale prices in the United States and Canada. More specifically, relative wholesale prices in the two markets move closely with the exchange rate.

In a recent set of papers, Gopinath and Rigobon (2008), Gopinath and Itskhoki (2010a), and Gopinath et al. (2010) use micro import price data collected by the BLS for the period 1994–2005 to provide evidence of incomplete exchange rate pass-through at the dock even conditional on prices being changed. While incomplete exchange rate pass-through per se is consistent with evidence on variable markups, it can arise from other sources of real rigidities, as previously discussed. Gopinath and Itskhoki (2010a) document a positive correlation between the frequency of price adjustment for a good and exchange rate pass-through conditional on price adjustment. They argue that this positive correlation is consistent with variation in markup elasticity across firms and cannot be consistent with other sources of firm heterogeneity. Neiman (2010) uses the same BLS import price data to document that, consistent with the greater importance of the strategic complementarity channel for arm's-length transactions as compared to intrafirm transactions, for differentiated products intrafirm prices are characterized by more stickiness, less synchronization, and greater exchange rate pass-through.

Finally, there are papers that evaluate the response of retail prices and wholesale prices for the same good to an exchange rate shock. Gopinath et al. (2009) use scanner data on retail and wholesale prices for stores of the same supermarket chain in the United States and Canada and find that, in response to an exchange rate shock, movements in relative retail prices in a common currency are explained mainly by movements in relative costs and very little by relative markups. Goldberg and Hellerstein (2006) and Nakamura and Zerom (2010) find that, for beer and coffee sales in a supermarket store, the pass-through from exchange rate shocks to wholesale costs is incomplete but the pass-through from wholesale costs to retail prices is close to complete. In a recent study, Berger et al. (2009) match goods in the BLS import price index to those in the BLS consumer price index (CPI) for the period 1994–2007 and find that the *overall distribution wedge*, which is the percentage difference between retail and at-the-dock prices, does not vary systematically with the exchange rate, which implies a nearly complete pass-through from at-the-dock to retail prices.[9]

Summary. Overall, a consistent finding across studies in the closed and open economy literatures is that the variable markup channel of real rigidities is an important feature of the wholesale cost data but not of the retail price data. This is surprising consensus given the different approaches used in the closed and open economy literatures and the different data sets involved. In the terminology of Section II, the empirical evidence is consistent with $\Gamma_R \approx 0$ and $\Gamma > 0$. Given the feedback from wholesale prices s_t to retail prices p_t in equation (1), one could expect sluggish adjustment in wholesale reset prices to generate slow adjustment in retail reset prices. The fact that Bils et al. (2009) find a negative persistence for overall reset-price inflation could then be consistent with either a small α or a large transitory variance for z_{it}, as long as these shocks are not purely idiosyncratic. In the next section we explore explicitly, using international price data, the dynamics of price adjustment both unconditionally and conditioning on exchange rate shocks.

IV. New Evidence on Real Rigidities

As discussed in Section III.A, Bils et al. (2009) find that regular inflation and reset-price inflation for retail price data are consistent with the absence of important real rigidities. In this section, we present evidence on the properties of regular inflation and reset-price inflation for import price data using the Bils et al. (2009) micro data on international prices. We then compare it to the properties of the inflation series, conditional on exchange rate shocks, which allows us to evaluate the conditional response of prices to a given aggregate cost shock. We then study the dynamic properties of price adjustment at the firm level.

First, we show that reset-price inflation for the import price data is less negatively autocorrelated as compared to that documented for retail prices. This is consistent with the conclusion that international prices depict higher real rigidities as compared to retail prices. Second, we present evidence regarding the sluggish response of price changes to exchange rate shocks. We do this in two ways. First, we project aggregate regular and reset-price inflation on lags of the exchange rate changes. We find that the autocorrelation of the fitted series is substantially higher as compared to that of the unconditional series. Second, using the micro data, we show that individual prices, conditional on changing, respond to exchange rate shocks that were realized prior to the previous price adjustment. Both pieces of evidence suggest a more important role for real rigidities as compared to the conclusions one can draw from the analysis of unconditional aggregate inflation series.[10]

While this evidence is supportive of the presence of sizable real rigidities, it does not discriminate among various sources of real rigidities. Therefore, we next try to assess specifically the importance of strategic complementarities in price setting. We do so by studying the response of the firm's prices to the shocks to its competitors. Our central result here is that the firm's prices respond strongly to the prices of its competitors and that this channel explains a significant fraction of exchange rate pass-through into prices.

The data used in this section are the micro import price data underlying the construction of the U.S. import price index. This covers the period 1994–2005. For details regarding the data, see Gopinath and Rigobon (2008).

A. *Reset-Price Inflation*

We follow Bils et al. (2009) in estimating the reset-price inflation series for U.S. imports. The log price of a good i at time t is denoted by p_{it}. The log of the reset price at time t for good i is denoted by p^*_{it} and defined as

$$p^*_{it} = \begin{cases} p_{it} & \text{if } p_{it} \neq p_{i,t-1} \\ p^*_{i,t-1} + \pi^*_t & \text{if } p_{it} = p_{i,t-1}, \end{cases} \tag{4}$$

where π^*_t is the average reset-price inflation of those goods whose prices change at time t. The inflation of the actual price series is referred to as *regular-price inflation*. In a Calvo pricing environment, where firms only differ in the exogenous frequency of price adjustment, the behavior of reset-price inflation will capture the extent of real rigidities. As discussed in detail in Bils et al. (2009), in the presence of real rigidities reset prices will adjust sluggishly, as firms have multiple price adjustments before they fully respond to a shock. The regular-price inflation series displays even greater persistence, as each firm waits for the random arrival of the opportunity to change its price. In the case of state-dependent pricing or variations in desired price responses across sectors, the behavior of measured reset prices is not as direct because there is selection of which firms change prices. Gopinath and Itskhoki (2010a) show that sectors that have a higher frequency of price adjustment also have higher long-run pass-through (less real rigidities). Consequently, the reset-price series is affected by those goods that change prices more frequently and pass-through eventually a lot more.

It is important to point out that the sample sizes in the import price data are not as large as in the CPI data and that given the low frequency of price adjustment the number of actual price changes used to impute the reset price series is low.[11] This would suggest that the import reset-price inflation series is more subject to noise as compared to the construct of Bils et al. (2009) for the U.S. CPI.

The persistence and volatility of the regular and reset-price inflation series within various subsamples are reported in table 1.[12] We measure persistence as the AR(1) coefficient for the series, and we report the standard deviation of the series as a measure of volatility.[13] The first row of table 1 reports these moments for consumer-price inflation from Bils et al. (2009). The rest of the rows provide these statistics for the BLS import-price data.[14]

Columns 1 and 2 of table 1 report statistics for the unconditional inflation series. For all subsamples considered, import-price inflation is

Table 1
Volatility and Persistence of Regular and Reset-Price Inflation

	Unconditional		Conditional on Exchange Rate	
	AR(1)	SD (%)	AR(1)	SD (%)
Regular-price inflation:				
Consumer prices	−.05	.14	...	...
Import prices	.51	.33	.55	.25
Dollar-priced goods	.56	.27	.79	.18
Market transactions	.43	.30	.70	.20
Reset-price inflation:				
Consumer prices	−.41	.95	...	...
Import prices	.02	1.60	.31	.82
Dollar-priced goods	−.04	1.20	.33	.75
Market transactions	−.03	1.70	.17	.91

Source: Statistics for consumer prices are from Bils, Klenow, and Malin (2009).
Note: Import prices exclude petrol classifications; the rows for market transactions include only dollar-prices goods. The last two columns project the inflation series on the current and 24 lags of the log changes of the U.S. trade-weighted exchange rate and compute the moments for the projected series.

more persistent relative to consumer-price inflation as calculated by Bils et al. (2009).[15] For example, for the dollar-priced imports, the persistence of inflation is 0.56, whereas for consumer prices it is close to zero (−0.05). The import-price inflation is also more volatile. A similar comparison holds for reset-price inflation. While Bils et al. find that reset-price inflation for consumer prices is negatively autocorrelated (−0.41), we find essentially zero autocorrelation for import prices (e.g., −0.04 for the dollar-priced imports). This difference in persistence of consumer-price and import-price inflation is consistent with the different nature of pricing at the consumer and intermediate-good levels (since most imports are intermediate goods).[16]

An important feature of the international data is that we can examine the response of the inflation series to a specific shock, namely, the exchange rate shock. This has advantages over just looking at reset-price inflation that aggregates (imperfectly in small samples) across idiosyncratic, sectoral, and aggregate shocks. We accordingly project the regular and reset-price inflation series on current and 24 lags of the log changes of the U.S. trade-weighted nominal exchange rate. We use the fitted values from this regression and estimate the AR(1) coefficient and standard deviation for the fitted series. The results are reported in the last two columns of table 1. In all cases, regular and reset-price inflation, conditional (projected) on the exchange rate shocks, exhibit more persistence.

For instance, in the case of dollar-priced imports, the conditional regular-price inflation series has an overall persistence of 0.79, while its unconditional persistence is 0.56. Similarly, for the reset-price inflation series the conditional persistence is 0.33, as opposed to the unconditional persistence of –0.04.

This evidence is consistent with the presence of multiple shocks of different degrees of persistence driving the inflation process. Under these circumstances, the unconditional persistence of the inflation series might not accurately reflect the underlying sluggishness in the micro-level price adjustment. In the next subsection, we present further evidence of the sluggish response of prices to exchange rate shocks by examining the behavior of individual prices and their response to lagged exchange rates changes.

B. *Micro Dynamics of Price Adjustment*

At the good level, we estimate pass-through into prices of exchange rate shocks realized during the most recent period of price nonadjustment and of those that were realized prior to the previous price adjustment. In the absence of real rigidities, all adjustment should take place at the first instance of price change, and hence the coefficient on the exchange rate change prior to the previous price adjustment should be zero.

Formally, we estimate the following regression:

$$\Delta\bar{p}_{i,t} = \beta_1 \Delta_{\tau_1} e_{i,t} + \beta_2 \Delta_{\tau_2} e_{i,t-\tau_1} + Z'_{i,t}\gamma + \varepsilon_{it}, \tag{5}$$

where i indexes the good and $\Delta\bar{p}_{i,t}$ is the change in the log dollar price of the good, conditional on price adjustment in the currency of pricing;[17] $\Delta_{\tau_1} e_{i,t} \equiv e_{i,t} - e_{i,t-\tau_1}$ is the cumulative change in the log of the bilateral nominal exchange rate over the duration when the previous price was in effect (which we denote τ_1). Similarly, τ_2 denotes the duration of the previous price of the firm, so that $\Delta_{\tau_2} e_{i,t-\tau_1} \equiv e_{i,t-\tau_1} - e_{i,t-\tau_1-\tau_2}$ is the cumulative exchange rate change over the previous (the one prior to the previous price change) period of nonadjustment. Figure 1 illustrates a hypothetical price series: if $\Delta\bar{p}_{i,t}$ is the price change between t_3 and t_{LL}, $\Delta_{\tau_1} e_{i,t}$ is then the exchange rate change between t_3 and t_{LL} and $\Delta_{\tau_2} e_{i,t-\tau_1}$ is the exchange rate change between t_2 and t_3. Finally, $Z_{i,t}$ includes controls for the cumulative change in the foreign consumer price level, the U.S. consumer price level and fixed effects for every BLS-defined primary strata (mostly two- to four-digit harmonized codes) and country

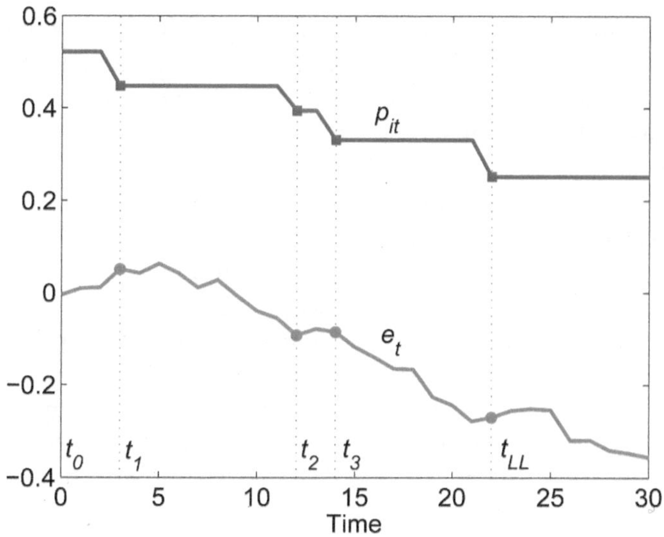

Fig. 1. Hypothetical good-level price series and nominal exchange rate

pair. We allow Z_t to include lagged foreign and domestic inflation. The standard errors are clustered at the level of the fixed effects. We restrict the sample to nonpetrol, dollar-priced goods and market transactions. Note that this specification requires the goods to have at least two price adjustments during their life. Since there are several goods that have only one price change during their life, we lose about 30% of the goods.

By conditioning on a price change we get past the period of nominal rigidity, which is essential to understanding the role of real rigidities. In a Calvo pricing environment, since the decision to change prices is exogenous, there are no selection issues to be concerned with. However, in an environment with endogenous frequency of price adjustment, conditioning on a price change will induce a bias in the exchange rate pass-through estimates, as it generates a conditional correlation between the exchange rate and the residual even if the unconditional correlation is zero. This is problematic if one tries to provide a structural interpretation to the coefficient. This is not our purpose here. We use this specification to provide a relation in the data between the response of prices conditional on adjusting to lagged exchange rate changes. Later we will estimate these regressions in the model-simulated data, where frequency is chosen endogenously, and infer how well models with real rigidities perform in matching the facts in the data. This exercise is accordingly similar to that of trying to match the behavior of the reset-price inflation series, a series that also is affected by selection issues. Furthermore, when the selection bias is strong, the pass-through coefficient on first adjustment (β_1) is biased upward while the pass-through coefficient on second adjustment (β_2) is biased downward, which makes it harder to identify the presence of real rigidities.

Table 2 reports the results from estimation of regression (5). We provide evidence for various subsamples of the data. Across all specifications we find that exchange rate shocks that took place prior to the current period of nonadjustment have a significant effect on current price adjustments. This is consistent with the existence of real rigidities in pricing. The strength of these lagged effects is much stronger than what would be suggested purely by the reset-price inflation series. The first row of table 2 points out that the elasticity of current price changes to lagged exchange rate shocks for dollar-priced goods is 0.08, which is only slightly smaller than the response to the contemporaneous exchange rate movement (equal to 0.11). The importance of these lagged effects is consistently present in all subsamples. For the

Table 2
Dynamic Response to Exchange Rate Shocks

	β_1	β_2	N	R^2
All countries	.11	.08	69,917	.01
	(.02)	(.01)		
Non-OECD countries	.06	.04	37,108	.01
	(.02)	(.01)		
High-income OECD countries	.23	.18	32,809	.02
	(.02)	(.02)		
Euro area	.22	.14	5,933	.02
	(.04)	(.03)		
Japan	.26	.24	4,249	.06
	(.04)	(.03)		
Canada	.28	.34	14,620	.01
	(.16)	(.05)		
Differentiated goods	.14	.10	21,360	.02
	(.02)	(.02)		
No missing prices:				
All countries	.10	.08	45,765	.01
	(.02)	(.01)		
High-income OECD countries	.19	.13	22,436	.01
	(.03)	(.02)		

Note: Items β_1 and β_2 are the pass-through coefficients at the first and second rounds of price adjustment, respectively; these are estimated from regression (5). Standard errors in parentheses are clustered at the country × four-digit sector level. N is the number of price changes in the sample. Results under "No missing prices" exclude from the sample all price changes that were followed or preceded by a missing price.

high-income OECD sample, the contemporaneous and lagged responses are 0.23 and 0.18, respectively. For the non-OECD sample, the pass-through rates are overall lower, but there are still important lagged effects. This is similarly documented for the euro-area countries, Japan, and Canada.

In the data there can be spells that have missing prices and where the new price follows or precedes a missing price. In this case the exact timing of the price change is not known, so lagged effects can arise from getting the timing wrong. The last two rows of table 2 check for the robustness of the results by including in the sample only those price changes that were not followed or preceded by a missing price. This changes the sample composition, but lagged responses are still strongly evident.

The results in this section are consistent with the evidence in Gopinath et al. (2010) that long-run pass-through is much higher than pass-through conditional on the first adjustment to the exchange rate shock. Here we present explicitly the dynamics and extend the sample to more countries.

We also divide goods into four equal-sized bins based on their frequency of price adjustment and estimate equation (5) within each bin separately. The purpose of this exercise is to evaluate if the importance of lags varies across goods with different frequencies of price adjustment. One conjecture may be that it is only the very high frequency goods that have multiple price adjustments to respond to a shock. In fact this is not the case, as we find that lags are important even for goods that adjust prices very infrequently: for example, the first quartile contains goods that adjust prices less than once a year, and in the first round the pass-through is 0.12, whereas it is 0.08 in the second round. This finding further assuages concerns about measurement issues with the timing of price adjustment.[18]

We also break the sample down by the end use of the product. Again, we find the second rounds of price adjustment to be significant for most end use categories. In the case of "Food, feed, and beverages" exported from the non-OECD countries (which dominate the sample of all countries in panel A of table 3), the pass-through is generally very low and insignificant from zero. In the case of "Consumer goods (nonfood and excluding automotive)," the dynamics are less evident. However, one should be careful about interpreting the results for this subsample because these goods more often have a fixed price during their life and then get discontinued and replaced. Since we do not observe price changes across discontinuations, we might be excluding important adjustments that take place at the time of product replacement.

Table 3
Dynamic Response to Exchange Rate Shocks, by End-Use Sectors

	β_1	β_2	N	R^2
A. All countries:				
Food, feed, and beverages	.05	.03	17,731	.01
	(.04)	(.02)		
Industrial supplies and materials	.13	.11	22,396	.02
	(.03)	(.02)		
Capital goods, except automotive	.16	.17	4,220	.05
	(.03)	(.03)		
Consumer goods (nonfood)	.05	.03	8,222	.01
	(.04)	(.02)		
B. High-income OECD countries:				
Food, feed, and beverages	.16	.15	5,207	.03
	(.04)	(.03)		
Industrial supplies and materials	.21	.25	13,089	.01
	(.05)	(.03)		
Capital goods, except automotive	.21	.22	2,587	.05
	(.04)	(.03)		
Consumer goods (nonfood)	.17	.03	2,915	.02
	(.06)	(.04)		

Note: See the note to table 2. Clustered standard errors are in parentheses.

Overall, the micro evidence is consistent with the aggregate level evidence of sluggish adjustment to exchange rate changes. This sluggishness is consistent with many forms of real rigidities, including variable markups, the Basu (1995) intermediate-input channel wherein each firm's output is used as an input in production, and sluggish response of other factor costs (like wages) to the underlying source of exchange rate shocks. Equivalently, it could arise from rational inattention or sticky information. The next subsection evaluates how the extent of product market competition affects the patterns of pass-through in order to identify the effects of strategic complementarities in price setting.

C. *Competition and Pass-Through*

In this section we evaluate the importance of the strategic complementarity in price setting for incomplete pass-through, using some measures that capture the pricing behavior of competitors and measures that capture the extent of competition within sectors. Ideally, one would need to perform this analysis with detailed industry data for each product and information on prices and market shares of different firms. These data, however, do not exist for the large number of products included in our study. Consequently, we use some proxies here, and they are necessarily imperfect. Nevertheless, we find evidence that is consistent with the presence of significant strategic complementarities at the firm level.

Trade-weighted versus bilateral exchange rate. First, we evaluate the response of each firm's pricing to its own bilateral exchange rate as compared to its response to the trade-weighted exchange rate. Movements in the trade-weighted exchange rate can be viewed as a more aggregate shock that affects a larger fraction of a firm's competitors, as compared to a shock that only affects the bilateral exchange rate. An alternative interpretation could be that prices of a firm that uses production inputs from the rest of the world are sensitive to the movements in the trade-weighted exchange rate because it affects the firm's costs.

More specifically, we estimate the following standard pass-through regression:

$$\Delta p_{k,t} = \alpha_i + \sum_{j=0}^{n} \beta_j \Delta e_{k,t-j} + \sum_{j=0}^{n} \gamma_j \pi_{k,t-j} + \varepsilon_{k,t}, \tag{6}$$

where k indexes the country, Δp is the average monthly log price change in dollars, π is the monthly foreign-country inflation using the consumer price index, n is the number of monthly lags, which varies from 1 to 24; $\Delta e_{k,t-j}$ is either a bilateral nominal exchange rate or the U.S. trade-weighted nominal exchange rate. Figure 2 plots $\sum_{j=0}^{n}\beta_j$ as a function of n for each case, where we estimate a pooled regression restricting the coefficients β_j to be the same across countries. Panel *a* of the figure plots the results for the all-countries sample, while panel *b* does it for the high-income OECD subsample. In both figures it is evident that the pass-through from the trade-weighted exchange rate exceeds the bilateral exchange rate pass-through, which is consistent with the hypothesis that firm's prices are responsive to cost shocks of firm's competitors. In further analysis, we find that this pattern is evident for countries in the euro area as well as the non-OECD countries, whereas it is less evident for Japan, Canada, and the United Kingdom.

We also perform the analysis using the individual price data, conditional on a price change. We evaluate the response to the bilateral exchange rate change since the last time the price was adjusted and to movements in the U.S. trade-weighted exchange rate that is orthogonal to the bilateral exchange rate for the country. More specifically, we run a first-stage regression, where we regress the trade-weighted exchange rate on the bilateral exchange rate. We calculate the residual and then estimate a second-stage regression, where we regress the price change, conditional on adjustment,

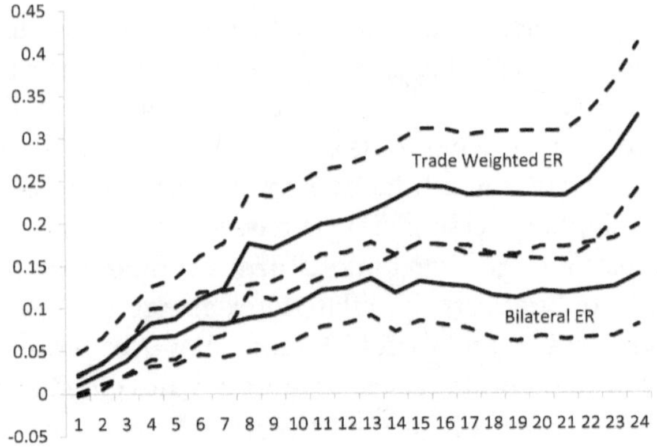

(a) All countries

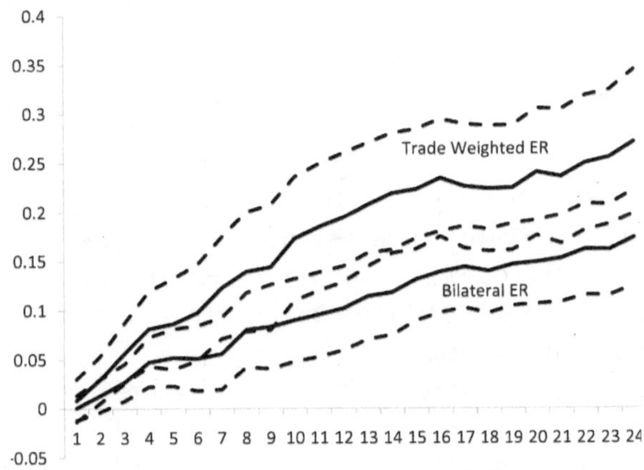

(b) High-income OECD

Fig. 2. Impulse responses to bilateral and U.S. trade-weighted exchange rate

on the cumulative change in the bilateral exchange rate and in the residual.[19] We include a control for the cumulative change in foreign country CPI inflation since the last price change. The results are reported in table 4. Consistent with the evidence in figure 2 using aggregate price changes, the effect of the residual is almost as large as the direct effect of the bilateral exchange rate, and in some cases it is even larger.

We should note that this evidence admits a number of interpretations. First, the sensitivity of prices to the trade-weighted exchange rate over and above the bilateral exchange rate is consistent with strategic complementarities in price setting when the competitors of the firm are exporters from other countries. However, it is also consistent with the fact that firms use production inputs imported from the rest of the world,

Table 4
Pass-Through of Bilateral and U.S. Trade-Weighted Exchange Rate

	Bilateral Exchange Rate	Trade-Weighted Exchange Rate	N	R^2
All countries	.11	.19	83,064	.01
	(.01)	(.02)		
Non-OECD countries	.07	.18	46,420	.01
	(.02)	(.02)		
High-income OECD countries	.22	.17	32,809	.02
	(.02)	(.05)		
Euro area	.27	.31	7,856	.03
	(.03)	(.07)		
Japan	.21	.17	5,733	.02
	(.04)	(.06)		
Canada	.23	.12	16,221	.01
	(.12)	(.10)		
Differentiated	.12	.17	21,360	.02
	(.01)	(.03)		

Note: The first column reports pass-through conditional on price adjustment of the bilateral exchange rate shocks. The second column reports the pass-through of the component of the U.S. trade-weighted exchange rate orthogonal to the bilateral exchange rate (i.e., a residual from the projection of the trade-weighted exchange rate on the bilateral exchange rate). Clustered standard errors are in parentheses.

and a movement in the trade-weighted exchange rate could therefore represent a relevant cost shock for the firm. In what follows we test for strategic complementarities in price setting more directly.

Competitor prices. A more direct test of the presence of strategic complementarities is to evaluate whether changes in the competitor prices affect the pricing decisions of the firm. We do so by estimating the following regression:

$$\Delta\bar{p}_{i,k,t} = \beta_e \Delta_{\tau_1} e_{i,k,t} + \beta_I \Delta_{\tau_1} P^I_{k,t} + \gamma Z_{i,t} + \varepsilon_{i,t}, \quad (7)$$

where $\Delta\bar{p}_{i,k,t}$ is the change in the log dollar price of good i in sector k, conditional on price adjustment, and $\Delta_{\tau_1} e_{i,k,t}$ is the cumulative change in the log of the bilateral nominal exchange rate over the duration for which the previous price was in effect. Now $\Delta_{\tau_1} P^I_{k,t}$ is a measure of the cumulative price change by firms other than firm i in sector k.[20] We also estimate the same regression for the life-long change in the price of the good and refer to the coefficients in this case as *long-run pass-through*. In terms of figure 1, this corresponds to having $p_{t_{LL}} - p_{t_0}$ on the left-hand side of (7) and corresponding cumulative changes in variables on the right-hand side.[21] Finally, $Z_{i,t}$ represents the cumulative change in the

CPI in the foreign country. We again restrict the sample to nonpetrol, dollar-priced goods and market transactions. We include fixed effects for every BLS-defined primary strata (mostly two- to four-digit harmonized codes) and country pair; the standard errors are clustered at the level of the fixed effects.

The results are reported in table 5. The first row of each panel (labeled "No $\Delta_{\tau_1} P^I_{k,t}$") presents the results where we exclude any industry competition effect. The next two rows include industry price effects aggregated at the BLS-defined primary strata level (mostly two- to four-digit harmonized codes) and at the 10-digit harmonized code level, respectively. As is evident in all specifications, the effect of competitor prices is large and highly significant. Moreover, it significantly reduces the direct response of prices to the exchange rate shock. If one does a back-of-the-envelope calculation of the extent of strategic complementarities using expression (2) of our accounting framework in Section II, one obtains a measure of markup elasticity of $\Gamma \approx 1.5$ (from $\Gamma/[1+\Gamma] \approx 0.6$). This value is consistent with the required markup elasticity to match the evidence of incomplete long-run pass-through, as we discuss in Gopinath and Itskhoki (2010a) and Gopinath et al. (2010). Furthermore, note that the direct impact of exchange rate changes (β_e) still increases from the specification conditional on one price adjustment (panel A of table 5) to the life-long specification (panel B of table 5), even when we control for competitor prices. This suggests that, although

Table 5
Response to Competitor Prices

	β_e	β_I	N	R^2
A. Pass-through conditional on first price change:				
No $\Delta_{\tau_1} P^I_{k,t}$	.13	. . .	83,056	.01
	(.01)			
$\Delta_{\tau_1} P^I_{k,t}$ (primary strata)	.07	.61	78,942	.13
	(.01)	(.02)		
$\Delta_{\tau_1} P^I_{k,t}$ (10-digit harmonized code level)	.04	.61	59,972	.25
	(.01)	(.02)		
B. Long-run pass-through:				
No $\Delta_{\tau_1} P^I_{k,t}$	.31	. . .	16,145	.06
	(.03)			
$\Delta_{\tau_1} P^I_{k,t}$ (primary strata)	.13	.66	15,273	.24
	(.02)	(.03)		
$\Delta_{\tau_1} P^I_{k,t}$ (10-digit harmonized code level)	.16	.62	11,379	.34
	(.01)	(.03)		

Note: These are results from estimation of eq. (7). Standard errors are in parentheses. The coefficient γ on the consumer-price inflation in the foreign country also shrinks along with β_e when we include the control for competitor prices.

strategic complementarities are an important feature of price setting, they do not fully explain the delayed pass-through of exchange rate shocks and that there are other sources of real rigidity present in the data.

Sector concentration. Finally, we relate the incompleteness in exchange rate pass-through to certain sectoral features that proxy for the level of competition among importers. An important distinction between retail and wholesale prices is that the latter originate from business-to-business transactions. Consequently, the strength of bargaining power of the buyer can have an impact on the extent of pass-through. To evaluate this hypothesis, we use measures of concentration in the import sectors constructed by the Bureau of the Census. This includes a Herfindahl index for importers and a measure of the number of importers that make up the top 50% of trade using census data on all imports entering the United States. We estimate the following long-run pass-through regression in which we interact the exchange rate change with a measure of concentration (at the two- to four-digit level):

$$\Delta \bar{p}_{i,k,t} = \beta \Delta_{\tau_1} e_{i,k,t} + \psi(\Delta_{\tau_1} e_{i,k,t} \times C_k) + Z'_{i,k,t}\gamma + \varepsilon_{i,t}, \tag{8}$$

where the second regressor is the interaction of the exchange rate change with a given concentration measure. In $Z_{i,k,t}$ we include separate controls for the concentration measure, the change in CPI inflation (both stand alone and interacted with the concentration measure), and country fixed effects. All standard errors are clustered at the primary strata level.

The results are reported in table 6 for the two measures of concentration. While the point estimates in both regressions suggest that sectors that are dominated by a few large importers (high Herfindahl index and small number of firms in the top 50%) have lower pass-through from foreign firms, the standard errors on these estimates are large. Overall, the evidence is inconclusive. We also performed this exercise for pass-through conditional on first price change, as well as restricted

Table 6
Exchange Rate Pass-Through and Sectoral Characteristics

	β	ψ	N	R^2
Herfindahl index	.30	−.02	12,432	.06
	(.03)	(.02)		
No. importers in top 50%	.23	.02	12,435	.06
	(.02)	(.02)		

Note: Clustered standard errors are in parentheses.

the sample to differentiated goods only; in all cases we found no clear relationship in the data.

Summary. The presented evidence is consistent with an important role of real rigidities in the data, reflected in a sluggish response of prices to exchange rate shocks even conditional on prices changing. The reset-price inflation series, when conditioned on exchange rate shocks, also exhibits persistence. We further find that the response of prices is greater to trade-weighted exchange rate shocks as compared to bilateral shocks and that the response to competitor prices is significant. These last two pieces of evidence are consistent with the importance of strategic complementarities in price setting; however, they are also possibly consistent with other explanations. For example, the trade-weighted exchange rate can reflect changes in the prices of inputs imported from the rest of the world, while competitor prices may proxy for sectoral shocks, which are not reflected in the exchange rate and which are common across firms from a number of countries. Presumably the most direct evidence of strategic complementarity arises from studies of pricing to market that control for costs, as discussed earlier in Section III. The best description of our evidence is as important facts regarding the dynamics of price adjustment that should be matched by models of price setting. We turn to one such model in the next section.

V. Model

In this section we quantitatively evaluate a reduced-form sticky-price model with a retail sector and a wholesale sector. Consistent with the data, we allow for variable markups at the wholesale level and constant markups at the retail level.[22] In the existing monetary literature, there is typically no interesting distinction made between the retail and wholesale sectors. The goal is to evaluate the behavior of regular and reset-price inflation, both unconditional and conditional on aggregate shocks, as well as the dynamic response of good-level prices conditional on changing so as to compare it to the evidence in Section IV. We also evaluate the extent of monetary nonneutrality generated by this source of real rigidities.

The model generates sluggishness in response to monetary shocks in wholesale prices, and this feeds into the slow adjustment of retail prices. However, aggregate inflation and reset-price inflation exhibit little persistence, since their movements are dominated by more transitory shocks. However, conditional on monetary shocks or exchange rate–like shocks, inflation series exhibit considerable persistence.[23] This is consistent with the data. However, the model fails to match the slow dynamics in price adjustment documented in the empirical data. This suggests a need for an additional source of persistence in prices.

Similarly, the output series can exhibit significant monetary non-neutralities if the money growth process is sufficiently persistent. While calibrated real rigidities in the form of variable markups increase the size of the contract multiplier, their effects are modest unless they are coupled with exogenous sources of persistence.

We begin by laying out the familiar equilibrium conditions of the model; the details are relegated to appendices. We first consider the model with Calvo price setting (app. A) and later evaluate the robustness of the predictions in a menu cost model of price setting in the wholesale sector (app. C). We should clarify that this is only a numerical exercise where the empirical evidence disciplines some parameters of the model.

A. *Setup of the Model*

Wholesale sector. Wholesale firms use labor and a constant returns to scale production function to produce intermediate goods. Therefore, a wholesale firm j faces a constant marginal cost mc_{jt} (all variables in logs):

$$mc_{jt} = w_t + \phi_j e_t - a_{jt},$$

where w_t is the nominal wage rate and e_t captures an exogenous exchange rate–like shock that affects the wholesale firm with elasticity ϕ_j that varies across firms. Further, $a_{jt} \equiv \bar{a}_t + \tilde{a}_{jt}$ is the sum of an aggregate (wholesale-sector-wide) and idiosyncratic (firm-specific) shock to the firm; a_{jt} represents some combination of shocks to the marginal cost and the markup that affects the firm's desired price.

The desired log price of a wholesale producer equals a log desired markup over the marginal cost:

$$\tilde{s}_{jt} = \mu_{jt} + mc_{jt}.$$

By desired prices we mean prices that a firm would set if it could adjust prices every period in a given general equilibrium environment; desired price is not the same as a reset price, which is set for a number of future periods.

We assume variable markups that depend on the firm's relative price:

$$\mu_{jt} = \bar{\mu} - \Gamma(s_{jt} - s_t),$$

where $\bar{\mu}$ is the steady state level of markup, Γ is the elasticity of markup with respect to price, and

$$s_t \equiv \int s_{jt} dj$$

is (an approximation to) the price index in the wholesale sector. This specification is a first-order approximation to a more general model of variable markups. For example, it can be obtained from the Kimball demand with nonconstant elasticity (e.g., see Klenow and Willis 2006; Gopinath and Itskhoki 2010a) or a model of strategic interactions between large firms (e.g., see Atkeson and Burstein [2008] and the bargaining model in Gopinath and Itskhoki [2010b]).

Retail sector. In the retail sector, firms combine labor and intermediate goods supplied by the wholesale sector to produce a final good. Specifically, firm's i marginal cost is given by

$$mc_{it}^R = \alpha s_t + (1 - \alpha) w_t - z_{it},$$

where α is the production cost share of intermediate goods and $z_{it} \equiv \bar{z}_t + \tilde{z}_{it}$ is the sum of aggregate (retail-sector-wide) and idiosyncratic (firm-specific) marginal cost and/or markup shocks that affect the firm's desired price. Note that we assume that the exchange rate shock, e_t, does not affect the retail sector directly and that each retail firm uses a full bundle of intermediate goods as input in production.

We assume constant-markup pricing in the retail sector (e.g., monopolistic competition and CES demand), so that the desired price of firm i is given by

$$\tilde{p}_{it} = \bar{\mu}^R + mc_{it}^R.$$

In the notation of Section II, it is equivalent to assuming that $\Gamma_R = 0$. This assumption, along with $\Gamma > 0$, is consistent with the evidence discussed in Section III. In Gopinath and Itskhoki (2010b), we provide a bargaining-based model that can rationalize this difference.

Wage rate and real output. We assume that the nominal wage rate depends on the consumer (final-good) price level, p_t, and aggregate nominal spending, m_t:

$$w_t = \gamma m_t + (1 - \gamma) p_t, \quad \gamma > 0. \tag{9}$$

This reduced-form model of wages is common in macroeconomics (e.g., see Chari, Kehoe, and McGrattan 2000; Burstein and Hellwig 2007) and can be derived, for example, from a cash-in-advance model of money demand and the intratemporal optimality condition for consumption-leisure choice.[24] Smaller values of γ imply a more gradual response of wages to aggregate nominal spending shocks and hence are a stand-in for various unmodeled aggregate real rigidities, such as real wage rigidity (Blanchard and Gali 2007), segmented labor markets (Woodford 2003), and round-about production structure (Basu 1995).

With our definition of m_t as aggregate nominal spending, real output is given by

$$y_t = m_t - p_t.$$

Therefore, the extent of monetary nonneutrality can be measured as the persistence of y_t in response to nominal spending shocks, since in a flexible-price world exogenous m_t shocks have no effect on real output.

Exogenous shock processes. As commonly assumed in the literature (e.g., see Chari et al. 2000; Bils et al. 2009), nominal spending m_t follows an exogenous AR(1) process in first differences:

$$\Delta m_t = \rho_m \Delta m_{t-1} + \sigma_m \varepsilon_t^m,$$

where $\rho_m \geq 0$ is the measure of *exogenous persistence* in the model. All other exogenous shocks follow persistent but stationary AR(1) processes:

$$x_t = \rho_x x_{t-1} + \sigma_x \varepsilon_t^x,$$

where $x_t \in \{e_t, \bar{z}_t, \bar{a}_t, \tilde{z}_{it}, \tilde{a}_{jt}\}$. All innovations ($\varepsilon_t^m$ and ε_t^x) are mean-zero unit-variance i.i.d. (independent and identically distributed) random variables.

1. Calvo Price Setting

In the case of Calvo price setting, a given wholesale firm j adjusts prices with probability $(1 - \theta)$ each period, while for any retail firm i the adjustment probability equals $(1 - \theta_R)$. Up to a first-order approximation, at the instances of adjustment the firms set their prices to the discounted expectation of their future desired prices (see app. A for a formal derivation):

$$\bar{s}_{jt} = (1 - \beta\theta) \sum_{l=0}^{\infty} (\beta\theta)^l \mathbb{E}_t \tilde{s}_{j,t+l},$$

$$\bar{p}_{it} = (1 - \beta\theta_R) \sum_{l=0}^{\infty} (\beta\theta_R)^l \mathbb{E}_t \tilde{p}_{i,t+l},$$

where β is the discount factor, $\bar{s}_{jt}$ and $\bar{p}_{it}$ are the (theoretical) reset prices, and $\tilde{s}_{j,t+l}$ and $\tilde{p}_{i,t+l}$ are the future desired prices (derived above) for the wholesale and retail firms, respectively.

Under Calvo pricing assumptions, the dynamics of aggregate wholesale and retail prices are given, respectively, by $s_t = \theta s_{t-1} + (1 - \theta)\mathbb{E}_j \bar{s}_{jt}$ and $p_t = \theta_R p_{t-1} + (1 - \theta_R)\mathbb{E}_i \bar{p}_{it}$, where $\mathbb{E}_j$ and $\mathbb{E}_i$ denote the cross-sectional means. Combining these equations with the expressions for reset prices and substituting in the expressions for desired prices, we arrive at the familiar forward-looking Phillips curves—dynamic equations for aggregate wholesale and retail inflation (see app. B):

$$\Delta s_t = \beta \mathbb{E}_t \Delta s_{t+1} + \frac{\lambda}{1 + \Gamma}[\gamma(m_t - p_t) - (s_t - p_t) + \bar{\phi} e_t - \bar{a}_t], \tag{10}$$

$$\Delta p_t = \beta \mathbb{E}_t \Delta p_{t+1} + \lambda_R [\alpha(s_t - p_t) + (1 - \alpha)\gamma(m_t - p_t) - \bar{z}_t], \tag{11}$$

where the expressions in square brackets are the average marginal costs of retail and wholesale firms with w_t substituted in from (9). Note that all idiosyncratic shocks wash out from the aggregate price dynamic equations. The slopes of the Phillips curves equal $\lambda \equiv (1 - \beta\theta)(1 - \theta)/\theta$ and analogously for λ_R. Finally, $\bar{\phi} \equiv \int \phi_j dj$ is the sensitivity of the average wholesale marginal cost to exchange rate shock, e_t.

Dynamic equations (10)–(11), together with the specifications for the exogenous shock processes, fully describe equilibrium dynamics in the case of Calvo pricing. The solution to this dynamic system can be obtained numerically using a conventional Blanchard and Kahn (1980) method.[25] Finally, in the Calvo case, reset-price inflation can be measured simply as $\Delta s_t^* = (\Delta s_t - \theta \Delta s_{t-1})/(1 - \theta)$ and $\Delta p_t^* = (\Delta p_t - \theta_R \Delta p_{t-1})/(1 - \theta_R)$, since the adjusting firms are selected randomly. Given the equilibrium dynamics of the aggregate variables, we can simulate firm-level prices by using the expressions for optimal reset prices provided above.

Aggregating firm-level prices, we arrive at the sample measures of regular and reset-price inflation, the counterparts to the empirical measures studied in Section IV.

Nominal and real rigidities in the model. We now discuss the sources of nominal and real rigidity in the model. First, nominal stickiness enters through the Calvo parameters θ and θ_R that reduce the slopes of the Phillips curves (λ and λ_R) and increase the persistence of inflation. Real rigidities in the form of variable markups, as measured by Γ, further reduce the slope of the wholesale inflation Phillips curve and contribute to the sluggish adjustment of wholesale prices. Furthermore, aggregate real rigidities, measured inversely by γ, slow down the pass-through of monetary shocks into the marginal costs of both types of firms and reduce the slopes of the Phillips curves. Finally, the share of intermediate inputs in the final-good production costs α links retail marginal costs to wholesale prices and constitutes a channel through which sluggish adjustment in wholesale prices translates into persistence in retail prices.

2. Calibration

We calibrate the model to monthly data and summarize the benchmark parameters in table 7. We set the discount rate to 4% annually, which implies a monthly discount factor $\beta = 0.96^{1/12}$. We calibrate the money growth process and exchange rate process to the data. Specifically, we use the monthly BEA (U.S. Bureau of Economic Analysis) data on M2 supply to calibrate $\rho_m = 0.5$ and $\sigma_m = 0.25\%$. Other papers in the literature use different numbers for the persistence of money growth. For example, Chari et al. (2000) use $\rho_m = 0.57^{1/3} \approx 0.83$, while Bils et al. (2009) use $\rho_m = 0$. Therefore, for robustness we also simulate the model for $\rho_m = 0$ and 0.8. Next, we let the exchange rate follow a very persistent AR(1) process, with the standard deviation of innovation equal to $\sigma_e =$ 2% and autocorrelation parameter $\rho_e = 0.995$, consistent with the data on bilateral nominal exchange rates for developed countries.

We select the parameters for the idiosyncratic shock processes ($\tilde{\sigma}_a$, $\tilde{\sigma}_z$, $\tilde{\rho}_a$, and $\tilde{\rho}_z$) to match the micro data on price adjustment. Specifically, we set the persistence of idiosyncratic shocks to match the high autocorrelation of new prices in the BLS IPP (International Price Program, which reports U.S. import and export price indexes) data (0.77 for import prices), and we set the standard deviation of idiosyncratic shocks to match the absolute size of price adjustment (7.5% for import prices and 8.5% for consumer prices).[26] This results in the standard

Table 7
Benchmark Parameters

Parameter	Symbol	Value	Source
Discount factor	β	$.96^{1/12}$	Monthly data
Money growth process, Δm_t:			BEA data on M2
Volatility (%)	σ_m	.25%	
Persistence	ρ_m	0 or .5	
Exchange rate process, Δe_t:			OECD exchange rates
Volatility	σ_e	2%	
Persistence	ρ_e	.995	
Retail idiosyncratic shocks, $\tilde{z}_{it}$:			BLS CPI data
Volatility	$\tilde{\sigma}_z$	8%	Size of price adjustment of 8.5%
Persistence	$\tilde{\rho}_z$	.90	
Wholesale idiosyncratic shocks, $\tilde{a}_{jt}$:			BLS IPP and PPI data
Volatility	$\tilde{\sigma}_a$	10%	Size of price adjustment of 7.5%
Persistence	$\tilde{\rho}_a$	.95	Persistence of new prices of .77
Retail aggregate shocks, $\bar{z}_t$:			Volatility and persistence of CPI
Volatility	$\bar{\sigma}_z$	5%	regular and reset-price inflation
Persistence	$\bar{\rho}_z$	.50	(Bils et al. 2009)
Wholesale aggregate shocks, $\bar{a}_t$:			Volatility and persistence of IPP
Volatility	$\bar{\sigma}_a$	4%	regular and reset-price inflation
Persistence	$\bar{\rho}_a$	.75	
Calvo parameters:			
Retail	θ_R	.75	Duration of 4 months, CPI data
Wholesale	θ	.90	Duration of 10 months, IPP data
Share of intermediate inputs	α	.5	Nakamura and Steinsson (2010)
Wholesale markup elasticity	Γ	1.5	Evidence on pass-through
Aggregate real rigidities	γ	.75	
Sensitivity to the exchange rate shock	ϕ	.225	Gopinath and Itskhoki (2010a)

Note: BEA = U.S. Bureau of Economic Analysis; BLS = U.S. Bureau of Labor Statistics; CPI = consumer price index; IPP = International Price Program; PPI = U.S. producer price index.

deviation of idiosyncratic shocks equal to 10% and 8% for wholesale and retail prices, respectively, while the persistence is set to 0.95 and 0.9, respectively.

Next, we set the parameters for the aggregate shock processes ($\bar{\sigma}_a$, $\bar{\sigma}_z$, $\bar{\rho}_a$, and $\bar{\rho}_z$) to match the standard deviation and autocorrelation of the regular and reset-price inflation series, reported previously in table 1. This requires fairly large and transitory aggregate shocks at both the wholesale and retail levels (standard deviations of 4% and 5% and persistence of 0.75 and 0.5, respectively). These processes are a stand-in for all unmodeled shocks that hit the economy, including various economy-wide and industry-level marginal cost and markup shocks, as well as measurement error in prices.

We set the Calvo probabilities of nonadjusting prices (θ and θ_R) to match the micro data on nominal price durations. Specifically, we choose parameters to produce 10-month durations in the wholesale sector (consistent with the evidence in Gopinath and Rigobon [2008] and Nakamura and Steinsson [2008]) and 4-month durations in the retail sector (consistent with Bils and Klenow [2004]). Next, we calibrate γ, the slope of the wage equation (9) and the aggregate real rigidity parameter of the model. The literature uses a wide variety of values for γ, ranging between 0.1 in models with segmented labor markets and round-about production and 4 in models with no real rigidities and strong concavity in the utility function. We set the benchmark value for γ to be 0.75, and for robustness we also use a greater value of 1.5, so that these parameters lie on both sides of the strategic neutrality case of $\gamma = 1$ and depart only moderately from it. We view this as a conservative choice for an aggregate parameter for which we have little direct information.

We choose the benchmark value for markup elasticity to be $\Gamma = 1.5$. This number implies a 40% pass-through of idiosyncratic shocks and is consistent with the evidence in Gopinath et al. (2010) and Gopinath and Itskhoki (2010a) on long-run exchange rate pass-through of about 50%. Moreover, it is consistent with the coefficients on the competitor prices reported in table 5 of Section IV. We additionally evaluate the robustness of our results using the values of Γ of 0 and 4, the former being the case of constant markups and the latter being the case of strong strategic complementarities at the firm level.[27]

Finally, we set the share of intermediate inputs in the final-good production, α, to equal 50%, at the conservative end of the spectrum of calibrations considered in Nakamura and Steinsson (2010). The sensitivity of the aggregate marginal cost to exchange rate shocks is set to $\bar{\phi} = 0.225$, which is consistent with most domestic firms being unaffected by this shock directly while a small fraction of importers in the industry (e.g., 30%) are affected strongly by this shock (e.g., $\phi_j = 0.75$).[28]

B. *Simulation Results*

First, we study the persistence of regular and reset-price inflation generated by our model. We compute all inflation series as sample averages of the simulated firm prices using a procedure close to the one used on the BLS data in Section IV.[29] The results are reported in table 8 for different values of parameters ρ_m, Γ, and γ. The first two columns report the results for the final-good (retail) inflation series, the next two columns provide the results for the unconditional wholesale inflation series, and the last two columns provide the results for the projection of wholesale inflation series onto lags of exchange rate changes. For wholesale prices, we

Table 8
Persistence of Regular and Reset-Price Inflation

	Unconditional				Conditional on Exchange Rate	
	Δp_t	Δp_t^*	Δs_t	Δs_t^*	$\widehat{\Delta s_t}$	$\widehat{\Delta s_t^*}$
$\Gamma = 0$	.41	−.25	.64	−.23	.85	−.03
$\Gamma = 1.5$	.32	−.25	.82	−.14	.92	.10
$\Gamma = 4$	.37	−.28	.87	−.01	.91	.18
$\rho_m = 0$	.39	−.23	.76	−.19	.91	.17
$\rho_m = 0.8$	.48	−.14	.79	−.07	.86	.16
$\gamma = 1.5$	.37	−.27	.76	−.09	.87	.07
Menu cost	...	...	.29	−.89	.38	−.66

Note: The entries are AR(1) coefficients for each series (Δp refers to final-good inflation and Δs refers to wholesale inflation for the subsample of foreign firms with $\phi_j > 0$; * indicates reset-price inflation). In the last two columns, the series are the projections on the current and 24 lags of the exchange rate changes. All inflation series are sample averages of the simulated firm prices, approximating the procedure used in the data. The default parameters are the benchmark parameters from table 7 (i.e., $\Gamma = 1.5$, $\gamma = 0.75$, and $\rho_m = 0.5$).

use only the subsample of foreign firms, that is, those that are affected directly by the exchange rate shock (with $\phi_j > 0$), to make this exercise as close as possible to our empirical evidence in Section IV, which uses data on import prices.

The first pattern that emerges from table 8 is that the aggregate consumer-price inflation series may not be very persistent even when wholesale inflation is significantly more persistent. Second, wholesale inflation is significantly less persistent than the wholesale inflation projected on the exchange rate. Next we examine reset-price inflation. Both for retail and wholesale prices, reset-price inflation is negatively autocorrelated while, when projected on the exchange rate, the autocorrelation becomes positive. These patterns are consistent with the empirical findings in Section IV.A. In our calibration, negative autocorrelation of the reset-price inflation series arises due to sampling error combined with transitory semi-aggregate shocks affecting wholesale and retail pricing.

The results in table 8 are largely similar across different parameter values considered. Higher values of markup elasticity Γ result in a more persistent (wholesale) inflation series, particularly when projected on the exchange rate shock, while variation in γ and ρ_m has relatively little effect on persistence of the inflation series. There are no clear patterns in variation of retail price persistence for different parameter values. This is because in our calibration monetary shocks are not the key drivers of the inflation series in the short run (at the monthly frequency); this appears to be a reasonable description of reality.[30]

We next evaluate the extent of monetary nonneutrality produced by the model. Table 9 reports the half-lives of output in response to a monetary shock for different values of the parameters. Specifically, we calculate the AR(1) coefficient of the real output series when all shocks other than monetary shocks are shut down; based on this AR (1) coefficient, we back out a measure of half-life that we report. From table 9 it is evident that the model can produce a wide range for the extent of nonneutrality, with half-lives of output ranging from about 1 quarter to over 20 quarters. However, this variation is largely driven by ρ_m, the exogenous persistence introduced through the autocorrelation of the money growth rate. However, variation in the amount of real rigidity, Γ and γ, has a relatively modest effect on the extent of nonneutrality: an increase in Γ from 0 to 4 nearly doubles the half-life, while a decrease in γ from 1.5 to 0.75 increases the half-life by around 50%.

When we fix parameters at their benchmark values, the model produces a fairly large half-life of slightly below 8 quarters, while shutting down the variable markup channel drops the half-life to less than 6 quarters. Without exogenous persistence (i.e., $\rho_m = 0$), however, the model produces very little monetary nonneutrality (a half-life of around 1 quarter).[31] We conclude that the empirically calibrated variable markup channel of real rigidities goes a fair way in amplifying the real effects on output; however, without exogenous persistence its absolute effect is modest.

Note that the variation in the persistence of output deviation in the model is not very tightly linked to the persistence of inflation, which does

Table 9
Half-Life of Output in Response to a Monetary Shock (in Months)

	$\rho_m = 0$	$\rho_m = .5$	$\rho_m = .8$
A. $\gamma = 0.75$:			
$\Gamma = 0$	5.3	17.2	56.1
$\Gamma = 1.5$	7.0	23.7	83.0
$\Gamma = 4$	8.9	31.3	114.8
B. $\gamma = 1.5$:			
$\Gamma = 0$	3.6	11.8	40.0
$\Gamma = 1.5$	4.4	15.5	58.1
$\Gamma = 4$	5.4	19.8	80.0

Note: Half-life is defined as $\log(0.5)/\log(\rho_{y|m})$, where $\rho_{y|m}$ equals the AR(1) coefficient of output $y_t \equiv m_t - p_t$ conditional on monetary shocks ε_t^m (i.e., when other sources of shocks are shut down).

Table 10
Micro-Level Exchange Rate Pass-Through

	$\Gamma = 0$	$\Gamma = 1.5$	$\Gamma = 4$	Menu Cost
First adjustment	.61	.44	.35	.55
Second adjustment	−.05	.04	.07	−.08

Note: The entries are coefficients from the regression at the firm level (for wholesale foreign firms with $\phi_j > 0$) of price change conditional on adjustment on cumulative exchange rate change during the most recent and the previous price duration, respectively (i.e., a counterpart to regression [5] of Sec. IV). The menu cost uses $\Gamma = 1.5$.

not vary much with the amount of real rigidities or the extent of exogenous persistence. Therefore, fairly long periods of monetary nonneutrality can be consistent with transitory inflation dynamics and negatively autocorrelated reset-price inflation. Again, this is because monetary shocks are not the main drivers of inflation at very high frequencies.

Our final results evaluate the success of the model at capturing the slow response of firm-level prices to exchange rate shocks at the micro level, conditional on price adjustment. This is done for wholesale foreign price with $\phi_j > 0$ to approximate the empirical analysis of Section IV.B. The results are reported in table 10. When there are no strategic complementarities, the second adjustment is negative (due to some mean reversion that we assumed in the exchange rate process). When strategic complementarities are present, pass-through at the second round of price adjustment is positive; however, it is much smaller than it is in the data (see table 2), where the second rounds of price adjustment are almost as large as the first. This failure of the model persists even when we assume strong strategic complementarities ($\Gamma = 4$) or shorter nominal price durations (not reported). Although the model with strategic complementarities captures incomplete pass-through in the long-run, it predicts very fast dynamics of pass-through relative to the data. This leads us to conclude that our model misses some important sources of persistence, which may further contribute to the extent of monetary nonneutrality produced by the model. Matching the very slow adjustment of prices to aggregate shocks at the micro level that we document in Section IV is an important challenge that we leave for future work.

C. *A Menu Cost Model*

In this section we briefly describe the setup and provide the simulation results of a menu cost model of price setting. The details are relegated to appendix C, and further discussion of the estimation procedure can be found in Gopinath and Itskhoki (2010a). This exercise is important in order to evaluate the severity of the selection effects present in menu cost models and absent in the time-dependent pricing models.

We adopt a two-sector model (wholesale and retail, as above) with three types of shocks: idiosyncratic marginal cost shocks, semi-aggregate marginal cost shocks (a stand-in for exchange rate shocks) in the wholesale sector, and aggregate monetary (nominal spending) shocks. In order to maintain computational feasibility, we assume that retail prices are completely flexible. We introduce the variable markup channel, using the Klenow and Willis (2006) specification of the Kimball (1995) preferences. The rest of the setup is similar to the one discussed above in Section V.A.

With flexible prices, no strategic complementarities (e.g., CES [constant elasticity of substitution] demand), and no aggregate shocks in the retail sector, the final-good price level is given by $p_t = \bar{\mu}^R + \alpha s_t + (1 - \alpha)w_t$. The wage rate is still assumed to satisfy (9). These two equations allow one to solve for the final-good price level p_t and the nominal wage rate w_t as functions of aggregate nominal spending m_t and the wholesale price level s_t.

A wholesale firm j faces a marginal cost $mc_{jt} = w_t + \phi_j e_t - a_{jt}$, where a_{jt} is an idiosyncratic shock and e_t is the semi-aggregate shock that affects the firm with elasticity ϕ_j distributed on $[0, 1]$. The firm also faces a demand schedule with elasticity σ and the superelasticity (elasticity of elasticity) ε, evaluated when the firm's relative price equals one (for details, see Gopinath and Itskhoki [2010a] and app. C). This implies a desired markup of $\sigma/(\sigma - 1)$ with markup elasticity equal to $\Gamma = \varepsilon/(\sigma - 1)$. A firm maximizes its discounted present value by optimally choosing the instances of price adjustment at a menu cost κ and optimally resetting prices at these instances. This problem can be formalized with a standard Bellman equation (see app. C), which we solve numerically. We then use the derived policy functions to simulate a panel of prices on which we conduct similar empirical tests to those in Section IV.

For calibration we use the same benchmark parameters as in table 7. Additionally, we set $\sigma = 5$ and $\varepsilon = 6$ so that the level of wholesale markup is 25% and the elasticity of markup is equal, as before, to $\Gamma = 1.5$. The menu cost is chosen to match the duration of 10 months of wholesale prices that implies a $\kappa = 3.5\%$ of the steady state revenue conditional on adjustment (corresponding to total annual menu cost paid equal to 0.35% of annual revenues), a number consistent with the literature. Finally, in order to match the absolute size of price adjustment of 7.5%, we set the standard deviation of the idiosyncratic shocks to $\sigma_a = 6\%$.

To keep this section brief, we report the results only for the benchmark values of parameters, $\Gamma = 1.5$, $\gamma = 0.75$, and $\rho_m = 0.5$. The unconditional autocorrelation of the wholesale-price inflation is 0.29, and it is 0.38 conditional on the exchange rate shock, both numbers being substantially smaller than in the case of the Calvo model (see table 8). The corresponding reset-price inflation series is strongly negatively autocorrelated—with autocorrelation of –0.89 unconditionally and –0.66 conditional on the exchange rate shock—emphasizing the powerful selection effects of the menu cost models. This negative autocorrelation of reset-price inflation conditional on the exchange rate shock goes against our empirical findings in Section IV.

Similarly, in the type of micro-level pass-through regressions run in Section IV.B, the menu cost model generates a pass-through coefficient conditional on the first round of price adjustment equal to 55%, while the coefficient for the second round of price adjustment is −8%. This is also due to the strong selection effect of the menu cost models that dominated the persistence introduced through strategic complementarities in pricing. Recall that in the Calvo model these two pass-through coefficients were 44% and 4%, respectively (see table 10), and this is in contrast to our empirical findings that pass-through at the second adjustment is nearly as large as the first one. Finally, the half-life of output in response to monetary shocks is 15.1 months in the menu cost model, as opposed to 23.7 months in the Calvo model.[32] This illustrates a well-known fact that the selection effect of the menu cost models reduces substantially the contract multiplier relative to the time-dependent models of price setting.

Summary. A number of insights come out of our simulation exercise. First, transitory aggregate inflation series are consistent with a persistent response of prices to certain aggregate shocks, including exchange rate and monetary shocks. Second, properties of the aggregate inflation series may be largely disconnected from the size of the contract multiplier for monetary shocks. Third, quantitatively exogenous persistence appears to be more important than strategic complementarities in generating long half-lives and large contract multipliers. Although strategic complementarities work to magnify the size of the contract multiplier, their absolute effects are modest unless coupled with exogenous sources of persistence. Fourth, the analyzed models (in particular the menu cost model but also the Calvo model) cannot match the very sluggish dynamics of prices in response to shocks at the micro level conditional on adjusting prices. This suggests a need for additional sources of persistence that are lacking from the model.

Appendix A

Calvo Price Setting

In this appendix we derive a general log-linear approximation for the price setting equation and aggregate inflation dynamics (Phillips curve) in a Calvo model. Since these derivations are well known, we keep the exposition brief.

Consider a firm j with a real profit function $\Pi^j(x_j|S)$, where x_j is the firm's log price and S is the state of the economy.[33] The desired price of the firm is $\tilde{x}_j(S) \equiv \arg\max_{x_j} \Pi^j(x_j|S)$ with the necessary condition $\Pi^j_x(\tilde{x}_j(S)|S) = 0$, where the subscript denotes a partial derivative. We assume that the marginal cost of the firm does not depend on the price of the firm; that is, a firm faces a constant returns to scale in production where productivity depends on the state of the world. Then, we can decompose the desired price as

$$\tilde{x}_j(S) = \mu_j(\tilde{x}_j - x,\ S) + mc_j(S),$$

where $mc_j(S)$ is the log nominal marginal cost of the firm and $\mu_j(x_j - x, S)$ is the log (desired) markup, which we allow to depend on the relative price of the firm, with x denoting the log of the relevant price index.

A general first-order approximation to the markup can be written as

$$\mu_j(x_j,\ S) \approx \bar{\mu} - \Gamma(x_j - x) + \varepsilon_j(S),$$

where $\bar{\mu}$ and Γ are some constants (assumed to be common across all firms at the point of approximation) and $\varepsilon_j(S)$ is some linear function of the state S. It is natural to assume that $\varepsilon_j(S)$ is stationary, while $mc_j(S)$ is cointegrated with the nominal variables of the model. With this approximation, we can solve explicitly for the desired price of the firm:

$$\tilde{x}_j(S) = \frac{1}{1+\Gamma}[\bar{\mu} + mc_j(S) + \varepsilon_j(S)] + \frac{\Gamma}{1+\Gamma}x.$$

A given firm sets prices to maximize its discounted expected value. In a Calvo pricing environment, the firm may adjust its price in every period with exogenous probability $(1 - \theta)$. Therefore, we can write the problem of the firm recursively as

$$\bar{x}_{jt}(\mathbb{S}) = \arg\max_{x_j} \mathbb{E}\left\{ \Pi^j(x_j|S_t) + \sum_{l=1}^{\infty} Q_{t,t+l}(\mathbb{S})\theta^{l-1}[\theta\Pi^j(x_j|S_{t+l}) + (1-\theta)\Pi^j(\bar{x}_{j,t+l}(\mathbb{S})|S_{t+l})]|S^t \right\},$$

where $Q_{t,t+l}(\mathbb{S})$ is the stochastic discount factor for real variables, $S^t \equiv (S_0, \ldots, S_t)$ is the history of the states, and $\mathbb{S} \equiv (S^t, S_{t+1}, \ldots)$. The first-order condition for the price setting can be written as

$$\sum_{l=0}^{\infty} \theta^l \mathbb{E}\{Q_{t,t+l}\Pi^j_x(\bar{x}_{jt}|S_{t+l})|S^t\} = 0,$$

where we omit the explicit dependence on $\mathbb{S}$. Taking a first-order approximation of this optimality condition around a nonstochastic steady state with zero inflation, we obtain

$$\sum_{l=0}^{\infty} (\beta\theta)^l \mathbb{E}\{\bar{x}_{jt} - \tilde{x}_j(S_{t+l})|S^t\} = 0,$$

where β^l is the nonstochastic steady state value of $Q_{t,t+l}$. The price setting formulas in Section V.A are direct implications of this linearized optimality condition. Now, using the expression for the desired price, we have

$$\bar{x}_{jt} = (1 - \beta\theta) \sum_{l=0}^{\infty} (\beta\theta)^l \mathbb{E}_t \left\{ \frac{1}{1+\Gamma}(mc_{j,t+l} + \varepsilon_{j,t+l}) + \frac{\Gamma}{1+\Gamma} x_{t+l} \right\},$$

where we switched notation for conditional expectation, suppressed the explicit dependence on the state of the economy, and omitted the constant by implicitly relabeling the variables to denote the deviations from the nonstochastic steady state.

Finally, since the nominal marginal cost is possibly integrated, we need to scale this expression by some monetary variable cointegrated with the marginal cost. A natural candidate is the competitor price index x_t or a sector price level (in a number of models, including the Kimball demand model, the two variables coincide). We therefore define $x_t = \int_j x_{jt}dj$. With some manipulation, we rewrite the deflated price setting equation as

$$\bar{x}_{jt} - x_{t-1} = \frac{1-\beta\theta}{1+\Gamma}\sum_{l=0}^{\infty}(\beta\theta)^l \mathbb{E}_t\{mc_{j,t+l} - x_{t+l} + \varepsilon_{j,t+l}\} + \sum_{l=0}^{\infty}(\beta\theta)^l \mathbb{E}_t \Delta x_{t+1},$$

or in a recursive form:[34]

$$(\bar{x}_{jt} - x_{t-1}) - \beta\theta\mathbb{E}_t(\bar{x}_{j,t+1} - x_t) = \frac{1-\beta\theta}{1+\Gamma}(mc_{jt} - x_t + \varepsilon_{jt}) + \Delta x_t.$$

Next, with Calvo pricing, the dynamics of the aggregate price level can be written as

$$x_t = \theta x_{t-1} + (1-\theta)\mathbb{E}_j \bar{x}_{jt} \Rightarrow \Delta x_t = (1-\theta)\mathbb{E}_j\{\bar{x}_{jt} - x_{t-1}\},$$

where $\mathbb{E}_j$ is the cross-sectional average across all firms. Combining the above two equations and rearranging, we arrive at the traditional New-Keynesian Phillips curve:

$$\Delta x_t - \beta\mathbb{E}_t\Delta x_{t+1} = \frac{\lambda}{1+\Gamma}\mathbb{E}_j\{mc_{jt} - x_t + \varepsilon_{jt}\}, \quad \lambda \equiv \frac{(1-\beta\theta)(1-\theta)}{\theta}.$$

Equations (10)–(11) in the text are special cases of this Phillips curve with the expressions for marginal costs substituted in (note that the cross-sectional expectation averages out all purely idiosyncratic shocks).

Appendix B

Dynamics under Calvo Pricing

The aggregate dynamic system contains three equations—the two Phillips curves for the wholesale and retail prices and the aggregate wage equation—for three variables (s_t, p_t, w_t):

$$\Delta s_t = \beta\mathbb{E}_t\Delta s_{t+1} + \frac{\lambda}{1+\Gamma}(w_t - s_t + \bar{\phi}e_t - \bar{a}_t),$$

$$\Delta p_t = \beta \mathbb{E}_t \Delta p_{t+1} + \lambda_R[\alpha s_t + (1-\alpha)w_t - p_t - \bar{z}_t],$$

$$w_t = \gamma m_t + (1-\gamma)p_t,$$

where Δm_t, e_t, $\bar{z}_t$, and $\bar{a}_t$ follow exogenous stationary processes. This system can be solved using the conventional Blanchard and Kahn (1980) method, which results in the expressions for the endogenous variables (s_t, p_t, w_t) as functions of the shocks to the exogenous variables. This solution allows us to study the statistical properties of endogenous variable time series, including their volatility and persistence.

When the retail prices are set flexibly (i.e., $\theta_R = 0$ or $\lambda_R = \infty$), there exists a tractable analytical solution for the aggregate dynamics. We discuss it briefly here. In this case, the expression for the consumer price level becomes static:

$$p_t = \alpha s_t + (1-\alpha)w_t - \bar{z}_t.$$

Together with the wage equation it allows us to solve for p_t and w_t as linear functions of m_t, s_t, and $\bar{z}_t$. Substituting these expressions into the wholesale price Phillips curve, we obtain a second-order difference equation in $s_t - m_t$:[35]

$$\Delta s_t - \beta \mathbb{E}_t \Delta s_{t+1} = \kappa(s_t - m_t) + \xi_t,$$

where

$$\xi_t \equiv \frac{\lambda}{1+\Gamma}(\phi e_t - \bar{a}_t) - \frac{\lambda}{1+\Gamma}\frac{1-\gamma}{\alpha(1-\gamma)+\gamma}\bar{z}_t$$

is the summary measure of all shocks other than m_t and $\kappa \equiv [\lambda/(1+\Gamma)]\{\gamma/[\alpha(1-\gamma)+\gamma]\}$ is the summary measure of nominal and real rigidities in the model. This difference equation can be solved forward. Assuming for simplicity that ξ_t follows an AR(1), the process for $s_t - m_t$ is an ARMA(3, 1). Therefore, s_t is cointegrated with m_t and movements in m_t dominate the low-frequency movements in s_t; however, the short-run dynamics of s_t (around slow-moving m_t) may be dominated by transitory shocks to ξ_t. In particular, the MA component may reduce significantly the short-run persistence, while it does not affect the long-run persistence. This logic is consistent with the empirical findings of Stock and Watson (2007).[36] Finally, one can show that one of the AR roots is given by ρ_m, while the other root is decreasing in κ and converging to one as $\kappa \to 0$. Furthermore, one can show that these roots also drive the persistence of the output response to monetary shocks.

Appendix C

Menu Cost Model

Kimball demand. To simulate the menu cost model, we first need to specify the explicit source of variable markups. We generate variable markups by introducing the Klenow and Willis (2006) specification of the Kimball (1995) demand. The demand function for firm j in this case is given by

$$\psi(s_{jt} - s_t) = [1 - \varepsilon(s_{jt} - s_t)]^{\sigma/\varepsilon}, \quad \sigma \geq 1, \ \varepsilon > 0,$$

where s_{jt} is the log price of the firm and $s_t = \int_j s_{jt} dj$ is the sectoral log price index. In Gopinath and Itskhoki (2010a), we show that this price index is a valid second-order approximation to the ideal price index with this demand system. The price elasticity of this demand is given by

$$\tilde{\sigma} = \frac{\sigma}{1 - \varepsilon(s_{jt} - s_t)},$$

which equals σ when the relative price of the firm is one. With this demand, the desired price is equal to a markup $\tilde{\sigma}/(\tilde{\sigma} - 1)$ over the marginal cost. The elasticity of the markup is given by

$$\tilde{\Gamma} = \frac{\tilde{\varepsilon}}{\tilde{\sigma} - 1},$$

where

$$\tilde{\varepsilon} \equiv \frac{\varepsilon}{1 - \varepsilon(s_{jt} - s_t)}$$

is the elasticity of the elasticity of demand. Therefore, the markup elasticity evaluated at the relative price of one is given by $\Gamma = \varepsilon/(\sigma - 1) > 0$.

Problem of the firm. The real profit of the firm is given by

$$\Pi(s_{jt}|\mathbb{S}_{jt}) = \psi(s_{jt} - s_t)[\exp\{s_{jt} - p_t\} - \exp\{mc_{jt} - p_t\}],$$

where $\mathbb{S}_{jt}$ is the state vector for the firm, mc_{jt} is the log nominal marginal cost of the firm, and p_t is the final-good price level. As discussed in the text, the marginal cost of the firm equals

$$mc_{jt} = w_t + \phi_j e_t - a_{jt}.$$

Therefore, the state vector for the firm includes $(p_t, s_t, w_t, e_t, a_{jt})$.

We can write the firm's problem recursively as

$$V^N(\mathbb{S}_{jt}) = \Pi(s_{j,t-1}|\mathbb{S}_{jt}) + \mathbb{E}\{Q(\mathbb{S}_{j,t+1})V(\mathbb{S}_{j,t+1})|\mathbb{S}_{jt}\},$$

$$V^A(\mathbb{S}_{jt}) = \max_{\bar{s}_{jt}}\{\Pi(\bar{s}_{jt}|\mathbb{S}_{jt}) + \mathbb{E}\{Q(\mathbb{S}_{j,t+1})V(\mathbb{S}_{j,t+1})|\mathbb{S}_{jt}\}\},$$

$$V(\mathbb{S}_{jt}) = \max\{V^N(\mathbb{S}_{jt}),\ V^A(\mathbb{S}_{jt}) - \kappa\},$$

where V is the value of the firm, V^N is the value of the firm if it does not adjust its price, and V^A is the value of the firm if it adjusts its price; κ is the menu cost, Q is the stochastic discount factor for real variables (which we set to equal β in the simulation), and S_{jt} includes in addition the previous price of the firm $s_{j,t-1}$.

General equilibrium. We assume flexible prices for the final good and no aggregate productivity shocks in the final-good sector. This implies that $p_t = \bar{\mu}_R + \alpha s_t + (1-\alpha)w_t$, where $\bar{\mu}_R$ is the constant markup in the final-good sector. In turn, the wage is given by $w_t = \gamma m_t + (1-\gamma)p_t$. This allows us to solve for p_t and w_t as a function of m_t and s_t and reduce the aggregate state space to (s_t, m_t, e_t). The state vector for an individual wholesale firm additionally includes $(s_{j,t-1}, a_{jt})$. In the general equilibrium of the model, firms optimally decide to adjust prices given their current state vector and rational expectations about the evolution of the state vector, while aggregated individual firm pricing decisions are consistent with the aggregate dynamics of the wholesale price level s_t.

Simulation procedure. We iterate the Bellman equation for the firm pricing problem on the grid given a forecasting rule for the evolution of the state vector.[37] This produces a policy function for firm pricing decisions, which allows us to simulate a panel of firm prices. In each period of the simulation, we make sure that the wholesale price index is consistent with the firm pricing decisions (which constitutes a static fixed point problem). As a result, we obtain a time series for the equilibrium wholesale price level. Given this time series, we update the forecasting equation. We iterate this procedure until the forecasting equation converges. With the equilibrium forecasting rule we simulate a panel of firm prices, and we use it to estimate various statistical moments, as in Section IV. Additional details of the simulation procedure can be found in Gopinath and Itskhoki (2010a).

Endnotes

This paper was prepared for NBER's 25th Macroeconomics Annual conference, April 9–10, 2010. We thank the International Price Program of the Bureau of Labor Statistics for access to unpublished micro data. We owe a huge debt of gratitude to our project coordinator Rozi Ulics for her invaluable help on this project. The views expressed here do not necessarily reflect the views of the Bureau of Labor Statistics. We thank Jim Stock, Mark Watson, Ulrich Mueller, Chris Sims, Patrick Kehoe, the editors Daron Acemoglu and Mike Woodford, and our discussants Mike Golosov and Virgiliu Midrigan for comments. This research is supported by National Science Foundation grant SES 0617256.

1. See Bils and Klenow (2004) and Nakamura and Steinsson (2008) for evidence on nominal price durations in the U.S. Bureau of Labor Statistics (BLS) micro price data underlying the construction of the CPI index and Christiano, Eichenbaum, and Evans (1999) for evidence on real effects of monetary shocks.

2. For a precise definition, discussion, and examples of *real rigidities*, see the entry for that term by David Romer in the *New Palgrave Dictionary of Economics* (2008). The ability of real rigidities to magnify the effects of nominal price stickiness is often referred to as the *contract multiplier*, a term coined by John Taylor (1980) and commonly used in the macro literature (e.g., see Chari et al. 2000).

3. Of course, the exchange rate can have additional indirect (general equilibrium) effects via productivity or cost of inputs. We discuss this issue in more detail in Secs. III and IV.

4. In Sec. V, we combine this framework with specific models of nominal stickiness to study the quantitative predictions of dynamic price setting models.

5. Goldberg and Knetter (1997) provide a survey of the earlier empirical pass-through literature. The specification of pass-through regressions can either be in real or in nominal terms and accordingly include the real or the nominal exchange rate. Since the two move closely at most horizons, either specification gives similar results. Typical pass-through regressions also include some controls for the foreign cost level, such as the producer price index or the manufacturing wage rate.

6. See the literature following the seminal observation of Meese and Rogoff (1983).

7. *Reference price* (*cost*) is defined as the most often quoted price (cost) within a given time period.

8. Specifically, Fitzgerald and Haller (2008) find that, conditional on price adjustment in both markets, the common-currency price differential across the two markets moves nearly one-to-one with the nominal exchange rate. According to the descriptive model (2) of Sec. II, this is consistent with a $\Gamma \gg 0$ provided that the competitor prices s_t in the two markets move little with the exchange rate, as in the model of Atkeson and Burstein (2008).

9. Additionally, a recent study by Berman, Martin, and Mayer (2009) compares the extent of markup variability across French exporters of different size. It finds that larger exporters have lower exchange rate pass-through, which is consistent with a model in which both the level and the variability of the markup increases with the productivity

and hence size of the firm. Since exporting firms are typically larger, the implication of this finding is that the extent of markup variability can be greater in the international data than in the full sample of firms producing for the domestic market.

10. This feature is consistent with the evidence in Boivin, Giannoni, and Mihov (2009), which finds that, while overall disaggregated prices are volatile, they are sluggish in response to aggregate macro shocks.

11. In the sample that excludes petrol classifications, the median number of price observations per month is 6,335 and the median number of price observations whose price is different from the previous month is 770.

12. The small number of price changes limits the analysis to large groups of goods.

13. We estimate an AR(1) coefficient so as to compare our results directly to Bils et al. (2009). If, as argued by Stock and Watson (2007), CPI inflation is better modeled as an ARMA(1, 1) or an IMA(1, 1), then the first-order autocorrelation understates the long-run persistence of the series. We have estimated other measures of persistence, such as the variance ratio to the long-run variance of the series. Although these measures suggest greater persistence for the inflation series, our comparative results for the conditional and unconditional inflation still hold.

14. In all specifications we exclude petrol classifications. For each series, we use 2002 weights at the four-digit level to aggregate across prices. More precisely, for actual inflation, we estimate mean price change by four-digit harmonized code for each month, then we average across the different harmonized codes using weights at the four-digit level. For the reset-price inflation, we assume that at the start of our sample in January 1994 all prices were reset prices, which is an initial condition assumption. Then we follow the formula in eq. (4) to construct the reset-price inflation, π_t^*.

15. The Bils et al. (2009) sample period is longer, 1989–2008. Bils et al. exclude energy, fresh fruit and vegetables, and eggs. We report their results for the sample that excludes sales price.

16. As documented by Stock and Watson (2007), among others, the short-run persistence of consumer-price inflation decreased in the 1990s.

17. In the BLS database, the original reported price (in the currency of pricing) and the dollar converted price are both provided. We use the latter, conditional on the original reported price having changed. Since the first price adjustment is censored from the data, we also perform the analysis excluding the first price change and find that the results are not sensitive to this assumption.

18. Refer to Gopinath and Itskhoki (2010a) for a detailed analysis of pass-through conditional on first adjustment and pass-through conditional on many rounds of adjustment across goods with different frequencies.

19. The coefficient on the residual will be equivalent to the coefficient on the trade-weighted exchange rate obtained from regressing the price change on the bilateral and the trade-weighted exchange rate, but the coefficient on the bilateral exchange rate will be different across the two specification.

20. For each good *i* we calculate the average monthly import price change for all goods in the same 10-digit or BLS-defined primary strata classification, excluding good *i*. We then cumulate these price changes over time to arrive at an industry competitor price index for each good. In our main specification, we include nonadjacent price changes; that is, if prices are available for January and March but are missing for February, the price change in March refers to the percentage difference between the March and January price. We also perform an analysis in which we include only price changes across adjacent months; we obtain qualitatively the same results.

21. Results are unaffected if we exclude the first price change that can be censored. For more details on the comparison between life-long pass-through and pass-through conditional on first price adjustment, see Gopinath and Itskhoki (2010a).

22. In Gopinath and Itskhoki (2010b), we discuss a bargaining-based micro foundation for these reduced-form assumptions.

23. Note that our simple model does not rely on any mechanisms of differential response to aggregate vs. idiosyncratic shocks as, e.g., in Maćkowiak and Wiederholt (2009).

24. Specifically, a model with log utility of consumption and linear disutility of labor results in $\gamma = 1$, provided that there is no additional source of aggregate real rigidities. Golosov and Lucas (2007) derive the same specification in a money in the utility model.

Ball and Romer (1990) refer to this benchmark as the case of strategic neutrality. Aggregate real rigidities work to reduce the value of γ.

25. When final-good prices are flexible ($\theta_R = 0$), this dynamic system has a simple closed-form solution, which we discuss in app. B.

26. For details, see Gopinath and Itskhoki (2010a).

27. Our benchmark number of $\Gamma = 1.5$ is considerably smaller than the markup elasticity of 2.5 implied by the Klenow and Willis (2006) calibration.

28. For more details, see the calibration in Gopinath and Itskhoki (2010a).

29. We use a sample of 5,000 retail firms and 6,000 wholesale firms, 1,800 of which are affected directly by the exchange rate shock. With this sample size, low frequency of price adjustment, and large idiosyncratic price movements, the sampling error in average inflation series is nontrivial.

30. This feature is consistent with aggregate data where inflation is well approximated by an ARMA(1, 1) process with both large AR and MA roots (see, e.g., Stock and Watson 2007). While monetary shocks are likely to be responsible for the AR component (long memory, low-frequency movements), there needs to be a source of relatively large transitory shocks to explain the MA component.

31. This finding is consistent with the results in Carvalho and Nechio (2008) on the persistence of real exchange rates.

32. The approach to computing the conditional half-life of output in the menu cost model is different. Since we cannot simply shut down other sources of shocks in the menu cost model (as its dynamics is nonlinear in shocks), we estimate econometrically the impulse response of output y_t to current and lagged monetary shocks ε^m_{t-j} and then use it to compute the projection of output series onto these shocks. The reported number is based on the AR(1) coefficient for the projected series.

33. Since we look at the real profit function, that is, a profit function normalized by the price level in the economy, it is without loss of generality to assume that the nominal variables enter the sufficient state vector S only normalized by the price level. Therefore, we can treat S as having a stationary distribution even though monetary variables may be trending. For an example, see app. C.

34. This is the step that requires stationarity of the right-hand-side variables.

35. This is under the assumption of a unit root in m_t; otherwise, the difference equation is second order in s_t.

36. If ξ_t is absent from the model, the process for $s_t - m_t$ is an AR(2) and therefore s_t exhibits both high short-run and long-run persistence.

37. To ensure stationarity of the grids, we normalize all nominal variables in the model by m_{t-1}.

References

Atkeson, Andrew, and Ariel Burstein. 2008. "Pricing-to-Market, Trade Costs, and International Relative Prices." *American Economic Review* 98, no. 5:1998–2031.

Ball, Laurence, and David Romer. 1990. "Real Rigidities and the Non-neutrality of Money." *Review of Economic Studies* 57, no. 2:183–203.

Basu, Susanto. 1995. "Intermediate Goods and Business Cycles: Implication for Productivity and Welfare." *American Economic Review* 85, no. 3:512–31.

Berger, David, Jon Faust, John H. Rogers, and Kai Steverson. 2009. "Border Prices and Retail Prices." International Finance Discussion Paper no. 972, Board of Governors of the Federal Reserve, Washington, DC.

Berman, Nicolas, Philippe Martin, and Thierry Mayer. 2009. "How Do Different Exporters React to Exchange Rate Changes? Theory, Empirics and Aggregate Implications." Discussion Paper no. 7493, Centre for Economic Policy Research, London.

Bils, Mark, and Peter Klenow. 2004. "Some Evidence on the Importance of Sticky Prices." *Journal of Political Economy* 112, no. 5:947–85.

Bils, Mark, Peter Klenow, and Benjamin Malin. 2009. "Reset Price Inflation and the Impact of Monetary Policy Shocks." Working Paper no. 14787, NBER, Cambridge, MA.

Blanchard, Olivier J., and Jordi Gali. 2007. "Real Wage Rigidities and the New Keynesian Model." *Journal of Money, Credit and Banking* 39 (suppl. 1): 35–65.

Blanchard, Olivier J., and Charles M. Kahn. 1980. "The Solution of Linear Difference Models under Rational Expectations." *Econometrica* 48, no. 5:1305–11.

Boivin, Jean, Marc Giannoni, and Ilian Mihov. 2009. "Sticky Prices and Monetary Policy: Evidence from Disaggregated US Data." *American Economic Review* 99, no. 1:350–84.

Burstein, Ariel, and Christian Hellwig. 2007. "Prices and Market Shares in a Menu Cost Model." Working paper, Department of Economics, University of California, Los Angeles.

Burstein, Ariel, and Nir Jaimovich. 2008. "Understanding Movements in Aggregate and Product-Level Real Exchange Rates." Working paper, Department of Economics, University of California, Los Angeles.

Calvo, Guillermo. 1983. "Staggered Prices in a Utility-Maximizing Framework." *Journal of Monetary Economics* 12, no. 3:383–98.

Caplin, Andrew S., and Daniel F. Spulber. 1987. "Menu Costs and the Neutrality of Money." *Quarterly Journal of Economics* 102, no. 4:703–26.

Carvalho, Carlos, and Fernanda Nechio. 2008. "Aggregation and the PPP Puzzle in a Sticky-Price Model." Working paper, Federal Reserve Bank of New York.

Chari, V. V., Patrick J. Kehoe, and Ellen R. McGrattan. 2000. "Sticky Price Models of the Business Cycle: Can the Contract Multiplier Solve the Persistence Problem?" *Econometrica* 68, no. 5:1151–80.

Christiano, Lawrence J., Martin Eichenbaum, and Charles L. Evans. 1999. "Monetary Policy Shocks: What Have We Learned and to What End?" In *Handbook of Macroeconomics*, ed. John B. Taylor and Michael Woodford, chap. 2, 65–148. Amsterdam: Elsevier.

Dornbusch, Rudiger. 1987. "Exchange Rate and Prices." *American Economic Review* 77, no. 1:93–106.

Eichenbaum, Martin, Nir Jaimovich, and Sergio Rebelo. 2011. "Reference Prices, Costs, and Nominal Rigidities." *American Economic Review*, forthcoming.

Fitzgerald, Doireann, and Stefanie Haller. 2008. "Exchange Rates and Producer Prices: Evidence from Micro Data." Working paper, Department of Economics, Stanford University.

Goldberg, Linda S., and José Manuel Campa. 2010. "The Sensitivity of the CPI to Exchange Rates: Distribution Margins, Imported Inputs, and Trade Exposure." *Review of Economics and Statistics* 92, no. 2:392–407.

Goldberg, Pinelopi, and Rebecca Hellerstein. 2006. "A Framework for Identifying the Sources of Local-Currency Price Stability with an Empirical Application." Working paper, Federal Reserve Bank of New York.

Goldberg, Pinelopi, and Michael Knetter. 1997. "Goods Prices and Exchange Rates: What Have We Learned?" *Journal of Economic Literature* 35, no. 3:1243–72.

Golosov, Mikhail, and Robert E. Lucas Jr. 2007. "Menu Costs and Phillips Curves." *Journal of Political Economy* 115, no. 2:171–99.

Gopinath, Gita, Pierre-Olivier Gourinchas, Chang-Tsi Hsieh, and Nicholas Li. 2009. "Estimating the Border Effect: Some New Evidence." Working Paper no. 14938, NBER, Cambridge, MA.

Gopinath, Gita, and Oleg Itskhoki. 2010a. "Frequency of Price Adjustment and Pass-Through." *Quarterly Journal of Economics* 125, no. 2:675–727.

———. 2010b. "In Search of Real Rigidities." Working Paper no. 16065, NBER, Cambridge, MA.

Gopinath, Gita, Oleg Itskhoki, and Roberto Rigobon. 2010. "Currency Choice and Exchange Rate Pass-Through." *American Economic Review* 100, no. 1:306–36.

Gopinath, Gita, and Roberto Rigobon. 2008. "Sticky Borders." *Quarterly Journal of Economics* 123, no. 2:531–75.

Kimball, Miles. 1995. "The Quantitative Analytics of the Basic Neomonetarist Model." *Journal of Money, Credit and Banking* 27, no. 4:1241–77.

Klenow, Peter J., and Jonathan L. Willis. 2006. "Real Rigidities and Nominal Price Changes." Working paper, Stanford University.

———. 2007. "Sticky Information and Sticky Prices." *Journal of Monetary Economics* 54, no. 1:79–99.

Krugman, Paul. 1987. "Pricing to Market When the Exchange Rate Changes." In *Real-Financial Linkages among Open Economies*, ed. Sven W. Arndt and J. David Richardson, 49–70. Cambridge, MA: MIT Press.

Maćkowiak, Bartoz , and Mirko Wiederholt. 2009. "Optimal Sticky Prices under Rational Inattention." *American Economic Review* 99, no. 3:769–803.

Mankiw, N. Gregory, and Ricardo Reis. 2002. "Sticky Information versus Sticky Prices: A Proposal to Replace the New Keynesian Phillips Curve." *Quarterly Journal of Economics* 117, no. 4:1295–1328.

Meese, Richard A., and Kenneth Rogoff. 1983. "Empirical Exchange Rate Models of the Seventies: Do They Fit out of Sample?" *Journal of International Economics* 14, no. 1:3–24.

Nakamura, Emi, and Jon Steinsson. 2008. "Five Facts about Prices: A Reevaluation of Menu Cost Models." *Quarterly Journal of Economics* 123, no. 4:1415–64.

———. 2010. "Monetary Non-neutrality in a Multi-sector Menu Cost Model." *Quarterly Journal of Economics* 125, no. 3:961–1013.

Nakamura, Emi, and Dawit Zerom. 2010. "Accounting for Incomplete Pass-Through." *Review of Economic Studies* 77, no. 3:1192–1230.

Neiman, Brent. 2009. "A State-Dependent Model of Intermediate Goods Pricing." Working paper, Booth School of Business, University of Chicago.

———. 2010. "Stickiness, Synchronization, and Passthrough in Intrafirm Trade Prices." *Journal of Monetary Economics* 57, no. 3:295–308.

Romer, David. 2008. "Real Rigidities. " In *The New Palgrave Dictionary of Economics*, ed. Steven N. Durlauf and Lawrence E. Blume. Basingstoke: Palgrave Macmillan.

Stock, James H., and Mark W. Watson. 2007. "Why Has U.S. Inflation Become Harder to Forecast?" *Journal of Money, Credit and Banking* 39, no. 1:3–33.

Taylor, John B. 1980. "Aggregate Dynamics and Staggered Constracts." *Journal of Political Economy* 88, no. 1:1–24.

Woodford, Michael. 2003. *Interest and Prices: Foundations of a Theory of Monetary Policy.* Princeton, NJ: Princeton University Press.

Comment

Mikhail Golosov, Yale University and NBER

I. Introduction

The past 10 years experienced a boom in research on the behavior of nominal prices using micro data. Economists obtained access to a number of new data sets that had not been previously available. Two independent literatures have emerged. One of them, which takes root in closed economy macro and monetary economics, focuses on the behavior of domestic consumer and producer prices. The other one, coming from the open economy macro and international finance tradition, focuses on the behavior of prices of imported goods.

Although the focuses of these two literatures differ, both are typically motivated by the desire to understand whether prices exhibit real rigidity. Real rigidity denotes a variety of mechanisms that prevent real prices from fully adjusting in response to the shocks to firms' marginal costs, such as strategic complementarities, variable markups, and so forth. A substantial amount of real rigidity is required in workhorse monetary models to generate large and persistent effects of nominal shocks on the real economy.

The two literatures thus far have reached different conclusions about the presence and sources of real rigidities in the micro data. The closed economy literature finds little evidence of real rigidities. The open economy literature consistently arrives at the conclusion that real rigidities, especially in the form of variable markups, must be substantial in order to be consistent with the micro data.

In their paper, Gopinath and Itskhoki, starting from the open economy tradition, take the first step toward reconciling the findings of the two literatures. In the empirical section, they present evidence that import prices behave differently from domestic retail prices, which are often the focus of the closed economy literature. They argue that the key difference between the two data sets is the nature of the goods that are being analyzed. While the domestic literature typically focuses

978-0-226-00212-5/2011/2010-0502$10.00

on the prices of retail goods, most of the imported goods are intermediate. Gopinath and Itskhoki extrapolate the conclusion of the open economy literature and provide a theory of price determination in the final (retail) and intermediate (wholesale) sectors. The main ingredient of their theory is the assumption that price determination differs between the two sectors. While in the retail sector prices are set by monopolistically competitive firms with constant markups, in the wholesale sector, prices are set through bargaining. This implies that real rigidities are present in the wholesale sector but not the retail sector.

In my comments, I first examine the differences in approaches between the closed and open economy literatures. I will discuss to what extent the open economy approach can provide definitive answers about the presence of real rigidities. I will also examine the evidence on whether the behavior of import prices differs significantly from that of domestic prices. Finally, I will discuss the theoretical model and the outstanding issues.

II. Domestic versus International Prices

First, I briefly review the closed and open economy literatures and examine which results led the researchers to their conclusions about the presence of real rigidities in the data. The goal is not to give an extensive literature review but rather to highlight one important difference between open and closed economy literatures: the two literatures not only use different data sets for their analysis but also rely on different statistical procedures in making their inferences about the presence of real rigidities. Although suggestive, none of those procedures can give a definitive answer. For this reason, it is not clear whether the difference in conclusions is driven by the differences in the data that the two literatures study or is an artifact of inconclusive statistical methodology. One of the most important contributions of the paper by Gopinath and Itskhoki is to present a new set of results from the import price data that is directly comparable to those in the closed economy literature.

Most of the research in the closed economy literature uses a variety of data sets of domestic retail prices. One of the most commonly used ones is the U.S. Bureau of Labor Statistics (BLS) micro data on domestic consumer prices that is used to construct the consumer price index. Klenow and Willis (2006) and Bils, Klenow, and Malin (2009) used these data to argue that there is little evidence of the presence of variable markup or real rigidity more generally. In the absence of any measure of marginal costs, both papers had to rely on indirect inferences to detect whether prices adjust to the real shocks slower than what is implied by nominal rigidity alone.

Klenow and Willis (2006) examine whether there is any evidence of variable markups. They argue that, to be consistent with the data on relative price movements, variable markups must imply implausibly large idiosyncratic shocks and movements in the micro quantities. Bils et al. (2009) develop a procedure to test for the presence of real rigidity more generally. They use micro data to construct a "reset-price inflation" index. They show that a broad class of models with real rigidities imply that this index must have positive autocorrelation and low variance. Instead, in the data they find that the opposite is true—reset-price inflation is highly volatile and has a large negative autocorrelation.

The open economy literature traditionally focuses on a different set of moments to test for the presence of real rigidities. The main identifying assumption it uses is that changes in the exchange rates, either nominal or real, represent a good measure of the changes in the marginal costs of imports. This literature regresses current prices of good i imported from some country j on past and present changes in the exchange rate of country j. Researchers find that pass-through of the changes in the exchange rate to prices is modest even in the medium run of 1–2 years. Over such horizons, only 10%–30% of the exchange rate change is reflected in the price of imports.

Gopinath and Itskhoki present several new facts about incomplete pass-through that are generally in line with the previous findings of the literature. In my opinion, the main empirical results of their paper lie not in the pass-through regressions but in the results that are directly comparable to those in the closed economy literature. Before reviewing these in Section IV, I will briefly discuss which inferences can be drawn from the pass-through regressions and why they may be uninformative about the presence of the real rigidities.

III. Pass-Through Regressions

In order to interpret incomplete pass-through as evidence of the presence of real rigidities, one needs to assume that changes in the exchange rates are exogenous shocks. An exchange rate is a price of one country's currency in the units of another country's currency. This price is determined endogenously by a variety of shocks that affect each country. The nature of these shocks determine the optimal amount of pass-through by the firm. It is easy to write models in which incomplete pass-through is optimal even without real rigidities. Therefore, without taking a particular stand on which shocks lead to fluctuations in exchange rates and why—in the absence of real rigidities—they should imply complete pass-through, the interpretation of incomplete pass through regressions as a sign of real rigidities is problematic.

One can argue that in the short run exchange rate fluctuations are not affected by any fundamental factor but rather are driven by sunspot-like fluctuations. Gopinath and Itskhoki indeed say that "exchange rate movements are disconnected from most macro variables at the frequencies studied in the literature." This interpretation leaves a number of questions unanswered. Does this imply that trade volume and other quantities are completely unaffected by the movements in the exchange rates? Shall we study the pricing decisions of firms in the models that imply that exchange rates and aggregate quantities are uncorrelated? What is the optimal pass-through in such environments, with and without real rigidities?

It is hard to make progress without having an explicit model of the exchange rate fluctuations. I am sympathetic to the arguments that no such model is currently available and that the pass-through regression is a reasonable method given the available state-of-the-art tools. That said, it is unclear to me why a priori real rigidities are considered to be the most plausible explanation for incomplete pass-through.

IV. How Different Are International and Domestic Prices?

Since pass-through regressions are hard to interpret, an important question remains whether there are systematic differences in behavior between domestic and import prices. Here, Gopinath and Itskhoki provide novel evidence on the existence of such differences. Table 1 of their paper reports persistence and volatility of regular and reset-price inflation for import prices and compares these statistics to those for domestic retail prices computed by Bils et al. (2009). The main finding is that the import prices have both higher persistence and volatility than domestic retail prices.

The results reported in table 1 provide mixed evidence on the presence of real rigidities in the import price data. As Bils et al. (2009) showed, the autocorrelation coefficient close to zero for reset-price inflation, as found in import price data, can be consistent with models with and without real rigidities. However, models with real rigidities have difficulty matching the large volatility of the reset-price inflation implied by the data.

Gopinath and Itskhoki point to an important source of differences between the goods studied by the open and closed economy literatures.

While the majority of studies on domestic prices have focused on retail prices, most imported goods are intermediate goods. These results open the possibility that the behavior of retail goods and intermediate goods may follow different patterns and, in particular, that there may be real rigidities for intermediate goods but not for final goods. If that conjecture is correct, the closed economy literature has not found real rigidities simply because it has focused on the wrong set of goods and prices.

This possibility suggests a promising research agenda. While there exist micro data on the domestic producer prices, these have been studied much less than data on consumer prices. To the best of my knowledge, the only systematic study of both producer and consumer prices was done by Nakamura and Steinsson (2008), who found few systematic difference in the patterns of pricing behavior between the two sets of goods. To fully reconcile the findings of the open and closed macro literatures, one could run a consistent set of tests on all three data sets for domestic consumer, producer, and import prices. Such a study can show whether there are systematic differences among the different types of prices and whether the conclusions about real rigidities can be carried from import to domestic producer prices. This would be particular important since imports play a relatively minor role in the U.S. economy and any real rigidity present there will have a much bigger effect if it is present in domestic producer prices.

V. Theoretical Model

In their theoretical section, Gopinath and Itskhoki propose a novel theory to reconcile findings from the closed and open economy literatures. The cornerstone of their theory is the assumption that price-setting mechanisms are different in the retail and wholesale sectors. They assume that prices in the intermediate sector are set through bargaining, whereas in the retail sector, monopolistically competitive firms post their prices. These assumptions imply in their model that there are real rigidities in the intermediate sector but not in the retail sector. Therefore, an outside observer who focuses only on retail consumer prices will not be able to find evidence of real rigidities.

Their simulation results show that this model can be successful at reconciling the two literatures. Bils et al.'s (2009) tests on retail prices reject the presence of real rigidity even when a significant amount of it is present in the wholesale sector. The same test performed on wholesale prices is consistent with the evidence from the import prices that

Gopinath and Itskhoki reported in the empirical section of the paper. Pass-through regressions indicate a limited pass-through.

Although consistent with the micro evidence, their model of variable markups does not lead to significant amplifications of monetary shocks. Relative to the benchmark without real rigidity, the half-life of the impulse response to monetary shock is only 50% higher in the preferred calibration of variable markups. Since monetary shocks lead to small and transient impulse responses in models without real rigidities, such amplification is not sufficient to make the model consistent with the vector autoregressive evidence on the effect of monetary shocks on the real economy.

The hypothesis that pricing behavior is different in the retail and intermediate sectors is interesting and promising and can lead to important discoveries about transmission mechanisms for nominal and real shocks. So far, the data on the pricing of intermediate goods have been relatively unexplored, and their detailed analysis may find confirmation of this hypothesis. At the same time, producer prices may conceptually differ from consumer prices, and many traditional assumptions from consumer theory may no longer apply for the prices of intermediate goods.

If we assume that intermediate prices are set as a result of bargaining between firms, it is not clear that the recorded price is a correct measure of the marginal cost of purchasing the good for the buyer. In many settings, it is natural for the firms to negotiate both the price and the quantity of the transaction. In such situations, prices measure the average cost for the buyer but not the marginal cost. The marginal costs are hard to measure even if one has information on both prices and quantities negotiated between firms. At the same time it is the responses of prices to changes of marginal costs rather than average costs that are the key for amplification of monetary shocks in many models.

The repeated nature of the interactions between firms represent another problem. As has been recognized since at least Barro (1977), observed nominal prices may not be allocative. If the real price decreases due to rigidity in nominal prices, firms may not adjust production and the quantities they sell if they expect buyers to compensate them in the futures for real losses incurred in current periods. While in anonymous retail markets such possibilities are unlikely, they may exist in the intermediate-goods markets, in which a small number of buyers and sellers are engaged in repeated transactions over long periods of time. Without our knowing the details of such interactions, observed nominal prices shed little light on the behavior of real quantities.

VI. Concluding Remarks

Gopinath and Itskhoki took an important first step toward bringing together two literatures that focus on closely related questions. Although a lot more work is needed to fully reconcile the two, this paper ultimately makes the contribution of pointing researchers toward a promising direction of future research.

References

Barro, Robert. 1977. "Long-Term Contracting, Sticky Prices, and Monetary Policy." *Journal of Monetary Economics* 3, no. 3:305–16.

Bils, Mark, Peter Klenow, and Benjamin Malin. 2009. "Reset Price Inflation and the Impact of Monetary Policy Shocks." Working Paper no. 14787, NBER, Cambridge, MA.

Klenow, Peter, and Jonathan Willis. 2006. "Real Rigidities and Nominal Price Changes." Working Paper no. RWP 06-03, Federal Reserve Bank of Kansas City.

Nakamura, Emi, and Jon Steinsson. 2008. "Five Facts about Prices: A Reevaluation of Menu Cost Models." *Quarterly Journal of Economics* 123, no. 4:1415–64.

Comment

Virgiliu Midrigan, *New York University*

This paper offers an excellent survey of recent empirical work studying the comovement between prices, costs, and nominal shocks. In addition, it presents interesting new evidence that sheds light on the mechanisms that account for the sluggish response of prices to nominal shocks. The authors' main focus is on how consumer prices of imported goods react to nominal exchange rate changes.

The paper is organized around two themes. The first theme is that real rigidities play an important role in accounting for the observation that retail prices are sticky. Two observations lead to this conclusion. First, imported-good prices react little to movements in nominal exchange rates even for firms that reset their prices. Second, reset-price inflation (a measure of the rate at which firms would like to change their prices absent nominal rigidities) is persistent.

The second part of the paper attempts to decompose the sluggish response of retail prices to nominal shocks into two components: a markup adjustment and cost rigidities. The authors argue that markup adjustments play a relatively minor role. Rather, stickiness in wholesale prices accounts for the bulk of the stickiness in retail prices. Again, several observations lead to this conclusion. First, quantitative studies by Klenow and Willis (2006) and Burstein and Hellwig (2007) find that models with markup variation cannot jointly account for the comovement of quantities and prices in the data. Moreover, nominal rigidities alone cannot generate much variation in markups since prices are quite flexible in the retail price data. Second, empirical studies of micro price data on retail prices and wholesale costs find that retail price stickiness is primarily driven by stickiness in wholesale costs: while wholesale prices are sticky, retail prices tend to respond quickly to changes in wholesale costs. (See the work of Goldberg and Hellerstein [2008], Nakamura and

978-0-226-00212-5/2011/2010-0503$10.00

Zerom [2010], and Eichenbaum, Jaimovich, and Rebelo [2011].) Finally, the authors offer new evidence that wholesale prices (at-the-dock prices of imported goods) react slowly to nominal shocks, as well as evidence of strategic complementarities at the wholesale level. I organize my comments around these two themes of the paper.

I. Are Real Rigidities Important?

The authors' first finding is that real rigidities account for the bulk of stickiness of prices in the data. They define real rigidities as "mechanisms that dampen price responses of firms because of factors such as strategic complementarities in price setting, real wage rigidity, and the dependence of costs on inputs prices that have yet to adjust, among others." In other words, real rigidities are anything other than nominal rigidities (menu costs that prevent nominal prices from changing too often) that generate a sluggish response of prices to shocks. Hence, when the authors argue that "real rigidities" account for the bulk of stickiness of prices in the data, they really mean that nominal rigidities play a minor role. Since prices change frequently in the data, and since even those prices that change do not seem to react much to nominal exchange rate changes, these findings reinforce the conclusions of much earlier work.

I briefly review here some evidence from my own work with Patrick Kehoe in which we document a similar pattern using international bilateral price data. We show in Kehoe and Midrigan (2007) that models with nominal rigidities imply a tight relationship between the degree to which a good's price is sticky and the extent to which that good's relative price fluctuates across countries. For example, a simple version of the Calvo model predicts that the international relative price of good i evolves according to

$$q_{it} = \lambda_i q_{it-1} + \lambda_i \Delta e_t,$$

where q_{it} is the real exchange rate of good i, λ_i is equal to one minus the frequency with which the price of good i changes, and Δe_t are changes in the nominal exchange rate. This expression shows that when λ_i is lower, so that prices are more flexible, real exchange rates for that particular good are less volatile and less persistent. In contrast, as λ_i increases toward unity, real exchange rates track nominal exchange rates closely.

We use sectoral price data from the U.S. Bureau of Labor Statistics (BLS) and Eurostat to test these predictions of the model. We use data for the United States, Austria, Belgium, France, and Spain on the frequency with which prices adjust for 66 consumption goods (sectors).

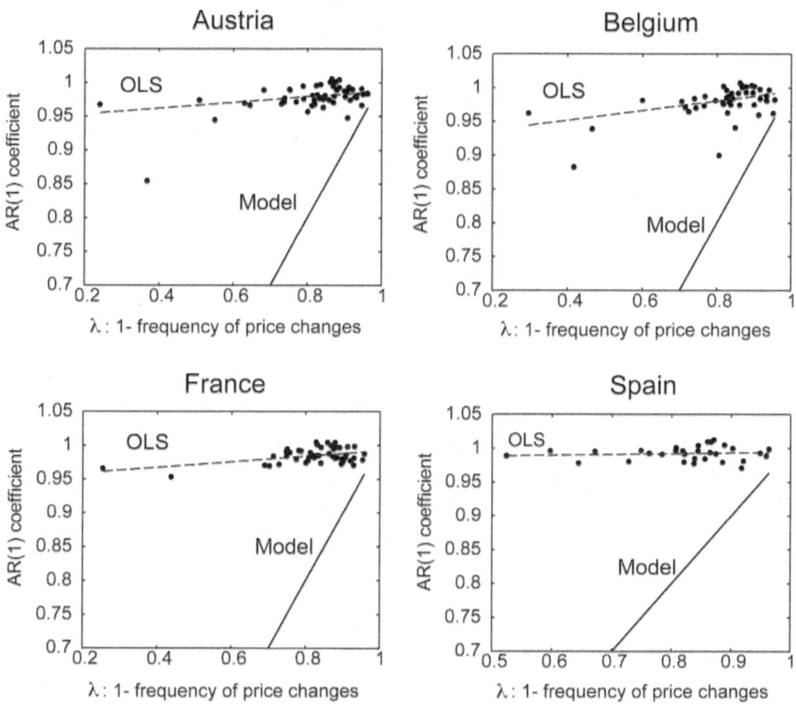

Fig. 1. Stickiness versus persistence

These data are derived from primitive data on the prices of specific items used by the BLS and the European countries' statistics institutes in order to construct data on the consumer price index. We also use monthly data on good-level real exchange rates for the European countries in our sample against the United States.

Figure 1, reproduced from Kehoe and Midrigan (2007), shows how the sticky price model accounts for the persistence (as measured by the serial correlation) of sectoral real exchange rates in the data. Notice that while the model predicts that persistence increases one for one with stickiness, λ_i, the data show a much weaker relationship. In particular, the model predicts that goods with flexible prices are characterized by little persistence in real exchange rates, while in the data all goods have a very volatile real exchange rate, pretty much regardless of how frequently their prices change. Thus, nominal rigidities alone cannot account for the persistence of real exchange rates in the data.

Clearly, the model's predictions can be brought closer in line with the data by introducing variable markups or factors that dampen the response of costs to nominal shocks. For example, a version of the model with sticky wages in which wages change once every 1.5 years can indeed account for the relationship between the persistence of real exchange rates and the frequency of price changes in the data. In this model, however, sticky costs (i.e., real rigidities), rather than sticky prices (menu costs), account for the bulk of the variation in real exchange rates. Goldberg and Hellerstein (2008) and Nakamura and Zerom (2010) reach similar conclusions, using an alternative methodology and data.

The authors argue in Section IV of their paper that the high persistence of reset-price inflation they document in the import price data is evidence of large real rigidities at this level in the supply chain. In contrast, they interpret the evidence of Bils, Klenow, and Malin (2009) that reset-price inflation for retail prices is much less persistent as evidence against the importance of real rigidities at the retail level.

I disagree with this interpretation. In particular, although I find the concept of "reset prices" introduced by Bils et al. (2009) (essentially a measure of what prices would have been absent nominal price rigidities) useful in disentangling the role of nominal rigidities, the persistence of reset-price inflation is not a useful measure of real rigidities. In New Keynesian models the persistence of reset-price inflation (or inflation for that matter) is mainly a function of the nature of aggregate shocks and the nature of monetary policy. (See, e.g., Clarida, Gali, and Gertler [1999], who show that under optimal monetary policy the rate of inflation is proportional to the exogenous shocks in the economy and thus inherits the persistence of those shocks.) Browsing table 8 in the Gopinath and Itskhoki paper, one reaches the conclusion that a similar feature characterizes their own model economy. In particular, as they raise the parameter Γ that determines the strength of real rigidities from 0 (no real rigidities) to 4 (large real rigidities), the serial correlation of inflation barely changes (it drops from 0.41 to 0.37), as does the persistence of reset price inflation (it drops from −0.25 to −0.28). Hence, even in the model the authors study, real rigidities have no visible effect on the amount of inflation persistence.

Despite this caveat, I still find the concept of reset price suggested by Bils et al. (2009) useful. In particular, real rigidities are used in the New Keynesian literature because they ensure that the models (i) account for the correlation between prices and nominal shocks and (ii) account for the low correlation between inflation and output in the data. Since these two features of the data are what real rigidities are designed to explain, the relevant questions are (i) what is the correlation between reset prices and nominal shocks, and (ii) what is the correlation between reset price inflation and output? These latter statistics, in contrast to inflation persistence, are clearly influenced by the degree of real (and nominal) rigidities in the model and can thus be used to disentangle the role of menu costs from other factors.

II. Sources of Real Rigidities

Having established that nominal rigidities account for little of the price stickiness in the data, the authors then go on to search for the relevant mechanisms that account for the sluggish response of prices to nominal shocks. In particular, is the imperfect comovement of prices and nominal shocks accounted for by sticky costs or rather by variable markups? Are these features mostly prevalent at the retail, wholesale, or manufacturer level?

The authors argue that their reading of the literature and their own empirical findings suggest that sticky wholesale prices account for the bulk of the price stickiness of consumer prices in the data. They base their conclusions on the observation that wholesale prices change infrequently in the data and do not comove with change in nominal exchange rates much, whereas retail prices track movements in wholesale prices very well.

I argue that such evidence must be interpreted with care. First, the average wholesale cost that is typically available in the data is not necessarily equal to the retailer's marginal valuation of those goods. Since retail prices are a markup over the maginal valuation (or cost) of goods, the latter object is the relevant object for empirical analysis. The average acquisition cost may not be necessarily equal to the marginal valuation for a number of reasons. For example, if wholesalers offer nonlinear pricing tariffs or if contracts specify both prices and quantities, the buyer may value an additional unit of the good more than the price at which it has actually purchased the other goods. Similarly, quantity adjustment costs may drive a wedge between transacted prices and marginal valuations. Although such wedges would affect the retailer's pricing decisions, they are not incorporated in the typical measures of wholesale costs used in empirical work. Overall, since statements about costs are really statement about quantities, our understanding of real rigidities would benefit from additional information on quantities.

In work with Oleksiy Kryvtsov (Kryvtsov and Midrigan 2010), we use information on inventories in order to decompose the role of markups and costs in accounting for the sluggish response of consumer prices to nominal shocks. We show that if costs of production are indeed sticky and markups do not vary much, a model with inventories predicts that retailers would take advantage of the stickiness in costs and strongly accumulate inventories when costs are low. In contrast, in the data, inventories react slowly to such shocks: although inventories are mildly procyclical, they are much less volatile than predicted by models in which sticky costs play an important role. We thus find an important role for variation in markups (rather than sticky costs) in accounting for the behavior of consumer prices. In particular, for models with inventories to match the dynamics of inventories in the data, it must be the case that costs are fairly sensitive to nominal shocks and that variation in markups accounts for the bulk of the stickiness of consumer prices.

III. Conclusions

The observation that prices change very frequently in the data has led economists to conclude that nominal price rigidities are rather unimportant in accounting for the stickiness of prices at the aggregate level. Rather, cost rigidities of various forms play a much more important role in current New Keynesian models of the business cycle. I argue here that such conclusions are premature. First, as pointed out by Kehoe and Midrigan (2010), the high frequency of price changes is not really evidence against the importance of sticky prices: a vast majority of price changes in the data are temporary, and such temporary price changes do not contribute much to the flexibility of the aggregate price level. In fact, we find that a standard menu cost model must have a frequency of price changes of about 12 months for it to reproduce the real effects of money shocks in our model in which prices change once every 4 months, as in the data, but in which we also match the frequency and special nature of temporary price changes in the data. Second, research by Carvalho (2006) and Nakamura and Steinsson (2010) has shown that heterogeneity in the frequency of price changes also amplifies the extent of nominal rigidities. Finally, data on costs must be interpreted with care, since prices in long-term relationships are not necessarily allocative. Contractual agreements, adjustment costs, or nonlinear tariffs generate a disconnect between the observed costs and the true shadow valuation of the good. Since statements about costs are essentially statements about quantities, I argue that a greater focus on the quantity data is necessary in order to disentangle the role of markups and costs in accounting for the dynamics of prices in the data.

References

Bils, Mark, Peter Klenow, and Benjamin Malin. 2009. "Reset Price Inflation and the Impact of Monetary Policy Shocks." Working Paper no. 14787, NBER, Cambridge, MA.

Burstein, Ariel, and Christian Hellwig. 2007. "Prices and Market Shares in a Menu Cost Model." Photocopy, Department of Economics, University of California, Los Angeles.

Carvalho, Carlos. 2006. "Heterogeneity in Price Stickiness and the Real Effects of Monetary Shocks." *B.E. Journal of Macroeconomics* 2, no. 1:1–56.

Clarida, Richard, Jordi Gali, and Mark Gertler. 1999. "The Science of Monetary Policy: A New Keynesian Perspective." *Journal of Economic Literature* 37, no. 4:1661–1707.

Eichenbaum, Martin, Nir Jaimovich, and Sergio Rebelo. 2011. "Reference Prices and Nominal Rigidities." *American Economic Review*, forthcoming.

Goldberg, Pinelopi, and Rebecca Hellerstein. 2008. "A Framework for Identifying the Sources of Local-Currency Price Stability with an Empirical Application." Photocopy, Department of Economics, Yale University.

Kehoe, Patrick, and Virgiliu Midrigan. 2007. "Sticky Prices and Real Exchange Rates in the Cross-Section." Photocopy, Department of Economics, New York University.

———. 2010. "Prices Are Sticky after All." Photocopy, Department of Economics, New York University.

Klenow, Peter, and Jonathan Willis. 2006. "Real Rigidities and Nominal Price Changes." Photocopy, Department of Economics, Stanford University.

Kryvtsov, Oleksiy, and Virgiliu Midrigan. 2010. "Inventories, Markups, and Real Rigidities in Menu Cost Models." Photocopy, Bank of Canada and New York University.

Nakamura, Emi, and Jon Steinsson. 2010. "Monetary Non-neutrality in a Multi-Sector Menu Cost Model." *Quarterly Journal of Economics* 125, no. 3:961–1013.

Nakamura, Emi, and Dawit Zarom. 2010. "Accounting for Incomplete Pass-Through." *Review of Economic Studies* 77, no. 3:1192–1230.

Discussion

Gita Gopinath initiated the session by responding to Michael Golosov's discussion. She began by commenting on the issue of the endogeneity of the exchange rate. She stressed that the paper made assumptions common to the literature on exchange rate pass-through. The first assumption is that, from a firm's perspective, exchange rate shocks are shocks to the costs of the firm that are not affected by the firm's pricing decisions. The second assumption says that the exchange rate shocks are orthogonal to other shocks that affect the firm, and she emphasized that this does not imply that exchange rate shocks are driven by sunspots. It just means that the fundamentals that might cause movements in the exchange rate are, from the firm's perspective, orthogonal to everything else affecting firm's pricing decision. She also noted that they could write and solve the model with an endogenously determined exchange rate. She argued, however, that such models are usually poor models of the exchange rate.

Next, Gopinath described the costs and benefits of using producer prices. On the one hand, she noted that it is the relevant price to use. On the other hand, she argued that since exchange rate shocks have trivial effects on producer prices, the advantage of using exchange rate shocks as sizable shocks affecting the firm disappears.

Gopinath also commented on the issue of whether prices are allocative, which was raised by both discussants. She noted that the prices are not list prices but rather a part of contracts. According to Gopinath and Rigobon (2008), a contract typically specifies a price and a quantity range that can be bought at this price. Thus, the buyers can choose their desired quantity within this range. Moreover the behavior of prices is consistent with monopolistic price setting.

Gopinath then turned to some issues raised by Virgiliu Midrigan. With respect to the variable markup interpretation of the real rigidities they found, Gopinath noted that they are careful about this at every point in the paper. She added that there is one piece of evidence in favor of variable markups that is not in their paper: a firm selling the same

978-0-226-00212-5/2011/2010-0504$10.00

product produced at the same plant to different markets often charges different prices to different markets. As to the alternative interpretation of the correlation of price changes with sector-specific inflation rates, she argued that the sector-specific shocks interpretation that Midrigan proposed was mentioned in their paper.

Oleg Itskhoki offered two additional comments. First, he repeated that the papers in the closed economy literature first assume a specific channel of real rigidities and then adjust the parameters of the channel such that it explains the long duration of effects of monetary disturbances on output. He stressed that, in their paper, they first use data to estimate the specific channel and then input the estimate into the model to see how important this channel is. He noted that the calibration in their paper uses a smaller elasticity of variable markups than that used in the work by Klenow and Willis (2006). On the one hand, this saved the authors from running into problems of counterfactual predictions for micro prices. On the other hand, the authors did not get as much of the real nonneutrality as Klenow and Willis got.

Second, Itskhoki claimed that it is very hard to get the long-lasting effect of monetary disturbances on output. He argued that, with their real rigidity mechanism, prices are more sluggish; however, this is still far from matching the sluggishness of prices at the micro level. Thus, he concluded, they are missing something in explaining micro prices.

Robert Hall pointed to a lack of understanding of the fundamentals of retail pricing of consumer goods. He thought that one cannot interpret the choice of how to run a retail business as a simple menu that is presented by the producer. The producer should be thought of as a principal in a principal-agent relationship. He gave an example of BMW of North America, which is a separate company that is buying from the parent company, BMW AG. However, the former does what the latter tells it to do. Next, he turned to the role of negotiations in price setting. He noted that, in modern bargaining theory, the generic bargaining model is an alternating offer bargain and that Nash bargaining can be achieved as a special case of it. He believed that the alternating bargain offer is a more realistic description of the way bargaining occurs compared to Nash bargaining. He concluded his comment by suggesting that the separation of agency transactions from those that have a bargaining character would be the first step in this research.

Daron Acemoglu remarked that *real rigidities* and *variable markups* are not exactly clear terms because there are many micro models that could be consistent with these two concepts. Acemoglu proposed to choose a particular micro model that is consistent with variable markups and estimate it using the data that the authors have, if the model can be identified with this data.

Gopinath replied by saying that they do not have sufficient data to do this exercise. She argued that any model that builds a little more structure would have predictions about market share and the elasticity of demand. However, the authors do not have market shares data. She added that, apart from the industry from which the good is coming, they do not have any quantity data. She pointed to a paper by Nakamura and Zerom (2010) that answers this type of a question for the coffee industry. Itskhoki added that once the model is linearized, any source of variable markups looks the same. Thus, the only prediction from the linearized model is the sensitivity of a price to competitors' prices. Itskhoki also mentioned that the prices in the data are quite variable and that the exchange rate is only a small component of the price movement. This makes it hard to distinguish among different models.

Hall made a comment that, in case of the Dixit-Stiglitz aggregator, the actions of players are determined simultaneously in equilibrium. Thus, conditioning on the play of others as a determinate of the firm pricing decision is not appropriate in empirical investigation. Itskhoki answered by noting that the prices are staggered. When they look at the price adjustment in the current period, they condition on the cumulative price change of the other firms in the previous periods.

Ariel Pakes expressed skepticism about whether industrial organization has good models to address the questions that are important to the authors of the paper, partly because of focusing on very different questions. He gave an example of the auto industry, where he said that industrial organization economists fit the cross-sectional variance of prices almost perfectly, yet they cannot capture the behavior of prices over time. He noted that the dynamics of pricing of durable goods in particular is a very hard problem, as it involves a double-nested fixed point: the behavior of consumers depends on what they perceive that producers will do, while the behavior of producers similarly depends on what they perceive that consumers are going to do. No one can compute a model like that, he said, and it is unclear what the way forward should be.

Jon Steinsson proposed explanations for the result that there is a big difference between the persistence properties of regularly reset prices in the U.S. Bureau of Labor Statistics (BLS) IPP (International Price Program) data as opposed to the consumer price index (CPI) data at monthly frequencies. He started by noting that measurement error may be important in interpreting such results because it can bias the estimates down to zero or potentially to –0.5. He justified this point by saying that the authors document bigger persistence of the CPI inflation rate at lower frequencies than monthly. He noted that the BLS IPP data set has a smaller sample; thus, one could expect that the bias could be bigger in this data set. However, for these data, the authors got the opposite result. Steinsson claimed that the measurement errors may bias the estimates less in the case of IPP data because of the properties of this data set. First, there are fewer price changes in this data set. Second, and more importantly, there are no sales in IPP data compared to CPI data. This can lead to estimating higher persistence. Gopinath responded by saying that they mentioned in their paper that the particular coefficient that they measure on reset-price inflation depends on the noise in the data. If there is noise, one is likely to get a biased-downward estimate. She also argued that they compared the persistence estimated from IPP data to the persistence estimated from CPI data set after removing sales from the CPI. Thus, sales should not explain the difference in the estimates. Gopinath added that the unconditional reset-price inflation does not provide much information about the amount of the real rigidities. She stressed that the takeaway should not be that the unconditional reset-price inflation in the IPP data set is more persistent than the one in the CPI data set. Rather the conclusion should be that the series does not provide enough information about the extent of real rigidities. Itskhoki responded by emphasizing that the more direct way of measuring real rigidities is to look at the actual micro prices and to document how long it takes for the micro prices to adjust.

John Taylor pointed out that the pass-through varies depending on the stance of the monetary policy, and, specifically, the pass-through is smaller for a low inflation regime. He wondered if this is something the authors could exploit in looking for the effects in different models. Next, he agreed with the point that the terminology *real rigidity* is not very useful. Itskhoki responded by saying that it could be a misleading term. There is nothing rigid about real rigidities; it is just some amplification mechanism built into these models. This could be purely conventional parts of the model that can be present in flexible price models that one does not consider a rigidity by itself. It is just a mechanism that, given stickiness in price setting, makes the price adjustment more sluggish. It is a label for anything that makes prices move slowly in response to shocks.

Jordi Galí made a suggestion on the problem of potential endogeneity of the exchange rate. He proposed that the authors rerun their regressions instrumenting the exchange rate using, for instance, the Christiano, Eichenbaum, and Evans (1999) fitted monetary policy shock. He argued that the shock has been shown to have large effects on the dollar exchange rate. He added that this could be a way to condition on the specific driving force. Itskhoki replied by saying that the benefit of working with international data is that you do not need to do any procedures to identify the underlying shocks. However, it is a possibility if one believes that the residuals that are picked up are a good measure of the exogenous shocks.

Deborah Lucas wondered how exchange rate hedging by firms affects the results of the paper. Gopinath said that the mechanisms that they have in the paper play out even if a firm could hedge the currency risks because the hedging contracts do not affect the marginal costs in this model.

6

Oil, Automobiles, and the U.S. Economy: How Much Have Things Really Changed?

Valerie A. Ramey, *University of California, San Diego, and NBER*
Daniel J. Vine, *Board of Governors of the Federal Reserve System*

I. Introduction

Between 2002 and mid-2008, the average real price of gasoline in the United States increased more than twofold after having risen only modestly in the preceding 15 years. Not surprisingly, this run-up led to renewed interest in the effects of oil shocks on the U.S. aggregate economy. Hamilton's (1983) seminal paper documented the negative effects of oil shocks on the aggregate economy, and numerous papers since that time have extended or questioned the strength of these effects.[1] Most recently, several authors have argued that the effects of oil price shocks on U.S. aggregate activity have declined since the mid-1980s (e.g., Blanchard and Riggi 2009; Edelstein and Kilian 2009; Herrera and Pesavento 2009; Blanchard and Galí 2010). These papers have variously attributed the decline to improved monetary policy, a smaller share of oil in production, or more flexible labor markets. Empirical work has also shown that a more muted response in the consumption of motor vehicles to energy price shocks has played a large role in obtaining these results (Edelstein and Kilian 2009).

This paper reexamines the extent to which the impact of oil shocks on the aggregate economy—and on the motor vehicle industry in particular—has changed over time. We first discuss the array of energy cost measures that authors in the literature have used to define oil price shocks, and then we survey the theoretical contributions from a number of dynamic stochastic general equilibrium (DSGE) macro models that include various roles for oil in the economy. Using these models, there are a number of structural parameters that reasonably could have changed over time and reduced the potency with which oil price fluctuations depress aggregate output.

978-0-226-00212-5/2011/2010-0601$10.00

However, all of these macro models assume that the price of oil reflects the true cost of energy for firms and consumers. While much of the recent empirical work uses published measures of oil or gasoline prices as an indicator of the strength of the oil price shocks, we find that these measures neglect the impact of the shortages that occurred in the critical 1973–74 and 1979 oil shock episodes, due to price controls.

Using two oil shock measures that include the effects of both price and nonprice rationing, we reexamine the evidence from vector autoregressions (VARs) that oil disturbances have had less impact on the real economy in the past 20 years than in the preceding decades. The results show that the responses of motor vehicle consumption and aggregate output to shortage-adjusted oil price shocks appear just as great during the last couple of decades as they were in the 1970s and early 1980s. However, even the new measures imply that the impact on nominal variables has become noticeably muted.

Why has there been so little change over time in the response of motor vehicle consumption to oil price changes? We find that, despite the many innovations in the way the U.S. economy produces and uses motor vehicles that have occurred over the past 40 years, the primary channels through which oil prices directly affect motor vehicles have not changed much over time. Namely, we present evidence that the recent increases in gasoline prices have caused just as much anxiety in consumers now as was observed 40 years ago, and the shifts in demand across vehicle size classes have also been as disruptive to motor vehicle capacity utilization since 2000 as they were in the 1970s and early 1980s.

The paper proceeds as follows. Section II reviews the data available on various measures of oil prices and discusses how modern DSGE models accommodate the role of oil in the economy. It also presents evidence that the presence of energy price controls and gasoline shortages in the 1970s may cause problems in empirical work because published prices in that era do not reflect the true cost of energy. Using measures that include the cost of shortages, we find no evidence of weaker effects of oil shocks on the real economy. Because we find that the motor vehicle industry plays a central role in the propagation of the oil shocks, the remainder of the paper studies this industry in detail. Section III examines the role of the motor vehicle industry in the overall economy. Section IV discusses how gas prices affect vehicle demand, and Section V shows the ways in which these shocks affect production. Section VI concludes.

II. Oil Shocks and the U.S. Economy

We begin by reviewing the behavior of several key measures of oil prices over the past few decades. After describing how macro DSGE models have been used to understand the role of energy costs in the economy, we present evidence that price controls may have led to a wedge between the published price of oil and the true cost of oil during the large oil price shocks in the 1970s. Using VARs that are similar to those estimated by Edelstein and Kilian (2009) and Blanchard and Galí (2010), we then show how mismeasurement of the true cost of oil in the 1970s may have caused the appearance of structural instability in the impulse-response functions of real output to oil price shocks. Using cost measures that account for shortages, we find that the impulse-response functions have not changed much over time.

A. *Overview of Oil Prices*

Figure 1 displays three oil price measures: the producer price index for crude petroleum (PPI-oil), the refiner acquisition cost of imported oil (RAQ), and the consumer price index for gasoline (CPI-gas). Hamilton (2003, 2009) typically uses the PPI-oil measure, and Mork (1989) and Barsky and Kilian (2002) use versions of the RAQ measure.[2] Unfortunately, the RAQ measure starts only in 1974.[3] We include the CPI-gas measure because several authors have shown that gasoline is a large share of U.S. petroleum consumption, and gasoline prices are also the most relevant energy price measure for the automobile sector.[4]

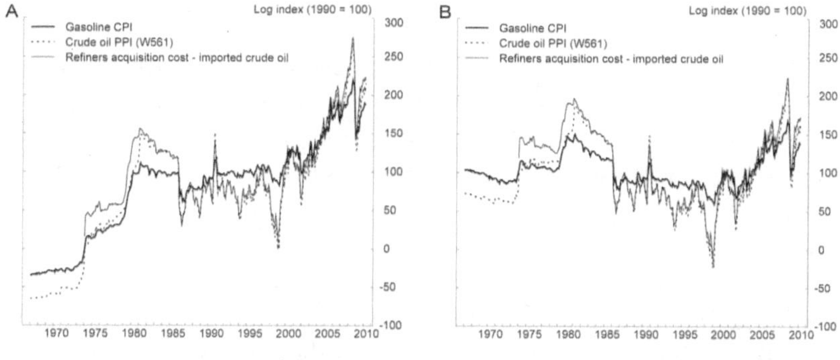

Fig. 1. Petroleum prices, January 1967 through March 2010. *A*, Nominal price indexes; *B*, real price indexes. Data come from the Bureau of Labor Statistics. The real indexes normalize the changes in petroleum prices by the changes in headline consumer price inflation. Refiners acquisition cost data begin in 1974. For each series x, the log index is calculated as $100 + 100[\log(x(t)) - \log(x(1990))]$.

Oil and gas prices—displayed in log current dollars in figure 1*A* and in log real index points in figure 1*B*—have risen notably at several points in history. Four episodes stand out in particular: first, the real price of gasoline rose 27% between October 1973 and May 1974, the result of an even larger rise in the price of crude oil after the Yom Kippur War. After falling back a bit over the next 4 years, the price of crude oil began to rise again at the end of 1978. By the spring of 1980, the Iranian Revolution and the Iran-Iraq War led to losses in crude oil production that pushed up the price of imported oil 71% and the price of gasoline 46%. Between 1982 and 1985, the nominal price of gasoline grew only modestly until Saudi Arabia abandoned production quotas and the price of crude oil plunged.

Real gasoline prices continued to trend lower after 1985, and, by the end of the 1990s, real gasoline prices had receded to record low levels. This pattern changed abruptly at the beginning of 1999, when the Organization of Petroleum Exporting Countries (OPEC) members phased in several cuts to production quotas. The real price of gasoline surged 43% by the summer of 2001 before the weakening world economy put downward pressure on crude oil prices. The relief was short lived, however. Gas prices began to rise again in early 2002, when political turmoil in Venezuela shut down much of the country's crude oil production; real crude prices climbed 588% and gasoline prices climbed 127% by summer 2008, and then they collapsed when the financial crisis spread from the housing sector to the rest of the economy and interrupted aggregate demand.

B. *Oil Shocks in Macro DSGE Models*

Economists take a keen interest in oil prices because these episodes of steep increases in prices were often followed by recessions. The literature has introduced into macro models four principle channels through which oil or energy shocks can lead to recessions: (i) energy serves as an important input to production; (ii) energy is an important consumption good; (iii) changes in energy prices lead to costly shifts in demand across sectors; and (iv) the policy response to oil price shocks includes monetary tightening, a move that depresses output. Often layered on top of these channels are forces that multiply and propagate the effects of oil price shocks on aggregate output, such as real wage rigidities (e.g., Bruno and Sachs 1982; Blanchard and Riggi 2009; Blanchard and Galí 2010), imperfect competition (Rotemberg and Woodford 1996), variable utilization rates (Finn 2000), vintage capital effects (Atkeson and Kehoe 1999; Wei 2009), and multiplier effects created by externalities across firms (Aguiar-Conraria and Wen 2007). We will briefly discuss each of these channels and point out which parameters in these DSGE models are suspected to have changed over time.

1. Energy as an Input to Production

Berndt and Wood (1975), Bruno and Sachs (1982), and Pindyck and Rotemberg (1983) were among the first to study energy price shocks in a framework that accommodates energy as an input to production. The strength of this channel is limited, however, by the small share of energy in total production costs, even in the 1970s. Finn (1991, 2000) modifies the standard model to reflect the notion that the energy requirements of installed capital are often fixed, and thus energy must be used in fixed proportions to capital use. This feature makes output more sensitive to increases in energy prices.

In many of the models mentioned above, a decrease in the amount of oil required to produce a unit of output would reduce the effect of oil shocks on the aggregate economy. This result suggests that increases over time in the fuel efficiency of many types of production technology may have weakened the relationship between oil price and real output. In addition, structural parameters not directly related to the use of energy can also affect the transmission of energy price shocks in DSGE models. For example, Blanchard and Galí (2010) show that a decline in the rigidity of wages in these types of models reduces the effects of oil price shocks on output.

2. Energy as a Consumption Good

In addition to the consequences of reduced output in general equilibrium, increases in oil prices also have direct effects on demand. First, oil shocks can lead to declines in demand for goods for which consumption is complementary with purchases of oil. Hamilton (1988) and Wei (2009) use models of demand for motor vehicles to show this effect. Second, oil shocks introduce uncertainty into the outlook for future energy prices, and increases in uncertainty can dampen demand for goods if purchases are costly to reverse (Bernanke 1983). Third, for energy-consuming capital goods, increases in the price of energy change the desired characteristics of the capital in use. Because the energy efficiency of the existing stock of consumer durables available in the short run is largely fixed, demand for new goods can shift between products in an exaggerated fashion and reflects the widening differential in the relative cost of ownership between different types of goods. For motor vehicles, smaller and more fuel-efficient models naturally become more desirable.

In these types of models, one parameter that has likely changed over time is the energy efficiency of consumer durable goods, including motor vehicles and other appliances. When energy efficiency rises or the share of these types of goods in total consumption falls, then we would expect the impact of oil shocks on output to diminish.

3. Sectoral Shifts and Costly Factor Mobility

Several papers have investigated sectoral shifts as a way in which oil price shocks affect the aggregate output. Davis (1987) and Hamilton (1988) both suggest that oil price shocks have a bigger effect on output if the shocks induce sectoral shifts and factor adjustment is costly. Bresnahan and Ramey (1993) argue that oil shocks can lead to disruptive sectoral shifts, even within narrowly defined industries. They present empirical evidence that shifts in demand between size classes of automobiles disrupted output in the U.S. automobile industry during the 1970s.

In the context of the multisector models, it is not clear that the structure of the economy has changed in a way that would weaken the transmission of oil price shocks through the sectoral-shifts channel. We find evidence in the motor vehicle industry that this channel remains quite potent.

4. Monetary Policy Reaction Functions

Bernanke, Gertler, and Watson (1997) argue that the endogenous response of monetary policy to an increase in oil prices is an important part of the outsized declines observed in output, a result they showed by using a structural VAR and counterfactual experiments with different monetary policy rules.[5] Using a calibrated DSGE model, Leduc and Sill (2004) find that 40% of the decline in output that follows a positive shock to oil prices reflects the systematic component of monetary policy.

To look for changes in policy parameters over time and assess whether these changes may have reduced the impact of oil shocks on output, a number of papers have either simulated monetary DSGE models or estimated monetary structural VARs. Blanchard and Riggi (2009), Herrera and Pesavento (2009), and Blanchard and Galí (2010) all find evidence that oil price shocks have had less impact in recent decades, in part, because of the changes in monetary policy.

To summarize, the theoretical literature has suggested a variety of ways in which oil shocks affect the economy. Some of these effects could be weaker now, while other effects could easily be as strong.

C. *The Importance of Nonprice Rationing in the 1970s*

In the models described above, it is assumed that the price of oil reflects the true acquisition cost of energy for firms and households. While the literature on the effects of oil shocks has debated the merits of various measures of oil prices and whether the effects are nonlinear, much of it has missed a potentially important change in the degree to which oil prices reflect oil disruptions.[6] In particular, other than Mork (1989), macroeconomists have not paid much attention to the embargoes, price controls, and shortages that marked the oil price disturbances in the 1970s. Helbling and Turley (1975) document that price controls were first imposed on the U.S. domestic oil industry in August 1971 as part of the general imposition of price controls. The controls on other sectors of the economy were phased out, but the controls were made more stringent on the domestic oil industry in response to the OPEC embargo of October 1973. These complex controls, which imposed a price ceiling on "old" oil that was lower than the one imposed on "new" oil, led to significant disruptions in the production of domestic oil and held the average domestic price of crude oil below the world price. Most of the effects of these controls were felt in the markets for gasoline and diesel fuel. According to some estimates, 20% of the gasoline stations ran out of gas during the height of the crisis (Frum 2000).

Pisarski and de Terra (1975) detail the policy responses to the embargo in various European countries. While most European countries did not impose the types of price controls imposed in the United States, they responded with other sorts of controls, such as bans on Sunday driving (Germany, Italy, Netherlands, Switzerland) and limits on gas purchases (Great Britain, Netherlands, Sweden, Switzerland). Almost all countries imposed lower speed limits.

Multiple oil and gas price controls also helped produce shortages after the Iranian Revolution of 1979. In April 1979, President Carter announced gradual decontrol of oil prices but proposed a windfall profits tax. In January 1981, President Reagan signed an order leading to the complete deregulation of oil and gas prices.

To quantify the additional cost imposed on consumers by nonprice rationing in the 1970s, Frech and Lee (1987) use data on urban and rural traffic patterns in California and estimates of the price elasticity of demand for gasoline from Lee (1980). They estimate that the time cost of the queues added between 13% and 84% to the price of a gallon of gasoline between December 1973 and March 1974; the additional time cost implicitly paid by consumers between May 1979 and July 1979 varied from 6% to 33%. Thus, the price index for gasoline shown in figure 1 potentially understates the true cost of gasoline quite severely in periods affected by the two oil shocks of the 1970s.

The PPI-oil measure suffers from the same problem because of the price controls on domestic crude oil. The refiners' acquisition cost of imported oil used by Barsky and Kilian (2002) comes closer to measuring the world price of oil. However, this measure still does not capture all of the additional costs imposed on the U.S. economy by distortions caused by price controls and the entitlement system. The reason is that price controls cause inefficiencies and deadweight loss that are larger than the gap between actual prices and market-clearing prices.[7]

In order to capture the true cost of gasoline during these episodes, we propose two new variables: the first variable augments published gas prices with estimates of the additional time cost during the periods of gasoline lines. In particular, we use the average of the rural and urban estimates from table 1 in Frech and Lee (1987), which compares the time costs per gallon to the published price per gallon of gasoline for the months of December 1973 through March 1974 and May 1979 through July 1979. All told, rationing is estimated to have added between 8% (in July 1979) and 67% (in March 1974) to the shadow price of a gallon of gasoline.[8] Using these estimates, we construct a shortage-adjusted index for the real price of gasoline, which is shown as the dashed line in figure 2.

Because the rationing-by-queue cost estimates likely capture the effect of shortages imperfectly, we also consider a second measure—the special question posed by Thomson Reuters and the University of Michigan in the Survey of Consumer Sentiment. Respondents to the monthly survey are asked several questions related to car-buying conditions. The survey tracks the portion of respondents who cite the price of gasoline or possible fuel shortages as a reason that car-buying conditions are poor.[9] This measure is shown in figure 3. The portion of consumers that expressed anxiety over fuel prices ramped up sharply at the time of the oil price shocks in the 1970s and early 1980s. Although the rise in real gas prices was much greater in the 2000s than in the 1970s and early

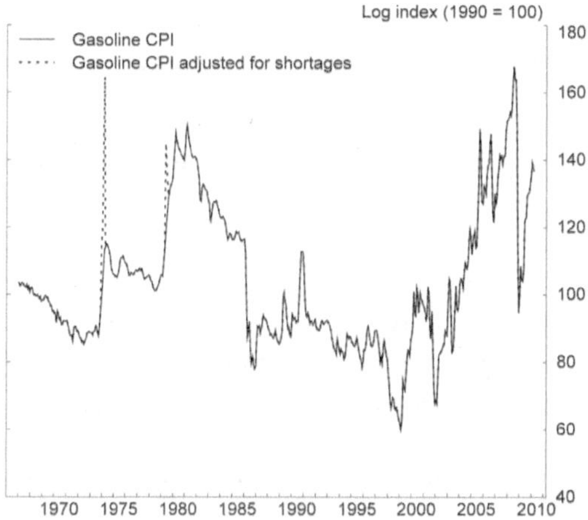

Fig. 2. Real gasoline prices, January 1967 through March 2010. Dashed line represents the CPI (consumer price index) for gasoline augmented with the shadow cost of waiting time in gas lines in 1973, 1974, and 1979 as estimated by Frech and Lee (1987). The log index is calculated as in figure 1.

1980s, the consumer sentiment variable hit similar peaks in both periods. A CNN opinion research poll conducted in June 2008 found that consumers were more concerned about long gas lines than about high prices (CNNMoney.com, June 10, 2008). This may explain why the run-up in

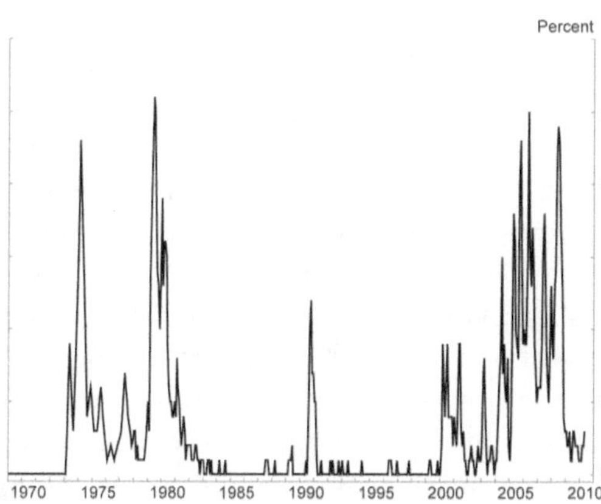

Fig. 3. Consumer sentiment toward gasoline, January 1970 through April 2010. Share of respondents to the Thomson Reuters and University of Michigan Survey of Consumer Sentiment who cite high gasoline prices or shortages of gasoline as reasons that car-buying conditions are poor. Gasoline price question was asked on a quarterly basis before January 1978, and the series was extrapolated to a monthly frequency by the authors.

gas prices in the 2000s, although bigger than the run-ups in earlier episodes, did not cause a larger effect on consumer sentiment.

D. *The Responses of Output, Consumption, and Prices to Oil Price Shocks*

Using the published measures of energy prices and the two variables that account for nonprice rationing in the 1970s, we now revisit the evidence used to suggest that aggregate activity has been responding less to energy price shocks in recent years than it used to in the past. The energy price measures we consider are as follows: (1) CPI-gas, (2) Hamilton's (2003, 2009) "net oil price increases," (3) CPI-gas that has been augmented with the time cost of rationing by queue, and (4) the measure of consumer attitudes toward gasoline prices and fuel shortages.[10] Our strategy is as follows: first, we show that the impulse-response functions from VARs estimated by Edelstein and Kilian (2009) and Blanchard and Galí (2010) do not change much if published gasoline prices are used in place of the authors' original energy price measures. Second, we show that the impulse-response functions based on gasoline price measures that account for the effects of shortages present a different story.

We begin by estimating a VAR that is similar to the one used by Blanchard and Galí (2010). The VAR system we estimate is

$$Y_t = A(L)Y_{t-1} + U_t. \qquad (1)$$

In the VAR estimated by Blanchard and Galí with quarterly data, Y_t includes the nominal price of oil, the CPI, the gross domestic product (GDP) deflator, nominal nonfarm compensation, real GDP, and nonfarm business hours. In other specifications, they also included the federal funds rate. In our version of their analysis, Y_t is built from monthly observations of the following variables (in order): (i) a selected version of one of the oil shock variables, (ii) the CPI, (iii) nominal wages of private production workers, (iv) industrial production, (v) civilian hours, and (vi) the federal funds rate. Function *A(L)* is a matrix of polynomials in the lag operator *L*, and *U* is a vector of disturbances. All variables except the sentiment measure and the federal funds rate are in logs. The shock to oil prices is identified using a standard Cholesky decomposition. We include a linear time trend and six lags of the variables. The data are monthly and span 1967:1–2009:12.

Blanchard and Galí (2010) compare samples that are split between 1983 and 1984, which is the typical split for studies of the Great Moderation.

Table 1
The Peak Effects of Oil Shocks on U.S. Variables

	Estimation Period				
	January 1967 to December 1985		January 1986 to December 2009		
	Peak Effect (1)	Month of Peak (2)	Peak Effect (3)	Month of Peak (4)	Ratio (3)/(1)
Nominal gas price:	1.000	3	1.000	2	
Industrial production	−.202	24	−.091	20	.45
Hours	−.099	26	−.035	32	.35
CPI	.184	19	.051	25	.28
Hamilton measure:	1.000	1	1.000	1	
Industrial production	−.005	24	−.002	11	.41
Hours	−.002	26	−.001	24	.39
CPI	.003	13	.001	2	.25
Gas price adjusted for the cost of shortages:	1.000	1	1.000	2	
Industrial production	−.072	25	−.091	20	1.27
Hours	−.038	27	−.035	32	.92
CPI	.084	20	.051	2	.61
Consumer sentiment about gas:	1.000	3	1.000	1	
Industrial production	−.002	27	−.003	31	1.67
Hours	−.001	27	−.002	37	1.97
CPI	.002	15	.001	2	.30

Note: Impulse responses are based on vector autoregressions (VARs) with monthly data. The variables include (1) a selected oil price measure, (2) industrial production, (3) hours, (4) the headline consumer price index (CPI), (5) nominal wages, and (6) the federal funds rate. The VARs included six lags and a linear time trend. Shocks to oil prices are defined using a standard Cholesky decomposition with oil ordered first. The oil shocks are standardized to be the same size in each sample period. The standard deviations for the shocks to each oil price measure are as follows: the nominal gas price shock is .013 in the early period and .038 in the late period. The shock to the Hamilton measure is .797 in the early period and 1.751 in the late period. The shock to the gas price adjusted for the cost of shortages is .045 in the early period and .038 in the late period. The shock to gasoline sentiment is 1.364 in the early period and 2.028 in the late period.

Edelstein and Kilian (2009) study samples split between 1987 and 1988. We choose a split between 1985 and 1986, as this date is between the dates used by these authors, and it also coincides with the rather dramatic change in the nature of the oil market that occurred in 1986.

We summarize the results in table 1. As an alternative to showing dozens of impulse-response functions from various permutations of oil price measures and estimation periods, table 1 shows the peak response of key macro variables to a shock in each oil price indicator in each period.

The shock has been normalized so that the size of the increase at its peak is equal to one in both periods. It is important to note, however, that the standard deviations of the (nonnormalized) shocks to nominal gas prices and to Hamilton's net price gain measure are more than twice as high in the second period as in the first period. In contrast, the standard deviation of the shocks to the shortage-adjusted gas price is roughly constant across the periods, whereas the standard deviation of the shocks to the measure of consumer sentiment toward gasoline is about 50% higher in the second period.

The key comparison in table 1 is the ratio in the last column. For a given shock in the gas cost variable, it shows the ratio of the peak response of the other variables in the second period to the peak response in the first period. The results for both the standard nominal gas price measure and Hamilton's nonlinear measure show that the responses of both industrial production and hours are less than half as large in the second period as in the first period. The response of inflation appears to have declined by an even larger proportion than did the real variables. In contrast, when either the real index of gas prices adjusted for the cost of shortages or the measure of consumer sentiment about gas prices/shortages is used as the oil price indicator, the peak response of industrial production becomes greater in the second period than in the first period. For hours, the response remains slightly less in the second period than in the first period if we use as the oil price indicator the shortage-adjusted gas price index, but it becomes greater if we use the measure of consumer sentiment.[11] However, the response of inflation is still lower in the second period than in the first period, even if the shortage-adjusted gas price index or the gasoline sentiment measure is used as the oil price indicator.[12]

To examine more formally the relationship between consumer sentiment toward gasoline and the various gasoline price measures, we estimate a number of bivariate VARs and compare the relationship in the early and the late periods. We find that shocks to the published CPI for gasoline appear to have an effect on sentiment in the early period that is about twice as large as the effect in the late period. In contrast, shocks to the shortage-adjusted gasoline price index have about the same peak effect on sentiment in each period. This evidence suggests that the presence of shortages in the early period is the key difference between shocks to gasoline sentiment and shocks to the published CPI for gasoline.

Edelstein and Kilian (2009) find that much of the decline in aggregate activity (or aggregate consumption, more specifically) that follows a jump in oil prices comes through demand for motor vehicles. They also show that this channel has weakened over time, thereby reducing the effect of oil shocks on aggregate activity. Because this result is even more likely to have been affected by the presence of market distortions in the 1970s, we also reestimate a VAR similar to the Edelstein and Kilian (2009) model, using our shortage-adjusted measures for the true cost of gasoline.

We estimate a trivariate VAR, in which Y_t is defined by (i) one of the oil cost indicators, (ii) the log of real total consumption excluding motor vehicles, and (iii) the log of real consumption of motor vehicles. In the first set of results, we use as an energy price indicator the Edelstein and Kilian (2009) measure of the purchasing power lost to increases in retail energy prices: this measure scales the changes in real energy prices by the share of energy in consumption expenditures.[13] In the second set of results, we use as an oil cost indicator the consumer sentiment toward gasoline. In each set of results, we estimate the VAR in two sample periods: 1967:1–1985:12 and 1986:1–2009:12. We normalize each shock so that the peak responses of the shock variable are equal to one in each sample period.

Figure 4 shows the estimates, with filled circles indicating when the estimated response is more than 2 SD from zero and open circles indicating when the response is between 1 and 2 SD from zero. The panels to the left show responses that use the Edelstein and Kilian purchasing-power series as an oil cost indicator, and the responses to the shocks are largely consistent with those originally reported by Edelstein and Kilian. Specifically, the response of total consumption falls less sharply in the second sample period than in the first sample period, although the responses are not statistically significant in either period. To the degree that the response has changed, the bottom-left panel shows that most of the change comes from the consumption of motor vehicles: the response in the consumption of motor vehicles is much less in the second period (*dashed line*) than in the first period (*solid line*).

The right panels in figure 4 show the impulse responses obtained when the consumer sentiment toward gasoline serves as the oil cost indicator. Several comparisons here stand out. First, the responses of consumption to these shocks have not diminished between the early and the late periods; this holds true for the consumption of motor vehicles and the consumption of all other goods and services. Moreover, the responses in the second period appear to be more persistent than those in the first period. Second, the responses based on these shocks are statistically significant, an indication that real activity is more closely related to consumer

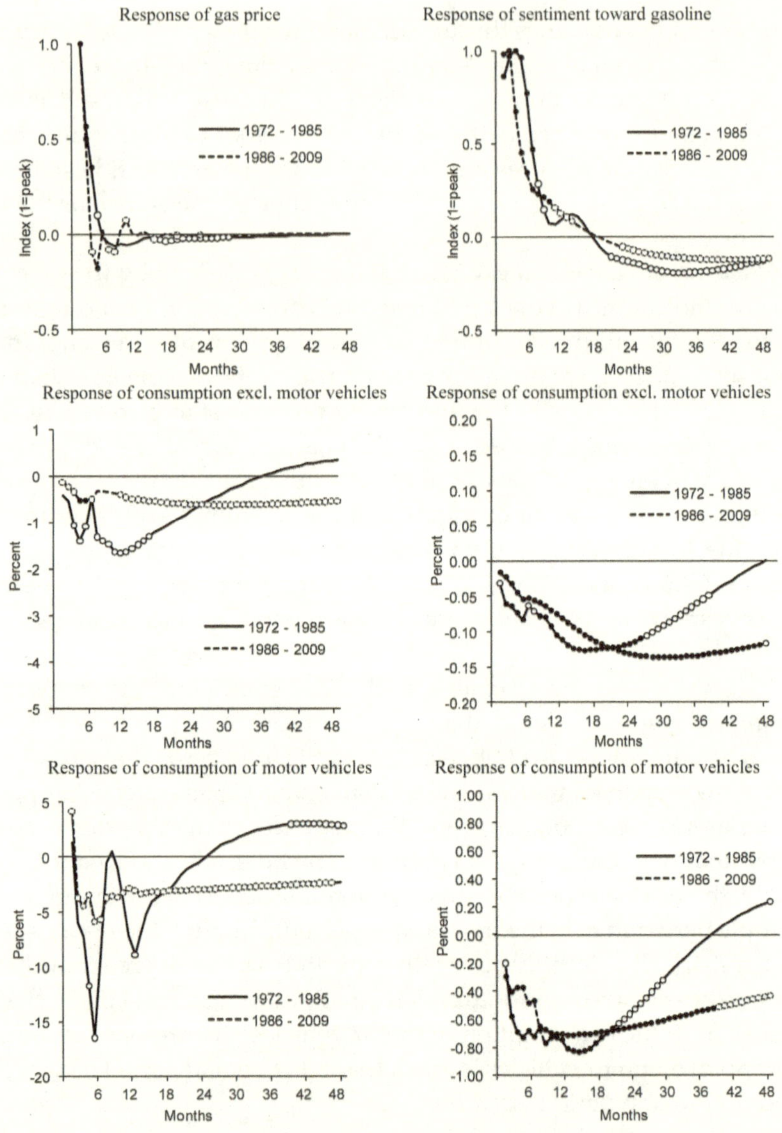

Fig. 4. Responses of consumption to two gasoline shocks: shock to the gas price (*left*) and shock to sentiment toward gasoline (*right*). Filled circles indicate periods in which the responses are more than 2 SD from zero, and open circles indicate periods in which the responses are between 1 and 2 SD from zero.

perceptions of the price of gasoline and its availability than it is to published fuel prices. And third, the decline in consumption of motor vehicles after a gasoline price sentiment shock is many times larger than the response of consumption excluding motor vehicles.[14]

For comparison, we also estimated the impulse response on the basis of other measures of energy prices. Using the Hamilton measure of net oil price increases, the responses show a significant muting between the early and the late samples. If we use the shortage-adjusted measure of gasoline prices, we find results qualitatively similar to those obtained using consumer sentiment toward gasoline as the oil cost indicator. The responses to oil shocks are only slightly smaller in the second period than in the first period; the peak impact on total consumption is 0.9 in the second period relative to the first and on motor vehicle consumption is 0.8.

To summarize, when oil price shocks are measured as the shocks to the published price index for gasoline, the Hamilton net increase in oil prices, or the Edelstein and Kilian purchasing-power measure, we confirm the results from the literature that oil shocks have much less of an impact on the economy after 1985 than they did up until 1985. In contrast, when we measure oil shocks as either the shocks to the price of gasoline adjusted for the cost of shortages or the shocks to consumer sentiment toward gasoline, we find that the impact of these shocks on real activity has either diminished only slightly or become larger in the later period. Finally, all measures of energy price shocks produce results that suggest the motor vehicle industry is a key part of the transmission mechanism between oil shocks and real activity. Thus, the remainder of the paper presents evidence that, although the motor vehicle industry has changed in many ways over the past 40 years, this sector continues to act as an important propagation mechanism between oil price shocks and real activity.

III. The Contribution of the Motor Vehicle Sector to the U.S. Economy

The contraction in the size of the Detroit three automakers in recent decades often leaves the impression that the contribution of the auto industry to the U.S. economy has declined significantly. In this section, we present some measures of the contribution of the entire domestic motor vehicle industry (the portion operated by the Detroit firms as well as the portion operated by other firms) to the U.S. economy and to the business cycle.

Figure 5 shows two measures of the contribution of motor vehicle output to U.S. GDP: Panel *A* shows the quarterly values of a statistic commonly referred to as "gross motor vehicle output," and panel *B* shows annual estimates of the domestic value added of motor vehicle

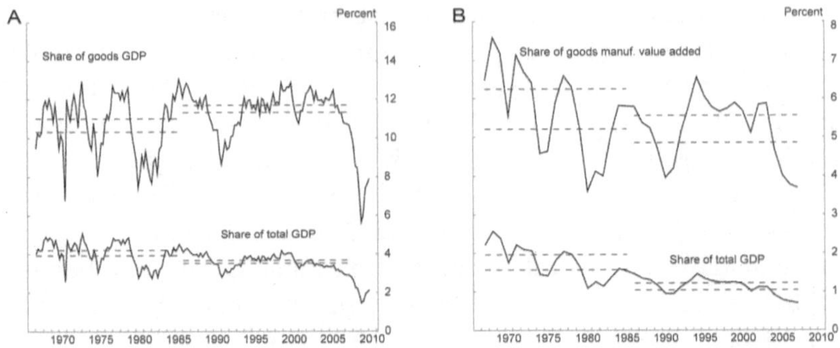

Fig. 5. Motor vehicle industry in the U.S. economy. *A*, Output, 1967:1–2009:4; *B*, manufacturing value added, 1967–2007. Dashed lines represent 95% confidence intervals for the sample means in two periods: 1967–85 and 1986–2007. Expenditure shares are based on nominal data. For value added, motor vehicles and parts are defined on a North American Industrial Classification System basis from 1977 through 2007; earlier periods are plotted as best changes from the standard industrial classification definition. Goods manufacturing includes agriculture, forestry, fishing, and hunting; mining; construction; and manufacturing.

and parts manufacturing, a narrower view of the industry's contribution to GDP.[15] The lower line in each of these panels displays each measure of output as a share of total GDP, and the upper line plots these measures as a share of either goods GDP (for gross motor vehicle output) or total value added from goods manufacturing (for motor vehicle and parts manufacturing value added). Shares are calculated from nominal expenditures data reported in the NIPAs. The dashed lines in the figure represent the 95% confidence interval for the sample mean of each line in two sample periods: 1967–85 and 1986–2007 (before the financial crisis had affected vehicle sales).

Two features in figure 5 are worth noting: first, motor vehicle output drops abruptly in recessions, and many of these recessions followed large increases in gasoline prices. As shown in table 2, the motor vehicle sector alone accounts for between 14% and 22% of the variance of the quarterly changes in real GDP, depending on the time period. Even after the Great Moderation, these figures continue to exceed the moderate size of the motor vehicle sector.

The second feature of the graph that is worth noting is that the size of the motor vehicle industry as a share of the U.S. economy does not show a downward trend that is as striking as one might expect. As a share of total GDP (fig. 5*A*, *bottom line*), motor vehicles represented about 4% of the U.S. economy between 1967 and 1985, and that figure declined to

Table 2
Fluctuations in Real Gross Domestic Product (GDP)

	Share of GDP (%)	SD (% Quarterly Change, Annual Rate)	Share of GDP Volatility (%)
Goods and services:			
1967–85	100	4.3	100
1986–2007	100	2.1	100
1986–2009:3	100	2.5	100
Goods:			
1967–85	37	9.2	54
1986–2007	30	5.0	51
1986–2009:3	30	5.6	50
Motor vehicles:			
1967–85	4.0	38.1	22
1986–2007	3.5	19.2	14
1986–2009:3	3.3	24.9	16

Note: Data are from the National Income and Product Accounts. Share of GDP volatility attributable to each component is calculated as 100 less the variance of growth contribution of GDP, excluding each component relative to the variance of total GDP. Figures for the early period exclude 1970:4, when a long strike severely reduced motor vehicle output and sales.

3.5% between 1986 and 2007. As a share of the goods-producing sectors of the U.S. economy, however, motor vehicle output actually increased between the two periods, from about 10.5% in the early sample to about 11.5% in the more recent sample. Manufacturing value added gives a similar picture: motor vehicle and parts manufacturers accounted for 5.7% of U.S. manufacturing value added in the 1970s and early 1980s, and this share slipped to 5.2% in the more recent period. However, as shown by the dashed lines, the decline between the two periods is not very pronounced relative to its high volatility.[16]

All told, the motor vehicle sector has been a modest but relatively stable share of the goods-producing sector over the past 40 years, and the declines that have occurred in its contribution to total GDP mostly reflect an increase in the size of the services sector. Most important, the auto industry continues to induce swings in aggregate activity that far exceed its modest size.

IV. Oil Shocks and the Demand for Motor Vehicles

We now describe theories of how gasoline prices affect vehicle demand and then present evidence in some detailed auto industry data that consumers adjust their vehicle-buying patterns in response to changes in gasoline prices. In addition, we show that this behavior has not changed much over the past 40 years.

A rather large literature has developed—much of it in the late 1970s—to analyze how households respond to changes in gasoline prices by making adjustments to their vehicle stock and to their driving behavior (e.g., Dahl 1979).[17] More recently, Wei (2009) casts the vehicle-purchasing decision in a general equilibrium framework, in which households invest in transportation capital with a particular level of fuel efficiency and then combine it with gasoline to produce the good that ultimately enters their utility functions—personal vehicle travel. Because consumers are forward looking, changes in gasoline prices lead to dynamic effects on the vehicle stock and average fuel efficiency.

After a gasoline price shock, households respond in the short run mostly by reducing travel, although estimates from the literature suggest the response in the short run is quite low (e.g., Hughes, Knittel, and Sperling 2006). Over long horizons, households adjust their vehicle technology and reduce further their consumption of gasoline. Using her DSGE model calibrated to U.S. fuel and vehicle consumption data, Wei (2009) finds that vehicle purchases and total miles traveled decline after a permanent shock to gasoline prices, although the equilibrium fuel efficiency of new vehicles increases.

These theories suggest that permanent increases in gasoline prices lead households to reduce vehicle travel in the short run and then to replace their vehicle stock in the long run. In the very long run, gasoline prices can also affect where households choose to live and work.

To see the effects of these decisions on vehicle travel over the past 40 years, figure 6 plots total vehicle miles traveled per household in the United States between 1970 and 2009. Two features in the figure are noteworthy. First, households nowadays consume a significantly larger amount of travel than they did in the early 1970s: the average household drove approximately 1,500 miles per month in 1970, and that figure has increased 50%, to almost 2,200 miles per month during 2000–2007. Second, households do cut back on travel when gasoline prices increase, although part of the decline in travel likely also reflects the deterioration in the broader economy that also occurs at these times.

While households now drive more each month than they did in the early 1970s, they do so in vehicles that are, on average, more fuel efficient. Figure 7 shows data from the U.S. Department of Transportation on the average fuel efficiency of the registered stocks of cars and light trucks (which include sport-utility vehicles [SUVs] and vans). As seen in the plot, the average fuel economy for each type of vehicle has increased over the sample, although much of the gains occurred in the 1980s, after the United States introduced Corporate Average Fuel Economy standards

Fig. 6. Vehicle distance traveled per household, January 1970 to October 2009. Data on vehicle miles are from "Traffic Volume Trends," Office of Highway Policy Information in the Department of Transportation. Data on the number of households in the United States are from the U.S. Census Bureau. Data were smoothed with a 12-month moving average.

that were met by reducing the average weight of cars and introducing some technological improvements to engine design.

One feature of figure 7 that receives lots of attention is the marked slowdown (or near halt) in the rate of improvement for average fuel economy that occurred in the 1990s. This was an era of relatively cheap

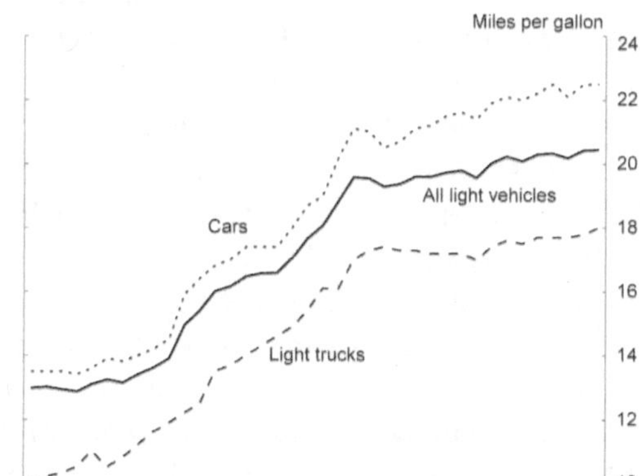

Fig. 7. Average fuel economy for the U.S. light vehicle stock, December 1970 to December 2009. Data are from the U.S. Department of Energy (2009). Data points for light trucks for 2003 and 2004 were interpolated. Light vehicles include cars and light trucks.

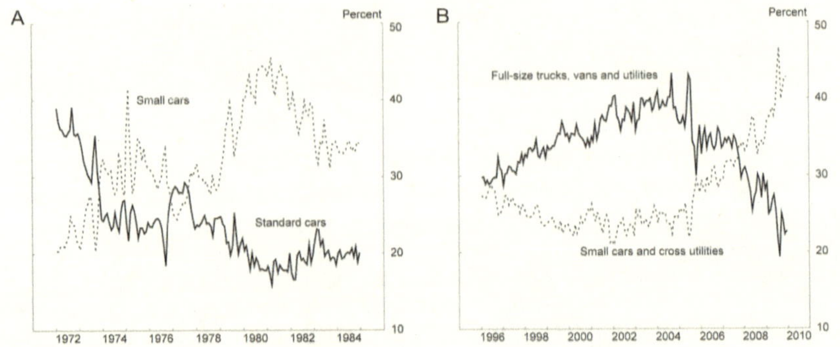

Fig. 8. Domestic sales shares for selected vehicle segments, percentage of domestic vehicles sold. *A*, January 1972 through December 1984; *B*, January 1996 through November 2009. Shares are calculated from U.S. sales of domestic light vehicles, which are defined as those produced in North America. The category "small cars" includes compact and subcompact cars; "standard cars" includes full-size and luxury cars. Cross-utility vehicles are small utility vehicles assembled on car chassis.

gasoline, and, likely as a result, demand shifted away from cars and toward larger SUVs.[18] Studies that more carefully take into account vehicle size and engine horsepower, such as Knittel (2009), conclude that the technological frontier of fuel-economy/vehicle-weight/engine-power possibilities continued to expand over this period, but these improvements are obscured in aggregate data by the shift in sales across vehicle size classes.

Shifts in vehicle demand across vehicle size classes often occur when gasoline prices move dramatically, a stylized fact that was discussed by Bresnahan and Ramey (1993). To see evidence of this, figure 8 shows the domestic market shares of vehicles of various sizes.[19] Figure 8*A* shows the key market shares in the 1970s and early 1980s. The domestic market share for standard-size cars fell noticeably in 1973 and did not stabilize until almost 2 years later.[20] When the second oil price shocks hit in 1979, this market share fell even further. The market share of small cars moved in the opposite direction on both occasions.

Figure 8*B* shows market shares of key vehicle segments in the 2000s. The patterns in market shares since 2000 have been similar to those observed in the earlier episodes of sharp gas price increases, although the scope of the variety of products available has grown considerably since the 1970s. The market share of full-size pickups, utility vehicles, and vans fell more than 15 percentage points between its peak in 2004 and early 2009. Small cars and the new cross-utility vehicle segment picked up most of this market share.[21]

V. The Response of Motor Vehicle Production

Shocks that affect motor vehicle sales often lead to changes in the rate of production that are quite abrupt, and the high level of volatility in motor vehicle production has been studied extensively in the literature on inventories and production scheduling. It is well understood how changes in aggregate vehicle demand can lead to reductions in production. In this section, we show how changes in the composition of demand, such as those induced by gas price increases, can lead to further declines in output.

We begin by presenting an inventory model in which segment shifts lead to capacity mismatches and thereby reduce output. We then study this channel, using detailed auto industry data by vehicle size class. We find that segment shifts are an important channel through which oil shocks affect the U.S. motor vehicle industry and that the importance of this channel has not declined much over time.

A. *Segment Shifts and the Constraints on Capacity*

Bresnahan and Ramey (1993) speculated that a shift in demand from one vehicle segment to another, with no decline in overall demand, can lead to a decrease in production and capacity utilization. They also argued that the variance of days' supply (i.e., the inventory-sales ratio) across segments reflects mismatches between capacity and demand for vehicles in some segments.

In order to formalize this hypothesis, we consider a simple model of a profit-maximizing monopolist who sells cars to two segments of demand. For each segment *i*, the monopolist chooses the price, P_t, and schedules production using regular time hours, RH_t, and overtime hours, OH_t. These choices determine expected sales, S_t, and expected end-of-period inventories, I_t. The firm maximizes the expected present discounted value of profits, given as

$$\Pi_0 = E_0 \sum_{t=0}^{\infty} \beta^t (P_{1t} S_{1t} + P_{2t} S_{2t} - \mathrm{Cost}_t). \tag{2}$$

The costs of production and inventory holding are given by

$$\begin{aligned} \mathrm{Cost}_t &= \gamma \mathrm{RH}_{1t} + \gamma \mathrm{RH}_{2t} + \gamma\omega \mathrm{OH}_{1t} + \gamma\omega \mathrm{OH}_{2t} \\ &\quad + \frac{1}{2}\alpha_1 (I_{1t-1} - \phi S_{1t})^2 + \frac{1}{2}\alpha_2 (I_{2t-1} - \phi S_{2t})^2. \end{aligned} \tag{3}$$

Inventory stocks evolve according to

$$I_{it} = I_{it-1} + \mathrm{RH}_{it} + \mathrm{OH}_{it} - S_{it}, \quad i = 1, 2, \tag{4}$$

and the use of regular time hours is limited by the capacity constraints:

$$\mathrm{RH}_{it} \leq K, \quad i = 1, 2. \tag{5}$$

The parameters of the model satisfy the following restrictions: $0 < \beta < 1$; $\gamma > 0$; $\omega > 1$; α_i, $\phi_i > 0$; $K > 0$.

Relative to the familiar linear-quadratic production-smoothing model, the inventory-holding costs in equation (3) are the same, but the marginal costs of production are somewhat more complicated: marginal costs in this model are flat when the monopolist uses regular time hours but rise when the firm must increase its workweek of capital and use overtime hours or a second shift. This assumption induces a key asymmetry in marginal costs.

Finally, the sales processes for segments 1 and 2 are described by the following equations:

$$S_{1t} = \theta_A - \theta_B P_{1t} + u_t^{\mathrm{seg}} + u_t^{\mathrm{agg}}, \tag{6}$$

$$S_{2t} = \theta_A - \theta_B P_{2t} - u_t^{\mathrm{seg}} + u_t^{\mathrm{agg}}. \tag{7}$$

There are two types of demand shifts in these sales equations: the first, u_t^{seg}, is a variable that shifts demand away from one segment and toward the other, while the second, u_t^{agg}, is a variable that shifts the demand curves for all types of vehicles in the same direction. We assume that each of these shift variables follows an AR(1) process as shown in the following equations:

$$u_t^{\mathrm{seg}} = \rho u_{t-1}^{\mathrm{seg}} + \varepsilon_t, \tag{8}$$

$$u_t^{\mathrm{agg}} = \rho u_t^{\mathrm{agg}} + \eta_t. \tag{9}$$

The autocorrelation parameter ρ lies between 0 and 1, and the shocks ε and η are white noise.

An increase in gasoline prices affects vehicle sales through both u_t^{agg} and u_t^{seg}. To study the effects of the second type of shock—the shift in sales between segments—we simulate the model and evaluate the optimal paths of key choice variables. To calibrate the simulation, β and ϕ_i are set to match the averages observed in the data for interest rates and days' supply for light vehicles. We choose values for K, θ_A, θ_B, and γ to generate a price elasticity of demand of -1.5 at the steady-state level of output, a figure that is in the range of empirical estimates for total vehicle demand.[22] Finally, we set α_i and ω so that the premium on overtime hours or second-shift hours is 10%.[23] The simulation considers shocks that shift the intercept of the demand curve by 10%, with $\rho = 0.75$.[24]

Because plants face the same cost function in each segment, the effects of an aggregate shock on inventories and production are the same in each segment. And, because the inventory-sales ratios change by equal amounts in each segment, the cross-section variance of the days' supply remains zero. This is not the case for shocks that shift demand between segments, a scenario that is shown in figure 9. If demand for segment 1 cars shifts up and demand for segment 2 cars shifts down by an equal amount, total production falls because the rise in output in segment 1 does not fully offset the fall in output in segment 2. The asymmetric response of production reflects the increase in marginal costs that occurs at the capacity constraint. Mirroring this pattern, the price of vehicles in segment 1 rises by an amount that is different from the decline in the price of vehicles in segment 2. All told, segment shifts reduce total production, sales, and capacity utilization, and they drive up the variance of days' supply across vehicle segments.

Some of these results depend critically on the increase in marginal cost that occurs when production exceeds the level of capacity.[25] If costs were instead quadratic, as is assumed in the standard production-smoothing model, then marginal costs would be linear, capacity utilization would have no effect on production costs, and segment shifts would not reduce total production.[26] The variance of days' supply would still increase in the case of quadratic costs, but the asymmetric response of production to positive and negative demand shocks requires the marginal cost function to exhibit some curvature.

B. *Evidence of Capacity Constraints and Segment Shifts in the Auto Industry*

To see the effects of segment shifts in the detailed auto industry data, figure 10 plots day's supply for vehicles in selected size classes in the early and the late periods. In the earlier period, days' supply of standard cars grew to uncomfortably high levels at the time of both oil shocks, and days' supply for small cars moved down. Similarly, in the later period,

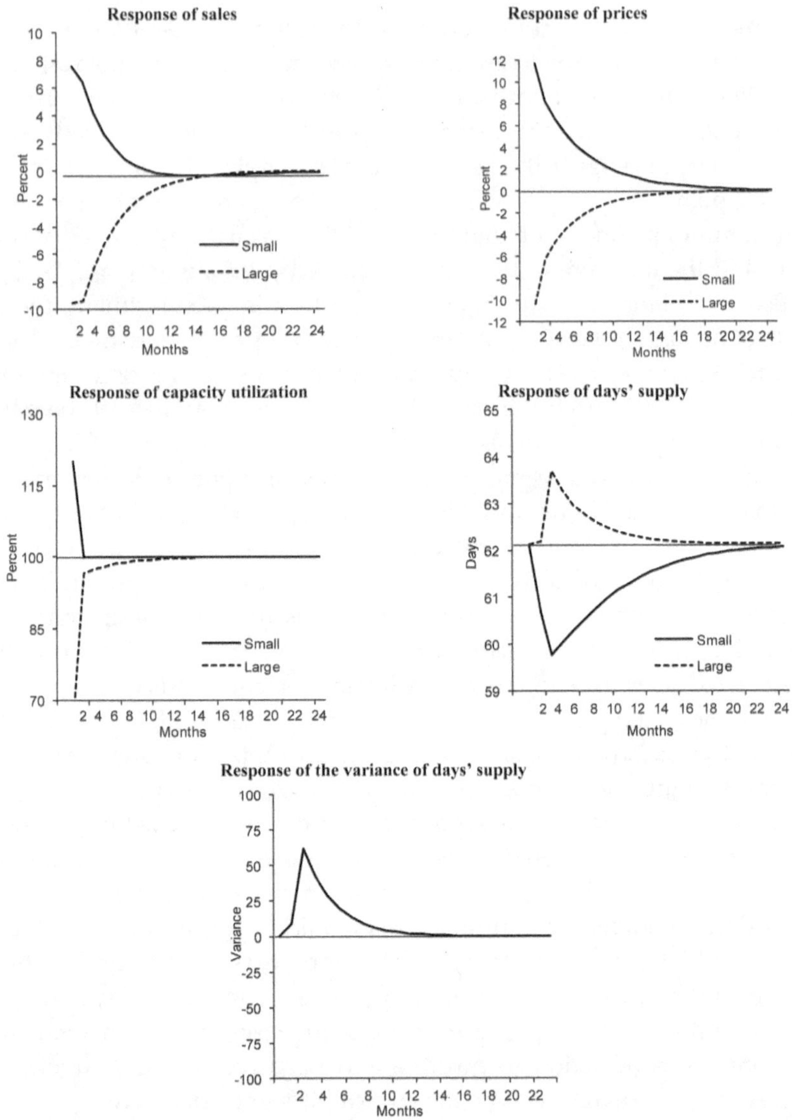

Fig. 9. Responses to a segment-shifting shock to sales. Impulse responses from the production model presented in equations (2)–(9) are shown.

days' supply for full-size trucks, vans, and utility vehicles climbed to critically high levels between 2000 and 2008, while days' supply for small cars and cross-utility vehicles moved down between 1998 and 2000 before edging back up in 2002. As the shift in demand between segments accelerated again at the end of 2004, days' supply for small vehicles

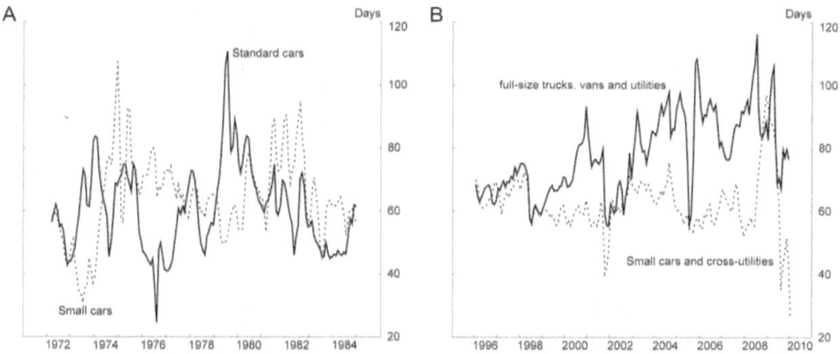

Fig. 10. Domestic days' supply of selected vehicle segments. *A*, January 1972 through December 1984; *B*, January 1996 through November 2009. Days' supply is calculated with end-of-month inventories and the 3-month moving average of sales. Inventories include finished vehicles held at dealerships and assembly plants and vehicles in transit. Domestic vehicles refer to vehicles produced in North America. "Small cars" include compact and subcompact cars, and "standard cars" include full-size and luxury cars. Cross-utility vehicles are small utility vehicles assembled on car chassis.

receded, and several of the models in these segments were reported to be in short supply.[27] The onset of the financial crisis in the second half of 2008 appears to have been a common shock that pushed up days' supply for almost all vehicle segments.

To measure these supply imbalances on a more general scale, we calculate the variance of days' supply across size categories, V^{DS}, that was described earlier. The formula is

$$V_t^{\mathrm{DS}} = \sum_{i=1}^{11} \frac{I_t^i}{I_t^A}(\mathrm{DS}_t^i - \mathrm{DS}_t^A)^2, \quad i = 1, 2, \ldots, 11, \tag{10}$$

where I_t^i denotes inventories on hand in vehicle segment i at the end of period t, I_t^A is the aggregate inventory stock, DS_t^i is days' supply for each segment, DS_t^A denotes aggregate days' supply, and i ranges from 1 to 11, covering five car segments (subcompact, compact, intermediate, full size, and luxury) and six truck segments (compact pickups, full-size pickups, small vans, large vans, cross-utility vehicles, and full-size utility vehicles). An increase the variance of days' supply across segments indicates that the imbalance between the composition of capacity and the composition of demand has become worse.[28]

The variance of days' supply is plotted in figure 11 from January 1972 to December 2009. Large spikes in the variance correspond quite closely with the increases in fuel prices discussed earlier. Also, the severity of

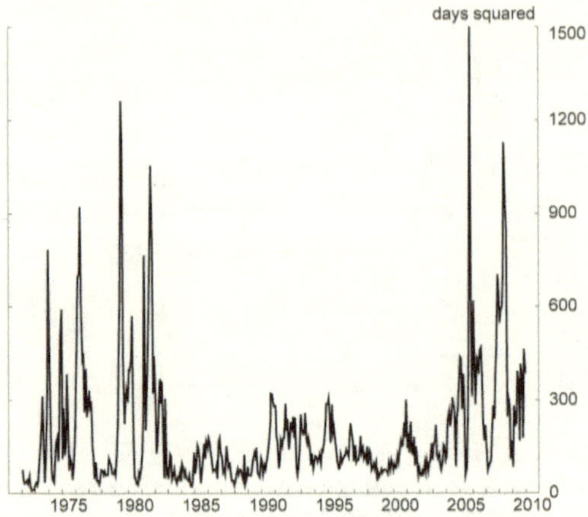

Fig. 11. Variance of domestic days' supply across vehicle segments, January 1972 through December 2009. Domestic days' supply is calculated from U.S. inventories and sales of vehicles assembled in North America. Variance is calculated across five car segments (subcompact, compact, intermediate, full size, and luxury) and six light truck segments (compact vans, full-size vans, compact pickups, full-size pickups, cross-utility vehicles, and standard utility vehicles).

some of the supply-demand imbalances that occurred after 2002 appear even greater than the magnitudes observed in the early 1980s.

To investigate the empirical relationship between these spikes in the variance of days' supply, the cost of gasoline, and movements in capacity utilization, we estimate a VAR in which Y_t includes four variables: (i) consumer sentiment about gasoline prices or shortages, (ii) aggregate days' supply for domestic vehicles, (iii) the variance of days supply across segments (defined in eq. [10]), and (iv) capacity utilization for light motor vehicle assembly.[29] The VAR also includes six lags and a linear time trend.

Oil shocks in the VAR play two roles: first, oil shocks reduce aggregate demand and dampen sales for all types of vehicles. In the production model described earlier, this role resembles the aggregate shock that drives up days' supply for the entire industry and reduces capacity utilization for all segments. Second, high gas prices lead to segment shifts in demand away from large vehicles and toward small vehicles. This role leads to mismatches in capacity and drives up the variance of days' supply across vehicle segments. Our production model also shows how shocks in this role can reduce capacity utilization when capacity constraints push up marginal costs for the products in demand.

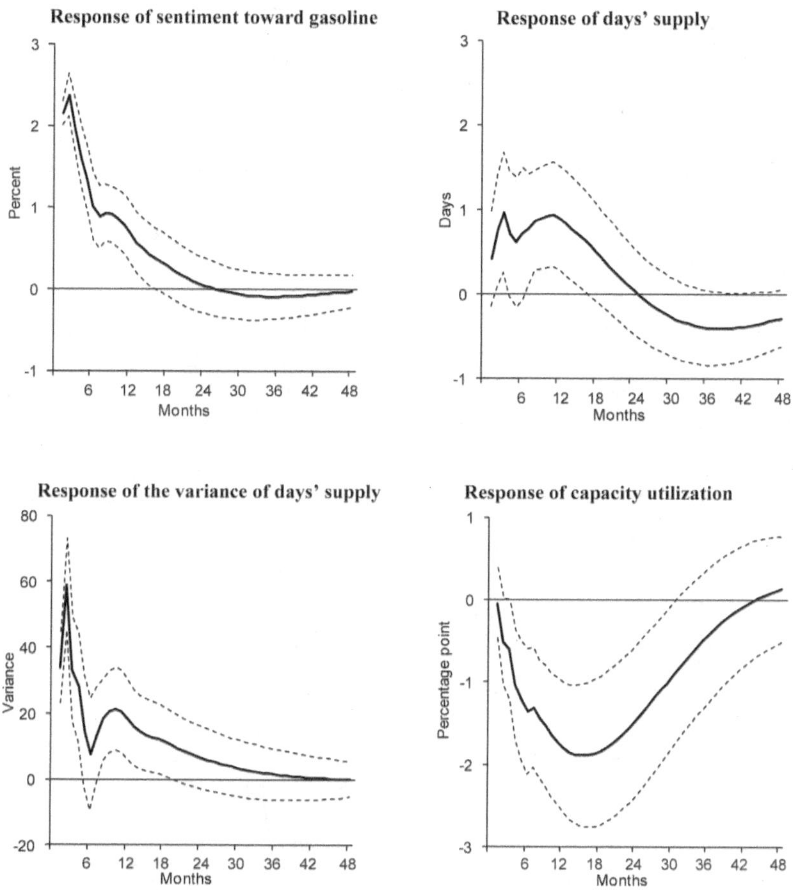

Fig. 12. Responses to a shock to consumer sentiment toward gasoline: combined sample, 1972–2009. Dashed lines enclose 95% confidence intervals.

Figure 12 shows the responses of the variables in Y_t to a shock to the measure of consumer sentiment toward gasoline (meaning a higher percentage of consumers were worried about high gas prices), which is ordered first in the VAR. The VAR is estimated over the full sample from January 1972 to March 2009. As seen in the figure, both the level and variance of days' supply increase after a sentiment shock, indicating that shocks to gasoline sentiment affect demand both as an aggregate shock and as a segment-shifting shock. According to the last panel, capacity utilization also falls significantly.

Has the relationship between these variables changed over time? To answer this question, we compare the impulse-response functions from

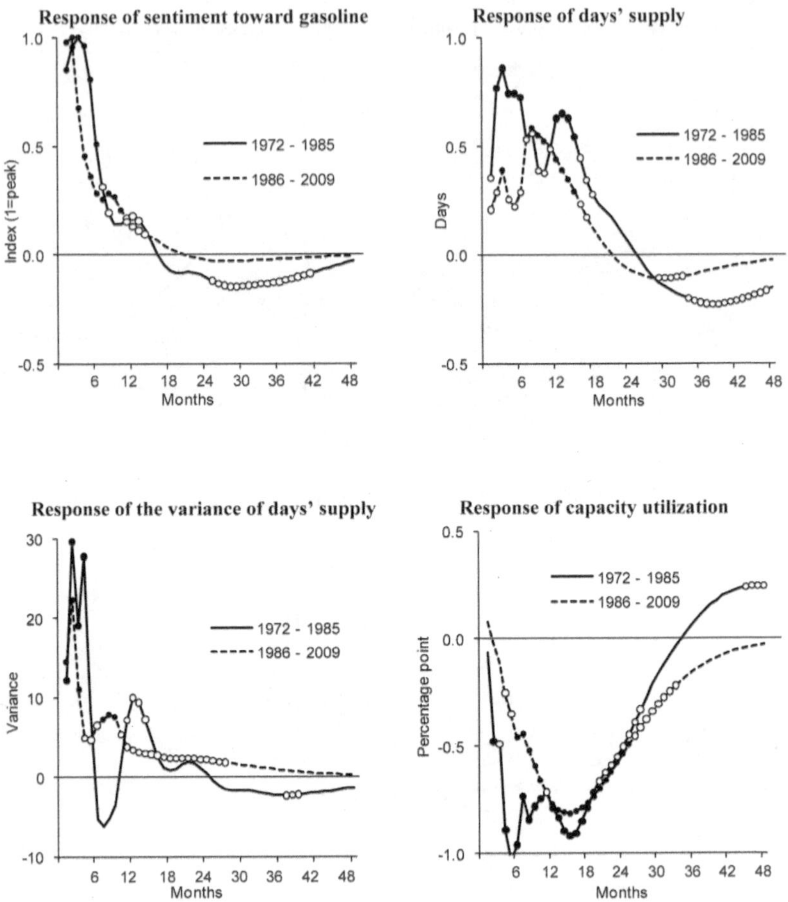

Fig. 13. Responses to a shock to consumer sentiment toward gasoline: split samples, 1972–85 and 1986–2009. Filled circles indicate periods in which the responses are more than 2 SD from zero, and open circles indicate periods in which the responses are between 1 and 2 SD from zero.

VARs estimated separately for 1972–85 and 1986–2009 and plot the results in figure 13. The shocks to consumer sentiment toward gasoline have been normalized to reach a peak of 1.0 in both periods. As seen in the figure, the peak responses of both the level and the variance of days' supply are about 30% larger in the early period than in the later period. The response of capacity utilization, however, is about the same in both periods.

Finally, using the VAR estimates and a set of counterfactual experiments, we parse the response of capacity utilization to oil shocks into portions that reflect the aggregate demand channel and the segment-shifts channel. In one experiment, we plot the response of utilization to a gasoline sentiment shock after we have shut down the segment-shifts channel by replacing the estimated coefficients of the days' supply equation in the VAR with zeros. The difference between the baseline response and this counterfactual response reveals the contribution of the aggregate demand channel to the transmission of gasoline shocks to capacity utilization. In a second experiment, we shut down the segment-shifts channel by setting the coefficients of the variance of days' supply equation to zero. The third experiment shuts down both channels.

Figure 14 shows the results of the each experiment; the solid lines represent the baseline response of capacity utilization to a gasoline sentiment shock, and the dashed lines represent one of the counterfactual responses. In the first panel, the counterfactual response is only half as large as the baseline response, a comparison that suggests the contraction

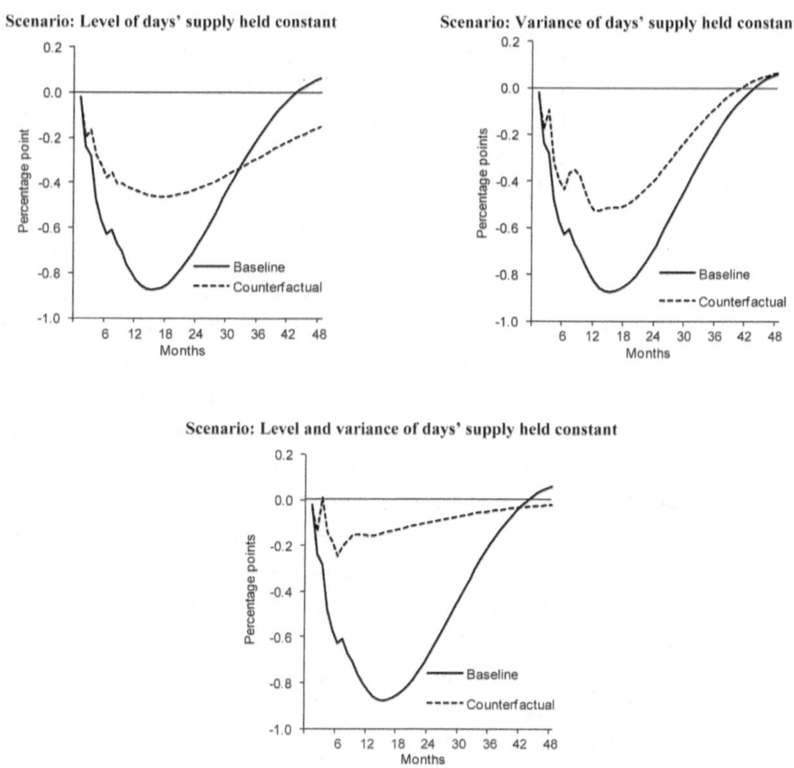

Fig. 14. Response of capacity utilization to shocks to consumer sentiment toward gasoline

in demand for all vehicles plays an important role in transmitting oil shocks to motor vehicle production. The counterfactual response in the second panel is also only about half as large when the segment-shifts channel is shutdown, indicating that this channel is also important. The counterfactual response in the third panel remains very close to zero, suggesting that omitted channels are not too important.

The counterfactual exercises indicate that the level and variance of days' supply channels are about equally important in transmitting oil shocks to motor vehicle output. These results imply that oil shocks have both aggregate effects and segment-shift effects. Moreover, the relationship between these variables appears to have been stable over time.

VI. Conclusions

This paper has studied the impact of oil shocks on the U.S. economy and its motor vehicle industry and has examined whether these relationships have changed over time. We have found that, once the costs of queuing are added to the prices paid for gasoline during the gasoline shortages in the 1970s, real output in the United States has been as sensitive to oil price shocks since the mid-1980s as it had been in the 1970s and early 1980s. The effect on inflation, however, has diminished over time.

We have also found that the motor vehicle industry plays an important role in propagating oil price shocks to the rest of the U.S. economy and that, despite the many innovations in the ways motor vehicles are produced and consumed, the primary channels through which oil prices directly affect demand for motor vehicles have not weakened much over time. Specifically, the abrupt shifts in demand across vehicle size classes that stem from oil shocks have been as disruptive to the supply-demand relationship in the motor vehicle industry since the mid-1980s as they were in the 1970s and early 1980s.

Our results may affect the debate over which changes in the U.S. economy have led to the decline in GDP volatility since the mid-1980s, or the Great Moderation. If the relationship between oil shocks and real output had, in fact, become weaker since the mid-1980s, then this stylized fact could have bolstered arguments that structural change had reduced the sensitivity of output to these types of shocks. Our results, to the contrary, suggest that this particular relationship has been stable over time. The diminished impact of oil shocks on inflation, however, may support the theory that monetary policy has played a role in reducing volatility. Finally, our results point to another change in government policy that may also have reduced the volatility of output since the 1970s: a decline in the propensity to use price controls.

Endnotes

The views expressed here are those of the authors and not those of the Board of Governors or the Federal Reserve System. Sam Ackerman provided excellent research assistance. We are grateful for comments from Daron Acemoglu, Jordi Galí, George Hall, James Hamilton, Chris Kurz, Ariel Pakes, and Garey Ramey, and we thank William Lee for sending us his papers. We also thank participants at the 2008 International Society for Inventory Research session, the NBER Twenty-fifth Annual Conference on Macroeconomics, and seminar participants at Statistics Canada and University of California, San Diego. Valerie Ramey gratefully acknowledges financial support from National Science Foundation grant SES-0617219 through the NBER.

1. See, e.g., Mork (1989), Hamilton (1996, 2003), Hooker (1996), and Barsky and Kilian (2002).

2. Blanchard and Galí (2010) use the price of West Texas intermediate oil, available from the St. Louis Federal Reserve (Economic Data—FRED, http://research.stlouisfed.org/fred2/). This series shares the same problems with the PPI measure that we will discuss below.

3. Barsky and Kilian (2002) extend it back to 1971, but we are worried about this extension, for reasons given below.

4. Also, Kilian (2010) highlights the importance of studying gas prices separately from crude oil prices.

5. Hamilton and Herrera (2004) questioned details of their specification. Bernanke, Gertler, and Watson (2004) responded, reestimating their model in a way that attempts to deal with this critique and finding results only slightly less strong than in their original paper.

6. See, e.g., the debate between Hamilton (2009) and Kilian and Vigfusson (2009).

7. For example, Frech and Lee describe inefficiencies in the allocation of gasoline across urban and rural markets. Similarly, Davis and Kilian (2009) show that the total inefficiency costs of price controls on residential natural gas in the United States was three times larger than was the estimate of the simple deadweight loss.

8. Frech and Lee's estimates are based on data from California only, so the question arises as to how California's shortages compared to the rest of the nation. According to the February 8, 1974, *Wall Street Journal*, there was no rationing in "New England north of Boston, much of the Midwest, Denver, Nevada, and Southern California. In Northern California, the word was okay on weekdays and in daylight, but otherwise watch out. There were long lines in Washington, D.C., and the Philadelphia area … and in New York and New Jersey, where things have been tough for quite a while now."

9. Other reasons consumers can give for this being a bad time for buying a car are (1) prices of cars are too high, (2) interest rates are too high, (3) cannot afford to buy, (4) uncertain future, and (5) poor selection or quality of cars.

10. The Hamilton measure is defined as the log change in the price index for gasoline relative to its previous 3-year high, if it is positive, or zero, if it is negative.

11. We do not show the response of nominal wages and the funds rate because their responses are not significantly different from zero, and the dynamic patterns swing from positive to negative in some cases.

12. The results are similar if we substitute the chained price deflator for personal consumption expenditures for the CPI.

13. We also considered a measure that scaled prices by the average fuel efficiency of the motor vehicle stock and the miles driven by households. The results were similar to those using the Edelstein and Kilian measure.

14. The relative magnitudes of the estimated responses imply that about 30% of the decline in total consumption that occurs 15 months after a gasoline price shock comes from the decline in motor vehicle consumption.

15. "Gross motor vehicle output" in the National Income and Product Accounts (NIPAs) is the retail value of motor vehicles sold to final consumers (households, businesses, and governments) and the wholesale value of vehicles invested in inventories. This series is adjusted for net exports of motor vehicles and has the advantage of capturing all of the value added from the production process as well as from the distribution of motor vehicles to final demand, including the wholesale and retail margins. This measure is not the same as "gross output of motor vehicles and parts" in the U.S. industry accounts, which is the sum of all sales and receipts in the industry, including sales of intermediate inputs to firms in other (or in the same) industries.

16. One additional measure of motor vehicle output that we examined (but do not report) is motor vehicle and parts output. This wider view of the industry is intended to help control for the value of imported intermediate inputs to motor vehicle production that have risen over time (see Kurz and Lengermann 2008; Klier and Rubenstein 2009). Using this adjusted measure, motor vehicle output was 12.5% of goods GDP in both the early and the late periods, and it declined from 4.75% of total GDP in the early period to 3.75% in the later period.

17. The Congressional Budget Office study from January 2008, "Effect of Gasoline Prices on Driving Behavior and Vehicle Markets," surveys much of the literature from the 1970s.

18. The average fuel efficiency of vehicles flowing into the stock each year (i.e., new sales) actually decreased during the 1990s, as the mix in sales shifted toward light trucks.

19. Figure 8 focuses on the market for domestically produced goods. An additional effect not shown in the graph is the shift to imported cars when oil prices increase; this move occurred in both the in 1980s and in the 2000s. The share of imported vehicles rose from about 15% in the mid-1970s to about 25% in the first half of the 1980s. The import share then fell back as foreign automakers began to establish manufacturing operations in North America, and the import share fell below 10% by 1996. The market share of imported vehicles turned up again in the late 1990s, and the share moved up from 17% in 2000 to 26% in 2009.

20. The domestic market share excludes vehicles imported from outside North America.

21. A cross-utility vehicle is a utility vehicle that is assembled on a car chassis. They are classified by the industry as a light truck.

22. See, e.g., Graham and Glaister (2002). Berry, Levinsohn, and Pakes (1995) find much higher elasticities (in absolute value) for particular models.

23. The statutory overtime premium is 50%, whereas shift premiums are typically 5%–10%. Trejo (1991) has found that the implicit overtime premium is substantially lower than 50%. Thus, our assumption of a 10% premium is within the relevant range.

24. The values of the parameters are as follows: $\beta = 0.997$; $\phi_i = 2.5$ for $i = 1, 2$; $K = 40$; $\theta_A = 100$; $\theta_B = 1$; $\gamma = 19.85$; $\alpha_i = 0.1$; and $\omega = 1.1$.

25. Several authors in the capacity utilization literature define full capacity as the point beyond which marginal production costs begin to rise too rapidly. See Klein (1960) and Corrado and Mattey (1997).

26. See, e.g., eq. (7) of Ramey and Vine (2006).

27. The patterns in sales and days' supply between 2000 and 2009 were influenced by occasional inventory clearance events, often targeted toward full-size trucks and SUVs. The Detroit manufacturers have typically dominated the full-size truck market segments and therefore faced significant loss in market share as sales of these vehicles sagged over this period. The large dip in days' supply in late 2001 reflects the advent of zero-interest financing, and the plunge in stocks in 2005 coincides with the extension of these firms' employee-discount programs to all customers.

28. In the theoretical model presented above, the variance of days' supply in steady state was zero because the parameters of the cost function were the same for each vehicle segment. In actual industry data, vehicle types often show distinct long-run average inventory-sales ratios. This implies that the cross-sectional variance can be positive in steady state.

29. The production theory presented above suggests that one should also include vehicle prices for each segment, but unfortunately we lack data on segment-specific vehicle prices over much of the necessary history.

References

Aguiar-Conraria, Luis, and Yi Wen. 2007. "Understanding the Large Negative Impact of Oil Shocks." *Journal of Money, Credit and Banking* 39 (4): 926–44.

Atkeson, Andrew, and Patrick J. Kehoe. 1999. "Models of Energy Use: Putty-Putty versus Putty-Clay." *American Economic Review* 89, no. 4:1028–43.

Barsky, Robert B., and Lutz Kilian. 2002. "Do We Really Know That Oil Caused the Great Stagflation? A Monetary Alternative." *NBER Macroeconomics Annual* 16:137–83.

Bernanke, Ben S. 1983. "Irreversibility, Uncertainty, and Cyclical Investment." *Quarterly Journal of Economics* 98:85–106.

Bernanke, Ben S., Mark Gertler, and Mark Watson. 1997. "Systematic Monetary Policy and the Effects of Oil Price Shocks." *Brookings Papers on Economic Activity*, no. 1:91–142.

———. 2004. "Oil Shocks and Aggregate Macroeconomic Behavior: The Role of Monetary Policy; a Reply." *Journal of Money, Credit and Banking* 36, no. 2:287–91.

Berndt, Ernst R., and David O. Wood. 1975. "Technology, Prices, and the Derived Demand for Energy." *Review of Economics and Statistics* 57:259–68.

Berry, Steven, James Levinsohn, and Ariel Pakes. 1995. "Automobile Prices in Market Equilibrium." *Econometrica* 63:841–90.

Blanchard, Olivier J., and Jordi Galí. 2010. "The Macroeconomic Effects of Oil Price Shocks: Why Are the 2000s So Different from the 1970s?" In *International Dimensions of Monetary Policy*, ed. Jordi Galí and Mark Gertler, 373–421. Chicago: University of Chicago Press.

Blanchard, Olivier J., and Marianna Riggi. 2009. "Why Are the 2000s So Different from the 1970s? A Structural Interpretation of Changes in the Macroeconomic Effects of Oil Prices." Working Paper no. 15467, NBER, Cambridge, MA.

Bresnahan, Timothy F., and Valerie A. Ramey. 1993. "Segment Shifts and Capacity Utilization in the U.S. Automobile Industry." *American Economic Review* 83:213–18.

Bruno, Michael, and Jeffrey Sachs. 1982. "Input Price Shocks and the Slowdown in Economic Growth: The Case of UK Manufacturing." *Review of Economic Studies* 49:679–705.

Corrado, Carol, and Joe Mattey. 1997. "Capacity Utilization." *Journal of Economic Perspectives* 11:151–67.

Dahl, Carol A. 1979. "Consumer Adjustment to a Gasoline Tax." *Review of Economics and Statistics* 61, no. 3:427–32.

Davis, Lucas W., and Lutz Kilian. 2009. "The Allocative Cost of Price Ceilings in the U.S. Residential Market for Natural Gas." Working paper, University of Michigan.

Davis, Steven. 1987. "Fluctuations in the Pace of Labor Reallocation." *Carnegie-Rochester Conference Series on Public Policy* 27:335–402.

Edelstein, Paul, and Lutz Kilian. 2009. "How Sensitive Are Consumer Expenditures to Retail Energy Prices?" *Journal of Monetary Economics* 56:766–79.

Finn, Mary G. 1991. "Energy Price Shocks, Capacity Utilization and Business Cycle Fluctuations." Discussion Paper no. 50, Institute for Empirical Macroeconomics, Federal Reserve Bank of Minneapolis.

———. 2000. "Perfect Competition and the Effects of Energy Price Increases on Economic Activity." *Journal of Money, Credit and Banking* 32:400–416.

Frech, H. E., III, and William C. Lee. 1987. "The Welfare Cost of Rationing-by-Queue across Markets: Theory and Estimates from the U.S. Gasoline Crises." *Quarterly Journal of Economics* 102:97–108.
Frum, David. 2000. *How We Got Here: The '70s*. New York: Basic.
Graham, Daniel, and Stephen Glaister. 2002. "The Demand for Automobile Fuel: A Survey of Elasticities." *Journal of Transport Economics and Policy* 36:1–26.
Hamilton, James D. 1983. "Oil and the Macroeconomy since World War II." *Journal of Political Economy* 91:228–48.
———. 1988. "A Neoclassical Model of Unemployment and the Business Cycle." *Journal of Political Economy* 96:593–617.
———. 1996. "This Is What Happened to the Oil Price-Macroeconomy Relationship." *Journal of Monetary Economics* 38, no. 2:215–20.
———. 2003. "What Is an Oil Shock?" *Journal of Econometrics* 113:363–98.
———. 2009. "Yes, the Response of the U.S. Economy to Energy Prices Is Nonlinear." Working paper, University of California, San Diego.
Hamilton, James D., and Ana Maria Herrera. 2004. "Oil Shocks and Aggregate Macroeconomic Behavior: The Role of Monetary Policy." *Journal of Money, Credit and Banking* 36, no. 2:265–86.
Helbling, Hans H., and James E. Turley. 1975. "Oil Price Controls: A Counterproductive Effort." *Federal Reserve Bank of St. Louis Review*, November, 2–6.
Herrera, Ana María, and Elena Pesavento. 2009. "Oil Price Shocks, Systematic Monetary Policy, and the 'Great Moderation.'" *Macroeconomic Dynamics* 13:107–37.
Hooker, Mark A. 1996. "What Happened to the Oil Price–Macroeconomy Relationship?" *Journal of Monetary Economics* 38, no. 2:195–213.
Hughes, Jonathan E., Christopher R. Knittel, and Daniel Sperling. 2006. "Evidence of a Shift in the Short-Run Price Elasticity of Gasoline Demand." Research Report UCD-ITS-RR-096-16, Institute of Transportation Studies, University of California, Davis.
Kilian, Lutz. 2010. "Explaining Fluctuations in Gasoline Prices: A Joint Model of the Global Crude Oil Market and the U.S. Retail Gasoline Market." *Energy Journal* 31:103–28.
Kilian, Lutz, and Robert J. Vigfusson. 2009. "Pitfalls in Estimating Asymmetric Effects of Energy Price Shocks." Discussion Paper no. DP7284, Centre for Economic Policy Research, London.
Klein, Lawrence R. 1960. "Some Theoretical Issues in the Measurement of Capacity." *Econometrica* 28 (2): 272–86.
Klier, Thomas H., and James M. Rubenstein. 2009. "Imports of Intermediate Parts in the Auto Industry—a Case Study." Paper prepared for the conference "Measurement Issues Arising from the Growth of Globalization," Washington, DC.
Knittel, Christopher R. 2009. "Automobiles on Steroids: Product Attribute Trade-offs and Technological Progress in the Automobile Sector." Working Paper no. 15162, NBER, Cambridge, MA.
Kurz, Christopher, and Paul Lengermann. 2008. "Outsourcing and U.S. Economic Growth: The Role of Imported Intermediate Inputs." Paper prepared for the 2008 World Congress on National Accounts and Economic Performance Measures for Nations, Arlington, VA.
Leduc, Sylvain, and Keith Sill. 2004. "A Quantitative Analysis of Oil-Price Shocks, Systematic Monetary Policy, and Economic Downturns." *Journal of Monetary Economics* 51:781–808.

Lee, William C. 1980. "Demand for Travel and the Gasoline Crisis." *Transportation Research Record*, no. 764:38–42.
Mork, Knut Anton. 1989. "Oil and Macroeconomy When Prices Go Up and Down: An Extension of Hamilton's Results." *Journal of Political Economy* 97, no. 3:740–44.
Pindyck, Robert S., and Julio J. Rotemberg. 1983. "Dynamic Factor Demands and the Effects of Energy Price Shocks." *American Economic Review* 73, no. 5:1066–79.
Pisarski, Alan E., and Niels de Terra. 1975. "American and European Transportation Responses to the 1973–74 Arab Oil Embargo." *Transportation* 4:291–312.
Ramey, Valerie A., and Daniel J. Vine. 2006. "Declining Volatility in the U.S. Automobile Industry." *American Economic Review* 96, no. 5:1876–89.
Rotemberg, Julio J., and Michael Woodford. 1996. "Imperfect Competition and the Effects of Energy Price Increases on Economic Activity." *Journal of Money, Credit and Banking* 28, no. 4:550–77.
Trejo, Stephen J. 1991. "The Effects of Overtime Pay Regulation on Worker Compensation." *American Economic Review* 81, no. 4:719–40.
U.S. Department of Energy. 2009. *Transportation Energy Databook*. 28th ed. Washington, DC: U.S. Department of Energy.
Wei, Chao. 2009. "A Dynamic General Equilibrium Model of Driving, Gasoline Use and Vehicle Fuel Efficiency." Working paper, George Washington University.

Comment

Jordi Galí, *Centre de Recerca en Economia Internacional, Universitat Pompeu Fabra, Barcelona Graduate School of Economics, and NBER*

Valerie Ramey and Daniel Vine's contribution to the present *Macroeconomics Annual* volume should be seen in the context of a recent literature that has found evidence of more muted effects of oil price shocks in the 2000s relative to the 1970s. In a nutshell, that literature argues that while the order of magnitude of the two oil price hikes of the 1970s and those in the 2000s have been similar, their impact on both nominal and real variables appears to have been much larger in the former period (see, e.g., Blanchard and Galí [2010] and references therein).

Several explanations have been put forward regarding that evidence, including a smaller role of oil in the economy, greater wage flexibility, better monetary policy, and a more limited impact of oil price changes on the demand for motor vehicles, among others. Needless to say, understanding the nature of the changing effects of oil shocks is of great interest to macroeconomists. There are at least two reasons for this. First, the changing response to oil shocks may hold a clue as to the sources of the Great Moderation. Second, and given that large fluctuations in oil prices are unlikely to go away, it would seem important to know whether a repetition of the macro turmoil of the 1970s is possible.

Ramey and Vine's paper calls into question one of the premises of that literature, namely, the smaller impact of oil price shocks in the most recent period. In particular, the authors claim that the existing evidence on this issue may have been distorted by the use of oil price measures that ignore the costs associated with rationing. In order to support that claim, Ramey and Vine revisit some of the existing vector autoregression (VAR) evidence using two measures that are meant to proxy the effective cost of gasoline: (i) the augmented price of gasoline constructed by Frech and Lee (1987), which accounts for the time cost

978-0-226-00212-5/2011/2010-0602$10.00

associated with queues and (ii) a survey-based index of the fraction of consumers who cite the price of gasoline or possible gasoline shortages as a reason for car-buying conditions being poor. Ramey and Vine's findings using those alternative measures suggest that oil price shocks have not had significantly different effects on the level of activity pre- and post-1985. That is also true when they focus on the response of motor vehicle consumption, thus questioning the hypothesis of a key role of that variable in accounting for the more muted effects of oil price shocks in the recent period. The impact of oil prices on inflation, however, is estimated to be substantially smaller in the post-1985 sample, independently of whether the conventional or the alternative oil price measures are used. The latter finding is important when it comes to interpreting the results, as I discuss below.

In addition, Ramey and Vine suggest that a key mechanism through which oil price shocks are transmitted to the real sector—namely, their asymmetric impact on the demand for different types of vehicles—is still alive and well and does not seem to have experienced any significant change relative to an earlier period. In particular, both the level of car inventories and its dispersion across models display an increase of a similar magnitude before and after 1985, in response to a normalized oil price shock.

The findings of Ramey and Vine are likely to draw plenty of attention since they question the conventional wisdom about the changing effects of oil prices shocks. It is thus important to subject them to close scrutiny. The present comment seeks to contribute to that task by raising a number of questions that, in my view, have not been fully addressed in Ramey and Vine's paper.

I. Mismeasurement and the Importance of Oil Shocks

The adjustment of the gasoline price series to capture the cost of queues generates two larger spikes in that series, in the mid and late 1970s, respectively. Accordingly, if the adjusted series measures the "true" price, the VARs estimated using the unadjusted series will tend to overstate the response of any variable to an oil price shock during the early sample period (pre-1985), but it will give an accurate picture when estimated using post-1985 data (since the two oil price series coincide over the latter period). Some of the existing VAR evidence (e.g., Blanchard and Galí 2010) points to relatively small effects of oil price shocks on nominal and real variables during the Great Moderation period. Is that conclusion also shared by Ramey and Vine? If so, what do they attribute the turmoil of the 1970s to, if oil price shocks played such a small role? The authors do not seem to take a stand on this matter, beyond stating that the differences across sample periods largely vanish when the new series are used. Knowing whether oil shocks have been equally important in accounting for fluctuations in both periods would seem to be of great interest. Unfortunately, the analysis presented in the paper (which does not contain any variance decomposition) does not allow one to draw any conclusion on this matter.

However, if the gasoline price adjustment used by Ramey and Vine is unwarranted or exaggerates the true cost of fuel, the estimated responses for the early period will understate the true economy's response to an oil price shock. The fact that nonprice rationing does not seem to have affected firms' effective energy costs significantly is a possible reason for taking that possibility seriously since the cost channel is likely to be a key channel in the transmission of oil price shocks to activity.

II. On the Macro Relevance of the "Segment-Shifts" Hypothesis

The segment-shifts hypothesis, originally discussed in Bresnahan and Ramey (1993), relies on two key assumptions:

- Oil price rises shift demand toward fuel-efficient models
- Marginal costs for each model are convex (e.g., due to overtime).

As a result, a rise in the price of oil should generate an asymmetric price response, with the increase in the price of fuel-efficient models being larger than the decline in the corresponding price for less fuel-efficient models. Accordingly, the average price of cars would increase, causing a decline in demand, production, and capacity utilization.

Ramey and Vine provide evidence of higher dispersion in inventory-sales ratios across models, which is consistent with the first assumption above. But no evidence is provided of asymmetric price effects, which makes it hard to assess the merits of the second leg of the segment-shifts hypothesis. While time series for the price indexes corresponding to different categories may not be available, the authors could have estimated the variation in the average price of vehicles relative to other durable goods in response to oil price shocks, as well as the effects of the latter on the quantities of vehicles produced (again, relative to the quantity index for general durable goods), for the segment-shifts hypothesis yields clear predictions regarding those effects.

Note, however, that even if favorable evidence for such an effect on relative prices and quantities could be obtained, it would hardly demonstrate a significant role for segment shifts as a source of the overall decline in aggregate demand since an increase in the relative price of cars should lead, in itself, to a greater demand for other goods that might offset the decline in the demand for cars. In that case, other considerations would account for the drop in aggregate demand and production (e.g., a negative wealth effect due to the increase in the price of imported oil).

III. How Should One Interpret the "Inflation Exception"?

As discussed above, the use of alternative oil price measures does not affect the evidence regarding a possible differential impact of oil price shock on consumer price index inflation across sample periods. Ramey and Vine estimate that impact in the more recent period to be between one-third and two-thirds the size of the estimated impact in the earlier period. In other words, while the estimated effects of oil shocks on real variables do not seem to have declined over time when the alternative oil price measures are used, the same cannot be said for inflation.

Thus, even if one puts aside some of the questions and concerns raised above and becomes convinced by Ramey and Vine's new evidence, it should be clear that one should not infer from the latter that "nothing has changed" between the 1970s and the 2000s regarding the impact of oil price shocks. In particular, and as illustrated by figure 1,

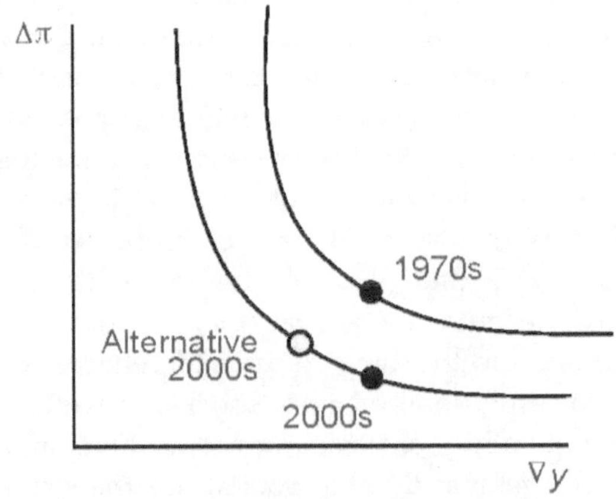

Fig. 1. Inflation-output trade-offs

the coexistence of a smaller impact on inflation with an unchanged effect on output implies an improvement in the output-inflation trade-off facing the Federal Reserve and, hence, the potential for a smaller response of both output and inflation to an oil price shock. Ramey and Vine's paper remains silent regarding the factors that could explain the improved trade-off.

IV. Final Remarks

The present paper by Ramey and Vine makes a welcome contribution to the literature on the effects of oil price shocks, by calling into question the conventional measures of oil prices used in that literature. Their findings suggest that measures that potentially capture the price as well as the nonprice costs of oil shocks imply significant differences in the estimated effects of those shocks. More research is clearly needed to evaluate the accuracy and desirability of the new measures and to provide stronger and more direct evidence on the relevance of the segment-shifts hypothesis. The authors should be commended for writing a paper that contains interesting and useful new evidence and that adds several new items to the research agenda on the effects of oil price shocks.

References

Blanchard, Olivier J., and Jordi Galí. 2010. "The Macroeconomic Effects of Oil Price Shocks: Why Are the 2000s So Different from the 1970s?" In *International Dimensions of Monetary Policy,* ed. Jordi Galí and Mark Gertler, 373–421. Chicago: University of Chicago Press.

Bresnahan, Timothy F., and Valerie Ramey. 1993. "Segment Shifts and Capacity Utilization in the U.S. Automobile Industry." *American Economic Review Papers and Proceedings* 83:213–18.

Frech, H. E., III, and William C. Lee. 1987. "The Welfare Cost of Rationing-by-Queue across Markets: Theory and Estimates from the U.S. Gasoline Crises." *Quarterly Journal of Economics* 102, no. 1:97–108.

Comment

Ariel Pakes, Harvard University and NBER

This paper focuses on the following question. Have the impacts of oil shocks on the aggregate economy, and on the motor vehicle industry in particular, changed over time? The basic difference between this paper and past work on this topic is that the current authors use measures of oil price shocks that include the effects on nonprice rationing. Using these variables, they conclude that "once the costs of queuing are added to the prices paid for gasoline, ... real output in the United States has been as sensitive to oil price shocks since the mid-1980s as it had been in the 1970s" and that "the primary channels through which oil prices directly affect demand for motor vehicles have not weakened much over time."

I will comment on the different sections of the paper in turn. My comments are mostly questions designed to push the analysis further, together with a few caveats on the purview of their results.

I. Initial Vector Autoregressions (VARs)

Their conclusions regarding the impacts of oil price shocks on the aggregate economy are based on comparing different VARs. They are all on monthly data with six lags and include, in addition to the price variable, the consumer price index (CPI), the gross domestic product deflator, nominal wages of private production workers, industrial production, civilian hours, and the federal funds rate. For price, one subset uses oil or gas price series taken from prior research, while the other uses either an adjusted price series (adjusted for the waiting time when there are price controls) or consumer sentiment data for oil and gas prices (explained in more detail below). The results that use the price series from previous research show differences in response of production and hours across the two periods. The results with their adjusted

978-0-226-00212-5/2011/2010-0603$10.00

price series indicated that production and hours response to the new price variables are the same or larger now then they were in the 1970s and 1980s. However, the impact of the new price variables on the CPI is still smaller in the more recent period.

Their is a statistical sense in which their new findings are not surprising. The production and hours variables used in their VARs are essentially the same as those used in the prior analysis, but in the new price series the magnitude of the gas price change in the early period has increased due to their adjustments. As a result, the impact of the price change in the early period must decrease. As for the CPI, as I understand it, the response of the monetary authorities to the price hike in 1973 was expansionary, while the response in the later years was not.

Are the economics puzzling? There is at least one sense in which they are. The early price changes were preceded by a long period of real oil price stability. The inflation-adjusted oil price in 1951 was $23.13 per barrel, and in 1972 it was $20.66. Moreover, the lowest price in the intervening years was $18.93, while the highest was $24.20.[1] So before 1973, both consumers and producers probably expected low and very stable gas prices over the relevant future: 1973 clearly changed this perception. It became evident that gas prices could increase sharply and that the increase need not be predictable from trends in the macroeconomy (as the Organization of Petroleum Exporting Countries demonstrated). Moreover, by the mid-1980s it was obvious that the most dramatic change in the gas price series after 1973 was the increase in the volatility, not the increase in the level, of prices.

So perhaps the first questions we should ask ourselves are, what are the likely impacts of the changes in the perceptions of future prices, and how are those impacts likely to feed through to the motor vehicle industry and the economy more generally? When perceptions (of the level and volatility) of future prices change, we might think that there would be changes in investment policies in the car companies and in other energy-intensive parts of the economy (airlines and aircraft production, electric utility generation, etc.) and by consumers. The impacts of these investments would likely take several years (more if they required new research outcomes) but should eventually change the nature of responses to future price movements (both by firms and by consumers through their purchases of durable goods).

The 6-month limit to the lag structure explains why we do not see the effect of these investments in the earlier period. However, I would have expected to see the effects of a changed investment policy built into the way consumers and firms respond to oil price shocks by the later period, and they do not seem to find it in the aggregate data. Of course, there are lots of factors that affect data at this level of aggregation, and the effects I am talking about might well have been countered by other processes.

II. The Motor Vehicle Industry

Next we have an analysis of the impact of oil and gas prices on the motor vehicle industry, which is considered "an important channel through which oil shocks affect" the economy. The authors begin by noting that although the motor vehicle industry does account for a smaller fraction of measured output in the later period than in the early period, its share only falls 10%–15% (depending on which measures one uses). I would argue that is not an insignificant fall, but they are clearly correct in thinking that the major changes in the automobile industry over this time period are not in its contribution to output. Rather the major changes are in (i) the firms producing that output and (ii) the type of product produced. Honda, Hyundai, Mazda, Mercedes, Nissan, Subaru, and Toyota all started manufacturing facilities in the United States after 1970, some in alliance with one of the "big three" U.S. companies. This change in the company composition of output was accompanied by a change in the location of motor vehicle production, which in turn changed the lives of a large fraction of our workforce. I understand that this is not the focus of the paper, but the change in company composition of output has had important effects on the economy.

The paper looks at the response of consumer's investments in motor vehicles to the gas price increases. An increase in the price of gas should have (interrelated) impacts on (i) the quantity of vehicles purchased, (ii) the types of vehicles purchased, and (iii) the amount of driving done with the current fleet. The authors provide a series of graphs that are informative in these respects, and I will go over (and add a bit to) a few of their results.

As they note, we might expect the price of gas to be more directly related to car-driving than to car-buying conditions. Figure 6 graphs vehicle distance traveled per household over time. It falls after 1973 and again after 1978. The surprise is the continual upward trend in driving thereafter (despite the fluctuations in gas prices). In 2007, the real price of gas is 10%–20% higher then it was in 1980, yet the miles driven are almost 50% higher. So gas prices are not terrifically successful in predicting miles driven, and even if they were, the relationship of miles driven to economy-wide production is not obvious.

More closely related to the impact of the motor vehicle industry on the rest of the economy is motor vehicle purchases. In particular, I want to look at how the interaction between consumer and producer investment incentives affected the types of cars purchased. To do so, I look at how the fuel efficiency of the new car sales responded to the gas price changes.[2]

The average miles per gallon (mpg) of the new car fleet actually fell after the gas price increase in 1973: from 16.2 mpg in 1972 to 15.7 mpg in 1974. The average mpg of the new car fleet did begin to rise thereafter, but that did not start happening until 1976. Real gas prices were falling between 1974 and 1976, but they were still higher in 1976 than in 1972.

We now move to 1978. The response of the average mpg of the new car fleet to the 1978 gas price shock was dramatically different. The average mpg of the new car fleet in 1977 was 19.5, but by 1981 it had increased by over 20%, to 23.7. It then goes up slowly to just over 27 in 1990. This, despite the fact that the real price of gas fell rather dramatically during those 10 years. The average mpg does fall slightly between 1990 and 2000 and then rise slightly after 2005, but none of the changes post-1990 are nearly as dramatic as those between 1972 and 1982.

There are at least two ways consumers can modify their auto purchasing behavior when either the gas price rises or there is a perception that future gas prices are more volatile. One is to delay purchasing. The other is to purchase a car with higher mpg. The car models available in 1973 were limited in their mpg rating; the consumer who wanted a family car simply did not have the option of purchasing one with high mpg. So if you did buy a family car, you bought a low-mpg car. The only possible real response to the gas price was to not buy a car, and this response was primarily chosen by low-income people who bought smaller cars with higher mpg. Hence, we have the fall in the average mpg of the new car fleet.

In the years between 1973 and 1978, (i) U.S. producers invested in high-mpg models, and (ii) foreign producers invested in the infrastructure required to market their high-mpg cars in the United States (dealerships, repair facilities, etc.). These two processes resulted in significant changes in the range of mpg available for different types of cars, and by 1978 the choice set facing consumers had changed rather dramatically. When the 1978 price rise occurred, the very low-income people continued to substitute out, but now the somewhat higher-income people could purchase family cars with higher mpg, and they did. This also explains part of the continual increase in miles driven in the face of rising gas prices; the cost of driving the extra miles was smaller in the later period.

Conditions in the car market did change over time in a way that changed how consumers' purchasing decisions responded to gas price changes and in a way that helps explain the relationship of driving behavior to gas prices. There is a question of precisely how the impacts of those investments filter through to aggregate data because the investments and their payoffs take time. It is clear, however, that the change did have significant impacts in the way we might analyze other policy scenarios (think carbon taxes and carbon emissions).

My guess is that similar responses happened in other industries. That is, the increments in capital stock should have been designed in a way that paid more attention to energy prices; in particular, given the volatility in energy prices, it should have been designed to accommodate variance in energy prices. If I had to guess where I would see this change in response most clearly, I would expect to see it in productivity figures.

Of course productivity also varies with the business cycle, and the two impacts might be hard to separate out in post-1972 data. But there were at least two recessions between 1950 and 1972 that had nothing to do with energy prices, and it would be interesting to compare the responses of the auto industry, and other energy-intensive industries, to those recessions and to their responses to the recessions that came after the gas price hikes. Another comparison that might help here is of the effect of gas prices on auto demand, and on general demand, in the United States to those effects in Great Britain. Presumably gas prices went up worldwide. However, Great Britain was an exporter of gas by the mid-1970s, so the increase in the price of gas should have been associated with improved economic conditions there (or at least not a noticeable decline). Thus, the comparison might throw light on whether the effect of gas prices on auto demand is through a decrease in real income or through an increase in the relative price of driving. It also might let us see whether the effect of auto demand on macroeconomic activity comes primarily through autos, per se, or through the effects of a contemporaneous increase of gas prices on "consumer anxiety," a topic I now turn to.

III. The Use of Consumer Sentiment Data

The authors show that recent increases in gasoline prices seem to have caused just as much anxiety in consumers now as we observed 30 years ago. The data here are very interesting. Not only does the anxiety variable track the gas price increases amazingly well, but it also registers increases in the later period of equal magnitude to those in the earlier period (and the earlier period was accompanied by lines at the gas stations and a war in the Middle East). Moreover, the "real activity is more closely related to consumer perceptions of the price of gasoline and its availability than it is to published fuel prices."

The anxiety variable is from the Thomson Reuters and University of Michigan Survey of Consumer Sentiment, and it tracks the portion of respondents who cite the price of gasoline or fuel shortages as the reason car-buying conditions are poor. An additional question asked is whether the next 12 months is a good time or a bad time to buy a car. I would have liked to have seen the two questions analyzed together, as that would give us a direct link between anxiety about gas prices and consumer car-purchasing decisions. Indeed, it would have been interesting to put the anxiety question together with other questions about consumer purchasing behavior, as that would have been a fairly direct link between anxiety about gas prices and consumer purchasing patterns more generally.

IV. Volatility in Gas Prices and Its Effects on Autos

The volatility in the share of motor vehicle output and the way it tracks recessions and gas price increases is striking (despite the fact that shares have not changed much). The paper uses the variance in days' supply across motor vehicle segments to measure mismatches across segments between capacity and demand. The argument is that much of the variance in days' supply is caused by (presumably unexpected) movements to segment demand, and that is caused by (presumably unexpected) shifts in gas prices.

Figure 11, which provides the cross-segment variance in days' supply, illustrates two facts:

- there was a marked increases in the variance in days' supply in periods when the gas price is rising, and
- there was no increase in the variance of days' supply when the gas price is falling (even when it fell rather sharply).

If missed segment-demand predictions due to unexpected changes in gas prices was causing the variance in days' supply, we should probably expect the variance in days' supply to respond to unexpected movements in price in either direction. One could argue that the 1973 and 1978 oil price shocks were caused by unpredictable political factors and that the fall in prices thereafter was predictable. However, the increase in gas and oil prices in the later period was largely a result of a continual steady growth in demand from India and China, so if seemingly predictable growth resulted in no increase in variance when prices were falling, should it not also have resulted in no increase in the variance in days' supply in the later period when prices were known to be rising (and the variance did increase in the later period)?

Of course optimal days' supply could respond differently to upward and downward shocks, or it could change with levels of demand for segments, or it could vary by segment for a given level of demand. The lesson is probably that, before we use this variable too intensively, we might want to look more deeply into what determines its value. I think it is clear that the series of adjustments that must be made to accommodate segment demand changes are costly (I am sure you would see that in profits) and can cause changes in capacity utilization. So, I do not doubt that there is an element of truth in the argument put forward here. However, to determine the timing and magnitude of the effect, we have to separate out perceptions from realizations and consider all the options for changing output available to management.

V. Conclusion

I think there is much left to be done here. The response of the economy, and in particular of the motor vehicle industry, to gas price changes is not only important for understanding the behavior of macro aggregates, but it is also important for understanding the likely implications of various policy scenarios (the carbon tax, exchange rate and tariff changes) and the political economy determining which of the possible policy issues will be implemented. What I have tried to make clear is that to answer such questions we need a deeper look into the institutional details of the important energy-using industries and the opportunities available to them for responding to energy price changes.

Endnotes

1. See "Historical Crude Oil Prices," InflationData.com, http://inflationdata.com/inflation/Inflation_Rate/Historical_Oil_Prices_Table.asp.

2. The authors do look at the fuel efficiency of the stock of vehicles. However, the response of the stock of vehicles will lag the response of the new car fleet, and it is new car sales that have the biggest direct effect on the economy.

Discussion

Valerie Ramey began by responding to Jordi Galí's comments. She stated her belief that the response of the economy during the 2000s to the conventional measures of oil shocks is the true response, while the response during the 1970s is overstated because conventional measures underestimate the true cost of oil in the 1970s. Then, she commented on the point that the new measure of oil shocks could have bigger errors, and this can explain the results that they got. She argued that they think the new measure is estimated more precisely since the standard error bands are narrower when the new measure is used. She also addressed the point on the decline in the effect of oil prices in many European countries despite the absence of rationing. She argued that this difference may be due to the increase in gas taxes in Europe. She said that a given change in crude oil prices has a smaller percentage change effect on gas prices there. She added that in the United States, gas taxes have not gone up very much, and, thus, this is not a part of the effect. In response to the question about the effect of rationing on firms, Ramey said that they could not find a lot of evidence that firms outside of transportation were affected by rationing. As to the possibility of different responses in the relative prices of different models of cars to oil shocks, Ramey agreed that their model would have implications on this. However, they did not have a good time series with detailed prices. Finally, she agreed with Galí that the evidence they provide points to an improved inflation-output trade-off.

Next, Ramey addressed comments by Ariel Pakes. She agreed that they provide a simple statistical explanation of the observed decline in the effect of oil shocks. They pointed out that the standard measures of the costs of oil or gasoline had errors because rationing is not accounted for. Once they account for the error, they get interesting results. She noted that the inclusion of 12 months of lags instead of 6 months

978-0-226-00212-5/2011/2010-0604$10.00

only increased the standard error bands. She added that with multivariable vector autoregressions (VARs), one gets dynamics continuing for longer than 6 months. She commented on why the miles driven in the 2000s are 50% higher than in the 1980s. She argued that two factors might account for that. First, the increase in housing prices led people to move farther from work. Second, the increase in female labor force participation led to longer commutes since spouses often work in different locations. Next, she agreed that it would be good to look at anxiety and how it affects other variables, acknowledging that they can do more with their consumer sentiment variable. As to the comparison of Great Britain and the United States, she noted that Bruno and Sachs (1982) documented that Great Britain had oil price controls in the 1970s; thus, the country is similar to the United States in this respect. Finally, she responded to the issue about the asymmetric response of the variance of domestic days' supply to changes in oil prices. She said that they do not know how permanent people regarded the change in oil prices. Vehicle purchases are likely to change if consumers expect oil price increases to be permanent. She added that in 2007–8, people thought that Chinese and Indian demand was going to keep increasing; hence, they expected the oil price to be permanently high. Thus, there is an increase in the variance of domestic days' supply during this period.

Next, Daniel Vine offered his response to the discussants' points. He noted that in an earlier version of the paper, they looked at the margins that the motor vehicle industry used to adjust output. In 1972–74, the industry used temporary measures to adjust output such as the reduction of overtime hours and temporary closure of plants. In 1979–80, the industry used a lot of permanent margins such as complete closure of plants. After the 2000 recession, temporary margins were used. However, in the beginning of 2006–7, a lot of plants were closed. This corroborates the view that perceptions regarding the persistence of the gas price changes are really important for determining how agents respond. He also mentioned that it is indeed surprising to many people that the auto industry is the same size relative to the goods-producing sector now as in the 1970s.

Daron Acemoglu raised the issue of distinguishing oil price changes from the costs of the oil price changes borne by consumers. The costs to consumers are the product of the average miles driven, car efficiency (miles per gallon), and the gasoline price. Consumers may change the miles they drive and the efficiency of the cars they buy in response to gasoline price changes. It can have offsetting effects on the costs to consumers. He wondered whether there is a way to distinguish this in a system with two driving variables: gasoline price and gasoline price corrected for rationing, miles driven, and efficiency. Ramey noted that much of the effect on motor vehicles is not the direct effect of oil but whatever oil does to the rest of the economy. She said that one of their counterfactuals shuts down all other channels such as disposable income, interest rates, and so on. They found that half of the effect is the direct effect of oil during the first year. However, it is less than a half after that.

Robert Hall worried that the authors overstated the extent to which rationing increased gasoline prices, both as to duration and as to amount. His personal recollection points to the weak enforcement of retail price controls. He argued that one could find a no-name gas station without a line that charged only 20–30 cents more compared to a brand-name gas station with a big line of cars.

Christopher House had two comments. He first raised the question of how to deal with the total number of observations the authors have. He worried that there were not many big observations in the sentiment data and in the oil data. He wondered whether the authors were concerned about whether they have sufficient variability. Next, he made a comment about the difference in the assembly and the output of the auto industry. While it is true that output as a share of goods gross domestic product (GDP) has not shown a big decline, it seems that as a share of the goods GDP, the value added in motor vehicles has gone from something above two to something less than one (fig. 5 in the paper). He insisted that the interpretation that the auto industry today is just as it was before should be presented with care. Vine noted that gross motor vehicle output does not double count shipments of the industry to itself. It values all vehicles at retail, and it values all the vehicles put into the inventory at wholesale, adjusting for net exports of motor vehicles. Thus, the measure captures the value added from the production and from the distribution to final consumers. The disadvantage of this measure is that it would include the imported intermediate goods, so, if the auto industry bought rubber and steel from abroad, that goes into gross motor vehicle output. Ideally, one would want to take out imported intermediates. One can do this, but it is very time consuming and may require many assumptions. Thus, they decided to present only two plots in figure 5: one is the value of the motor vehicles industry net of imported incomplete vehicles and another is the value added of motor vehicle assembly as a share of goods GDP. They argue that both measures look pretty stable.

7

Macroeconomic Lessons from the Great Deviation

John B. Taylor, *Stanford University and NBER*

Congratulations to the National Bureau of Economic Research on the twenty-fifth anniversary of the Macroeconomics Annual conference series, and thanks to all the editors over the years—Stanley Fischer, Olivier Blanchard, Julio Rotemberg, Ben Bernanke, Daron Acemoglu, Kenneth Rogoff, and Michael Woodford—who have consistently encouraged research with a strong empirical content and policy relevance.

My remarks tonight focus on the macroeconomic aspects of the financial crisis. Most of my research over the past few years has been on the financial crisis. My approach has been empirical, examining data on interest rate spreads, money supply, consumption, and investment and simulating empirical models using the discipline of counterfactuals—basically the same approach used in the papers presented at the NBER Macroeconomics Annual conferences over the years. In these remarks I want to summarize the key findings in a few words, without the charts or tables, and then draw the implications both for macroeconomics as a field and for macroeconomics as a guide for policy. Since this is a Macroeconomics Annual meeting, I will focus on macroeconomic issues and not delve into regulatory issues.

Let me begin with an explanation of the title of my talk. I know economists use the word "great" too much, but I think it is quite fitting here. We all know what the Great Moderation was, and we have debated what caused it. Many have argued that good policy, especially good monetary policy, played a big role. And we all know what the Great Recession was and that it marked the end of the Great Moderation. You may not have heard much about the Great Deviation. I define it as the recent period during which macroeconomic policy became *more interventionist, less rules based, and less predictable*. It is a period during which policy deviated from the practice of at least the previous 2 decades and from the recommendations of most macroeconomic theory

978-0-226-00212-5/2011/2010-0701$10.00

and models. My general theme is that the Great Deviation killed the Great Moderation, gave birth to the Great Recession, and left a troublesome legacy for the future.

I. Great Deviation List

The policy actions and interventions that I would put under the rubric of the Great Deviation include the following:

- Deviation from the monetary policy of the Great Moderation, 2003–5
- TAF, created by the Federal Reserve, 2007
- U.S. discretionary fiscal stimulus, 2008
- On-again/off-again interventions of financial firms by the Fed, 2008
- Money market mutual fund liquidity facility, 2008
- Commercial paper funding facility, 2008
- U.S. discretionary fiscal stimulus, 2009
- G-20 fiscal stimulus agreement, 2009
- MBS purchase program of the Fed, 2009–10
- Trillion dollar European rescue package, 2010
- The ECB joining the rescue package by buying distressed debt, 2010
- The Fed joining the rescue package by making swap loans, 2010

That is a dozen already, and one could add more, including interventions by the federal government to encourage Fannie Mae and Freddie Mac to purchase high-risk mortgages, and decisions by U.S. financial regulatory agencies to let banks deviate from rules-based regulations by allowing risky off–balance sheet activity or by not monitoring the risk of complex asset-backed securities on the balance sheets. And there are also the many deviations from the rules-based Stability and Growth Pact in Europe, which are the cause of the crisis Europe is facing now. But let me focus on these dozen.

First on the list is the decision by the Federal Reserve during 2003–5 to hold its target interest rate below the level implied by monetary principles that had been followed for the previous 20 years. One can characterize this decision as a deviation from a policy rule, such as the Taylor rule, and in that sense it is a deviation from a more rules-based policy. Without this deviation, interest rates would not have reached such a low level, and they would have returned much sooner to the neutral level that they eventually reached. The deviation was larger than any other during the Great Moderation—on the order of magnitude seen in the unstable decade before the Great Moderation. One does not need to rely on the Taylor rule to conclude that from the perspective of many of the standard objective functions that monetary policy might seek to optimize, rates were held too low for too long. The real interest rate was negative for a very long period, similarly to what happened in the 1970s. The intervention was an intentional departure from a policy approach that was followed in the decades before. The Fed's statements that interest rates would be low for a "prolonged period" and that interest rates would rise at a "measured pace" are evidence of these intentions.

The low interest rates added fuel to the housing boom, which in turn led to risk taking in housing finance and eventually a sharp increase in delinquencies, foreclosures, and the deterioration of the balance sheets of many financial institutions as toxic assets grew rapidly. To test the connection between the low interest rates and the housing boom, I built a simple model relating the federal funds rate to housing construction. My research showed that a higher federal funds rate would have avoided much of the boom and bust.

The next intervention on the list is the Fed's term auction facility (TAF) created in December 2007. The purpose of the TAF was to reduce tensions in the interbank market that had risen sharply in August 2007. The TAF provided a way for banks to get loans from the Fed without using the discount window. After this facility was created, tensions in the interbank market—as measured by the spreads between the London Interbank Offered Rate (LIBOR) at various maturities and the overnight index swap (OIS)—abated for a while but soon shot up again. My view, based on research with John C. Williams (Taylor and Williams 2009), is that this new facility had little or no effect on these interest rate spreads. Measures of counterparty risk in the banking sector, such as the spread between secured and unsecured interbank loans, explain money market spreads very well. In my view, this policy intervention prolonged the crisis because it did not address the deterioration of the balance sheets at banks and other financial institutions. We now know that the banks were holding many toxic assets, but the problem was diagnosed as a liquidity problem.

The 2008 discretionary countercyclical fiscal policy action—the Economic Stimulus Act of 2008—is next on the list. This action was also a deviation from the type of policy that was used in the Great Moderation, a period in which there was a near consensus among economists that such discretionary policies were not effective and could be counterproductive. As part of this stimulus, which was passed in February 2008, checks were sent to people on a one-time basis, and aggregate disposable personal income jumped dramatically though temporarily. The objective was to jump-start consumption demand and thereby jump-start the economy. However, aggregate personal consumption expenditure did not increase by much at all around the time of the stimulus payments. This is what the permanent income theory, the life cycle theory, or modern new Keynesian models predict from such a temporary lump-sum payment.

The most unusual and significant set of interventions were the on-again/off-again rescues of financial firms and their creditors. The interventions started when the Fed opened its balance sheet to rescue the creditors of Bear Stearns in March 2008 and then made loans available to Fannie Mae and Freddie Mac. The Fed's interventions were then turned off for Lehman, turned on again for AIG, and then turned off again when the Troubled Asset Relief Program (TARP) was proposed. These interventions clearly did not prevent the panic that began in September 2008 and in my view were a likely cause of the panic, or at least made the panic worse. Could the unpredictable nature of these interventions have been avoided? If the Federal Reserve and the Treasury had clearly laid out the reasons behind the Bear Stearns intervention as well as the intentions of policy going forward, then people would have had some sense of what was to come. But no such description was provided. Uncertainty was heightened and probably reached a peak when the TARP was rolled out. Panic ensued and quickly spread around the world as stock market indices went down in tandem with the 30% drop in the Standard & Poors 500.

The panic halted when uncertainty about the TARP was removed on October 13, 2008. The original purpose of the TARP was to buy up toxic assets on banks' balance sheets, but there was criticism and confusion about how that would work. After the TARP was changed to inject equity into the banks rather than to buy toxic assets, uncertainty was reduced, and conditions began to improve, as measured by the LIBOR-OIS spread and other indicators such as the S&P 500. Market conditions then improved in other countries.

Other policy interventions were taken during the panic in late September and October 2008. The Fed's programs to assist money market mutual funds and the commercial paper market were helpful in rebuilding confidence. To be sure, the panic period is complex to analyze empirically because so much was going on at the same time. In addition to the Fed's actions, we had the Federal Deposit Insurance Corporation guarantee of bank debt and the clarification that the TARP would be used for equity injections.

After the worst of the panic was over there were more interventions. Another discretionary fiscal stimulus—the American Recovery and Reinvestment Act of 2009—was passed in February 2009. The amount paid in checks was smaller and more drawn out than the 2008 stimulus, but the impact was about the same: no noticeable effect on consumption. In addition, my analysis of the government spending part of the stimulus suggests that it had little to do with the turnaround in economic activity.

At the Group of 20 leaders summit in the spring of 2009, other countries agreed with the U.S. approach and passed their own discretionary fiscal stimulus packages—a contagion of deviations from rules-based predictable policies around the world. This is number 8 on my list, but it could be numbers 8–26. We are still learning about the impact of these packages, and a huge amount of empirical work is needed to determine their impact.

Other interventions were introduced by the Fed in the period following the panic, most significantly the Mortgage Backed Securities purchase program, which turned out to be $1.25 trillion in size. My view, based on empirical research with Johannes Stroebel (Stroebel and Taylor 2009), is that this program had only a small effect on mortgage rates once prepayment risk and default risk are controlled for.

Many of these policies have helped to create legacies of debt and monetary overhang. Moreover, the central bank interventions raise questions about central bank independence; the interventions are not monetary policy as conventionally defined, but rather fiscal policy or credit allocation policy. Unwinding the programs creates uncertainty, and there is a risk of inflation if they are not unwound. The fiscal interventions have resulted in higher debt levels, and they have redirected policy attention away from issues of long-term fiscal consolidation.

Nowhere is there more evidence of this legacy of debt as there is in Europe, where the debt problems of Greece, Portugal, and Spain worsened significantly since the crisis. Indeed the earlier interventions have led to more interventions: the 750 billion euro rescue package by European governments and the International Monetary Fund, the agreement by the European Central Bank (ECB) to buy distressed government debt, and the agreement by the Fed to provide dollar swap loans to the ECB to relieve pressure in the interbank market. I have added these echo interventions to the list. It is still too early to determine their impact, but the early movements in the interbank and exchange markets were not favorable.

II. Other Views

Of course others have different views of the Great Deviation. Ben Bernanke (2010), for example, argues that I use the wrong Taylor rule to measure the deviation from rules-based policies. He shows that the low interest rates in 2003–5 were not a deviation if you use a modified policy rule with *forecasts* of inflation rather than actual inflation. But the Fed's forecasts of inflation were too low in this period, which suggests that such a modified rule is not such a good one.

Some would say that the Great Deviation was needed. For example, the financial panic in the fall of 2008 and the Great Recession were so severe that policy makers had to take large unprecedented discretionary actions. But the first four action items on my list were taken before the panic of fall 2008 and before the recession that started in late 2007 turned into the global Great Recession.

Others might say that my research ignores mistakes in the private sector. Of course there were market problems of various sorts. Mortgages were originated without sufficient documentation or with overly optimistic underwriting assumptions and then sold off in complex derivative securities that credit rating agencies rated too highly. Individuals and institutions took highly risky positions through either a lack of diversification or excessive leverage ratios. But such mistakes do not normally become systemic, and in my view, the government actions tended to convert nonsystemic mistakes into systemic risks. The low interest rates led to rapidly rising housing prices with very low delinquency and foreclosure rates, which confused both underwriters and the rating agencies or made it easier for them to hide the mistakes. The failure to regulate adequately entities that were supposed to be, and thought to be, regulated certainly encouraged the excesses. As I mentioned, risky activities at regulated banks were allowed by regulators. Regulatory gaps and overlapping responsibilities added to the problem; these issues seem likely to be addressed in regulatory reform.

Still others might say that things would have been worse without the Great Deviation, that we would have had Great Depression 2.0 without the Great Deviation. I do not see hard evidence for this claim. If I could pick and choose from policies on the list, I would select the Fed's actions for the commercial paper market and money market funds, but those actions would not have been needed were it not for the preceding items on the list.

III. Macroeconomic Lessons

What are the implications of the Great Deviation and the subsequent events in the global macroeconomy for the field of macroeconomics? The recent crisis gives no reason to abandon the core empirical "rational expectations/sticky price" model developed over the past 30 years. Whether you call this type of model "dynamic stochastic general equilibrium," "new Keynesian," or "new neoclassical macroeconomics," it is the type of model from which modern monetary policy rules and recommendations were derived. Along with rational expectations came reasons for predictable, rulelike policies: time inconsistency, credibility, and the Lucas critique, or simply the practical need to evaluate macro policy as a rule. Along with the sticky prices came specific monetary rules that dealt with the dynamics implied by those rigidities as fit to actual macro data. This is the type of model in which robustness of policy rules could be checked as it was in the NBER *Monetary Policy Rules* volume (Taylor 1999). These models did not fail in their recommendations for rules-based monetary and fiscal policies. I have to disagree with Narayana Kocherlakota (2010) when he says that "macroeconomists let policymakers down ... because they did not provide policymakers with rules to avoid the circumstances that led to the global financial meltdown" (5). The rules were provided. Policy makers took a different, more discretionary approach.

It is easy to criticize the rational expectations/sticky price models by saying that they do not admit enough rigidities, have only one interest rate, or do not have money in them. But we should not confuse useful simplified versions of models, which frequently boil down to only three equations, with more detailed models used for policy. By focusing on such smaller simplified models, Woodford (2003), for example, is able to derive many useful theorems. For practical policy work those simplifying assumptions are relaxed. Many of the rational expectations/sticky price models examined in the study by Taylor (1999) or by Wieland et al. (2009) are more complex models that have time-varying risk premia in the term structure of interest rates, an exchange rate channel, and more than one country.

Of course, macroeconomists should try to improve their models in whatever ways they think can make them more useful for policy makers. Many have been working on improving our understanding of the credit channel, a worthy task that goes back to the research of Brunner, Meltzer, Tobin, Bernanke, and Gertler. An implication of my research findings is that we need to do more work on "political macroeconomics." In particular, we need to explain and understand why policy makers moved in such an interventionist direction despite the research that stressed predictable rulelike monetary and fiscal policy. Once we understand that, practical solutions should follow.

One possible explanation is that policy makers had genuine doubts about the practical relevance of the research on policy rules. In this regard I am reminded of the 1992 Macroeconomics Annual conference. It was the same year that I presented the paper that contained what would come to be called the Taylor rule. At that conference I commented on a paper by Ben Bernanke and Rick Mishkin (1992). They were raising doubts about the use of rules for the policy instruments and making the case for a considerable amount of discretion in monetary policy making. They said that "monetary policy rules do not allow the monetary authorities to respond to unforeseen circumstances" (184). I dissented from that view in my comments, referring to research on policy rules in which the instruments of policy adjust to contingencies (Taylor 1992).

Another explanation is that in a practical policy setting, policy makers sometimes try to do more than the underlying economics suggests is possible. In this regard let me close with a statement that Milton Friedman made in congressional testimony over 50 years ago. I drew this quote from the famous debate between Friedman and Walter Heller (1969, 48) in which Friedman refers to his 1958 testimony at the Joint Economic Committee. According to Friedman,

> The available evidence ... casts grave doubt on the possibility of producing any fine adjustments in economic activity by fine adjustments in monetary policy—at least in the present state of knowledge. ... There are thus serious limitations to the possibility of a discretionary monetary policy and much danger that such a policy may make matters worse rather than better. ... The basic difficulties and limitations of monetary policy apply with equal force to fiscal policy. ... Political pressures to "do something" ... are clearly very strong indeed in the existing state of public attitudes. The main moral to be had from these two preceding points is that yielding to these pressures may frequently do more harm than good. There is a saying that the best is often the enemy of the good, which seems highly relevant. The attempt to do more than we can will itself be a disturbance that may increase rather than reduce instability.

Endnote

Written and updated version of after-dinner remarks at the twenty-fifth Macroeconomics Annual conference, National Bureau of Economic Research, April 19, 2010.

References

Bernanke, Ben. 2010. "Monetary Policy and the Housing Bubble." Speech at the annual meeting of the American Economic Association, Atlanta, January 3.

Bernanke, Ben, and Frederic Mishkin. 1992. "Central Bank Behavior and the Strategy of Monetary Policy: Observations from Six Industrialized Countries." *NBER Macroeconomics Annual* 7:183–227.

Friedman, Milton, and Walter Heller. 1969. *Monetary vs. Fiscal Policy: A Dialogue.* New York: Norton.

Kocherlakota, Narayana. 2010. "Modern Macroeconomic Models as Tools for Economic Policy: Annual Report Essay." Federal Reserve Bank of Minneapolis *Region* (May), 5–21.

Stroebel, Johannes, and John B. Taylor. 2009. "Estimated Impact of the Fed's Mortgage-Backed Securities Purchase Program." Working Paper no. 15626 (December), NBER, Cambridge, MA.

Taylor, John B. 1992. Comment on "Central Bank Behavior and the Strategy of Monetary Policy: Observations from Six Industrialized Countries" by Ben Bernanke and Frederic Mishkin. *NBER Macroeconomics Annual* 7:234–37.

———, ed. 1999. *Monetary Policy Rules.* Chicago: University of Chicago Press (for NBER).

Taylor, John B., and John C. Williams. 2009. "A Black Swan in the Money Market." *American Economic Journal: Macroeconomics* 1 (January): 58–83.

Wieland, V., T. Cwik, G. Mueller, S. Schmidt, and M. Wolters. 2009. "A New Comparative Approach to Macroeconomic Modelling and Policy Analysis." Unpublished manuscript, Center for Financial Studies, Frankfurt.

Woodford, Michael. 2003. *Interest and Prices.* Princeton, NJ: Princeton University Press.

www.ingramcontent.com/pod-product-compliance
Lightning Source LLC
LaVergne TN
LVHW100249210926
848480LV00003B/875
9780226002132